TOWER STORIES
The Autobiography of September 11ᵗʰ

REVOLUTION
PUBLISHING

Damon DiMarco

www.towerstories.org

Portions of the proceeds have been pledged to Secret Smiles Charity, New York.

Published by Revolution Publishing
115 W. 29th St. New York, NY 10001

Cover Design by Ben Peterson
Page composition/typography by Ben Peterson

ISBN: 0-9748684-5-0

FIRST EDITION

10 9 8 7 6 5 4 3 2 1

"Strange is our situation here upon earth. Each of us comes for a short visit, not knowing why, yet sometimes seeming to divine a purpose. From the standpoint of daily life, however, there is one thing I do know: that we are here for the sake of each other, above all, for those upon whose smile and well-being our own happiness depends, and also for the countless unknown souls with whose fate we are connected by a bond of sympathy. Many times a day I realize how much my own outer and inner life is built upon the labors of others, both living and dead, and how earnestly I must exert myself in order to give in return as much as I have received and am still receiving."

- Albert Einstein

TABLE OF CONTENTS

Foreword

by Thomas Kean, Chairman of the 9/11 Commission

It is difficult to remember that day, but we must. Time has its own way of dulling the sharp edge of memory. Once the edge has been sufficiently blurred, the distorting colors of apocrypha swirl in, smearing the true image and creating a fable. A myth. Whatever it's name, the resulting picture is false. And yet people will believe it. In later years, they will have no choice. And therein lies the danger.

This book is unique for several reasons, not the least of which is that it allows our American people to speak for themselves regarding the terrorist attacks of September 11th. The events of that day are arguably the most traumatic ever to occur on American soil. There is ample evidence to support the need for a record such as this book presents.

After the Great Depression had ravaged the United States through the early part of the 20th century, President Roosevelt realized that our country needed more than an economic kick start. It needed cultural inspiration, as well. He assigned writers and journalists through the Federal Writer's Project to document the experiences of common people living through uncommon circumstances.

Roosevelt knew that a culture which cannot remember its past trials and transgressions will doom itself to repeat them. The memory of slavery, for instance, was fast slipping from the American consciousness. In some ways this was a sign of progress; in other ways it was potentially dangerous. The FWP documented the recollections of thousands of former slaves in what would later become the Slave Narrative Collection. Nearly a hundred years later, these narratives are still performed around the country as theatrical events; assigned as required reading for university courses; read for self-edification by curious citizens. They are a part of our cultural body of evidence against what was, and an inspiration toward a brighter future of what might be.

Some of our greatest works of literature were born of this need to bear witness. John Steinbeck's *The Grapes of Wrath*. Jack Conroy's *The Disinherited*. Studs Terkel's *The Good War*.

I'm proud and grateful to see this legacy continued.

*　　*　　*

What follows is not media spin, 5 second sound-byte, or a coldly-recycling film reel. It is a living time capsule of our nation's humanity.

The interviews contained in this book are seminal to our American history. Interestingly, they were conducted immediately following the attacks on the World Trade Center, before time had been granted a chance to blur the details. Reading them, you get the sense that there was just enough time between the Towers' collapse and the click of the recorder for people to catch their breaths and plant their feet on firm ground. Then they began to speak, directly and candidly. They spoke from their hearts, and I can't think they gave a single notion toward the idea that their words would be preserved forever. It was too confusing and painful a time to fumble with the weight of such ideas. Truth rings out in every word.

I hope this book remains in print for a very long time to come, because everyone should read it. Our children should read it. With regard to 9/11, we - as a people - cannot allow a myth to take root. We must ground ourselves in the reality of our pain if we have any hope of moving forward. And move forward we must.

*   *   *

One of the contributors to this book calls 9/11 "a Kennedy moment. . . Everyone knows where they were when John Lennon was killed. Everyone knows where they were when the Space Shuttle blew. It's a Kennedy moment. A Pearl Harbor moment." It's a valid observation. Perhaps it's even a key to understanding the workings of human consciousness. And so I invite you, this instant, to clear your mind and think back for a moment.

Where were you that day? Watching the video clips spool over and over again on the television . . . listening to your car radio while driving to work . . . waking up to a household exploding with confusion and chaos . . . calling friends, calling family . . . inside the Towers. . . outside the Towers . . . on the streets of New York City, or halfway across the world . . . wondering where your loved ones were. Wondering. Just wondering.

You were scared. You were angry. You were vulnerable. We all were.

But after that initial shock passed over us, what did you do then? Perhaps the most important message recorded in *Tower Stories* is written between the lines:

You made turkey sandwiches for rescue workers rushing down to Ground Zero . . . you donated goods . . . you sent money to relief charities . . . you held a perfect stranger while she cried . . . you walked the streets of Manhattan, looking for someplace, anyplace to help. . . you gathered together in mourning. You prayed. You hung on.

You went back to work. You picked up the pieces. And maybe, like me, you made eye contact with people you didn't know on the streets where you live and nodded. Only this time, as our glances met, a new door was opened between us. We were able to share in a quiet secret that everyone suddenly knew – that we are all, in our own way, survivors.

Move forward we must.

For we are Americans. This is our story. ℑ

AUTHOR'S INTRODUCTION

The photos you're about to view have all been donated by gracious photographers, both amateur and professional. The stories you're about to read are distilled from interviews conducted in the year following September 11th, 2001. In every case, great effort was made to capture the speaker's inimitable tone, viewpoint, and rhythm of speech.

If, while reading, you begin to imagine what the speaker looks like, or the particular gestures he or she might make to illustrate a point – if the voice you are experiencing begins to take on a life of its own in your mind – then perhaps this book's mission has succeeded.

The *Tower Stories* project sprang from the disturbing notion that the memory of September 11th might one day quietly fade from the consciousness of the world. The fact is that our human history crawls through the sands of time like a snake towing a trowel in its wake. Despite the best efforts we exert to preserve our tracks, they inevitably disappear, wiped clean behind us or forever blurred into causal statements devoid of human feeling.

What will future generations do with these statements? Perhaps they will ponder them as if reading a collection of ancient Zen koans, and attempt to extract a meaning which we ourselves could never distill.

Pearl Harbor was the event which prompted the United States to enter the Second World War . . . the Holocaust claimed the lives of six million people. . .JFK was assassinated in Dallas Texas. . .the first President of the United States was George Washington . . . Harry Truman dropped the bomb and the United States was attacked on September 11th, 2001. . .

And so on. Our species has an unsettling gift for boilerplating tragedy.

So the mission for *Tower Stories* was to create a book that was personal, real, accessible and non-partisan - something reflective of human nature as it manifested itself on the 11th – full of foibles and hubris; fear and longing; community, sorrow, and yes, a considerable amount of pride where heroism warranted it.

Or, if you prefer, the book's mission could be stated like this: write a book that someday we'll be proud to have our grandchildren read. So that, when they start to ask questions – and they *will* ask questions - we can pull a copy off the shelf, hand it to them, and say, "Here. Maybe this will help you understand. These are the voices of the people who were there, and I bet they'll tell you what happened much better than I can."

"Oh, and by the way? When you're finished reading, come find me and let's sit down together. We can talk for as long as you like."

Who knows? If we give our grandchildren free access to our history, they just might come up with better answers than we did. We might save them a few mistakes. After all, isn't that what we're here for? 🙎

Timeline of Events

Tuesday, September 11, 2001
Note: all times are offered in EDT.

The planes take-off.

7:58 AM: *American Airlines Flight 11 leaves Boston for Los Angeles.*
8:01 AM: *United Airlines Flight 93 leaves Newark for San Francisco.*
8:11 AM: *American Airlines Flight 77 departs Washington D.C. for Los Angeles.*
8:12 AM: *United Airlines Flight 175 leaves Boston for Los Angeles.*

The attacks on the Towers.

8:45 AM: *Flight 11 crashes into the North Tower of the World Trade Center. A burning hole is torn in the building.*
9:04 AM: *Flight 175 crashes into the South Tower of the World Trade Center. Now both buildings are burning.*

The first response.

9:15 AM: *President Bush makes his first statement about the attacks from Sarasota, Florida. He says the nation is the victim of an "apparent terrorist attack."*
9:18 AM: *The FAA shuts down all New York area airports.*
9:21 AM: *The Port Authority of New York and New Jersey closes all bridges and tunnels into and out of New York. The NYSE and NASDAQ stock markets close.*
9:40 AM: *The FAA grounds all flights in the United States, the first time in U.S. history that all airline operations have been stopped.*

The crisis continues.

9:45 AM: *Flight 77 crashes into the Pentagon; the White House and Capitol are evacuated.*
9:57 AM: *President Bush takes off from Florida.*
10:05 AM: *The South Tower of the World Trade Center collapses, showering escapees and emergency rescue workers with tons of rubble.*
10:09 AM: *Heavily-armed Secret Service agents are deployed around the White House.*
10:10 AM: *A section of the Pentagon collapses from the damage inflicted upon it. Flight 93 crashes in Somerset County, PA; cell phone accounts from passengers on board*

confirm that the plane was hijacked.

10:15 AM: *Some 11,000 people evacuate the United Nations.*

10:25 AM: *The FAA reroutes all international flights bound for the U.S. to Canada.*

10:28 AM: *The North Tower of the World Trade Center collapses.*

Further chaos . . .

10:44 AM: *Federal buildings in Washington, D.C. are evacuated.*

10:46 AM: *Secretary of State Colin Powell, in Latin America, makes plans to return to the U.S.*

10:53 AM: *New York primary elections are canceled.*

10:54 AM: *Israel evacuates its diplomatic centers.*

11:02 AM: *New York mayor Rudy Giuliani asks residents to stay home; orders evacuation of Manhattan south of Canal Street.*

11:15 AM: *The Center for Disease Control prepares emergency response teams.*

A long afternoon.

12:05 PM: *Los Angeles International and San Francisco International Airports are evacuated under the logic that they were destination airports of the four crashed planes.*

12:17 PM: *Immigration and Naturalization Services places U.S. borders with Mexico and Canada on the high alert status, but keeps these borders open.*

12:18 PM: *Major League Baseball cancels all games scheduled for that night.*

1:05 PM: *President Bush addresses the nation from Barksdale Air Force Base, Louisiana. He says that security measures have been put into place, and that the United States military is on high alert across the globe. He vows to "hunt down and punish those responsible for these cowardly acts."*

1:43 PM: *The Defense Department announces that battleships and aircraft carriers are being deployed around New York City, Washington D.C., and the East Coast.*

1:48 PM:: *President Bush leaves Barksdale Air Force Base and flies to a Nebraska military facility.*

2:30 PM: *The FAA makes an announcement that all commercial U.S. air traffic has been canceled.*

2:51 PM: *In New York City, Mayor Giuliani announces that subway and bus services have been partially restored. As far as the number of people killed in the attacks, Mayor Giuliani says, "I don't think we can speculate . . . more than any of us can bear."*

3:55 PM: *Mayor Giuliani notes the number of critically injured in New York City as having risen to 200, with 2,100 total injuries reported.*

4:09 PM: *7 World Trade Center, adjacent to the Twin Towers, is reported on fire.*

4:25 PM: *The New York Stock Exchange, AMEX and NASDAQ announce that they will remain closed.*

4:30 PM: *The President leaves Nebraska to return to Washington, D.C. Fires are still reported burning in the Pentagon.*

5:20 PM: *7 World Trade Center collapses. The 47-story building sustained heavy damages after Towers 1 and 2 collapsed. Nearby buildings are also on fire.*

5:30 PM: *U.S. officials announce that the plane which crashed in Shanksville, PA may have been headed on a collision course for the White House, Camp David, or the United States Capitol Building.*

A longer evening...

6:10 PM: *Mayor Giuliani asks New York City residents to stay home on Wednesday, September 12th.*

6:35 PM: *At the Pentagon, Defense Secretary Rumsfeld notes that the building is "operational" and hints at getting to work immediately on reconciling the attack.*

7:17 PM: *U.S. Attorney General Ashcroft announces that the FBI is looking for tips on the attacks.*

7:45 PM: *Reports confirm that at least 78 police officers are missing; 400 firefighters killed.*

8:30 PM: *President Bush addresses the nation, asking for prayers for the families and friends of the victims. He notes that the U.S. government will make no distinctions between terrorists who commit attacks and those who harbor terrorists.*

9:22 PM: *Reports from the Pentagon say that the fire there is contained, but not under control.*

9:53 PM: *Mayor Giuliani announces that no more rescue volunteers are needed, adding that he still has hope that people are alive in the rubble of the World Trade Towers.*

10:56 PM: *New York City police echo the Mayor's earlier sentiment that people are alive in the rubble.*

World Trade Center: Damage Assessment

Collapsed or Destroyed
1. One World Trade Center
2. Two World Trade Center
3. Marriott Hotel
4. Five World Trade Center
5. Seven World Trade Center

Partially Collapsed
7. Four World Trade Center
8. Six World Trade Center

Major Damage
6. One Liberty Plaza
9. East River Savings Bank
10. N.J. Kalikow and Co. Building and Millennium Hotel
11. Federal Building.
12. N.Y. Telephone Building.
13. Three World Financial Center
14. Two World Financial Center
15. One World Financial Center
16. St. Nicholas Greek Orthodox Church
17. 90 West Street
18. Bankers Trust

At The Towers

TOM HADDAD, 31, was working in his office, Suite 8901 on the 89th Floor of Tower 1, when the plane hit two stories above his head.

———

First, I heard the engine. It was incredibly loud. There were a couple of times when I'd been in the office late at night and I could hear thunderstorms, I could see lightning hitting the water - it was that kind of *boom*. Then the glass in my window started to vibrate like ripples in water.

The order of all this occurred to me later. For weeks after the plane hit, I was replaying the first 30 to sixty seconds over and over again in my head, trying to make order of it.

I got to work early that day. The day before, we'd made a major presentation to a banking client - we do a lot of internal work for banks, Citibank is our biggest client. Recently, we'd taken on the project of communicating the services available to employees after the merger of JP Morgan and Chase. We were putting together a campaign to educate them.

The client was interested in quick turn-around, so on the 10th of September, I was at the office until about nine at night. The following morning, I got into the office at about 7:30, still working on the campaign designs.

There were five people in the office that early: myself; Lynn, the head copywriter; the receptionist, Sabrina; another fellow from the art department, my friend Evan; and Frances, a lady from client services. I had just completed the designs and Lynn and I were discussing them at my computer.

My computer monitor was in the window well of my office, facing north. I had a great view from that window. In fact, if I craned my neck about a millimeter to the right, I could see the Empire State Building off in the distance.

I was sitting at my desk. Lynn was in the doorway to my office, heading out. I got up out of my chair to ask her to come back and look at the designs again when we were hit. I was thrown about three feet and hit the wall nearly horizontal. Lynn was thrown a good five feet out my door into the main design department. The entire office erupted into flames and total darkness.

All the power went out like flipping off a light. The sprinkler system popped on. When I came to everything was on fire except for a three and half foot path to the door. I was in that path and so was Lynn. Interestingly enough, Evan, Frances, and Sabrina were all in that same straight line. After talking about it later, we found out how lucky we were – everything around us burned.

I don't know if you've ever been in the World Trade Center, but it could really move a lot. I mean, on a windy day, the Towers would actually sway. I would hear the creaking from my office. Ceiling tiles would fall on you; it was fairly normal. When we were hit, all of the ceiling tiles dropped on us. We had just had construction done on the office to put up walls, including the wall to my office. One of the inter-office walls fell down.

* * *

I stood up, totally stunned. Lynn got up off the ground and yelled, "Thomas, what are you doing? Run!" She ran toward the front door.

The carpeting in the office was that gross kind of indoor-outdoor industrial carpet. If you scraped your feet on it, it would make this sort of *Vroooooooof!* noise that went right through you. My foot slipped on a piece of ceiling tile and I realized the glass from my window had blown into the office. That's when I turned and looked out the window.

I was stunned at how blue the sky was. The columns in the wall had stayed, but nothing else. I was open to the sky 89 stories in the air.

I turned back toward where Lynn had run deeper into the office and that's when I noticed the conference room wall had a very interesting pattern of fire running down it. Later I found out it was jet fuel leaking straight down from the ceiling.

* * *

Everything was strangely silent except for the constant high-pitched *whoop whoop whoop* of the fire alarm. We had done fire drills as a matter of routine working in the Towers. They'd always played announcements over the intercom system. Nothing now, though.

It was as if time started to move very slowly. I didn't run, I didn't hurry. I just strolled out of the office, absorbing my surroundings. I got to the front of our office's design department and caught up with Evan. He was as stunned as I was.

We walked toward the front reception area and the back wall behind the receptionist's desk was on fire. Sabrina was okay. She had been standing in that same straight line that kept all of us safe. But the front doors to the office had blown in and were on fire. And across the hall from our office was a ladies room. The wall was gone and you could see toilets. We were walking on tiles and glass.

Lynn ran through the front door and out into the hallway. We decided to follow her. We got about six feet out; I looked over to my right and couldn't see a thing because of the black smoke. The entire east side of the building was obscured and there was no air to breathe.

Evan and Sabrina were with me, Lynn was in front. But I thought to myself, "I don't know where Frances is." So I decided to turn back into the office. At this point, the fire was six feet high but there was a little spot on the door where there was no fire. I put my foot on there and crashed through.

I could hear Frances screaming from the copy room. The filing cabinets in the copy room had all gone down on top of one another. Now Frances is tiny. She stands maybe 4'11." And somehow she had managed to wiggle in between all these cabinets which were full of reams of 11 x 17 paper and hanging files. They had fallen in front of a door leading to the hallway and she was pulling on the door handle, screaming to get out. She must've panicked. She didn't realize that she couldn't open the door because a filing cabinet had fallen against it.

The cabinet was heavy but I threw it aside as if it weighed nothing. Pure adrenaline. Evan and Sabrina followed me, raising the rest of the cabinets and debris in front of the door. When we opened that door and got out, we turned the corner to go toward the elevators. We could hear Lynn's voice yelling to us, "Follow me, follow me!" We started running.

*   *   *

From fire drills as far back as the third grade I remembered we would have more air if we crawled. I yelled, "Everybody drop! Crawl to her!" We crawled past Kosmo Services, the office which shared a wall with mine.

I swear to you, that office looked like nothing had happened even though it was directly under where the plane had flown in. Their power was still on, their phones still worked. Some of the ceiling tiles had fallen and the books were jumbled around a little from the shelves, but it looked as if nothing had happened. I didn't understand it at all.

We crawled into Kosmo and there were five people in there including Walter, who owned the company. Lynn and Walter went out into the hall to see if they could find anybody. They found an elderly gentleman who was yelling, "Somebody please help me!" I don't know his name. I would see him in the elevator everyday but, like a lot of people who worked for companies on my floor, I never talked to them. Not even a 'hello' or 'how you doing?' They were just the people in the elevator.

There was nothing wrong with this man. He was just scared and in the dark out in the hall, so they brought him inside.

Lynn and Walter also discovered that all the doors to the stairwells were locked. Don't know why. I've heard that the doors lock automatically during an emergency as a mechanical function and I've also heard that the doors were kept locked intentionally to keep people from going into the stairwell to smoke. Each office was apparently equipped with keys but we didn't know it at the time. I found out later that the keys to the stairwell were in the receptionist's desk, which was on fire.

*　　*　　*

We had air in Kosmo's office, and after Lynn and Walter came back, we closed the door to try to keep the air clean. It had taken us maybe 15 minutes to get out of our office. I was still in a daze.

Now this is interesting: in my office, there was a radiator by the window. Every morning, I used to step up onto the radiator into the window well, put my head against the glass and look out and down. From that perspective, you could see everywhere, all of New York City.

In the Kosmo office, the first thing I did - I guess by instinct - was step up onto the radiator, put my head against the glass, and look out. I wasn't thinking that my own windows had just blown out. Occasionally, flaming pieces of the building would fall and hit the glass that I was pressing my face against.

Walter said, "Hey, you know? I don't think that's such a good idea."

I said, "Okay," and climbed down.

*　　*　　*

People started making phone calls. I called my wife, who works for NBC at Rockefeller Center, but she was still at the gym - she goes there on mornings when I go to work early. I left a message on her voice mail, trying my best to sound even-keeled. I said, "Ah, the building's exploded. Turn the TV on, we're probably on the news."

Then somebody had the great idea to turn on a radio. Simultaneously, Lynn was on the phone talking to a friend who was watching TV. We learned that a plane had struck the building. WNEW radio station was, in my opinion, making light of the situation. They were watching replays of the impact on TV, doing a play-by-play as if it were a sporting event. I decided that, since we were all freaking out and Frances and Sabrina were crying, I would get up and change the station.

That's when the second plane hit. Our building shook, and I was nearly knocked off my feet again.

*   *   *

We sat on the floor of Kosmo Services. I called my mom, but she wasn't home. I called my wife's machine again and left progressively nervous messages. There were actually four messages I later learned - the fourth message was a hang-up and I believe it was time-stamped at 9:14 am.

I hung up on that call because a guy from Operations came by and opened the office door. He was dressed in regular clothes but had a hard hat and a flashlight. He said that he'd just opened the stairwell and he told us, "Wait, and then follow me." But none of us waited. We saw the open stairwell and went for it.

Apparently, there were two Operations guys who had come up to look for people, but I only saw the one. One of them went down from our floor and the other guy went up, I assume to see if they could open more stairwells. I found out later that the guy who went upstairs didn't live; the guy who went downstairs did. Later on, I saw a television show on The Learning Channel, and I think I recognized the guy who went up as the Head of Operations, a Port Authority guy.[1]

We started down the stairs. There was nobody on them, it was eerie. There was just the 11 of us, five from my office, five from Kosmo, and the elderly guy. We were told later that everyone else on our floor had been killed.

*   *   *

When we reached the 82nd floor, someone said that the stairwell was blocked. We would have to cut across the building and find another pathway down. So we opened the door to the 82nd floor and started walking around, looking for another stairwell.

The floor was completely devastated. You couldn't see your hand in front of your face. The

---

[1]From other interview accounts, it is likely that this man was Frank DeMartini. Mr. Martini worked closely with Rick Zottola at Lesley E. Robinson, Associates. See RICK ZOTTOLA in the GROUND ZERO & THE VOLUNTEERS section of this book.

burning smell . . . I'll still occasionally catch a whiff of it for no apparent reason. Something tangy and pungent, similar to burning rubber. The floor was covered with piles of debris, collapsed plaster walls and big chunks of metal that looked like beams.

Somebody in our group got the idea to light our way through by turning their cell phone on and off. This little green light would come on in the black smoke and the phone's owner would wave it through the air around objects so that we could see where they were and crawl through them. Fire surrounded us everywhere, but you still couldn't see anything. You could only see the fire when you got right on top of it.

It was extremely hot. The sprinklers were on here, too - we were drenched. The fire emergency strobes would flash but we still couldn't see through the obscurity of debris.

When we got to the next stairwell, we started down again, and now we saw people. Occasionally, we would pass somebody going down. But we kept to the course and we kept to ourselves. We were tired and scared and very determined.

*   *   *

We got to the 78th floor Sky Lobby.[2] We encountered a railing of sorts, a long hallway that allowed us to keep going without actually going out onto the 78th floor. At the end of this hallway were two doors, side by side. Two guys were standing in front of them, yelling at each other.

The one door said "EXIT" on it with a sign pointing down. One man was saying to follow that sign, but the other man yelled, "No. I've done this before. This other door goes to the bottom. If you take the stairs with the EXIT sign, you'll have to cross the building again."

"I'm following the sign, I'm following the sign!" said the one guy.

The other guy said: "You do whatever you want, I'm going this way." They were angry. I didn't recognize either of them.

I was in the front of our group at this point. We had lost the people from Kosmo so there was just the five from our office and the elderly gentleman. I said, "I'm following this guy if he says the door goes to the ground." Not the guy who followed the sign, but the guy

---

[2] A Sky Lobby was a sort of dock that increased office space without having to put in more elevators. There were elevator banks at the base of each Tower that would go direct to the Sky Lobbies on 78 or 44. From there, you would take a local elevator to the floor you worked on.

who said, "I've done this before."

*   *   *

We entered another stairwell, but this one was flooded. Water was rushing ankle-deep in a constant flow down the stairs from the sprinklers or maybe from broken pipes. At some points the flow was so heavy that you had to hold on tight to the railing. It was incredibly hot and we were soaked.

In the stairs you would see items like a pair of shoes, a tie, an abandoned briefcase - as if someone had said, "Screw this, I don't need a tie anymore," and tossed it.

We encountered a lot more people around floor 50. Before that, we had seen small groups here and there, but there were actual crowds on 50. People would yell their floor number out as they went down to let people know who was evacuating. Not once did we hear anyone higher than our floor.

People were stopping and drinking Cokes, soft drinks and water from jugs. "Does anyone want a Dr. Pepper?" Uh uh. We didn't stop for anything or anybody. And we helped people; there was a couple of elderly women who were having trouble getting down the stairs at one point where the water was serious - we helped them get past that area. We weren't abandoning anyone and we weren't allowing how tired we were to affect what our mission was: to get the five of us the hell out of there.

*   *   *

We saw the first fireman on the 30th floor. He had his full gear on and a hose over his shoulder. I couldn't believe he had any energy to walk up the steps. He looked exhausted, ready to drop. He took his helmet off, someone poured water in it and he put the helmet back on his head with the water still in it. It was devastatingly hot.

There was no panic in the stairs, people weren't pushing. They were friendly and calm. We all thought that, by getting to the stairs, we'd be safe. We would get out. The fire was behind us, after all. It was just a matter of keep walking, keep walking. We still didn't know at that point what kind of devastation had taken place.

We'd been walking two at a time, but we experienced a back-up around the 50th floor. Occasionally, someone would come up the stairs and you had to make room for them - a fireman, a building manager, an occasional EMT. By the 30th floor, so many people were coming up that we were down proceeding single file. The line was moving slow, the water was moving fast. You had to hold onto the brackets that held the banister to the wall.

8

*   *   *

At about the 3rd floor there was a woman sitting in a chair in the stairwell doorway with two firemen by her side. She was in hysterics, saying she couldn't go anymore, she absolutely could not walk anymore. They were saying to her, "Please. You have to keep walking. You only have three floors to go . . ."

Two regular office guys were carrying a person in a wheelchair via a board slung between the wheels.

A door opened out onto the Plaza Level. Technically, this was floor 2, the courtyard between the two Towers. The Trade Center really had two ground levels, this Plaza Level and the true ground level at the bottom of the escalators. The huge glass windows of the plaza were still standing and there was a line of police officers stretching all the way back. The police were shouting to us, "Don't look out the window, just keep walking."

At this point, the five of us were separated; Frances and Sabrina had gotten ahead of us in the stairwell but I was still with Lynn and Evan.

*   *   *

A guy walked past me from behind and started through the plaza. He was bald and had a massive head wound that stretched all the way over his skull from temple to temple. It was pouring blood onto his white dress shirt.

A cop from the row yelled out to him, "Hey, buddy are you okay?" and ran forward from the line.

The bald guy says, in a heavy, matter-of-fact New York accent: "Yeah. I've had better days."

The cops started yelling, "If you have the energy, run! If you can, you gotta run!"
Lynn took off running down toward the escalator.

Time stopped dead for me, just as it had immediately after the impact of the plane. I was still walking, but I was completely hypnotized by what I saw through the windows in the plaza outside the building.

*   *   *

The Sphere[3] was smashed. It had a dent in it and a piece of the building on top of it. A large chunk of the building façade was right outside the window, blazing fire.

Occasionally you would hear this devastatingly loud *thumping*. At the time, I thought it was more pieces of the building falling, it didn't register. But there were these hunks and piles of meat on the ground . . . nothing I recognized as body parts. I found out later they were the remains of jumpers.

Somehow I kept walking and got to the escalator leading down to the Concourse Level. The escalator was stopped and filled with water about knee-deep at the bottom. All the glass leading out of the Concourse was broken. All the revolving doors? Broken. The floor was covered in glass. The line of police officers was staggered, directing traffic past the PATH[4] station, around a corner by the A Train to another escalator up to the plaza level. We exited outside to the Trade Center campus. I think we were on Church Street, just Lynn, Evan, and myself.

There were police officers yelling, "Don't look up, just keep going." Which is, of course, exactly when I decided to look up. I hadn't even thought of it until they said not to. That's when I saw we were standing directly in front of Building 2. I was looking straight up at a gaping hole with fire coming out of it, the same thing you've probably seen on the news.

We decided to walk across the street.

In front of an iron gate surrounding a church, Lynn said, "Whatever you guys do, don't leave me. I don't have any money or identification. I left my purse upstairs."[5] She was fairly calm, but nervous. We all were. Evan, at this point, hadn't really said anything. He's a pretty quiet guy. Then I heard the sound of the building starting to fall.

It was a creaking. Almost like when you have an upstairs neighbor and they're walking around; sort of like that, but really, really loud. And then thunder. I turned around and saw the building coming down. We were a block away.

The three of us ran in different directions.

---

[3]Sculpture by artist Fritz Koenig. A huge gold sphere made of steel and bronze, created in 1971 as a monument to world peace through international trade.

[4]Port Authority Trans-Hudson Corporation. A series of trains connecting points in New Jersey, notably Hoboken, to stations scattered throughout lower Manhattan.

[5]The church mentioned here was probably St. Paul's.

*   *   *

I ran straight up Dey Street and passed a 4/5/6 subway station. I turned to go in there, thinking I would be okay underground. But should I go down? Or try to find a building to get into – or a car to crawl under? In that split second of indecision, the cloud engulfed me. It came from the north, south, east, west. It came from above; every possible direction. I was standing in the middle of the street. There was nowhere to go.

The debris cloud hit me like a sledgehammer from all directions so I didn't fall over. Total blackness. No air at all. Then something hit me on the head.

I pulled my shirt up over my head. I couldn't see anyway, so what did it matter? I thought to myself, "I can't believe that after 80 flights of stairs, I'm going to die right here in the street." I was so tired. My knees hurt. Anytime I stopped moving, my legs would shake. I wanted to just sit down and let it happen.

But you know - just a couple of days before, I had made a promise to my wife that I would never leave her alone. How could I do that to her? I said to myself, "I love my wife. I'm gonna keep walking."

I remembered there had been a building right in front of me before the cloud came down. I started toward it, but walked straight into a parked car. I felt my way around it, kicking for the curb with my foot. Got up over the curb and onto the sidewalk. I was walking like Frankenstein with my shirt over my head and my hands out in front of me.

I walked into somebody who grabbed my hands and said, "Go this way." And then they let go and were gone.

I walked toward the left and into the rough stone wall of a building. I thought, "Okay, I'll just keep walking to the left and maybe I'll get to a door." I kept going and came to a corner. So I figured I'd turn the corner and follow the line of the building - eventually there had to be a door.

"Fuck it, I'm gonna walk forward."

Boom. I walked right into a revolving door and into the building.

*   *   *

I pulled my head out from inside my shirt and saw what must have been a thousand screaming people. I was standing in the building's lobby.

There was a fireman on his hands and knees in his bunker gear throwing up blood all over the floor. He looked up at me and his eyes were blood red; he looked at me like I was nuts. He handed me a Gatorade, still on his hands and knees. I was confused. I didn't know what was going on. I couldn't believe I was alive.

And he goes, "Just fucking drink it."

I had so much soot and ash in my mouth and nose. I took a swig, weird shit going through my head. A stranger hands me a drink after throwing up, I'm worried about germs? I decided to wash my mouth out with it rather than drink. I spat it out on the floor, which is when I noticed that the fireman hadn't really been throwing up blood. Like me – he was spitting out red Gatorade.

I noticed then that I was covered with ash an inch thick. I had gotten so wet from being in the building that everything stuck to me. A guy walked up to me saying, "Hey, are you okay? Are you okay?" He was totally clean. I handed him the Gatorade.

A policeman got on a bullhorn and said, "If there's anyone with any disability or asthma, follow my hand." And though there's a thousand people in the lobby, I see this hand poke up. I think, "I don't have a disability or asthma but I'm gonna follow that hand."

I worked my way through the crowd. People saw me and made a path. The mob split down the middle. I went through a back door and into an Au Bon Pain.[6] There were maybe ten police officers in there trying to figure out what to do next.

* * *

In retrospect, I had no idea where I was. I don't know the location of that building now, for instance. I haven't wanted to go downtown at all, but after seeing that special on CBS, I want to see the street again. I want to know where I was.[7] I wonder how far away I got.

When I was running from that building, I felt like Carl Lewis. That's the fastest I've ever run in my life. I have no idea how far I got.

---

[6] A chain patisserie.

[7] The Naudet brothers, a pair of French filmmakers, happened to be filming a documentary on the New York Fire Department on 9/11. The brothers captured some of the most extraordinary film ever taken on that day. The film aired on CBS in March of 2002.

In the Au Bon Pain, there was a case of Poland Spring water bottles and I took one of them along with a handful of napkins. I wiped all the debris out of my eyes and face. At this point, it hit me like a ton of bricks that I had no idea whether the people I was with had lived or died. Evan - I've known him since freshman year in college, we were roommates together. Lynn? She's been such a special friend to me at my job, like a confidante. I thought, "How could they have survived?" I'm sitting there in the Au Bon Pain with my bottle of water and I started to panic. I started to hyperventilate.

A police officer sat down next to me and she took my hand. "It's okay," she said. "Just let it out. You're experiencing post-traumatic stress syndrome."

I thought, "Post? I think I'm still *in* the trauma."

But she was nice enough to calm me down. Another officer on a bullhorn said, "We're evacuating this building. An officer will tell you at the door to walk right or left. Follow that direction."

I got to the door and the guy said to walk to the right, so I did. I started down the street through calf-deep piles of sand-colored building debris. Everything was weirdly quiet, almost as if my brain had taken in so much information that it had shut down. Even when the building was falling, there had been so much sound that it was if there was no sound at all. Like white noise. A drone.

I'm walking down the street, not knowing where to go, thinking that everybody I was with had died. I barely knew who I was, I was dizzy and disoriented, my speech is slurred. I'd been hit twice on the head, once in the office and once on the street. I had caught the wall of my office on my right temple and whatever had hit me in the street had caught my left temple. All I wanted to do was get uptown and find my wife. I knew where she worked and I said, "Even if I have to walk, I'll get there eventually."

So I started walking.

*　　*　　*

Someone in the street yelled, "Hey, these buses are going uptown."

There were three MTA buses waiting and the first two were jam-packed with people. The third bus looked newer, almost like the type you would travel long distances on. There was nobody on this bus, so I got in line - I was maybe the third person. I said: "If you're going uptown, that's where I'm going."

I walked to the back of the bus and sat down. I was numb. People were filing onto the bus, some were dirty and some were normal looking. A guy sits down in the seat in front of me, slumps down, sits up again, and then starts pounding on the glass window of the bus. He's yelling nonsense at the top of his lungs.

"This guy's lost it," I think.

He's down in his seat again and I notice in the reflection of the window glass that it was Evan. He had thought he'd seen me out on the street - a guy had walked past with a similar moustache and build. Evan was pounding the window to get my attention.

I got up, sat down next to him, and said, "You've got to be fucking kidding me. After all of this, here you are."

We hugged each other and I said, "Listen. For the rest of the day, we stick together."

The bus headed uptown. As we were making the turn off Park Row, Building Two fell. We heard it and the bus was completely consumed in the cloud. After it settled, we kept driving. We got to the UN[8] and the street was blocked by security so the bus couldn't go north anymore. As it turned to go cross-town, I looked at Evan and said, "Let's get out and walk to Rockefeller."

* * *

When we got to NBC, there was a security guard who said, "Who you looking for?"

"My wife."

"Well, they evacuated the building."

I felt like, now what? Where could she possibly be? The city is huge. I asked somebody on the bus if I could borrow their cell phone, but it wasn't working. Meanwhile another guy on the bus was giving everyone an in-depth description of people whom he had seen jump. I'm standing there, completely at a loss, I barely know who I am. I say to myself, "I'd better get to a hospital. I should really have someone take a look at me."

* * *

Evan hadn't been out in the dust cloud. He had been running and a door to some building

---

[8] The United Nations, located on 1st Avenue between 41st Street and 42nd Street.

opened up - someone had grabbed him and pulled him in just before the impact.

Lynn didn't get very far. The impact threw her into the gate of the church we had been standing by and people trampled her. They ran right over her. The whole left side of her body was a giant bruise, but somehow she managed to survive. She covered her face and crawled into the lobby of a building where she tied her shoe and left. Then she walked all the way across the Williamsburg Bridge.

* * *

From Rockefeller, we decided to walk west, I don't know why. We got to the Double Tree Hotel[9] and I thought they might let us use the phones. The people there looked at us as if we were nuts. In midtown, we were the only people covered in soot. We were space aliens who had been quickly thrust uptown by the bus; people walking from downtown wouldn't show up for another hour or so.

The receptionist behind the desk at the Double Tree looked at me and said, "You're dirty."

Uh huh. "Okay. I was just in the World Trade Center and I need to use your phone."

She just kept looking at me.

"I need. To use. Your phone."

She turns the phone around and I decide to call my wife's mother in West Caldwell, New Jersey, figuring that, if anyone knows where my wife is, she would. I've dialed this number thousands of times. But on that day I had to do it four or five times to get it right. I finally got through and my mother-in-law knew where to find my wife.

She had been evacuated from NBC and didn't know where to go. One of her co-workers had shown up to work late and had no idea what was going on, just that her building was emptying out. This co-worker had a cousin who worked in a building close by and they went there. Kim thought that if she went to another office, she would have multiple phone lines at her disposal. I called at about noon and 20 minutes or so later, she met me at the Double Tree Hotel.

We started to find a way home.

---

[9]In Times Square

*   *   *

I've been keeping to myself lately, spending a lot of time with my wife, Kim. We've been married three years in May. We met in high school, we've been together for over 13 years. I've been an emotional wreck. Not so much in breaking down and crying a lot. More like sudden mood changes.

I'll flash to anger like never before. I always had a short fuse, but I was able to keep it in check. Lately it seems as if, "Why bother?" I've been hideously depressed. I go from normal to extremes. From what I've read, it's post-traumatic stress, but you know what? I refuse to go to any counseling - for multiple reasons.

First, I don't think that they're going to suddenly make me better. It's gonna take time, a lot of talking and a lot of living. Second? I had a horrible experience with the hospital I went to on September 11th. The astronomical bills they've continually sent me even though my insurance paid for it.

I went to the hospital because I was hit in the head twice. First by the impact of the plane when it struck the Tower; I was thrown three feet across my office. Second, in the street - I was hit by the debris cloud pretty hard. Between the two, I got a concussion and barely knew who I was. I walked the streets like a zombie.

*   *   *

I say I don't talk to people. I say that I've pushed a lot of people away. Will that continue? I don't know. I'll tell you this: a lot of my friends come to me when they're having hard times and I'm their counselor. But I felt as if none of them were there for me when I needed them. Not that anybody could really be a counselor for this. The whole city is in need of counseling now. I'm being selfish.

I'm sorry that my friends are having problems with this and that. One guy I know – his marriage is breaking up and I'm sorry. But I don't have time for it right now. I keep thinking about the hundreds of bodies I saw. So instead of being an asshole, which I have great potential for right now due to my temperament, I haven't answered phone calls. I haven't responded to e-mails just so that I don't lash out at people.

It's safe to say that I'm trying to give myself space to take care of my own shit. I don't want to hurt anyone in the process. I went back to work the next week. They needed stuff done and I thought that it was a way for me to focus on something else. I was driving myself nuts sitting at home and once I found out that everyone from my office lived, I went back to work. Work sounded like a good idea.

I make a parallel between my situation and people who have seen combat. My grandfather was on the beach at Normandy. One time he told me what he witnessed there. Somehow he had managed to be a part of this horrific, historic event and maintain a normal life. He didn't allow the horror to overtake his person. I use that as a motivation; I won't allow this event to redefine me. It has and it hasn't, but I make the parallel that I'm not a victim, I'm a soldier. ℥

FLORENCE ENGORAN, 36, worked as a credit analyst at a securities firm on the 55th floor of 2 World Trade Center. She and her husband moved out of Manhattan six months previous to September 11th. "So many things happened in May of 2001," she says. "We had just purchased a house, we moved to New Jersey, and I found out I was pregnant."

———

On the morning of September 11th, at 8:40 am. I got a coffee in the lobby of the World Trade Center and went up to the 55th floor of Tower 2. Everything was normal. As I got off the elevator, everyone was standing around saying, "A small plane hit the other building."

We hadn't seen or heard anything. Usually when things like that happen,[10] people stop working and start milling around. So we were like, "What should we do?"

Some people said, "Oh just sit down, let's keep working, we have to get out some focus reports."

I had one of the five offices on the back wall. There was a big open area with cubes and then a big, huge window where you could see the Hudson River. Within a few minutes, we started to see flaming debris coming down in front of our window. Then the noise . . .

Huge boulders of concrete. Flaming pieces of paper. At first it sounded like it was starting to rain. But then it got so loud . . .

*   *   *

Now people were really stunned. I still had my coffee in hand. I didn't go back to my office to pick up my bag, I turned right around and ran to the fire steps. It wasn't a conscious thought. Not even, "Should I go to the elevators?" My mind was on autopilot: go to the stairs.

It was a panic situation. People were running. We had a trading floor attached to a section of our office - the traders were getting up and running to the stairs. I thought, "I'm five months pregnant, I'm gonna have to go down 55 flights." And these guys are running past me, pushing to get into the stairs.

The stairway was maybe wide enough for two people across. You either stayed to the wall or held on to the handrail. The woman behind me started to scream, "Go faster! Go faster!" I screamed back at her, "I'm pregnant, I'm going as fast as I can!" But other people were

---

[10]Apparently, it wasn't uncommon for small planes to hit the Towers.

saying, "Everyone calm down, relax. Just keep going down. Focus on walking." It probably took me five flights to realize I still had my coffee in my hands. I put it down.

*   *   *

I'd been having morning sickness. I was thinking, "What if I pass out? No one's gonna help me." I was pretty new at the office so I didn't know a lot of people. But these two guys I work with said, "Oh, there's Florence." One guy's name was Brimley, the other was Brian. I had only known them since May - they worked in the accounting department. We said, "Hi," in the morning and that was about it. But these two men said they were gonna stay with me the whole time down, which they did.

Announcements kept saying, "A small plane hit the first building. The incident has been contained there, you don't have to go down." In my head, I was not paying attention to this. I was thinking: "I'm on my way down, I'm going down. Tell me *later* that everything's okay."

Abby Bullock

We probably got to floor 20 when the second plane hit our building.

*   *   *

I held on to the handrail – the impact knocked people over if you didn't hold on. The building moved six to ten feet. Everyone stopped dead, the building was swaying so badly.

Up until that point people were thinking, "It's not us. It's not our building." Even though we were nervous and had seen the debris and wondered if our building might catch fire higher up, we thought we were safe. But when our building was hit people started to scream.

"What's happening?" Different people saying, "They're setting off bombs!" People were using their cell phones to call their families, but other people were starting to panic, saying, "Stop using the cell phones, maybe it's detonating bombs as we go down." Crazy things.

Then the lights went out. Concrete dust started to waft up the stairwell - you were breathing it in. People started to scream. No one was moving. You could smell the jet fuel, it smelled like gas.

When the building settled, people started to run down the stairs, pushing to go past. That lasted maybe a minute. Then people started to scream, "Stop running, we're shaking the stairwell!" – and people calmed down again. We covered our faces with napkins someone handed out. Water bottles were passed around so you could wet your shirt and cover your mouth. It wasn't a thick cloud of smoke, but you definitely had trouble breathing.

* * *

From the 20th floor down was an eternity. People were absolutely silent now where before they'd been laughing, figuring the danger was in the other building. Now they were more focused and scared, trying to walk down as fast as they could.

I had stopped maybe twice from floor 55 to 20 because it was so hot in the stairwell. I was sweating, I needed a breath. Brimley and Bryan still accompanied me. They kept saying, "Okay, we're gonna wait with you, and when you're ready, we'll start again." But after floor 20, it was, "I'm going down, no more breaks. If I pass out on the way, it's gonna have to be."

At the bottom of the stairwell, Port Authority workers were directing us through a passageway. "Okay! Make a left, then a quick right!" Then you opened this door and you were out on the Concourse.

Some people said, "Why are you making us go through the Concourse? We could have gone to the right and out Liberty Street. Why can't we go out those doors?" No one was answering. It was because the debris was falling.

In the Concourse, there were police officers and security guards at different points. I feel very bad because I think they must have been left in there when the building came down, you know? They got us all out, but they were still in there . . .

When I saw them, it hit me that this must be something so bad. Usually, what's the protocol in a fire? "Everyone calm down, no one run." But here they were telling you, "Run! Get out! Get out! Get out!" Pointing which way to go, through the Concourse. It was a weird way to go around. We used an escalator that made us go from the Liberty Street PATH train entrance down past the bakery, by the Nine West shoe store and out.

As we got to the top of the stairs by Nine West, there was a cop there, directing us. He said,

"Things are falling, stay under the building."

Then: "Okay, now! Run! Run!"

*   *   *

People ran. I don't remember things falling, though I know they were. I just kept running. I got across the street by St. Paul's church. Then I started to look around. I had lost Brimley and Brian. Were they in front of me? Behind me? I didn't want them thinking that they had to find me. Policemen were telling us to run across the street . . .

At that point I turned back, and got my first look of the buildings. And I saw something that didn't quite register. A necktie. On a man. In his suit. Jumping out of the building. I realized people were jumping out the windows.

I started walking up the street up to Broadway by the St. Paul's Church graveyard. There was this puddle of blood and . . . a mass with shoes and clothes in a pile. I looked at it and then I realized it was a body. It had to be someone either from the plane of someone who had jumped. I said, "Okay," and kept moving.

*   *   *

I stood up on the fence of the church graveyard so I could look back. Brian and Brimley were behind me and I flagged them down.

Then the three of us followed the crowd up to City Hall, but at once we thought, "What are we doing by City Hall? What if this is the next target?" So we wound through the streets and the next thing you know, we're at Federal Plaza. But the guards outside the Plaza were telling everyone, "Get away from this building. Get away." I guess they thought it might be a target, too.

We were on Thomas Street at that point, with Brian walking ahead. You would pass lines of people on payphones - maybe 30 people to a payphone. People were standing on line, way too close to the buildings.

Some man stepped out of a law firm and Brian said, "Can we come in?"

"Sure, sure."

He took us in.

*　　*　　*

They sat us down, gave us water. They let us use the bathroom, the telephones. Everyone was trying to get through on cell phones, but the circuits were dead.

I called my father in Long Island to let him know I was okay. I had to try him twice; on the third time, it went through. I probably made ten phone calls and that's the only one that went through.

I couldn't get my husband. I later learned that when he heard that a plane had hit the first building, he went down to the World Trade Center to see if he could see me coming out. He was standing under the building when the second plane hit, trying to call me at work, trying to call anyone. His cell phone wouldn't work, so he went back to his office, which was lucky. He would have been killed when the building came down.

Brimley and Brian said, "You stay here. We're gonna go to the corner bar and get a drink." At that time, this made a lot of sense. I was like, "That sounds like a perfectly good idea." And out they went. I guess they needed it so bad, they left the pregnant woman at the lawyer's office. But they didn't even make it to the corner when a police officer came to the door and started evacuating everyone from the building.

*　　*　　*

Across the street from the lawyer's office, people were lined up on a huge set of steps, looking up at the World Trade Center. And all of a sudden they started to scream.

"Everyone! We're gonna start to run again! Go up West Street! Get out of here!"

Everyone had been calm before in the lawyer's office. Now they panicked. I started to run again but I was so dehydrated, I passed out.

*　　*　　*

Two guys from the lawyer's office picked me up off the street. They asked the police, "Can we get an ambulance for her?" The police said: "There's none coming."

One of the guys said, "I've got my car here."

The other guy said, "Put her in. Drive."

So: one guy in the back with me and the other guy driving. And as we left, the guy with me turned and says, "Oh my God, there went the building." It must have been the second Tower. I heard people screaming.

So now, at that point, both buildings were down. And these two guys drove me to St. Vincent's Hospital.

* * *

Hundreds of beds were lined up outside St. Vincent's with nurses standing around waiting. Rows of empty gurneys four or five deep. I only saw one guy sitting in one.

There were already hundreds of people outside waiting to give blood. Someone had made makeshift signs that said 'A', 'O', 'B' and people were congregating around them. They put me in a wheelchair and they took me to the maternity ward.

They were concerned that I needed fluids; they wanted to see how the baby was. They said I was the only pregnant woman brought in from the Trade Center. 20 nurses milling around the nurses station, looking at the TV. But no one was coming, do you know what I mean? All these people waiting, but no one was coming.

I was extremely dehydrated. I had started a few contractions, but that was from the dehydration and the stress. Once they got fluid in me, everything settled down.

The nurses at St. Vincent's kept calling my husband on his cell phone until they finally got in touch with him. He came to the hospital trying to find me, but nobody knew where I was, they hadn't been admitting people properly, I wasn't in the system. So he started walking around trying to find me and eventually got to the maternity ward. It was probably one o'clock in the afternoon when we were reunited.

All the lawyers, Brimley and Bryan, everyone had told me, "Don't worry, your husband's not gonna go to the Tower, he's not gonna come look for you, he'll just walk away." But I said, "I know my husband. He's gonna look for me." I was worried he was standing there at the bottom of the building. Not until I saw him did I feel relieved.

* * *

Recounting this now, it's almost like normal. Like I'm telling a story. If you had seen me in the beginning, I would have been bawling my whole way through.

I'm in counseling. I wouldn't say I'm a hundred percent back to normal. I have trouble going over bridges and going through tunnels. But I'm slowly working myself back up. I've been back to the city. You tell yourself, "I'm a strong person, I'm tough." You don't think these things are gonna affect you the way they do.

The baby? She was having a few problems, but basically . . . she's in there, she's healthy, she's on her way. At St. Vincent's when they were looking at her on the monitor, they said, "Wow, she's really moving around." Well, why not? I walked down 55 flights and ran for at least a mile. And she was in there through it all, kicking around, moving. Running with me.

It's given me a connection to her. Before, September 11th, I wasn't talking to her. I didn't have that connection of, "Okay, little baby. Mommy's running. Just calm down." Now I do.

A few weeks after the attack, I thought, "Am I out of my mind bringing a child into this world?" Especially, too - she was diagnosed with fluid on the brain. "I'm gonna bring this child who's possibly handicapped into this crazy world? What do I tell her? 'People in this world will leave you when buildings are collapsing. They're not gonna help you. You're not gonna be able to get out.'" You see, my other source of guilt - there were so many handicapped people left in the building and they died.

But I'm dealing with that. Now, I definitely feel it's important she's here. Why should I not have a child? Why let horrible people who only know how to hate fill the world?

Fill the world with good people instead. It's important.

Emily Anne Engoran, the littlest WTC escapee, was born on February 18, 2002 weighing in at 8lbs 12.5oz. 🕭

NANCY CASS, 43, works for the New York Society of Security Analysts, Inc. [NYSSA] located on the 44th floor of 1 World Trade Center. She has been employed there for 16 years.

———

8:47 am. There were four of us inside one of the elevators on the east side of the building. I was the last one to step off on the 44th floor. I took four steps to my left, toward my office. There was a loud explosion and the building began to shake violently. People began to scatter.

I froze in place, not knowing which way to turn. One man got back into the elevator we had just stepped off - he looked frightened. The elevator was dark. I shook my head and told him, "No, don't get back in." He stepped out and ran around the corner.

I heard debris falling through the freight elevator. It got louder as it came down the shaft, closer to the 44th floor, like a ton of rocks being dropped through a long, long line of coffee cans. Then: a terrific *swoosh*, which was the freight elevator plummeting.

I thought something had malfunctioned with the electrical systems on one of the higher floors. The passenger elevators on the west side of the building had been out of order for the past five or six weeks and the elevator company had a crew of men working on the scene. I thought something might have gone wrong up there . . .

Then white smoke billowed out through the freight elevator doors. All of a sudden, flames forced their way through the opening.

This all happened in less than 15 seconds.

*　　*　　*

When I saw the flames shoot through the elevator doors, I turned and calmly said, "Fire." The people who had been in the elevator on the way up with me had run toward the second bank of elevators that went to the higher floors. Now they ran straight for the emergency exit and I followed.

I started down the stairs, moving pretty quickly. People were already moving down single file, everyone was calm. But then there was a bottleneck; I had to stop - this must have been somewhere around the 39th floor.

A few hysterical women were screaming. Men in front and in back of me kept calling for people to stay calm. We began to move again, slowly. We had to stop between floors to let people below us file out into the stairwell. Every time we stopped, I heard a woman from above shout, "Why are we stopped?! Why are we *stopped*?!"

It was on the 35th floor that I heard someone from below answer, "The doors are locked!" I remember thinking to myself, "What doors could possibly be locked going down an *emergency* exit?" A building maintenance worker who was behind me asked the same question out loud. Another maintenance worker said he had keys and started to go down. I kept thinking, "What doors are they talking about?" and "Lord, I hope he has the right key."

About five minutes later, we proceeded down once again. The smoke was starting to build up in the stairwell, an acidic smell. A young man two people in front of me took a travel pack of tissues from his shirt pocket. He pulled one out and passed the pack to the guy behind him. I remember thinking, "Oh please, let him pass me a tissue."

The young man looked at the man in back of me, started handing him the tissues. He realized I was watching him. He looked at me, then handed me the tissues. I took one. I thanked him. Then I passed the packet back.

*　　*　　*

We continued down, stopping at every landing. People were calm. Typical New Yorkers. Nothing much fazes us.

One of the men standing in the landing, three people behind me, said, "I wonder how many thousands of people are in this building."

I answered, "I don't know. Do you work here?"

"Yes."

"Oh. If you didn't, I was going to say, what a day for you to visit."

The men around me laughed politely. Nervously.

*　　*　　*

At the 33rd floor two black girls started to panic and broke away from the line somewhere above me. They ran down the steps and through the opened fire exit door. They left the stairwell and went back into the building.

A man standing on the landing said, "You shouldn't go there. Stay here." But the two girls shot through the open door and looked both ways, as if they were crossing the street. Then they ran off to the left.

The man said, "They shouldn't have done that."

I looked at him and said, "Hey, it's a woman's prerogative to do what they did." I gave him a 'what can you do?' shrug with my shoulders.

*   *   *

It was on that landing - the 33rd floor - when people from above started shouting, "Get to the left! To the left!" We all scooted to one side. I remember hearing some someone above me say: "Which left? Which way is *left*?" Then, people from below started shouting, "To the *right*! To the *right*!" That was a time of confusion. Left . . . ? Right . . ?

Someone from below shouted, "The firemen are coming, make way!"

We were all trying to get as close to the railing as possible. I found myself unable to squeeze in. I moved three steps down below to the landing to allow more room for the other people, but that landing was not a good place to be. I remember saying to myself, "You'll just be in someone's way. Go back to where you were." And somehow I managed to get back in place just as people from above started shouting, "Get to the wall. Get against the wall!"

There was now a clear path on the stairwell and two, then three guys broke the line from above and started running down. I thought to myself, "I can't believe it, what cowards these men are." I shouted, "Hey! We didn't clear this just for you to come down! Stop it! Stay there."

Then I saw men walking backwards down the stairs carrying something. These were not emergency workers, just your ordinary-looking businessmen. They were leading a woman, a burn victim.

*   *   *

I'll never forget the look in her eyes, the skin hanging from her burnt face, her arms, her hands. It was as if her skin had been peeled off her body. She was a black woman, but her body showed the wounded pink scars that will be with her for a lifetime. Her eyes were white and opened wide, staring straight ahead. She had that look of total bewilderment. Shock and horror. I stared in disbelief.

When she was right next to me, firemen appeared from below, hustling up the stairs. No one moved. There was a gridlock right in front of me. People started maneuvering around as the burn victim was led down the stairs. A split second later the firemen were dashing past me up the stairs.

They looked so young. They had a frightened look in their eyes. As they passed me, I leaned over the railing and shouted down: "Get a medic, this woman needs a medic!" I was hoping there would be some emergency medical technicians following close behind who could help the burn victim.

*　　*　　*

Just then, two older firemen appeared on the landing below. They were totally calm. They assured everyone that the smoke was not as bad below. I immediately assumed they were more experienced because one of them had gray hair and they both seemed as if they'd seen this type of situation a hundred times before. They asked everyone to stay calm, so I did.

I remember thinking, "These brave, brave men going *up the stairs.*" They had no idea what was facing them. How bad was the fire? And the equipment they were carrying: the hoses, the axes, the extinguishers. All heavy. You could hear them breathing in gasps. It was extremely painful for me to think they had to go up. But I realized they had a duty to do.

*　　*　　*

We continued to descend the stairs again, slowly. Stopping and descending. Stopping and descending. No one was saying anything. Everyone still appeared relatively calm.

At one landing there was a building maintenance worker who was holding a roll of paper towels in his hand, offering for people to rip off a piece. I told him that it was really nice thing for him to do and I took a piece because I didn't know what I would be facing further down. I was holding the towel it in my hand and rolling it around, nervously crumpling it into a small ball. I still have that piece of paper towel. It's in the shoulder bag I was carrying that morning.

*　　*　　*

At another landing, I glanced back at the man standing behind me. He had a gas mask on, covering his face. The gas mask was a vivid blue, not the army green one would imagine. It covered his nose and mouth. Where had *that* come from?

I said to him, "Hey, that's a pretty smart thing to have right now."

He told me he had been in the building in 1993 when terrorists had tried to blow it up. He went on about how he thought the building officials handled that emergency all wrong; he didn't think they were geared up to manage the situation, so he'd prepared himself to deal with something similar.

I thought that maybe he was taking this notion to the extreme and I didn't say anything more to him.

At some point during my descent, I heard rumors trickling down the staircase that a plane had hit the building. I was used to seeing commuter planes flying around from my office window, so I thought, "That could be possible. Something could have happened to the pilot, something could have malfunctioned on the plane."

*　　*　　*

At about the 4th or 5th floor, a fireman told us to start going down one by one. There was an overflow of water cascading down the staircase. I remember hearing some women mumbling about taking their shoes off. I moved past them, thinking, "Why are you stopping? Just go, it's only water."

I grabbed the railing and thought, "All I have to do is get out of here."

It was very dark on the last few steps leading to the fire exit. At some point during my descent to the lower floors, the lights had gone out. I stopped, not knowing where to go. I found myself alone, and looked around. Where did the men go who were in front of me? Where did the people go who were in *back* of me?

I turned my head to the right and noticed a light from outside growing dimmer. A door was closing. I ran down the hall toward the light with both arms outstretched.

*　　*　　*

I pushed on the door lever and stumbled out onto the Plaza level. This level is one floor above the lobby or street level of the Trade Center. You could walk outside from here to an enormous courtyard called the Austin J. Tobin Plaza.

There was a huge sculpture representing the world in the middle of a fountain. Souvenir vendors set up shop out there for tourists to buy trinkets. There was outdoor seating for noonday and evening concerts and sidewalk restaurants where people could enjoy their morning coffee or cigarettes as I would often do. There were cement benches where you could sit and people-watch or just listen to the water as it flowed over the side of the fountain. The Port Authority spent an enormous amount of money landscaping that plaza. Every month they would bring in flowers, trees, shrubs, and plants. The landscape would change with the seasons.

I stood there, inside the building, looking out the three-story high windows onto the Plaza. I saw huge chunks of glass; twisted beams of black, gray, and red steel that were the size of small cars; large pieces of white metal. Scraps of paper flew through the air as if caught in a breeze. Glass, steel and metal were scattered everywhere.

Still under the impression that a commuter plane had hit the building, I thought about the demise of the pilot and his passengers. I was stunned by this whole scene. I looked at my watch. It was 9:15 am.

A voice off to my left, brought me back to my senses. "Come this way, come this way!" It was a World Trade Center security guard standing at the far north end of the Plaza level. I tried to run toward him but my knees buckled and I stumbled. I don't exercise regularly, but I didn't think the descent down the 44 flights would have had that great an affect on my legs. I limped toward him.

The guard said, "Go that way," pointing again to my left and toward the west side of the building. There was a door that would lead me outside and over to the sky-bridge, which is a glass-enclosed walkway to the World Financial Center. I walked quickly past him toward the door and looked back. No one was behind me. Where did the people who were with me go?

*　　*　　*

That was when I saw Daisy, the bookkeeper from my office and I yelled to her. "Daisy!"

I went to her and took hold of her by both arms. I asked if everyone from the office got out, she said that everyone did. Then she said that she thought Wayne, the Executive Director, and Mary, an accountant, had gone to check the offices for other people. She said that Tara, my assistant; Mark, the A/V technician; and Maria, an administrative assistant, were with her when she had left the office. But they had been separated while going down the stairs.

"Great," I said. "Everyone's out. Let's get going."

She said, "Wait, I've got to put my shoes on."

"Daisy, I can't believe you stopped to take them off." I thought she was silly to take her damn shoes off. They're only shoes.

I stood there, holding her up, while she put them back on her feet.

*   *   *

As we started to go for the door, the security guard suddenly shouted, "Stop!"

I turned around and saw a girl coming from around the corner I had just rounded. She froze. I looked up. The glass chandeliers were falling. I grabbed Daisy and placed my right hand over her head, my left hand over mine. My elbow was on her neck and I pushed her to the side of the building.

We were so close to the door leading out. I remember thinking, "If we can just make it across to World Trade Center 6. If we stand right up against the outside wall, we'll be okay." There was an overhang that protects you from the rain and snow where I would smoke my morning cigarette before going inside to work. Now it would protect us from the falling debris.

"Daisy, come on. Let's go."

*   *   *

We ran out the door, across the breezeway between the two buildings, and banged up against the glass wall of Building 6. We stood there for a moment, safe. I looked up toward the sky. I could see debris falling all around us. Paper was floating down like a ticker-tape parade. I looked straight ahead and could see a revolving side door about a hundred feet away from us. I said to Daisy, "Come on, we can make it." And we ran for it.

We went straight for the revolving doors and Daisy said, "Here! We can go through here." There was an open door right before the revolving doors and we dashed inside.

Once inside the sky-bridge that connects 6 World Trade Center to the World Financial Center, I put my right arm over Daisy's shoulder and took hold of her left. We walked across the sky-bridge. At one point, we tried to fast-walk, but Daisy said her legs were sore. Mine, too. So we just walked. The bridge wasn't crowded. Again, I wondered: "Where did the people go?"

*   *   *

About halfway across the bridge, I spotted Leslie, a friend whom I had met while commuting on a bus a few years back; I had bumped into her about a month back outside the West Street entrance to the Trade Center, where people go to smoke. She had recently started working for Kemper Financial/Insurance on the 36th floor.

Leslie was holding onto an older woman the same way I was holding onto Daisy. We both looked at each other, smiled nervously and shrugged.

We finally got to the entrance of the World Financial Center. The Winter Garden was right in front of us. The Winter Garden was an indoor atrium which houses very tall palm trees. It could almost be described as an indoor version of the Austin J. Tobin Plaza. (*Plate 1*)

We were standing at the top of the marble staircase that grandly cascaded down to the main floor and I thought about the many brides I'd seen being photographed from those sweeping steps. It was a beautiful staircase, a beautiful setting.

I heard a voice from below saying, "Go toward the exit. Keep moving down, go toward the far exit." Which would put us on the waterside of the World Financial Center.

*   *   *

Daisy and I headed down toward the marble staircase. I looked to the right of me and Leslie and I gave each other a 'here we go again' kind of shrug. We smiled weakly and got on our way. Leslie and the other woman walked off to the right, toward an escalator; Daisy and I went down the stairs. At this point, I lost sight of Leslie.

Once outside the World Financial Center, Daisy and I stopped, turned around, and looked toward the sky. Both Towers were in flames and smoking.

There were wrought-iron tables and chairs set outside under the trees for patrons of the dockside restaurants at the World Financial Center. I said to Daisy, "Let's sit here, we can rest for a while and watch what's going on." I remembered how, back in '93 when a bomb went off in the underground garage of the Trade Center, I'd walked casually from my office on Broadway to the corner of West and Liberty Streets and stood there watching the chaos of firefighters, policemen, and rescue workers. Now I wanted to watch the Towers and take in history while it happened.

I took a seat and looked through my purse for a cigarette. I pulled one from the pack and looked up, realizing I couldn't see anything because of the trees. I said to Daisy, "Let's move to another table for a better view." Daisy and I moved out from under the trees and looked up.

I said, "My God . . ."

The hole in the Tower was huge. It was only at this point that I realized it hadn't been a commuter plane that hit; it was a commercial jet. Now we could see the destruction, the enormous amount of smoke pouring out of the Towers.

Leslie appeared beside me and nudged my arm. "There you are," she said, relieved.

I looked at her and smiled nervously. I introduced Daisy to Leslie. Now, the three of us were standing there, staring as a body fell from the sky on the left side of Tower One.

*　　*　　*

The body appeared from under the smoke and tumbled down in a cartwheel motion, I'll never forget that. Cart wheeling down from the sky toward the ground.

I was horrified by the thought that someone was jumping from the Trade Center. Horrified. I said something like, "I can't believe someone would jump."

Leslie looked at me and said, "There's already been at least ten people. I've seen at least ten."

I looked at her, dumbfounded.

When we looked up at the Towers again, more people were jumping. I don't know how many people I saw . . . but I do remember seeing someone who looked as if he were trying to fly from the right side of 1 World Trade Center to the top of the Marriott Hotel – his arms outstretched like Superman. The images of those people falling from the sky . . . my God. What about their families?

This large black woman standing near us suddenly spoke out loud, to no one in particular. "It was two planes hit the buildings."

I looked at her and said, "No way."

She looked at me and said defiantly, "It was *two* planes."

I looked up at the building again and thought, "This woman is crazy. No way could two planes hit the buildings. One plane must have hit, and the way it impacted Tower 1, high up - it must have plunged and ricocheted into Tower 2." That made sense to me.

But this woman, whoever she was, said, "It was terrorists."

This time I turned and looked her in the eye. "What? No way."

She screwed her face up. Her eyes got real narrow, as if she were shooting arrows from them. In a very flat and odious voice, she said, "It was terrorists." This gave me a very eerie feeling. It was spooky.

In a soft voice, I said to Daisy and Leslie, "Let's move away from here, we don't need to hear this."

I thought: "Why is this woman standing here trying to incite panic among the people gathering?"

The three of us backed away, closer to the edge of the Hudson River.

* * *

The three of us had cell phones. We started pulling them out to make calls. I really didn't know whom to call, so I thought I'd call my Mom in Florida.

I talk to my mother every day, but usually early in the evening while driving home from work. I knew that she'd be leaving her house soon to catch a plane that would bring her to New York to visit relatives; she and I were to meet over the weekend. "What the Hell, why not?" I thought. I'd surprise her with an early phone call and tell her what happened at work.

My call didn't go through. Daisy and Leslie couldn't get through to anyone, either. I looked around and saw some men with cell phones to their ears. So I walked over to one and asked, "Are you getting a signal?"

He said, "No."

I asked another. This man also said no.

Leslie stopped in her tracks and said, "Hey, the cell towers were on top of 1 World Trade Center."

Of course they were. That's why our calls weren't getting through.

*   *   *

I thought, "Well, there's no reason to stand around. There's nothing to see that I won't be able to watch on the evening news. And there's no way that anyone's going back to work today, not after this."

I turned around and I couldn't believe we were so close to the commuter ferryboats going over the Hudson River to New Jersey. We were right next to the railing leading down to the docks. I told Daisy and Leslie, "Follow me." I looked to my right and saw masses of people pushing their way onto the dock. I found an opening at the railing and thought that, if we just continued to move forward and stayed right where we were next to the railing, we'd be able to board easily. (*Plate 2*) Because I'm taller than Daisy or Leslie, I moved them ahead of me so I could keep an eye on them - like a mother duck does to her ducklings when she moves them from one location to another.

Miraculously, we slid into the line and onto the dock where there was a line of people standing in line to buy tickets.

I remember Leslie was worried about not having money - she said she needed to find an ATM machine. I said, "No way am I standing in this line, let's go." I'd never taken the ferry before, but I said, "There's no way they could possibly be worried about checking tickets."

There were too many people pushing onto the boat – like a bunch of people storming the stage at a concert to get an autograph from their favorite rock star. I looked around and saw that there was one boat with hardly anyone on it. I said, "Let's get on that one. I heard someone say they're both going to Hoboken, New Jersey."

*   *   *

As we approached the boat, I asked one of the ferry workers. "To Hoboken . . . right?"

He said, "No, this one's going to Jersey City. The boat across the way is Hoboken."

Thank God I thought to ask. Daisy said she'd take the Jersey City ferry since her daughter lived there; she could stay with her. I said, "Okay, take care."

Leslie and I moved our way across the dock to the other ferry. Again she said she needed to find an ATM machine. I said, "Don't worry. They're not checking tickets. Let's get on and go."

* * *

I started to get a little nervous at this point. The boat was filling up fast in front of us and I was worried there wouldn't be enough room. Then a ferry worker yelled to the people on board, "Move back, make more room! Move back!" The next thing you knew, we were on board.

Leslie was still in front of me. I wanted to get to the upper outside deck so I could continue watching the Towers, but there were three men blocking the way to the stairs - one standing in front of the stairs and two more sitting on the steps. I thought, "Why are they just watching all these people push their way in? Why won't they move to allow more people on board?"

The man sitting on the highest step held his head in his hands. He looked disheveled, in despair. I stood there for a moment looking at him, wanting to ask if he was okay. He was most likely in shock. But I was still being pushed from behind.

Leslie and I made our way toward the back of the boat. There were rows of wooden benches similar to the pews you see in a church positioned three across that ran the length of the boat. Leslie saw a woman she knew sitting in one of the middle rows and told me she was going to her. I went to the very rear of the boat and sat in the last row next to a window.

There was a group of five businessmen hanging around the back. I couldn't help but overhear their conversation. They were talking about what had happened. I heard one of them say, "Two planes."

I turned around and asked, "Was it really two planes?" and one of the guys said, "Yes."

I lowered my head and shook it in disbelief. During the ride to Hoboken, I kept looking out the window. Both Towers were smoking and I was silent and numb. Now *I* was in shock.

* * *

When I got to Hoboken, I hopped a train to Berkeley Heights. I was staying there for the week with my cousin, John, because I had three daytime conferences and three late-evening committee receptions scheduled for the week.

On the train, I found a seat across from a young Indian woman and sat down. We looked at each other and gently smiled 'hello'. We didn't say anything, words weren't needed.

A young man wearing a Yarmulke sat on the aisle facing me. We looked at each other. Just a blank stare. I watched him bring out this little prayer book. Again, he looked at me and I blinked my eyes, nodding my head up and down, hoping that he'd get my signal to say whatever he was going to say aloud. He must have understood because he started reciting a prayer in Hebrew. The woman in front of him turned in her seat to listen.

Even though I didn't understand a word he was saying, I knew that it was a prayer for those poor people in the planes and in the Trade Center. And somewhere during his prayer, I started reciting the Lord's Prayer.

He finished. We looked at each other. I smiled a little smile and I knew he understood it for a thank you. I kept reciting the Lord's Prayer for a long time.

*   *   *

At one point I remember thinking, "All of my shoes are gone." I never wore good heels to the office. I commuted in comfortable shoes like penny loafers or sneakers. I kept about 15 pairs of shoes in one of my desk drawers, blue shoes and red shoes, purple shoes and tan shoes. Beige shoes. Green shoes. I had sandals with big high heels and sandals with low, short heels. I must have had five pairs of black shoes. All gone.

Then I realize how stupid it is for me to think about my shoes. What about all our office equipment? We finally got a great postage machine and now it's gone. All of our computers; all of our membership records; all the paper work I'd ever generated. Gone.

Then it hits me. My God. The people.

And then I know. I know that those brave firemen who passed me going up the stairs - never came back down.

And I think, "God bless this country. God bless us all." ℥

JAN DEMCZUR, 48, came to the United States from Poland in 1980 and worked as a window cleaner in the World Trade Center every day for ten and a half years. On September 11ᵗʰ, with only his bucket and cleaning tools, Jan helped a group of men escape from a stalled elevator in the north Tower shortly before it collapsed.

Mr. Demczur speaks in a soft, charming Ukrainian accent that turns words like 'squeegee' into 'skveegee'.

———

I worked six a.m. to three in the afternoon and I had a routine. I knew where to start in the morning since a lot of floors are closed that early. I knew a lot of the security guards since I'd worked in the Trade Center so long. They would open the doors with their keys and let me do my job.

That morning, I had already finished a couple of floors: the 48ᵗʰ, 49ᵗʰ, 50ᵗʰ. I went up to the 92ⁿᵈ and 93ʳᵈ floors, also routine. Then I did the 77ᵗʰ.

At a quarter after eight, I decided to break for breakfast. I took the elevator from the 78ᵗʰ floor Sky Lobby to the 44ᵗʰ. Then an escalator down to the 43ʳᵈ floor to the cafeteria to get a coffee and some Danish.

I was eating and thinking of where I would go next. I would usually start on the upper floors by that point in the morning and work my way down. So I decided to go do the 70ᵗʰ Floor. I finished my breakfast, maybe 20 to nine, and went back to work.

* * *

I went back to the 44ᵗʰ floor and took an express elevator to the 70ᵗʰ floor. There were five gentleman riding inside the car with me. They pushed buttons for their own floors: 68, 73, and 74. I didn't push mine, because someone was standing in front of me.

The door closed. We were going up, but not so fast. Then, I felt something was wrong. I said, "This elevator's going down." We didn't reach the 68ᵗʰ Floor. Everybody looked at me because I was in uniform.

At the time, the plane had hit the building but we didn't know anything about it. The building shook a little bit from side to side, but that was all. We felt a little swing, nothing unusual.

I hit each button, thinking that maybe the elevator would stop at different floors. But it was still going down. I hit the emergency intercom button and there was ringing on the other end, but the elevator was still going down. I screamed to the guy on my right side, "Push the red button." He was still staring at me. I repeated it again, and then he pushed the button. The elevator stopped, but we had no idea where we were.

*   *   *

A few minutes went by and a man started talking on the intercom.

He said, "What happened there?"

I said, "We're in a car. Something's wrong, we dropped a couple of floors."

"Which floor are you stopped on?"

I said, "I don't know, they don't show it."

At the same time, smoke started coming up from the bottom.

The man on the intercom said, "We have a problem on the 91st floor. That's what I heard. Something hit the building."

We started yelling to him, "Are you going to send somebody to help us?"

Then the intercom stopped working and we were on our own.

*   *   *

We didn't have any information. There were six guys in all. One tall guy, George - I knew him. I'd see him two or three times a week in the cafeteria, on a floor, in a Sky Lobby. He started pounding on the roof to open the hatch, like in the movies when you see someone in an elevator try to jump from one car to the next. George was pounding, but he couldn't get it open.

Another guy, John Paczkowski, opened the elevator doors. And we saw a wall with a big number 50.

Two of the other guys complained because smoke was coming in. They said: "Close the doors, close the doors!"

I said, "I don't know if that's a good idea."

We closed them, but smoke still came in. And I said, "We have to open the doors because in 15 minutes we might pass out on the floor."

So we opened them again. I had my wooden stick and it fit exactly between the doors, the perfect size. It's like a broomstick; I use it to reach higher windows or inside-the-glass partitions. It's about four, four and half feet long, between three-quarters to an inch thick. That stick kept the doors open.

I put one hand on the wall and said, "Wow. This is drywall. That's not gonna be so bad. Usually this is three-quarters of an inch thick." So we started kicking it.

*   *   *

Two guys kicked but we couldn't break it. I said, "Something is wrong. I can't believe we can't break sheetrock. Usually, you just cut it with a knife and break it like paper."

I turned back to the group and said, "Does anybody have a knife?"

Everybody looked at me, "No, no."

I looked in my pocket. I said, "Maybe we can work with the squeegee." I grabbed it and started chopping a hole in the drywall. Just a little hole so we could start to break it. I was trying to figure out how thick the wall was.

I chopped and through a layer of sheetrock one inch thick and said, "Look at that. I don't usually see a one-inch thickness." But sometimes they use that in office buildings, I guess.

I saw another piece of sheetrock behind the first and I started chopping deeper. We did that second piece of sheetrock, but there was another behind that one. I was surprised at this.

Three guys switched with each other, each taking a turn with the squeegee, digging deeper. We made a hole maybe two inches wide and one inch high.

Finally, I took the squeegee from the third guy and I start banging it. I felt it go through. I said, "Wow. That's three layers, each one-inch thick." And we started kicking. But the hole we'd made was too small and the wall didn't give up.

*   *   *

We didn't panic or get scared because we didn't know exactly what had happened. We just got busy digging the hole. It was quiet. We got wet with sweat. There was the smoke, and the wind was blowing powder from the sheetrock into your mouth and eyes and nose.

The first thing I thought was that the elevator had gone down because of some local building problem. When the smoke started coming out, I changed my mind a little, but I didn't expect something as big as what I later learned had happened.

We cut wider from side to side, maybe 24 inches. On both sides of the sheetrock was a metal channel that held together sheets of drywall. The gentleman behind me picked up the squeegee's handle, which I had taken off before, and he started scratching at the wall. He was using whatever he had, and he was doing pretty good. He cut through one layer and maybe half of the next.

While I was cutting, my squeegee fell out and dropped onto the other side. I was very upset with myself. The guys behind me didn't know that my squeegee fell down and I didn't tell them. I just looked at the gentleman scratching with the handle. He was exhausted. I grabbed the handle from him and started to cut through another layer in the middle of the wall.

I turned back to the group and said, "Gentlemen, two men have to kick at the same time. Now we should be able to break it."

I had shoes with rubber soles. Not very good to kick with. I looked at George; he was a tall guy with a size 10 ? shoe. I said, "You try to kick. Your shoe is leather, it is better to kick with."

He turned around and supported himself against the other side of the elevator. Turning back, he kicked like a horse a couple of times, really hard. With John Paczkowski, also. The two men, kicking together.

*   *   *

After a couple of kicks, George's foot went through. We all started kicking around the edges to make the hole bigger and bigger. I grabbed the pieces and pulled them down. Finally, we made a hole big enough for me to look through. But when I did, I said, "It's dark." Behind the wall, there was a space maybe eight to ten inches. And beyond that there was another wall.

The next wall was corrugated metal 2 x 4 and sheetrock. I took it to be the inside wall to an office space and thought, "Well, there's usually only one piece for that." So we kicked a couple of times again and felt the sheetrock crack. We heard tiles spill out on the other side of the wall. I looked through the hole; you could see sinks and toilets. I said, "This is a men's bathroom."

We made this second hole and a skinny guy, Alfred, said, "Let me get through. Maybe I can get through first."

I thought, "Right. You guys have been standing in the back, now you want to go first." I was tired. But I looked at him and said, "Okay. Go ahead."

He went halfway through the hole and came out in the bathroom over the sink. He could only move so far, so half of him was in the elevator and half of him was in the bathroom. He started yelling, "Push me! Push me!"

That was one question I remember someone asking in an interview. "You weren't scared? You were halfway in the bathroom and halfway in the elevator? That elevator might have moved down and cut you in half."

I don't know. You don't think that way when you're doing something like that.

*   *   *

We pushed Alfred through. When he was out, I said, "There's another bank of elevators. Check them and see that nobody got stuck there."

Alfred said, "Okay, okay."

He left and went into the hallway, took the elevator down to the 44th Floor Sky Lobby and returned with some civilians and firemen. They had a key to the elevator. But by the time they returned, we had already made a bigger hole and everybody was out. I took my bucket and John Paczkowski had his laptop.

The firemen said, "Okay, guys. Hurry up."

*   *   *

We were inside that elevator for like, 45 minutes. When the plane hit, it was a quarter to nine or something? Now it was probably 9:30. We got out on the 50th Floor. When the firemen came up, they saw five guys standing around, and they were surprised.

Some of the guys from our elevator went to the stairway. I saw a sign that said not to use the elevator when there's fire or an emergency, but two firemen were inside the elevator along with the gentleman who carried the elevator key - in an emergency, you have to have a special key to operate the elevator. I didn't want to go in there, I wanted to use the stairs. But the fireman was yelling at me, "Move it faster."

I don't know what I was thinking. I jumped in and they brought us down to the 44th Floor.

I still had water in my bucket and, on the Sky Lobby, there was a plant, you know? Lots of flowers. I dumped this water onto the plants because I didn't want to carry it down. I said, "Let them grow." It was only for one second. Very quick. I don't know what I was thinking. I said, "Who knows? Beautiful flowers. Don't want them to dry out."

*　　*　　*

On the 44th Floor, I went to the stairway and met the rest of the guys from the elevator. We started walking down, and at first, we didn't see anybody on the stairway. But two or three floors down there were a lot of people, so many that you couldn't move. It was going very slow. I just counted floors and wondered, "How long is it gonna be until we get down?" There were people evacuating from the lower floors, that's what was taking so long.

It was foggy and wet in the stairwell. I heard two guys talking about how two planes had hit. One gentleman who worked up on the 68th floor said, "Don't worry about what happened now, worry *later*. We'll find out what happened when we get down."

I wasn't really concerned with what had happened. I was thinking that maybe the two planes had hit each other in the air and the parts fell on the building or something.

We walked down the staircase very slowly.

*　　*　　*

On the 17th floor or maybe the 15th floor, somebody was yelling, "Help! Help!" The door was open from the inside hallway to the stairway and I saw a nice gentleman in a white shirt with a briefcase. I said, "What happened?"

He said, "There's two people over there. I need help." But it was dark and I was scared. I was already tired.

I saw two firemen and said to them, "This guy says two people over there need help."

One fireman went over to help. By that point there were a lot of firemen around. As we were going down, a lot of firemen were coming up.

When I was on the 12th Floor, I heard a very loud noise. Unbelievable. Smoke was coming up. I got oxygen twice from firemen on the stairway.

I was carrying my bucket down all this time and people were telling me, "Leave it." But I said, "I like this bucket. I've had it for nine years. I got this bucket for a purpose."

The supervisors at my job always told me, "Have two different buckets, a round bucket and a little rectangular bucket." But before, when I was working with a round bucket, I had to stick both hands down in the water. With this bucket, I just had to stick one hand down. It was very convenient. All the guys I worked with learned a lesson from me. I told them, "Take this bucket from me and try working with it today. See how easy it is to wet the glass." I wanted to keep the bucket for retirement.

But I saw the smoke coming out the doors and I said, "I have to leave it." I took the rag from the bucket and the handle from the squeegee.

*   *   *

I heard this loud noise on the 12th Floor and it scared me good. I was thinking maybe a transformer had blown up or something. Some fireman started yelling, "Go back up!" and I was running from the 12th Floor to the 15th Floor. But the people higher than me said, "What are you doing?"

I said, "The guy's yelling 'Go back up'."

They said, "No, no, no! It doesn't matter what happens. Go down."

So I turned around and went back down.

It was dark. You couldn't see anything. But there were a couple of firemen with flashlights saying, "Where is the exit here?" One of them turned to me and said, "You work here."

I said, "I *was* working."

"Do you know where the exit is?"

I said, "Move your flashlight on the wall and I will try to recognize which floor this is."

He started moving from one side down to the middle. I said, "Here is the exit." Because I saw the door was open and I recognized the slop sink where I usually dumped the water I washed windows with. It was the 3rd floor.

We went through the door.

*   *   *

There was powder on the floor maybe two, three inches deep like snow. Everything was twisted and broken. The big glass walls of the first floor, the panes of the lobby that had stood 16 feet high, were shattered. There was a lot of falling debris that could hit you on the head. I only recognized we were in the lobby after I saw the security gate where we slid our ID cards to enter the building each day.

I turned right. In the front of the building was a big vestibule. The visibility was low because of all the smoke, but I recognized the direction that the West Side Highway was in. I started calling, "We're supposed to go this way, it's more safe this way. If we go the other way, I think it's too far to the exit."

We ran from the Towers. I followed two firemen out a revolving door. Another one stood outside and yelled, "Hurry up, hurry up!" And another fireman was there holding a hose. He said, "Hey, come over here. Get some water."

I washed my mouth and face. A medical assistant grabbed my arm and took me maybe ten feet away. He said, "Sit down." They gave me an oxygen mask and I put it on. There were a lot of people sitting there.

I didn't know what was going on. I lifted my head and looked at the building on fire. I said, "Wow, that's gonna be bad. The top floors are gonna be burned." But I also thought, "They're gonna renew it and we're gonna come back."

I started looking for the other building. I thought maybe I was at a bad angle, maybe it was behind the other building. I asked another guy with an oxygen mask on, but he didn't say anything. So I asked another guy, and he said the South Tower was down.

I said, "What do you say?"

He repeated, "The building is down."

When he told me, my skin froze. And my hair. I was thinking I was gonna go gray. I can't believe it - that big, strong building went down. All 110 stories.

*   *   *

I had only been sitting there a very short time when firemen started yelling to the medical assistants, "Take those people far from here. More people are coming from the buildings and we need the space."

I picked myself up and started to move. There was a big policeman - I knew from the Port Authority. Often, I'd see him in the elevator on the 88th Floor, a nice guy. He started yelling like crazy, like someone put a knife in his throat or something. I'm looking at him and saying, "What's going on?"

Then I looked behind me and saw the antenna on the top of the Tower turning upside down. The whole building started to come down. I wasn't even two blocks away.

I ran. I didn't know - was the building gonna fall on its side? Which side? I turned around to keep my eyes on what was going on behind me. I took off the mask and left the bottle of oxygen. I saw the building wasn't going over on it's side, it was collapsing on itself like a stack of pancakes.

I tried to go as far as I could. Maybe four blocks. But I was shaking, I couldn't walk. I felt as if something had exploded in my head. Everything - my head, my hands, my legs - was shaking. My voice was breaking, I couldn't talk. Probably . . . definitely, I was in shock.

*   *   *

Some guy came to me and said, "What's your name?"

I replied, "Jan."

He got closer to me and I said, "What's *your* name?"

He said, "George." The same guy who was with me in the elevator.

He'd gotten out of the Tower a couple minutes earlier than I had, and he told me what he had heard from firemen and policemen. That one plane had hit one building, another plane the other. One plane had hit the Pentagon. He told me there were four more hijacked planes in the air, and that F-16s had shot a plane down. He was scared.[11]

---

[11]Various accounts from this time show that rumors had already begun to spread through the streets of Lower Manhattan. These rumors listed the number of attacks in wildly varying numbers, locations, and severity.

George had a cell phone and he'd called his wife. I said, "Can you call my wife for me?" I gave him the number but I screwed it up. I must've been in shock. I held the cell phone and tried to talk, but I couldn't get through.

He said, "Where are you gonna go?"

I said, "I'm gonna go to my wife. She doesn't know if I am alive or not." She was working on 2nd Avenue between 13th and 14th Street, not far from where I was.

I'm from New Jersey and so is George. He said, "I heard that ferries are taking people from New York to New Jersey. I'm going there and somebody's gonna come with a car to take me home."

So he went his way and I went mine.

*   *   *

I went to my wife's work place. She had known what was going on because she had tuned into the television and radio. She was happy I was alive, but still very upset. I confirmed all the information I hadn't known for sure before - the two planes, the buildings collapsing, the Pentagon.

I was disturbed significantly. The beautiful place where I'd worked for so long had come down. To me, it was a second home. The commute from my house was only 25 minutes away but I liked working there because I liked all the friendly people and the many tourists that came to visit.

I would hear so many different languages. People would come to me and ask, "Can you translate? Do you speak this language?" I speak very good Polish, Ukrainian, Russian and English, so I could help a lot of people. And if I didn't understand them, I always knew someone who could.

I had known so many people who worked in the Towers. My friends. A lot of people were killed, and – at that point - I didn't know who was alive and who was not.

My wife and I took a train and then walked to 12th Avenue where they were taking people across the Hudson River in ferries to reach New Jersey.

*   *   *

The boat dropped us in Hoboken and I started feeling pains in my chest. There were a lot of policeman, firemen, and ambulances where we landed. I was holding my chest and someone asked, "Sir. Are you alright?"

I said, "Not really."

He said, "Come here," and put me in a wheelchair. He wheeled me to a stretcher and medics checked my blood pressure. They decided to take me to the hospital.

There were nice people all around me at the hospital who told me that I had low oxygen in my blood. They put me on oxygen for two and a half hours until my level got normal. The doctor was laughing with me, saying, "You're going to live."

I said, "Yeah, but I don't know for how long."

I was in bad shape. I was in shock. I didn't feel safe, I was scared. I was freezing. I felt pressure in my head, like something had broken inside. But finally, they said I could go home. While my wife looked for a taxi, I asked a lady police officer near me "Were you working at the World Trade Center?"

She said, "No."

She asked me where I was from. I said, "I was there."

And she said, "What happened?"

I told her about the elevator and how I got out. Behind her was another man, who was listening as I talked to her. He said, "What's your name?"

I said, "Jan."

"I'm the chief of the medical supplies for the Hoboken Fire Department. Where do you live?"

I said, "In Jersey City."

"That's not far away," he said. "Come on. I'll take you home." Very nice guy. He brought us home and was so happy he could help.

*   *   *

I was home by 9:30 in the evening. There were a lot of messages on my answering machine.

My brother called from Poland after he saw everything on television. "Please call home. We don't know what happened to you." Long-distance wasn't working until the next day so I bought a telephone card and got a connection overseas to my mother and father in Poland. When they first picked up the phone, my father couldn't talk. He was crying. He heard me and handed the phone to my mother. "I'm so happy I've heard you," she said. "I couldn't sleep all night. My pillow was all wet." Finally, she knew I was alive and the rest of the family called each other with the news.

*   *   *

How am I doing now? I don't know. I'm much better. I went to group counseling with other people who worked at the World Trade Center. Everyone had their own story. But after a while, a lot of people dropped out and went to personal counseling. I did also, I still go every other week. I also see a psychiatrist once a month. It helps me and I take pills every day.

The first month, I couldn't sleep. Maybe an hour or an hour and a half each night. I was so tired, I couldn't eat. I had no appetite, no energy. Everything was bothering me - like the sounds of ambulances, police, even the sounds of planes in the air. If someone took out their garbage and made a noise with the cans, that would bother me. I'd see the faces of my friends, who later on I learned had been killed.

Three policemen I knew pretty good; a couple guys from my crew. Altogether, we lost 27 people from my union - I didn't know them all, but I knew eight or nine. Other businessmen and people I knew from the floors - I saw them in some pictures in the newspaper.[12] I try to sleep, but it is still coming out.

Right now, I do not work. When will I go back to work? I don't know. The union is working on it. I hope they find a place for me that's convenient. Not a dangerous place, not after what's happened to me. People understand. The bosses? They know life. I don't need their respect, but they should understand what I've been through.

When will it all get better? As time goes by. For me, it'll probably take the rest of my life. I was there and I saw this. I know what happened.

And now, we're at war. But this is only the beginning. At any time, something could happen; if not here, then somewhere else - in a different state or a different country. The ter-

---

[12]The New York Times ran a daily section for many weeks called Portraits of Grief which presented a dignified memorial to the people lost in the Towers. The page shared photos alongside well-written short pieces celebrating the lives and personalities of the deceased.

rorists have a strong connection and the job is not done.

This is the blackest day in the history of America. ဒ

ARLENE CHARLES, 46, came to the U.S. from the island of Grenada over 30 years ago. She worked as an elevator starter on the 78th Floor of Tower 1, a few floors below where the first plane slammed into the building at 8:48 am.[13]

Arlene speaks with a lyrical island accent. Occasionally, she exhales a spirited "hooooo!" before plunging into a difficult memory. She gives the impression of a practical and able woman.

———

I went to work at six o'clock that morning on the 78th Floor. That wasn't my normal spot, but one of the other ladies called in because she was on vacation. My friend, Carmen Griffith, was with me along with my friend James Rutherford.

Everything was going well until we heard that explosion. *Boooom!* Like everything in the building started shattering. I didn't know what had happened. I don't know if it was like whiplash or what, but the strength just left my body and I went down, lying down flat on my face. I was scared.

I heard this lady screaming and I thought to myself, "Damn. Who is that screaming like that?"

Then the woman's voice screamed out, "Arlene! Please help me!"

I said, "Who is this?"

She said, "It's Carmen! Can you help me?"

I said, "Carmen, I'm scared. But let's talk to each other. We'll talk to each other and follow each other's voices."

We had to follow each other's voices because everything around me was black smoke. You couldn't see anything on the 78th Floor.

*　　*　　*

Now all of us elevator starters have a radio, you know? While all this was going on, people

———

[13] An elevator starter monitors the elevators in a building. If someone gets stuck in a car, the elevator starter tracks where the car has stopped, coordinates the efforts to free anyone trapped inside, and ultimately greets the people once the car doors are finally opened.

were calling me on my walkie-talkie from downstairs and all over the place. I couldn't answer at the time, I was so scared. I guess they thought I was dead because I wasn't responding. But when I finally answered they told me to get out of the building. I told them I was trying to find Carmen and couldn't leave her.

As if I could see anything. The air began to clear out a little and I could see that both the windows that faced Church Street and West Street had popped open. Shattered. We were open to the air 78 stories up.

Carmen stumbled into me and she was screaming and bawling. She was on fire.

Over the walkie talkie, they told me again to leave the building.

"Carmen's on fire," I said.

* * *

What had happened to her . . . she said she was in the elevator, taking people up to Windows on the World. The explosion happened at the same time she closed the door. The car couldn't move anywhere, everything was standing still. But she's an elevator operator, so she knows how to take her hand and open the door. That's when she got burned. She had six people in the car with her and she turned around to make sure they were okay when a ball of fire flew right in her face and burned her.

She didn't know what happened to the people in the car. She didn't know whether they got out or not. Everything happened so fast.

She had crawled to me, with me calling to her, saying, "Follow my voice." She was literally on fire when she reached me. Her face was all red. Her fingers peeled back. No skin left.

* * *

I was so scared. I led Carmen around and we came upon this security guard for the floor. I said, "Can you help me with Carmen, please?" But I think he was scared himself, he just disappeared and I don't know which way he went. I don't know if he made it out of the building or what. I never saw him or heard from him again. He was a new guy, I didn't really know him.

Then this man came and helped me with Carmen. He told us to come to his office. Meanwhile, I'm trying to call downstairs to find out what's going on and the people on the radio kept repeating, "Arlene, just get out of the building!"

I said, "Well, I have Carmen here with me and I can't get out."

They asked me, "Where's Rutherford?"

Rutherford was on the 106th Floor. He had gone to bring some people up there before the explosion. He didn't make it.

I kept on calling downstairs, but I couldn't get no answer. Carmen told me, "Arlene, I don't want to die like this, let's get out of here."

*   *   *

Now this woman showed up who worked for the Port Authority on the 88th Floor. Her name is Audrey. I said, "How did you know where we were?" She said she had just passed Carmen and me on the floor right before the attack. She said she'd heard Carmen screaming after the attack and didn't want to leave us. She followed the noise until she found the office where me and Carmen were.

Carmen kept screaming that she was burning and Audrey helped me put water on her skin, but it was all . . . it was all . . .

Audrey helped me get Carmen to the stairs and we climbed all the way down to the 30-something floor. I don't know really know which number it was.

*   *   *

These two guys passed us in the stairwell and one of them gave me his shirt and wet it with some water. We applied it to Carmen's face and the rest of her. She was still crying out that she was burning - she wanted the water to cool her off. Some firemen passed us on the way up, as well, and they opened the hose and wet us down.

A man saw us - two ladies struggling to help one another down the stairs - and he asked us if we needed help.

"Yes. Thank you. Very much."

They kept calling me on the radio and I kept on telling them what floor we were on. It was ridiculous. At that time, I didn't know that the second plane had hit. We were just trying to get out.

Finally, we reached the concourse, having walked all the way down from the 78th Floor, and

I couldn't walk anymore. I threw myself down and some lady said, "Oh my God, somebody give her some water."

One of my co-workers, Alan Stephano, came and gave me some water. He and a guy named Vito picked me up and brought me outside to an ambulance.

*   *   *

They asked me if I wanted to go to a hospital. I said no. All I was thinking was that I wanted to get home to my family, to my kids. They'd been calling me on my cell - for some reason it was working, don't ask me why. My little cousin had been at work and she kept calling me. I said to her, "Alhana, I'm getting out, I'm trying to get out. Stop calling me. Just go tell my father, my aunt, and everybody that I'm okay."

But she kept calling, wanting to make sure I was out of the building.

I got out of the ambulance just as Building 2 started crumbling down. I had to start running for my life again. I ran inside a building and I felt like the whole city was falling apart. I didn't see nobody I knew. I saw this guy and I begged him, "Please don't leave me," because I was scared.

"No," he said. "I'm not leaving you. I'm not leaving you."

*   *   *

It turns out I walked all the way to the Brooklyn Bridge and across. I walked so far, my legs wouldn't work the next day. I walked all the way to Dean Street and 3rd Avenue, my neighborhood. I found a phone and called my aunt. She told me to stay where I was, a cousin would come to pick me up. He came, but it took him almost an hour with the traffic. I didn't have my pocketbook. I didn't have no money. Everything vanished in the fire.

My cousin took me to my aunt's house and I got a shower. I didn't have a house key, that was gone, too. I had to wait for my kids to come home. But my 13-year old son Jamahl had run away from school when he heard about the Towers. He knew I worked in the building and he thought I'd died. At lunchtime, he'd left the school and they couldn't find him. The administrators were really worried. They knew I worked in the Trade Center, too.

The school kept on calling my house. They couldn't find me, they couldn't find my son's sister or my step-daughter, Sharon. She's a cop and had to go in to work. When they finally got hold of me, it was nine o'clock at night. I answered the phone and someone asked to speak to Jamahl.

"Jamahl?" I said. "Who's speaking?"

It was the Principal at the school. And when I told him who I was he was so happy. They'd been worried about Jamahl since he'd left, knowing why he'd gone, knowing that he thought he'd lost me.

*   *   *

Sometimes, when I tell people that I made it down from the 78th Floor, they can't believe it. And Carmen, the fact that she made it down with me is a miracle. They took her to Long Island Hospital. Her husband was in the building during the attack, too, and they couldn't find each other. They eventually transported him to the same hospital. It was so funny. The same day they moved him to that hospital, the <u>Maury Povich Show</u> came and picked me up to take me to see Carmen. I hadn't seen her since the 11th.

Right now, I'm on workers' compensation. Our union is helping us out a lot; the company is working with us to get everybody back to work. A lot of people are back already. We've got good people in our union, a good president and a good vice-president. Thank God for that. If we didn't have the union, I don't know what I'd be doing right now. We never expected this to happen.

We knew everybody in that building. It was like a family. Since we were in charge of the elevators, we'd say "Good morning" or "Good night" to nearly everyone we came across. We saw them every day. The people in Cantor Fitzgerald?[14] We saw them every day.

This is something I'll never get over. Never. I came to this country 30 years ago. I love this country. But this wasn't what I expected, you know? ⚡

---

[14]Cantor Fitzgerald, one of the strongest bond trading firms in the world, lost approximately 700 of its 1000 employees in the attack. By September 19th, 2001, the firm's management had made a pledge to distribute 25% of the firm's profits each quarter for five years. They further committed themselves to paying for ten years of healthcare and benefits for those families and loved ones who had lost family in the attack.

GABRIEL TORRES, 30, is a security officer who manned the lobby entrances and various checkpoints throughout the Trade Center complex. He monitored the traffic of office workers passing by. His post was mainly in Building 5. He says: "The World Trade Center was a high-risk place. We used to get bomb threats all the time. Anytime an anniversary of the 1993 bombing passed, somebody would call and say they had a bomb."

––––––

September 11th started like a normal day. I used to get to work at five a.m. for the 5:30 roll call. Then at six they dispatched me to the Concourse level of 5 World Trade.

I saw the people I normally see and said hi, talked to them. I knew a lot of people by name. Where my post was, they had a newsstand right in front of the E train - they had a Mrs. Field's Cookies shop. The lady there used to give me chocolate-chip cookies.

Everything was quiet. Around 8:45 I was talking to a co-worker when we heard a loud *bang* but we didn't pay no mind to it. It wasn't close to us; it was a faraway bang. We thought it came from construction outside. You know how they have those big metal plates that cover the ground during road repairs? We thought somebody had dropped one of those.

Seconds later, people came running down the hallways of the Concourse and I thought, "What the hell's going on?" I tried to ask somebody. I could have sworn I heard somebody say, "Gun!" and so I'm thinking that some madman is running around with a gun in the Concourse. I told people, "Come over here! Come over here!"

A couple minutes go by and I still didn't know what's going on. I saw one of my co-workers who worked in the lobby of Tower 1 come around the corner holding his arm. He was real busted up and bleeding on the back of his head.

I yelled at him, "What the hell happened?" And he said, "I don't know, an explosion." So now I thought this was about a bomb.

I sat him down and tried to talk to him. I called on my walkie-talkie, but the radio was mass confusion. Everybody was calling at once and I heard a lot of screaming, someone saying, "Get off the radio!" But I said, "No, I got a guard over here that's hurt. He's a mess." So they sent the EMS.

My supervisor came with them and she told me, "Look, we gotta start evacuating these people. A plane just hit the building."

* * *

This co-worker of mine from Building 1 told me this:

He was at the turnstiles where people swipe their security cards to enter the Towers. When the plane hit, some elevators shot down to the main floor and broke through the wall he was standing in front of. The wall exploded, hitting his arm and head.

I said, "Oh my God," and I told the people at Mrs. Fields and the newsstand that a plane had hit the building. I started getting them out.

Then I said to myself, "Hold on, let me run off and call my Mom." My cell phone wasn't working, so I went to the payphones. After a while, I finally got through. I called my Mom at her job and said, "Mom. Yo, there's something going on here, a plane hit the building."

She goes, "I know. We're watching it on TV. You gotta be careful. Get outta there."

I said, "Mom, I'm here doin' my job. I gotta do what I gotta do. But God forbid - if I don't make it - call my wife and tell her I love her. Tell my son."

At that point, my Mom went crazy on the phone. And then the line went dead.

* * *

The F and D[15] got on the loudspeaker and, for some reason, told the people in Building 2 that everything was okay. They thought it was just an accident. A lot of people went back up to their offices. Minutes after that, the second plane hit but I didn't hear it, I was in the Concourse evacuating people.

I saw people come out with skin missing. Bleeding. Smoke. Ba ba ba *ba*, you know? And I'm like, "Awww, shit." I'm talking to myself, "This is crazy." Thinking it must be some kind of dream.

One of my co-workers, a tall, African guy name of Ajalah Godwin - he decided to walk over to Building 2 to evacuate people and see what was what. A lot of my supervisors and co-workers were in that area before the buildings came down. They'd been trying to figure out what was going on. As I watched Ajalah go, someone told me another plane had just hit the

---

[15]Fire and Safety Director

Pentagon. So I ran over to Ajalah, told him the news, and said, "Be careful."

He looked at me and said, "What's going on?"

I thought about staying with him but I ran back to Building 5 and kept evacuating people.

Must've been a couple of minutes later . . . that's when Building 2 started coming down.

*   *   *

It was like out of a movie. All I heard was the noise: *Wwwwhhhhhhooooooooooouuuuuuu*. The wind, the pressure, coming for you. The lights in the Concourse - from a distance, I could see them going off, little by little, coming towards me. I thought it was another plane coming through the building, right over me.

"Holy shit."

I dove under the pay phones in the Concourse. As soon as I did, everything flew past me. People. Debris. I was balled up with my head down, screaming, "Oh my God, what's going on?" The wind. The pressure of the building coming down. It was blowing everything and everybody away. Windows blew out from the stores around me.

Then? Everything got quiet. Nothing but smoke and fire. You couldn't see anything. I touched myself. I was okay.

*   *   *

I heard a female co-worker. She was screaming. It was Sergeant Winters; I recognized her voice. I'm like, "Sandra! Is that you?"

She was calling me by my last name, "Torres, Torres! Come get me!"

I said, "Sandra, I can't find you."

She goes, "Follow my voice."

I followed her voice, crawled over to her, and picked her up. She's a pretty big girl, but I picked her up. I said, "Look, we're gonna have to start walking outta here." We started toward the Building 5 entrance on Vesey Street. Toward that way, there were 30 or 40 people all grouped up.

One girl was hysterical, screaming. This guy was gonna slap her, but I said, "No, no. Y'all gotta calm down. You're gonna get us all killed." Another co-worker - a good friend of mine - William Fields, was also there. Me and him started talking, and William said, "We gotta get these people outta here." So we told everyone, "Everybody's gotta hold hands and walk slowly."

The entrance that me and Sandra had been walking toward was blocked off. So we went back to the entrance of 5 World Trade where the Warner Brothers chain store was. We all held hands, and little by little we started walking over the debris to the escalators.

Once we got there, I had the people go up one-by-one. The last person was my friend William Fields. He said, "Come on, come on."

But I said, "No, I want to stay and see if there's anymore people."

*   *   *

As he went up, I saw two firefighters come up from the E train area.

They said, "Who are you?"

"I'm security for the building, I just got some people out. I'm trying to look for more."

One of them tells me, "We don't know our way around here. Can you help us?"

I said, "Sure, I know this place like the back of my hand."

He gives me a fire extinguisher and we started looking around. A lot of stuff was on fire, burning rocks and debris. We yelled out, "Hey! Hello! Is anybody here?" But we didn't hear nothing.

We got to the part on the Concourse where escalators led down. One of the firefighters asked, "What's down there?"

"That's the PATH train."

He says, "You think there's anybody down there?"

"I don't know. We can check to make sure."

We went down to the platform where they had stores. The firemen had two little flashlights, but they weren't doing a whole lot in the dark and smoke. I said, "There's a parking area between Building 1 and Building 6. Maybe people are over there."

"Hello? Anybody here?" Nobody's answering.

It was dark in that parking area, we couldn't see a thing. Mind you, that area was right next to Building 1 and we weren't in there five minutes when that Tower started coming down.

We heard that same noise I'd heard the first time: *Wwwwhhhhhhoooooooooouuuuuuu.* I already knew what it was and I went to dive, not knowing there were doors right in front of me - the underground entrance to Building 1.

As I dove forward, the two doors exploded off their hinges. One of them smashed me in the face.

* * *

I had all this stuff on top of me. Debris, the door, rubble, dust. The firefighters were a little ways from me and they didn't get injured because they had their rough suits on. They called out to me, "Are you okay?"

I said, "Yeah. But I got this door on top of me."

I threw the door off me. I was down on my knees. I said, "I'm okay." But when I stood up, I started bleeding from my forehead. "We gotta get outta here," I said. Trust me when I sawy we all just wanted to leave.

I took off my shirt and held it to my head. We looked for the way out. We tried to make it back the way we came down, but it was difficult - the escalators were totally mangled. There was rocks and debris and fire all around. Everything was destroyed. So we tried climbing up, twisting and turning ourselves over debris. We thought we were headed back to the main Concourse where the stores were, but it was so dark and smoky that we didn't really know where we were.

* * *

We heard a helicopter, looked up, and we could see the sky. I said, "Wow, we're either outside or in a building with no roof and if we're in a building with no roof, that's dangerous because the building's gonna collapse and we're gonna die." The helicopter kept blowing the smoke around in swirls.

I looked to my left and saw the fountain and the ball they had in the middle of the fountain. "The Sphere?" I said. "Oh my God, look! That's the fountain. We're outside." The wind started clearing up and I saw Buildings 5 and 6. That's when I knew we were in the Plaza. We had somehow managed to climb through a hole and make it outside.

I kept thinking, "I hope these buildings don't collapse." That's all I kept thinking.

We stood there for maybe an hour in the middle of a blasted city block full of twisted metal, cement, rocks, and fire. And we screamed, "Help! Help!"

* * *

I had a hole in my leg and didn't even know it. I must have got it when we were down in the Concourse, but it didn't register because I was so pumped up on adrenaline. While we're sitting there on these rocks and screaming, I was holding my shirt to my face and little by little I began to feel this pain in my right shin.

"Damn. What's going on?"

I looked down and saw a hole in my pants and through it, a hole in my leg. I could see the bone. So I cut a piece of my undershirt off and wrapped it around my leg to stop the blood.

We were just sitting there breathing all this smoke. One of the firefighters gave me a cloth, a dickey that he had around his neck. It's an item they use like a hood to protect themselves from the smoke - he gave me his.

The other firefighter said, "Let me try to find a way out." And he climbed up on this mountain of debris and went over to the other side until we couldn't see him anymore. We kept calling out, "Are you okay?" and he would holler back, "Yeah." But he found out there was no way to get out – the debris just kept rolling on and on forever - and he came back. (*Plate 3*)

* * *

As time went by, we heard people moving around in the area and we yelled, "Help!"

"Hey! Who's over there?"

We saw a firefighter in the distance on top of some debris and we got real happy.

Some firefighters went underground, back into the Concourse. It turns out that a part of it was still good. They worked their way up through another hole and called for us. We kept calling, "Here! We're over here!"

A firefighter standing on part of the Plaza threw us a rope. We had to climb up this metal thing; he gave us the rope so we didn't fall. We climbed and he pulled us up. From there, they brought us back down into the Concourse through the hole they'd made, and we made our way through the underground again, out through the N/R subway train at Cortlandt Street. In the station I remember we had to go down one set of stairs and up the other side, like if you were transferring from the downtown to the uptown train. We exited and came out in front of the Millennium Hotel.

*   *   *

When I got outside? Everything was mass destruction. Buildings were on fire, some were collapsed. People were running back and forth. There was a fire truck and a bus right there, all burned up. Just horrible. I was speechless.

I laid myself down on the ground. Some people grabbed me and dragged me to the Duane Reade pharmacy store on Broadway. Some medics looked at me. They cut off my pants and wrapped my leg, my head and my elbows - I had glass and cuts in my elbows. They said, "Is there anybody we can call for you?"

I said, "I need to call my Mom. She probably thinks I'm dead."

One of the guys calls and tells her, "Your son is alive. He's a little banged up, but he's alive."

I spoke to her, started crying on the phone. "Mom, I'm okay. I'm here. I just gotta get out."

*   *   *

I looked up and asked someone, "How do I get outta here?"

"There's no traffic going in or out of Manhattan. None whatsoever. What you need to do is sit there and take it easy."

I said, "Look, I'm not just gonna sit here. I've got to go home to my wife. My son's at my Mom's place. I gotta leave." I was very persistent.

But they were telling me, "Don't go nowhere." They thought I was delusional or something. "Stay, stay, stay."

Being stubborn, I walked out of the building. Mind you, I had a hole in my leg. I'm limping.

I have my uniform on - there's blood, smoke, my face is black from the soot. I walked over the Brooklyn Bridge 'cause that was the only way to go. There were very few people on the bridge, they weren't letting anybody back and forth. The police were very busy handling other people. They tried to stop me, but they took a good look and said, "If you want to go, go."

I was stressed out already, I said, "Fine, I'm going." And I walked over, limping and everything. I looked like a monster.

*   *   *

As I went over the bridge, there happened to be a reporter from the *Daily News*, taking pictures of me like I was a movie star.

Click, click. "Sir! Sir!" The reporter got me really mad because he came up and said, "Hey, my name is so-and-so, I'm with the *Daily News*. Are you okay?"

"Yes."

"Can you tell me in your own words what happened?"

I looked at him. I wanted to throw him off the bridge. But with whatever little strength I had left, I started going off on him.

"No, no," he said. "Please. I didn't mean it like that."

"Do me a favor? Get away from me."

I continued walking to the other side.

*   *   *

They had a lot of police in that area, not letting anybody go across. When I got there, the cops looked at me. "Are you sure you're okay?" They sat me down.

"Yes, yes. I just need to go to the 88th Precinct. My Moms works there and I need to see her." One of the cops turns around and says, "That young lady over there works for the 88th."

I looked at the girl and she knew me. "Oh! You're Lydia's son. Jump in the car."

*   *   *

They drove me to the hospital and took me into the emergency room right away - started checking me to see if I had any broken bones, a concussion, anything like that. Then they started stitching me up. My mom called my wife and she came down, too.

I don't like hospitals. I was freaking out. And my Mom - she wasn't hysterical, but you could see in her face that she was nervous. So I started cracking jokes. My wife said, "Oh, you're hurt." But I said, "Don't worry, baby. The good stuff's still intact." The nurse and the doctors were laughing and one nurse asked me, "How can you be cracking jokes when you almost died?"

I said, "Well, I'm here now, so I'd better make the best of it."

*   *   *

Stories went around. My little sister thought I was in a coma. She thought that part of my head had been removed and all that was left of me was body parts. Everybody was calling her and she told them, "Yeah, he's in a coma," and that got everybody crying. My grandmother in Puerto Rico thought I was dying.

There was more confusion because my stepmother - my father's wife - worked in Building 1. She didn't make it. My stepmother and my wife have the same name: Vivian. So my stepbrothers and sisters called my aunt asking, "Did you talk to Gabriel and see if our mom got out?"

My aunt called my Mom and said, "How's Vivian?" My Mom, of course, said, "Vivian's here with him." Meaning my wife.

My aunt, thinking of my stepmother, said, "Good, good." And she called all the kids, saying, "Your mom's fine." They were real happy.

But later on, my aunt called again and said, "Vivian's not home yet, where is she?"

My Mom said, "She's still here." Again, meaning my wife.

"Oh, good. I'll tell Pauly and John."

And that's what gave my mother the clue. She said, "Who are you talking about?" My father has the same name as me, too, Gabriel, so everybody in the family calls me by my nickname: Pepsi. My Mom said, "No, I'm talking about Pepsi's Vivian. I thought you meant my son's wife."

"No, I meant the other one."

"You mean she's still missing?"

Now the kids were really depressed. They thought their mother was alive but now they weren't sure.

*　　*　　*

Vivian worked on the 28th Floor for Blue Cross/Blue Shield. The people from her office say that she never made it in to work. Judging from the time she left her house on the morning of the 11th, she should have arrived at the Towers right when everything started. So I think she was either standing in front of those elevators when they exploded, or she was on one of them. People said those elevators smashed down flat to about two inches high. Nobody on them would have had a chance.

It hit me very hard. When the attack happened I forgot she worked there. I was running around, trying to help people, thinking about my wife, my son, my Moms. So many things. To this day, I think, "If I had remembered, I would have run over to Building 1 to try and help her." But then I probably would have died when the building came down.

It's like I told my wife. "I know it's not my fault. But I feel bad. And I don't want my stepbrothers and stepsisters to hate me because I made it out and their mother didn't."

*　　*　　*

My son was baptized on his birthday, September 16th, five days after the attack. We had made plans prior to the World Trade Center coming down. I went to the rehearsal on Friday; the baptism was on Sunday. I had stitches by then. I was limping around on a cane.

As I entered the church, the lady who does the rehearsals, Ms. Negron, was speaking about the people in the World Trade Center: "Let's bow our heads down and offer our condolences and prayers for the people who lost their lives." I heard this as I was walking closer and closer.

Ms. Negron looked up and said, "Oh my. What happened to you?"

I said, "I'm one of the people from the Trade Center."

65

She turned to the crowd and said, "Look. We have one here!"

People were looking at me with these "oh my God" expressions. Like, "This guy actually made it to church?" I couldn't say nothing. I was speechless.

Baptizing my son was the happiest thing for me. A big tragedy, but a great event to happen afterward. It brightened up my spirit, you know?

If I had died, he wouldn't have known me. Other kids would ask him: "Who's your father?" And he'd have to say: "I don't know He died when I was one year old."

That's a sad thing to think about and that's exactly what ran through my mind. ℥

NICK GERSTLE, 24, worked at Verizon as a construction technician and splicer.[16]

———

I was at work in Brooklyn and heard about the attacks on the radio. Our foreman called us up and told us to go to a C.O., which is where huge computer networks handle the telephone switching.[17] There are dozens of C.O.'s around the city - that's how the telephone network is built. Cables connect your home or business to central offices; then central offices connect to other central offices. Like tentacles going in and out of a brain.

Pulling into our office, I asked my foreman if there was any kind of volunteer effort being done within our company. He said, "It's too early, it just happened a few hours ago. Watch TV and if they need you for the Red Cross, you can volunteer that way."

It wasn't enough for me.

*   *   *

I just went down there. I didn't know if the trains would go there or if I would be allowed to help. The company certifies me every year in CPR and first aid - that's one of the things that motivated me to act. And I'm a pretty big guy. I knew they'd need people who could move things, especially people with the knowledge that I have and the training Verizon provided me. Even if they had me just handing out water, I'd have done it to make a difference.

I took the N/R subway and I had to change trains a couple times to make it into Manhattan. The train runs above ground into the city[18] and as we went over the bridge, we saw the smoke billowing out from the Towers. It was horrifying. People were looking at in awe, crying. Mothers were crying, they knew their families, their kin were in the buildings. The first stop that let off in the city was Canal Street.

As soon as you got out, you got a sense that nothing was as it was supposed to be. Basically, from Canal down to the Trade Center, I had to find "holes" in the police barricades where people would say, "You can go through with that pass." I kept showing my ID and telling them I was first-aid certified. Some cops would let me in, some wouldn't. If they wouldn't

---

[16]Phone cables run on poles or underground. A splicer climbs to the top of a pole or crawls beneath a manhole cover to gain access to a problematic line. He locates trouble in a cable which might contain a bundle of up to 1200 wires and repairs it by hand.

[17]C.O. – central office

[18]From Brooklyn.

Sheperd Sherbell

let me in, I'd walk a block and I'd try another police officer. I worked my way in like that.

*   *   *

Finally, I made it to a temporary triage center, by a college near the Brooklyn Bridge. When I went in, there was no power, just emergency workers that had gotten injured. I asked for gloves and they gave me a little mask - not the type that would stop anything. But it still helped. I got a firefighter jacket from a Burger King on Church Street near the Trade Center that had been made temporarily into a headquarters. I also got some heavy-duty gloves. I knew that in order for me to go in, I needed protective gear. I just had the shirt on my back.

*   *   *

As I walked down Broadway . . . I can't even begin to describe it. Three inches of layered soot on the street. The surrounding area was wet from fire hoses. It was like the war zone from that film *Terminator 2*.

I was on Broadway waiting with hundreds of firefighters and a small group of volunteers. There were Marines standing next to us. I saw them getting ready to go into the debris field. Half an hour later, when I finally got into the debris myself, I found that group of Marines again. They had found two Port Authority cops trapped 15 feet under the rubble.

*   *   *

You could see one cop's hand sticking out of the debris. The hand was alive and wiggling. The cop called up to us and said that his partner was down there with him and wasn't doing so well.

There were three Marines with me and we tried talking to them. "Hey guys. Don't worry." I remember one of the Marines saying, "By this time tomorrow, you'll be somewhere on a beach, sipping a drink."

We started digging. We didn't have any tools, so we used our hands to dig away at the rubble. I looked down into the hole at the two men and said, "Anybody order pizza?" I was trying to lighten up the mood.

I'm sure that those two cops will remember me. "So *you're* the guy who said that." The mood was too much for that.

I'm glad I had the fireman's jacket and gloves. Some parts of the rubble were very hot. Some of the I-beams were glowing. I was scared but at the same time, there was so much camaraderie you didn't feel the fear. You're under the rubble, you hear these guys saying, "Don't let us die. Don't let us die."

And I thought, "Don't worry. I'm right down here with you. If you go, we all go."

*   *   *

The area wasn't organized at all. It wasn't like someone was in charge and giving orders: "You, you, and you! Go there!" It was more like, "Okay . . . I'm going in." Whatever you could find, whoever you could get to go in with you. You just did it.

I remember some of the guys who were down there. There was a volunteer fireman from Maryland. He told me he had heard what had happened and put a siren on his car. He'd driven from Maryland to New York in an hour and a half. The trip usually takes four hours, so he must've done a hundred miles an hour the whole way.

I remember another volunteer, a Hispanic guy from Long Island. He didn't go into the rubble with us, he knew his fire company was responding and he was going to wait for his equipment to arrive.

Like I said, the hole those cops were in went about 15 feet down. It was a small hole with a huge I-beam sitting on top holding up the concrete and rubble so it wouldn't collapse onto the men. We formed a line from the rubble pile to the street and began bringing tools in. It was unbelievable. Amidst the smoke and rubble and darkness, flickers of light from fires all around.

When the professionals came, I told them I was a volunteer, and they ordered me out. They said they needed space to get the emergency personnel in. But I stayed next to the hole.

Then I started to feel nauseous. I couldn't breathe. I was only able to use 50 percent of my lungs. It was around 12 o'clock noon.

A fire lieutenant asked me if I was fine. I said, "Yeah. Yeah." But 10 or 15 minutes later, he saw me again, this time I was gasping for air, down on one knee. He said, "Hey guy. You gotta get out of here." I wanted to stay there as long as I could, but I'm glad he told me to go. When I was evacuated, they still didn't have the two cops out. They were just starting to bring them up.

*   *   *

I started stumbling out of the rubble, gasping for air. I couldn't fill my lungs. If it wasn't for the line of firefighters giving me air from their oxygen tanks, I don't think I would have made it.

It was a long way to get back; the rubble was a mammoth field of smoking hills. The hole where the cops were was in the middle of the Trade Center area. All the way out, you were jumping over I-beams, climbing over things. If it wasn't for the thick gloves they gave me, my hands would have been burned. You were careful not to step in holes, you didn't know what was down there. A lot of times, you looked down and all you saw was glowing red.

I paused for oxygen at least twice. You know the air tanks the firemen have? The second time I got air, I used that for five minutes. It was really heavy though and I had to drop it. I was so exhausted; I couldn't even hold on to that tank.

There was one last hill before me. When I got to the apex of it, I could see firemen below moving everywhere. It was like looking down from a plane and seeing these little ants. It was a great feeling when I saw it.

Once I got down the hill, they had gurneys ready. Firemen were helping me, giving me their shoulders to lean on. I collapsed on the gurney.

Two doctors were working on me as they moved the gurney at about 15 miles per hour to the triage area. I was amazed. I'm a pretty heavy guy. They had to lift me up at times to get me over debris, but they did it.

*   *   *

I was in the hospital two days later when I heard about those two cops on the TV news. They got them out just fine. Man, that felt good to hear.

At the hospital, they treated me for smoke inhalation. I had burned my lungs and throat pretty badly. They gave me some steroids. They'd torn my shirt off and I needed a new one before they'd let me out. I didn't want to wait, but they told me, "No, no. You *have* to wait." I said, "Okay," and sat down for 40 minutes.

They finally gave me a clean shirt and I was about to go when Mayor Giuliani walked in. One of his aides saw my fireman's jacket and said, "Wait right here. Mayor Giuliani wants to see you." The Mayor came to console injured firemen and here I was, a telephone worker who *looked* like a fireman.

He was really nice, with a smile that made you feel like he was your dad. He looked at me for a couple seconds, shook my hand, and said, "Tell me what happened."

I told him my story. That I was a volunteer who worked for Verizon and how I was part of the group that helped rescue the two Port Authority cops. He started pumping my hand, saying, "Wow, you're a really great person."

The NYPD and FDNY Commissioners were there, too.[19] They both congratulated me. I guess it's true that the NYPD Commissioner doesn't smile at all. He had this stern look on him the whole time; I'm sure he had a lot on his mind that day. I told him that, I remember that he said, "What's your name again?"

I said, "Nick Gerstle."

"One more time?"

"Nick Gerstle."

Now I know why he asked that. A day later, he had a meeting with Verizon Vice Chairman Larry Babbio and told him that he'd met me, and that I was a hero; that's the story I heard.

I'd taken off work without leave, so I called my foreman and said, "I'm over here at the hospital and my lungs are messed up."

He said, "The whole company knows about it. I've got VP's calling me about you. Don't worry about it."

*   *   *

I was discharged around nine that night and I went to my sister's house in Queens. We watched the rescue efforts from there. But I thought, "I can't be here. I want to go back and help."

---

[19]Bernie Kerik and Thomas Von Essen.

So, Wednesday night I left at six, took a train, and got to Ground Zero around eight o'clock. I stayed there 'til six or seven the next day. The fireman's jacket helped me get downtown through the barricades again.

While I was walking past Canal, I saw a police van going to the site and I waved him down. They thought I was a fireman. That's how I got through all the blockades.

The second time I was there, things were much more organized. We weren't inside the smoke this time, we were outside the rubble. They didn't want anyone going in because it was too dangerous.

After that second adventure, I went home, fell asleep, and didn't wake up for a long time.

*   *   *

Right now, it's December.[20] I'm back at work repairing special circuits, the lines that go to stockbrokers and businesses. We've been set up at a facility we call "Verizon City" since virtually the day after the attacks – it's a temporary camp downtown in an old parking lot that our company's real estate people came upon and said, "Hey, we need this space." Our company's built construction trailers and a garage for service vehicles and tools.

A lot of lines are down and we're making sure data gets through. A lot of translation problems in the lines have to be re-programmed. It's tedious work, a lot of paperwork. We estimate that the whole restoration will take most of 2003.

I'm just happy to be here and part of the work.

*   *   *

It's a great feeling to think that I helped rescue those men. There weren't that many people pulled from the rubble; I think only four people were rescued that way of all the thousands who were killed. Such a tragedy.

Before? I was just another person. Now, I am a good person. If something happens, I know I have the guts to go jump in there and help. What I took away from this experience is "do whatever you can do to help." Don't think. Just go. **$**

---

[20] 2001.

HOMICIDE DETECTIVE Y, 38, of the New York City Police Department. He works out of an East side precinct which covers all investigations south of 59ᵗʰ Street in Manhattan. Detective Y has been on the force for 18 years; he served as an undercover narcotics officer for five. Before joining the force, he pulled a three-year stint in the Marine Corps. He is a big, affable man with unstoppable energy, a real New Yorker who talks with his hands and tells you exactly what's on his mind.

———

I'm on the wagon. I'm drinking water. I gotta lose weight. I gained like, ten, 15 pounds since the attack. A lot of it has to do with the long hours put in at the precinct. There were tons of food brought to the station house. A busy time. If you're not at the Morgue or at the Fresh Kills landfill or down at Ground Zero you were sitting in the office, working. Eating. For about a week, we were on duty all the time.

We're officially treating the attack on the Towers as a homicide case. A gigantic homicide, some three thousand strong. Basically, in a homicide investigation, you're trying to collect enough evidence to bring to the DA²¹ so you can make an arrest. Initially, the 1ˢᵗ Precinct had the homicide case, but then, right away, it became a federal case. We were handling the initial investigation, doing the grunt work - then the feds came in and took over. The FBI. The "Famous, But Incompetent," I call them. Or "Forever Bothering Italians", depending on where you grew up. You can quote me on that.

Most NYPD guys feel the same way about them. Most of these feds aren't street people, they're college graduates. They have a degree in accounting. What the fuck does that have to do with the street? It gets in the way; they got no common sense, no street smarts. I mean, I can talk to a person for ten, 15 minutes and get a sense for what type of person he is. But I've done numerous interviews alongside FBI agents. Just the way they question people? Man, are they missing something.

You've got some guy from Iowa coming over here to interview people from the streets of Manhattan and it doesn't work. I was born and raised in Brooklyn. I have a sense for this city. These guys? Yeah, there are some good federal agents, but if you ask around, most of the good ones are ex-cops. *They* know how to communicate.

But I don't want to get into the feds. Please. It's just gonna piss me off.

---

²¹District Attorney.

*   *   *

I been on the force 18 years. I could retire if I want when I get my 20 years in. But I won't. I like it. What I do now is like being the CEO of a company. To me, homicide is the ultimate crime. Everything else? Not exciting. You steal something from someone? That can be replaced - money, property, whatever. Can you replace a life?

You see bodies, you see killers, you see assholes in my business. If you let a case get to you emotionally, that's when the problems start. You're working a child murder or an elderly person is killed? That's when it gets to you. When you get a storeowner that gets killed when somebody holds him up? Any normal person that has no business getting whacked? That's the stuff that gets to you.

But if a street person gets killed? You take that as being part of the street. You're a wise guy,[22] you get whacked? You're a drug dealer and somebody kills you? You're robbing somebody's store and you get shot? Hey, you're in the game and that's part of the game.

It's the innocent people that get to you, and that's why September 11th was such a giant wake up call for this country.

*   *   *

I want to say this: to me, freedom is not free. A lot of people don't realize that. These liberals! They have this attitude that we shouldn't bother anybody. "Leave everyone alone." Look at what happened to the U.S.S. Cole.[23] The liberals and Clinton didn't do a goddamned thing about that. And the message sent was, "You can do whatever you want to this country and we won't do anything back." These are the liberals I'm talking about here, not the working class people who know what it is to make a living.

What I mean about freedom is not free is that . . . if you get to a checkpoint and you get stopped? Don't complain about it. Or when you get on a plane now and you're being frisked, you gotta take off your shoes? Don't complain about it. I just got back on a plane from Los Angeles, right? And coming back, the pilot of the plane only showed one ID at

---

[22]A member of organized crime.

[23]The U.S.S. Cole was docked in Aden, Yemen for a scheduled refueling on October 12th, 2000 when a terrorist bomb ripped a huge hole in the hull of this Arleigh-Burke class destroyer, killing 17 crewmen and seriously injuring 39 others. As part of the official Judge Advocate General's investigation of the event, Secretary of the Navy Richard Danzig was quoted as saying: "We must account for why 17 people under our charge died, and why many other people, material, and interests within our responsibility were lost. In the process, we cannot avoid our own responsibility for what the terrorists achieved. We owe it to those who suffer to provide the comfort of explanation, to the best of our abilities."

the gate. Security wanted two. So they put him through the search like anyone else. The pilot was not too happy about that. You know what? Fuck him. That's for *your* safety.

A lot of people don't feel that way. And you know where that comes from? Being born in this country and thinking you can do whatever the fuck you want, whenever you want.

Civil rights and "you can't touch me". Bullshit. Tell that to the three thousand victims at the Towers. Or tell that to the families of the victims.

*   *   *

You know, the same thing goes for when you're working homicide. I mean, say that . . . Jesus, knock on wood, but say that somebody in your family gets killed. Do you want me going the extra step and maybe not worrying so much about how the killer feels about his civil rights when I'm conducting my investigation? Or would you rather I get the job done? God forbid, your brother or your mother or your sister gets killed. You want me talking to their murderer in a *nice* manner, making it easy for them to get away with it? Or do you want results? If I gotta break your balls to get results, I'm gonna do it.

You treat people accordingly, though. I only break balls if I have to. See, if you start out high? You got no place to go from there. You gotta start out here.[24] Then? According to where the conversation goes, you adjust accordingly. If you *earn* the respect, you *get* the respect. If you *act* like an asshole, you get *treated* like one.

*   *   *

A wake up call, I'm telling you. Liberals? They're the most annoying people on the face of the earth. To me, they're in La-La Land. It was two or three days after the attack and I'm driving down 42nd Street. There's people out there protesting us bombing Afghanistan. I'm at the point now where I'm older; I don't get as uptight like I would've. But those people? They don't look at the big picture. They don't realize that they're able to protest only because they're in this country and they're allowed to. They got these signs out: "Two wrongs don't make a right." What the fuck are you talking about? Are you a mental midget?

I got an idea! Why don't we let the terrorists do whatever they want and leave them alone so they can attack us again?

And those people? I guarantee that none of them were down there at the World Trade Center when the attack happened. They didn't see the after effects. I guarantee that no one

---

[24]He thumps his gut with an open palm.

who was down there turned around and held up a sign saying, "No more war."

You know what I call a conservative? "A liberal who got robbed."

*　　*　　*

Was *I* down there that day? Yes. What happened was this:

Homicide detectives work what's called a turn-around tour. We work two four-to-ones from four in the afternoon to one at night. Then two eight-to-fours which run eight in the morning to four in the afternoon. So when you work your third shift, you get off at one in the morning and you gotta be back at work by eight. We sleep at the precinct, that's the turnaround part. September 11th was the morning we slept over, so we were up and working.

My partner and I were in the racks.[25] We get up, my partner looks at his beeper and says, "Oh shit. Look at the date. It's 9/11. 911 – like the emergency code. I wonder if we'll catch a homicide today."

I says, "Hey. You never know." And we brushed it off. This is eight o'clock in the morning.

We go upstairs and we get a phone call from our detective bureau to respond down to the World Trade Center. "A plane hit the World Trade Center." When we initially heard it, we thought it was one of those Cessnas that went off course. We turned on the TV and said, "Holy shit. Now *there's* a problem."

There were six of us working and we split up. Three guys went in one car, three guys went in another. At any given time, you've got five detectives and a sergeant. So my whole team went down.

I was driving. We took the FDR[26] down, I guess 'cause I knew it would be easier to go around the Trade Center. But the second plane hit as we were heading down. We didn't see it, we *heard* it. Then we got near the Brooklyn Bridge, *then* we saw it. Or rather you could see what was left of it, the Towers, through the outline of the city. That's when we said to each other, "Holy shit. This is *not* an accident. We've got problems."

We went down by the Battery Tunnel, went around that loop, and parked the car underneath the overhang just outside the Tunnel. I figured, if we had to get outta there,

---

[25]Station house bunks where overnight personnel can catch some sleep.
[26]The Franklin Delano Roosevelt Drive runs along the east side of Manhattan.

that was the best way - there was no way to bring the car up any closer. We got out and started walking up West Street, a couple blocks south of the south Tower.

*   *   *

It's a mess. There's cops everywhere. Fire trucks pulling up. EMS was there, treating people who were injured with cuts. There was glass all over the place, you were afraid to walk. I saw one body on the ground that was already covered. Somebody had put this yellow poncho over it.

We had our shields[27] out on the lapels of our suit jackets, but it was mayhem. We're trying to tell people, "Get the Hell out! Get the Hell out!" But some people just weren't getting it. I don't know if you want to call it shock or stupidity; people were just sitting there. They were strolling along as if they were going to see a play. I'm like, "Let's get going. What are you doing? We *have* to be here, you don't. Get the fuck outta here! Move your ass!" Nobody really paid attention.

So. Three of us stuck together. We made a pact when we got down there that we would stay with each other because it was total mayhem. But I says, "You know, this'll sound funny, but I gotta go to the bathroom in the worst way." I'd had two cups of coffee that morning, which I normally wouldn't have.

I do a part-time job further south of the Towers on Trinity Street and I says, "Hey, you know what? Why don't we go over there to my job, and I'll use the bathroom. I'll get on the phone to find out where all the detectives are gonna be."

See, we didn't know where everyone was. Turns out all the detectives were on the north side of the Towers; we were the only morons on the south side. We started walking down Greenwich Street, straight south.

We got to Thames Street when we heard a rumble, sounded like an explosion. We look, and there's the building starting to come down. We start to run. And as we're running, this thick cloud comes down and covers us. It's like being in a wind tunnel. Everything turned black. We were literally blown off our feet - it picked us up off our feet and threw us. We landed and none of us could breathe. The smoke, the concrete dust was so thick. It burned our eyes.

*   *   *

---

[27] Police badges.

77

Now I always carry a hanky.[28] Always. So what I did was I kept passing it back and forth so we could all breathe through it. I knew where we were and I knew we had to get south in order to get away - south was where the water was. Near the water, I figured it'd be a little easier to breathe. So we held onto each other's belts and I basically led the way.

One of the guys with us - not my partner but the other guy - he couldn't breathe, he has asthma. We were getting a little nervous for him. I wanted to pick him up and carry him out but he didn't want that. Me? I can understand that. He's a man.

It was like walking around at midnight. You know those little street carts where you get your cup of coffee? We didn't see one of these things until we walked right into it. Totally deserted. We went into it and got water, poured it on the hanky. We took a few bottles of water with us and kept passing the hanky back and forth. We kept moving.

*   *   *

A guy appears out of nowhere, walking next to us.

He says, "'Scuse me. Am I all right? Am I all right?"

He's got a big cut across his forehead over his right eyebrow. A middle-aged man, late fifties.

I say, "Listen. You're all right. You just got a bad cut. You're going to need stitches." The cut was covered in filth.

So we rinsed it off with the water bottles. I wasn't gonna give him the hanky, I hate to say it, that was all we had. "Listen," I says. "Put something against your head to stop the bleeding and follow us."

At this point, we were a couple of blocks further south and you could see a little better. There were people running around us, you could make them out. We didn't want to run because you still couldn't really see what was in front of you; we could've run into anything.

A female hooked up with us, too. She saw our shields, I guess. She said, "Do you mind if I come with you guys?"

"No. Go right ahead. We're just gonna try to get to the water."

---

[28]He gestures to the pressed white handkerchief in the breast pocket of his suit jacket.

So that's what we did. We walked toward the water. And little by little the air started to clear.

*   *   *

I'd called my wife on the cell phone when I got down there to the Trade Center. This is about ten, 15 minutes before the Tower collapsed.

I said, "I'm right underneath the South Tower. It's mayhem down here. I can't talk to you."

She wanted me to find her brother who works on Barclay Street, very close by. He was on his way to work and nobody could get hold of him. She gave me his cell phone number and, of course, I couldn't get through.

But I had just spoken to her and she was watching all this on TV. She knew I was at the South Tower. Then the building fell. She thought I was killed in the collapse. I didn't realize this until I finally got through to her four hours later. She was hysterical. I been married 15 years. I got an 11-year old daughter at home.

When I'm finally talking to my wife, I made her go to my daughter's school. I said, "I don't care what you gotta do, I want you to pull her out of school." She's in a Catholic School in Staten Island. But, you know? When I saw this happen, I didn't know what was gonna happen next. What other kinds of attacks? Schools? Bridges? I knew we were in a lot of trouble and it wasn't over. So I took precautions for my own family.

What was going through my head during all of this was, "We're in for a lot of shit. We, *the country*, are in for a lot of shit." Because if they attacked here? If they could bring the Towers down?

We didn't even know about the Pentagon at that time, or the other plane in Pennsylvania. We didn't have radios, we didn't know what was happening. But I said to myself, "Life, as we know it, has totally changed."

*   *   *

We walked from where the first Tower was all the way down to Water Street and Battery Park. We meet up with a lieutenant I know from the detective bureau and a chief I know. They just happened to be there, directing people to walk up the FDR Drive.

They're like, "See this building on the corner? This building's gotta be evacuated, there's still a lot of people in it." We're trying to get everyone out, but they're saying things like, "Well, the building personnel told us we should just stay where we are." It was the most frustrating, aggravating thing. It was like being in a comic strip. You just couldn't understand what the fuck these people were thinking - I mean, these are educated people, they have white-collar jobs. You'd figure they'd have a little common sense.

I said, "Listen, the Towers just fell. Get your asses out of here. Manhattan is obviously a major target, I don't think they're gonna attack Brooklyn, know what I mean? Get the fuck outta here." And we're trying to get them to walk over the Brooklyn Bridge - just get them outta the buildings! We didn't want anyone in buildings.

At that point, my partner panics because he hears a jet overhead. I says, "Relax. Take it easy. That's one of ours."

"How the fuck do *you* know?" he says.

"I spent three fuckin' years in the Marine Corps. I know what the Hell a fighter jet sounds like. Trust me. And if I'm wrong - if the terrorists got hold of a fighter jet - we ain't got a prayer in Hell anyway, so don't worry 'bout it.."

But, then, if they had fighter jets, they wouldn't have used commercial planes. They would've attacked with missiles or something like that. This is all going through my mind while we're down by Battery Park.

*   *   *

Now we start walking up Water Street 'cause we understand there's a temporary police headquarters set up by Pike and South over by the Pathmark Grocery Store. We learned about it through a radio one of the guys had, so we started walking toward there.

We didn't realize how bad we looked. But we're covered from head to toe in soot and the dust. As we're walking, people are looking at us. And the weird thing was . . . we would look at each other, but we never really thought, "*I* must look like that, too." I guess we must have been in shock a little. Plus there was this instinct of let's-get-to-where-we-gotta-go-so-we-can-start-doing-something. I wanted to get in the game. Up until then it was like: okay, this is a fight. Now it was time to get in the game and take a swing at someone.

We get all the way up to Pike? Cherry? One of those streets over there. And this uniformed guy starts screaming, "Get back! The bridge is gonna blow! Get back! Get *back*!"

We start running for our lives, my shoe goes flying off, I get a cramp in my leg. My partners are ahead of me, I'm slowing down. They're screaming at me, "Come on! Come on!" It was insane.

"Go! Don't worry, go!"

"We're not leaving you!"

This is all when we were walking underneath the bridge . . .

Turned out somebody had left a truck on the bridge and just walked off. They assumed it was a truck filled with explosives. But nobody was gonna get close enough to it to try and figure it out.

*   *   *

We got to the temporary headquarters. Everybody saw us. They were all, at the point, in uniform.

They said, "Listen, there's a decontamination unit set up behind the Pathmark." So we went, and they literally hosed us down from head to toe with our suits still on. We were just covered. They washed out our eyes with solution and our eyes looked like demons' eyes, they were so red. We finally relaxed and were able to get something to drink. And we finally got hold of one of our supervisors who told us that everybody was gonna muster at Church Street. So we start to walk, now from the east side back over to the west side.

We're walking through Chinatown, sopping wet in our soaked suits. And Chinatown's going about their business as if nothing happened, selling fish heads and fucking rice. You can look into the backdrop of the skyline, and all you see is this plume of smoke. But in Chinatown, it's like it's a different world and nobody cares.

Me and the guys looked at each other like, "What the fuck is going on here? Are we in a different city?"

I mean, not to degrade the Chinese. But I was a little offended by it. I was a little *pissed* to be honest with you.

"What the fuck is *wrong* with you people? Do you realize what's going on?"

*   *   *

We didn't realize that the three of us were among the officers reported missing from the NYPD. Our partners thought we were dead. At Church Street, when they saw us, everybody hugged each other. "Are you all right?"

"Huh? Yeah, we're all right."

Meanwhile they'd all gone through the same type of deal over on the north side of the Towers.

One of the sergeants from the detective bureau, for instance. He got his leg run over by a van. He dove underneath a van when the Towers fell and it ran him over. He ended up spending about a month in a Jersey hospital, they took him over there with a harbor launch and he's doing real good now, thank God.

* * *

All the stuff that happened afterwards? Maybe that was the worst. At my daughter's school, they lost six parents. Three firemen plus a woman and two men who worked in the Trade Center. That's a big nut when you consider it's a small school, only two grades per class.

That night, going home . . . I remember it being so eerie going across the Verranzano Bridge. Quiet. All the tollbooths were up. No lights. It was all black. We had gone to the hospital to get treated and I had to be back at work at four the next morning. I got home at 12 midnight. I walked in, both my wife and my daughter were up. They gave me a big hug and a kiss - it was good to be home. But I wanted to get back to work.

My daughter understands what's going on. Not because she's my daughter do I say this, but she's very intelligent. Her attitude was, "What do they want, these people? Why don't we just give them what they want so they'll leave us alone?"

I asked her, "What do you think they want?"

And she says, "It can't be that important for us not to give it to them."

She doesn't have a mean streak in her.

* * *

I broke down one night later on. We had a party at the house and I had been drinking. Everybody that was there, none of them were cops. Everybody's talking about the World Trade Center, whether the information we receive is accurate. And I didn't want to hear it. I was like, "You people don't know what the fuck you're talking about. I'm in the middle of this shit. I know what's being found, I know what's *not* being found. I'm at the Morgue . . ."

I drank myself into oblivion. After everybody left, I went upstairs.

A good friend of mine was killed in the Towers and every day I checked the Morgue to see if they had found him. They haven't found him yet. We were partners in Narcotics from '92 to '96. He'd been in the Marine Corps the same time I was in, we just didn't know each other at the time. We were very close. I found out he was missing that second day, Sept. 12th, and I knew that anyone missing was dead. Just after being down there and seeing that devastation, I know that.

I broke down. My wife came upstairs, she had heard me sobbing. My daughter started to come in the room, but I turned over and my wife said, "No, it's okay, honey. Daddy doesn't feel good." My little girl knew something was up. You think kids don't know. But they do.

My daughter didn't really see me too much. And that's good, because I never want her to see me upset. Because to me, it shows weakness. And I never want her to see weakness in me. I don't want her to ever worry that I'm not there to protect her. She always says she wants her mother. But when something happens, she wants her daddy. I never want her to see me vulnerable and think that Daddy won't be there.

*   *   *

The attack on the Towers is technically a homicide and our office started working on tips coming in. Stuff like, "I know this Arab who said he wasn't going to work on September 11th and he wouldn't tell me why." We didn't have a homicide in the city for a week following the 11th. We didn't have a homicide in Manhattan South for almost a *month* after the attack. I guess people had other things on their minds. So our job was to track down these leads.

Now this is where my problem with the FBI comes in. We would go out on a tip and find out that two FBI agents had already been there. It's like, "Let me ask you a question, what the fuck's going on here? Either we're gonna work together or *not* work together. But don't waste my fucking time."

The leads were being filtered into a command center, then they were being filtered back out. If it was something that took place in Manhattan South, we went out on it. If it was something that took place in Brooklyn, the Brooklyn detectives went out. But all these leads went through the command center where the FBI analyzed them.

On one tip, the guy was a pilot. An Egyptian. He was staying in a hotel in midtown. Someone called in to say he'd overheard this guy had said, "The skyline's gonna change" or something like that. The fact that he was Egyptian and a pilot made him suspicious so we went to visit. That's when we found out the FBI had already been there.

I said, "Lemme call this FBI agent." I had his number.

I got him on the phone and said, "Did you talk to this guy?"

He says, "Yeah."

"Well, what did he tell you?"

"Not much."

"Well, how'd you talk to him? What'd you say to him? How'd you question him?"

"Well . . . you know . . ."

"No," I said. "I guess maybe I don't."

I went back upstairs to question the guy myself. He didn't understand the point to the investigation. "Why are you bothering me?" he says. "Leave me alone, I don't bother nobody. I really don't have time for this, I'm going to brunch with my friends."

And that's when I got a little hefty with him. Apparently the FBI guy didn't get that way with him, 'cause as soon as I got a little heated he kinda understood that we weren't fucking around. I said, "I'm gonna throw you out the fuckin' window in about two seconds if you don't shut the fuck up and answer my questions. You think I'm playing? You try me. I'm in no fuckin' mood for your shit, okay?"

At that point, we thought there was five thousand people dead from the Towers. So I said, "You think I'm gonna listen to *your* bullshit today? I'll throw you out that fuckin' window so fast your head'll spin." What can I say? He came around. He sat down and shut the fuck up and answered my questions.

But you know, the FBI didn't do that. It's not in their book, that's a street thing. I don't mean to be mean. But you gotta show people you're not playing games.

Turns out that the whole lead was a joke, a get-even thing.

*   *   *

The Egyptian went through where he was, what he'd been doing on the 11th. I could tell by looking at him that he might have been homosexual. So I says, "Are you gay? Were you with any lovers recently? What's the story?"

I'm not shocked by anything like that. You gotta be an asshole if you're shocked by that sort of thing, especially if you're a detective in New York City. I mean, if the guy thought he was gonna shock me by telling me he was gay, well . . . you'd better get yourself some Rice Krispies and have a good breakfast, 'cause it's not gonna bother me. I seen it all. I told him that.

He told me he'd gone out to a few clubs and been with a few different lovers in one night. I said, "All right, fine, no problem, no big deal. I just need to know all this."

I said, "Do you know all these guys' names?"

He says, "No, I don't." And I *knew* he don't. For that community, that's a lifestyle that happens a lot. We've worked plenty of homicides with gay individuals that sleep with three, four men a night and not even know their names. You know what? If I could do that with women, I'd do it. I mean, that's a great lifestyle if you can do it.

So when the guy told me he didn't know the guys' names, I believed him. But I don't think the FBI would have believed him. They never even got to that fuckin' point! Again: I don't mean to throw a blanket on all FBI agents. But the majority of these guys couldn't find their asses if they had a map in their back pockets, know what I mean?

As it turns out, the Egyptian was homosexual and a lover of his was trying to get even with him by giving a bogus tip. We wound up getting a lot of those.

And the fact that the feds were going on these leads before we got them meant that they were trying to upstage us. It's frustrating. The right hand don't know what the left hand's doing. And when we ended up telling our bosses what was going on, they pulled us from the cases. They said, "Well, if this is what's going on, then we're wasting our man power."

Now look: I know nothin' about Al Quaeda cells. I'm no expert on terrorism. But you know what? I learn pretty quick. I know how to get information, that's my job. I'm good at what I do, and everybody I work with is good at what they do. You don't want to tell me what's going on? Fine. Then tell me who to interview and tell me what you want to know and *I'll* talk to them.

But the Feds took everything over. And we went back to work on the active homicides we had prior to the attack.

*   *   *

We also did the Fresh Kills landfill, sifting through the debris from the Trade Center, hoping to find body parts, identification, the black boxes - which are actually orange.[29] In the beginning, we found a lot of body parts.

The area up there was set up like a military camp. We had tents set up with designations: BODY PARTS, BONES, IDENTIFICATION, PAPERS. All of them in separate spots so you could drop off whatever you ound and it could be analyzed. Some of the stuff we found that we thought was human flesh wound up being meat from a refrigerator. And some stuff that we thought was meat from a refrigerator wound up being human flesh. They had scientists up there who could tell the difference.

We'd bring the stuff over in buckets; we were dressed up in the Tyrex suits with the gas masks. You can't appreciate that type of work until you do it.

And then we were assigned to the Morgue, on 1st Avenue and 30th Street. As the bodies and body parts came in, each thing had to go to a different area. If you had an arm, it went to the area where the arms were. If you had a leg, it went to the leg area. Torsos - they all went into refrigerated trailer trucks and they had teams of detectives escorting body parts to wherever they had to go, just to make sure everything was done in a proficient manner. It's a pretty good system.

If a fireman or a cop's remains came in, there'd be a ceremony. We'd all line up. A flag would be draped, then somebody would fold the flag in the right manner. The remains would be saluted and then the body would be taken in. Most of the time, there really wasn't much of a body, but it's something for the family.

To describe the way the bodies are? You can't. When you see homicides, you see accidents, all kinds of different deaths . . . which I have seen . . . it didn't prepare me to see the destruction

---

[29] An airplane's supposedly indestructible Flight Data Recorder (FDR) and Cockpit Voice Recorder (CVR): useful tools that aid airline disaster investigations. The boxes cost from $10,000 to $15,000 each and can reveal events that immediately precede in-flight disasters. Boxes use magnetic tape or solid-state memory boards to record data which is then dumped into a Crash-Survivable Memory Unit (CSMU) which can store up to two hours of CVR audio data and up to 25 hours of FDR flight data. Solid-state FDRs can track up to seven hundred flight parameters in larger, modern aircraft; this includes data pertaining to acceleration, airspeed, altitude, flap settings, outside temperature, cabin temperature and pressure, and engine performance. Both boxes are generally stored in the rear section of an airplane.

of bodies from the World Trade Center. What happened with those people . . . it lives with me every day. We homicide detectives don't leave it. We're always around it. Cops and firemen are still right in the middle of this shit.

*   *   *

You walk into that Morgue and the smell hits you. If you've ever smelled bad meat? Times that by a hundred - that's the only way I can really describe it. If you've never smelled it before, once you do, you'll never forget. And once you know it, if you walk into a room and you get hit with that smell you know there's a body in the room.

Every dead body is different; it depends on the temperature, the time of year, ventilation. There's a lot of factors. It's essentially the same goddamned smell, but at different levels.

You get a guy that's been dead for two weeks in an apartment that's a hundred degrees . . . *that's* got a certain smell. It's hard to explain.

*   *   *

I don't think I have much of a story. A lot of people went through a lot more. People who got injured, hit with glass, people who got cut. You know, if I hadn't gone to the bathroom? When we went back the next day to get our car, had we been standing there? We would have been dead. We escaped narrowly with our lives.

I lost six very good friends, cops and firemen. To me? I believe, "If your time's up, your time's up." I was always kind of a believer in that. But after the attack, I knew it. And knowing that? Personally, it makes it a littler easier.

I've been in shootings. I used to think that I had a destiny when I went into a firefight or knocked on a door. But I have an attitude now where I'm always careful, I always do my tactics . . . when my time's up, it's up. And there's nothing gonna change that.

You say to yourself, "What if I *didn't* have to go to the bathroom? What if I *hadn't* had somewhere to go downtown? What if I *didn't* go to the Towers that day?" A lot of what-ifs. We laugh about it. But things happen for a reason.

*   *   *

As far as the way people treated the cops after the attack? In my 18 years, I've never seen that kind of admiration. The hellos on the street. People coming up to us - kids coming up with pictures they'd drawn, pictures of the Trade Center with aptions that read, "We love you, New York City Police," and "Thank you so much for what you're doing." They're handing these to us. Heartbreaking. It was just heartbreaking.

See, usually? Everybody loves firemen and everybody hates cops, that's what it boils down to. Firemen don't give you a summons. Firemen don't lock you up. But I seen this guy on an interview who was down at the Trade Center that day, working in one of the firms. He said, "I used to walk by the police all the time and I took them for granted. I don't do that no more."

What this city turned into after the attack happened was the most beautiful thing I've ever seen. I was shocked. For a while, everybody was, "Hey, how are ya?" Concerned about each other - what we used to call *esprit de corps* in the Marines. A camaraderie. But things are back to normal now. People are back to being assholes. Now everybody's back to, "Fuck you, get out of my way, I got my own business to attend to."

*　*　*

I'm offended by that viewing ramp they built.[30] Handing tickets out to people, whatever the fuck it is. I'm offended seeing tourists down there snapping pictures. Maybe I'm being a little sensitive, but to me, that's a giant tomb. A gravesite. I take offense to these fuckin' European scumbags coming here taking photos like it's a fuckin' circus attraction. A carnival. How would a family member feel knowing people are taking pictures of a loved one who's not home yet?

I want to say to them: "What are you folks taking a picture of? Do you have any idea what you're looking at?"

But what are you gonna do? People are gonna be people. That's human nature. The asshole factor's always out there. 🔥

---

[30]To accommodate the growing number of tourists interested in visiting Ground Zero, the city build a viewing ramp overlooking the site.

OUTSIDE THE TOWERS

ANNA BAHNEY, 26, works at The New York Times. *Anna had a peculiar experience on September 11ᵗʰ. While most of lower Manhattan was fighting like mad to get out of the city, she was fighting like mad to get back in.*

―――――

I live in Williamsburg, Brooklyn. My alarm went off at 8:30 a.m. and I was listening to NPR on the radio. I opened my eyes, turned over in bed and looked out the window. I remember thinking, "This is an alarmingly beautiful day."

The radio said that there was a fire up on top of one of the World Trade Towers. And my response was, "Time to make the donuts." Meaning: today was going to be a big news day.

I was actually scheduled to work on news at the National desk that day. A building fire would technically be a Metro story. But the way the desks worked, I knew that a story like that would eventually trickle down to National. So I wasn't tearing out the door. I figured I had a little time.

I got up, went through my morning routine. I had the radio on in the shower. When I got out of the shower, they were already interviewing an eye witness who said she saw a plane, and that the plane was kind of veering off toward Brooklyn, as if it wanted to go towards the airport. But then she saw it go into the building. So we knew then that it was an attack.

I turned on the television. You could see the smoke coming out of the one building. And then there was this moment - like one of those subliminal clips they put in movies to make you buy Fritos or something. You saw this dark shadowy object coming toward the front Tower. You could see it, but you almost couldn't *consciously* see it, do you understand? It was so shocking. And then my whole TV went black.

That's when I knew this was serious.

*   *   *

I didn't freak out. I just kept saying to myself, "This is serious. This is serious." I knew this was a deliberate attack. The TV came back on and I continued to watch and eat my cereal.

They cut to a split screen; they had "New York" and "Washington." I had this sudden image of 18 cities up there. New York, Washington, Chicago, Boston, San Francisco, Los Angeles. All of them. I was afraid somebody was gonna come on and say, "These places have been hit, too, and they're taking over."

Then the pieces started falling into place: two airplanes in New York, another one at the Pentagon. I knew I had to get to the office. But by this time, they were saying that the bridges in New York had been shut down as well as the subway systems. No traffic in or out of Manhattan. And I'm thinking: "I *have* to get to Manhattan. I *have* to get to the *Times* office."

My boss Erika called and said, "Hey, have you heard about this?"

"Yeah, I've heard about this."

"Are you gonna make it in?"

I could just imagine the frenetic energy in the *Times* office, how they would need people. A lot of people who work at the paper live in the suburbs and even more remote areas.

"Yeah, I'm leaving now. The bridges are closed, the subway is down. I'll do what I can."

*   *   *

The *Times* building is near 42nd and Broadway. The only access into Manhattan is the Williamsburg Bridge, which is on Delancey Street, 40-plus blocks away to the South. I normally take the L train to 14th Street, then the N/R up to Times Square. But none of those trains were running.

I had on blue jeans, a white T-shirt and sandals. Since I didn't know what I was getting myself into, I changed into walking shoes. I got my backpack and put in a big bottle of water. I was very, very calm. Like thinking, "I'm packing for destruction. Okay." I put in an extra shirt, which I thought I might need to cover my face. And I packed some bagels, a notebook and some pens. I set off walking down the street.

I was still at home when the first Tower fell; I saw it on TV. There weren't that many people on the streets. I got the feeling that they didn't know. That they either weren't listening to the news or they weren't understanding it. Or maybe they didn't care. No one looked terrified. But then, I guess I was really stressed out, too, and I didn't think that *I* looked terrified. Maybe they were looking at me the same way.

*   *   *

This drunk was standing on the street, talking to himself. I remember thinking, "*He* doesn't know what's going on. I wonder when he's going to figure it out."

91

I continued walking. There were radios on in the delis and some cars on the streets. I'm hearing things as I'm walking: "The second Tower has fallen. Children will be held in school. President Bush is criss-crossing the country in a plane." I tried to call the *Times*, but my cell phone was dead. I kept walking.

I got to the train station and there was mild chaos there because people were still trying to get to work. They didn't understand the severity of the situation. "Where are the trains? What's going on?" Around the train station, Williamsburg is a very artsy, urban hipster area. The kids who couldn't get to work had sat down in the cafés. Like I said, it was a beautiful day.

I went to see if I could walk over the Williamsburg Bridge.

* * *

I walked through a Puerto Rican area and the news from the radio became all Spanish. But I could hear "Giuliani" and I could hear "American Airlines." I could hear "World Trade Towers" and I could hear "President Bush." There were many more people on the streets in this neighborhood. There was a lot more chatter in this area.

Finally I got to the bridge. By this time I'd met lots of people who were asking, "Is the train closed?"

I said, "Yeah, it is."

"What should we do?"

"Well, I'm gonna walk to the bridge."

So now there's more people moving with me in that same direction.

* * *

I got to the bridge and there was a footpath, a ped-way that went up. There's a white sawhorse barricade across it with three policemen there and about a hundred people gathered at the foot of it. People were petitioning the cops.

"My child is over there."

"My father is over there."

"I live just on the other side."

"I just need to get across."

The police were saying, "No, no, no, no, no."

One of the policemen was Hassidic, one was Latino and one was Polish. They're saying, "No" to people in various languages. I'm looking for a way to bypass them and get across.

There were lots of people trying to use their phones. One person would get a connection, then eight people would try to use that cell phone. There were offers to exchange money - this man held out five dollars saying, "Please, let me use the cell phone. Please." But no one was charging anything. A woman saying, "No. Here. I'm finished. Use this."

It was an incredible rumbling going on, all these people trying to get across, trying to communicate. And then this tall, black man ran out of the crowd and right up to the policemen. He said something to them and he showed them a card. He was allowed to step onto the bridge and cross.

I asked some people who were closer to the front what had happened. They said: "The only people allowed to pass are members of the press and hospital workers." I had my *Times* card so I showed it.

"Look," I said, "I have to get there, I have to get to work." There was no question after that. The police just said, "Go ahead."

Meanwhile there were torrents of people coming down off the bridge from Manhattan. On the Manhattan side, they were letting people start across the bridge in heats. A group would come across, then there would be nobody for a while. Then another group. Then no one. A bunch of people had just come across as I was allowed to pass through. It was like walking through a mob.

But once I got passed them, I took off running.

*   *   *

I ran up the ramp and up the stairs and started across the bridge.

There were hundreds and hundreds of people walking toward me. Businessmen, storekeepers and their families. Old people. It was if the whole island of Manhattan had been tipped on its side and dumped out onto the bridge.

As I'm running, this guy shouted, "You're going the wrong way!" But I kept going. By the time I reached the middle of the road, this group had thinned out and I was alone again on the bridge.

At that point, I could actually see what I was running to. I saw the two, distinct columns of smoke and the . . . nothing. The Towers just . . . weren't there. I ran harder for what seemed like a long time.

*   *   *

When I got to the other side, there was a policeman standing guard before you hit the off ramp down to the streets of Manhattan. When he saw me, he kind of bolstered himself up. Just the two of us on this bridge. A doughy sort of cop. A middle-aged man gone sort of round in the middle, balding, with a moustache. He looked terrified and alone.

At first, he postured himself like, "You're going the wrong way, what's your reason for crossing?" I showed him my card and he completely changed. He looked so vulnerable.

There was a moment of silence and he said, "What do you know?"

I didn't know anything. I was clueless myself. But I told him what I'd heard on the radio, having walked as far as I had. "Vice-President Cheney holds office while the President is moving to a safe location."

He said, "Oh." And he looked down. We were both quiet for a minute.

And then? I don't know why I did this. I'm not a religious person, I'm not Catholic. But what I really wanted to do was cross myself, though I have no spiritual, traditional reason to do that. So I touched my hand to my forehead. I offered the man a salute. A benediction, I guess. A gesture of respect I wanted to give to him. Something. Because I appreciated him standing on that bridge so much, being vulnerable.

And I said, "God bless you."

And he said, "God bless *you.*"

I ran down the stairs.

*   *   *

At the bottom of the stairs there was another barricade and thousands of people waiting to go up and cross. The crowd spread from the very start of the pedestrian bridge back down Delancey, which was shut down across all four lanes of traffic. All the way back past Essex, past the streets whose names I don't know. Plus traffic from all the cars on the tributaries to the Williamsburg Bridge. Lots of trucks backed up in a gridlock. Lots of people in cars, stuck there, nobody moving. Everyone had their radio on.

I had made it into Manhattan. But what now?

I tried to use my cell phone again and I called into the office. It worked. I talked to Erika and said, "Look. I'm in Manhattan. I'm down here. Does the Metro Desk need anything?"

She said, "Hang on, I'm gonna transfer you."

I talked to an editor at Metro and repeated, "I'm down here on Delancey Street, do you need anything?"

And they said, "*Oh* yeah."

It's a pretty tight ship at the *Times*. They had already dispatched a lot of reporters and they had things covered for the most part. But the sort of over-arching things that they would need: the sights, the sounds. They wanted to know about the ad-hoc crisis centers that were being set up. They wanted interviews with people who had actually seen and/or participated in rescues. They were very specific about all that, and I said, "Okay."

*   *   *

Right where you come down from the bridge, there's a firehouse, which you can see from the top of the bridge. I backtracked to there. A woman there was hooked up to some sort of oxygen mask. She was dressed in business attire with her purse at her side. She was covered in dust. Her purse was black, but with the dust it had turned white. She was sitting there by herself, breathing into this mask.

Three firemen were standing nearby and I talked to them. I said, "Are you with this house?"

They said, "No, we're from Queens." The firemen from that house had already been sent out and these men had been brought in to cover them. They had their trucks and their ladders with them, the idea being that they would rotate out when the house came back in.

These guys knew what was going on. They had seen the pictures on TV, same as all of us. And they were waiting in that firehouse, knowing they had to go down there when and if these men came back.

The lid was on. They were so nervous. They were pacing back and forth, there was a rat-tat-tat to their conversation. They just had to keep talking, keep talking. They told me, "Yup, we've been here, we know *this* is what's happening, we know *these* people are coming back, we're waiting, we don't *really* know what's going on." They didn't have much information. They just had this raw-nerve energy.

I took some notes and kept walking.

*   *   *

I saw a group of business people coming toward me with cloths over their faces.

I said, "Where were you?"

They had been in a building near one of the Towers, and were covered in debris.

I walked down toward Chinatown. No cars. All the streets are shut down. It was a pedestrian free-for-all with everybody heading north and east, away from where I was going. I was still going in the wrong direction.

There was this young, blonde woman crying on the street corner. She was with another young, blonde woman who was consoling her. The crying woman had all these keys in her hand, as if she'd just run out of her house. The two women were standing there when all of a sudden this police car covered in debris - it's like snow - swerved up and came to a screeching halt in front of them.

A guy jumped out. He was covered in debris, too; there was dust all over his hair. He ran to the crying woman and embraced her, lifted her off the ground and spun her around while the other woman stared. The couple pressed their foreheads against each other and talked, saying private words. Then the officer got back in his police car and drove away.

I said, "Is that your husband?"

The crying woman could barely talk, she's sobbing. "No. That's my boyfriend. He was working down there and he has to go back."

I took more notes and kept walking.

*   *   *

Most places I passed were shut, but I found some delis open with their radios on and people gathered around listening. Some places had telephones, water, and toilets and if they had these three things, they put up signs. "TELEPHONE." "WATER." And "TOILETS." Here were the beginnings of my makeshift crisis centers.

Several churches had these signs out front and people were going into the buildings. Along the Bowery, Methadone clinics and halfway houses were taking people in. I kept walking faster toward the traverse of the Manhattan Bridge.

It was still a free-for-all with people walking in all different directions. This big crowd passed me, and suddenly, right before me, is one of my co-workers, Jesse, this guy that I sit next to every day who also works in Culture. We see each other and stop. We give each other a big hug. This is a person I work with; I certainly wouldn't under normal circumstances go up to him and give him a hug on the street.

I had seen more people in that one morning than I had probably seen during my whole time in New York. Masses of humanity. But in all that, I had been anonymous. Jesse was the first person I ran into that I knew from my life before the attack. And even though we were all, everyone in New York, witnessing what was happening together - even though there was a bond, a friendship of sorts - it was almost not validated because they hadn't been there *yesterday*. They hadn't been part of my life, my routine. Seeing Jesse was like validating that this wasn't a dream. This *was* my life. I was *here*. There. Right where it was all happening.

Jesse had been dispatched down to the scene to gather information. We exchanged brief words of, "I'm doing this, I'm doing that." He was going off to Brooklyn to visit churches who were serving people who'd fled the city. We said good-bye and he went along his way.

*   *   *

I ended up walking through Chinatown and I got as far as Canal Street before I was stopped at a checkpoint of barricades. The authorities had a bunch of emergency vehicles lined up. Policemen on the street. I circled around for a bit.

Eventually, I ended up sitting on a curb in front of a firehouse in Chinatown.

It was still a beautiful day. And in Chinatown, I watched construction on a shop. Men were painting the doorjamb and the doors. Some shops were open and kids were playing ball.

I sat in front of this firehouse, waiting for the fire teams to come back so I could interview them. Waiting. And waiting. And waiting.

*   *   *

Some of the firemen were from Westchester.[1] I found out that different teams who'd come into the city from the outlying regions to volunteer were brought to a command center up in Harlem and then dispatched down to individual houses throughout Manhattan on a rotation plan. These men, too, had that nervous energy I'd seen in the guys from Queens.

Finally, the team I was talking to loaded up and headed out. I remember seeing them climb onto the fire truck. They didn't know where they were going. But they smiled and everyone on that street cheered them as they drove off. They waved to us. I decided to walk more.

By now it was almost three o'clock in the afternoon and I figured I'd be needed more in the office. I had a long walk ahead of me, so I decided to start.

Was I tired? I don't know. I had sat down for a while. I hadn't really eaten anything. But I was charged. Charged but calm. Fully cognizant. Everything was very clear.

*   *   *

I was walking north on 3rd Avenue when I saw this man walking ahead of me in jeans and a T-shirt. On his left leg, from about the middle of the thigh down, his jeans were ripped. Gone. He had a big bandage across his leg above his knee. Blood was seeping through.

I asked him, "Can I talk to you for a moment?"

He said, "Sure." I found out what happened.

He was a livery driver who delivered supplies for the Mayor's office. He'd been at City Hall; his truck was out on Broadway when the planes went into the Towers. He'd watched them. People had started screaming and running as the buildings fell. He ran with them.

---

[1]Westchester County lies in the heart of the Hudson River Valley, directly north of New York City. It can be reached within minutes by train from Grand Central Station in Manhattan. The county's southernmost tip, which includes towns like Yonkers and Mount Vernon, touches the northern border of the Bronx. Westchester is filled with historic sites, rolling acreage, golf courses, parks, beaches, and quaint towns. It is a popular, upscale suburb for people who work in Manhattan.

But the power of the falling buildings had caused all the windows along Broadway - around John Street and Church Street - to explode.

Somebody had screamed, "Everybody get down!" And everybody had. Then the shrapnel and smoke washed over them. The driver said it was like a flood of water, but it wasn't falling down. It was falling up, seeping up toward everyone on the streets.

After the major stress of the impact passed, the driver said that people started checking each other out. There was an elderly couple near him, so he was helping the woman because she thought she had hurt a bone in her hip. The elderly man was helping his wife . . . suddenly someone looked at the driver and said, "Your leg. Are you okay?"

He looked down at this huge gash in his leg. He hadn't known what caused it. Glass? Or metal? Something. The wound had torn his jeans leg off, ripped right through it. You could see the bone. He's here helping these people and someone tells him, "No, *you* need to get in the ambulance *first*. You're bleeding."

They got him in the ambulance and he went directly over to St. Vincent's Hospital. I tried to get a gauge for how the hospital was treating the severity of the victims, so I asked the driver if he had been treated immediately. He said, "Yes. I went right in and they put 22 stitches in my leg." Four hours later I found him walking down the street.

Under normal circumstances, you know - if there had been an accidental fire or an explosion and someone had sustained that sort of injury - they would have been kept in the hospital. But apparently no one had the facilities and the resources to do that. His injury was deemed 'walkable', which is all that anyone could do at the time; there were no cabs or trains running.

That's what a lot of the crisis centers I saw were about. People had these injuries that weren't completely life-threatening so . . . they left them to recover in relative quiet.

This man was walking down the street, kind of in a daze. Laughing as he told me his story.

I said, "Well, where are you going?"

He lived in Brooklyn, but he had no idea how he was going to get home.

*   *   *

At 8th Street, I took the N/R subway train up to 42nd and went to the *Times* office. The energy at the paper was palpable as I walked in. The old warhorses at the *Times* always bemoan that nowadays the place is so placid and tranquil. They don't have the rat-tat-tat of typewriters anymore; you don't have to yell into your telephone in a noisy newsroom. They pine for those days that have been replaced by computers and soft, digital phones. But that day, I got a feeling of what it must have been like in earlier years. People were yelling for copy. The noise level was pitched way above the norm.

There were maps spread out and everyone was so focused, directing each other. People from the Metro Desk were debriefing people like me. Before I headed up to the office, I had called in my interviews. Usually they have one news assistant on the Metro Desk who answers the phones and handles copy. That day there were 11 manning the phones, tracking the reporters, taking transcriptions from staff who called in. Similarly, the National Desk usually has one news assistant. That day they had eight.

It was "rally the troops." Everyone was there. Management had even called in people who *used* to work at the *Times* six months previous. Culture reporters were going down to the site and covering stories. It was an amazingly generous performance, I thought.

*   *   *

They brought in food. And thus began my two weeks '*Times* diet.' For the next two weeks I was in the office from nine in the morning until nine at night or beyond. We were given three meals a day. Bagels in the morning, sandwiches for lunch. Greek salad and cookies and some sort of chicken thing for dinner - all catered. In the end, it kind of became a joke. The employees of the *Times* are largely stockholders in the company. So two and half weeks into this feeding plan, people were like, "As a stockholder in the company, I think we can cut out the catering now."

But that first week, it was necessary. So many places weren't open and people were too busy to get something to eat on their own. I think there was also an emotional component. Everything was in such an uproar, you had to stop once in a while and have someone tell you, "Okay. It's lunch time now." You needed to have some consistency.

And there's a hard core to journalists who've worked their way up the ladder to write for *The New York Times*. These people live for their work. Things like food and sleep kind of fall by the wayside during times like the attack. People became very tight. You're working together, spending 12 hours a day together, eating your meals with each other. And so much information is passing back and forth. In the following days, documents would come in containing 16 terrorists' names. Another document came in with 19 more.

Meanwhile, I'm working on the National Desk. That first week, flights weren't going anywhere. The breaking stories in Florida[2] were on a national scale. We're calling our reporters in Atlanta and Houston and telling them, "Just get in your car and drive. We don't know where you're going, just drive to Florida. That's where the story is." We're trying to coordinate information from the FBI and from other sources, trying to figure out who these terrorists are and what their connections are. Meanwhile, we're also trying to figure out who was killed in the attacks.

The advent of all the posters and missing flyers that were seen all over the city? I had been dispatched one day to go down to the Armory and collect as many flyers as possible so that we could start a list of the missing.

*   *   *

I'd been holding myself together, maintaining objectivity, doing two jobs at once. Then, one day in the newsroom – all at once I just . . . stopped, and looked down.

In one hand, I had a fax listing the bank account numbers, the addresses, the frequent flyer numbers and the social security numbers of 19 dead terrorists. In the other, I had the photographs, job descriptions, names and family breakdowns of eight dead civilians. It was overwhelming.

I walked away for a little bit. I didn't cry - and I *do* that. I cry a lot, that wouldn't have been unusual. I just didn't have any tears at that moment. I was beyond them, I think.

*   *   *

This whole thing stripped the country down to its fundamental operating procedures. The terrorist attack happened and we found ourselves asking new questions. Do baseball games need to happen? No. Football games? No. Stock market? No. Do we need the flag? No. Transportation? Not so much, no . . .

Do we need a President? Yes. Do we need firemen? Yes. Policemen? Yes. We needed to hear from Rudy Giuiliani. We need direction.

It also stripped a person down on an individual level, right down to a personal basic operating procedure. Emotions, for instance. Do I need them right now? No. Do I need to get this work done? Yeah. Do I need to talk to people? Yeah. Do I need to eat food? Yeah. Sleep? A little. When I can.

[2]In the days that followed September 11th, many terrorists involved with the hijacking of the four airliners were traced to Florida flight schools and other locations in the state where they had planned their tactics and trained themselves.

I realized so much about myself through this process by having the extraneous stripped away. All the social formalities, all the fears. All of the luxuries of life that we take for granted. ∫

JESSE LUNIN PACK, 28. A native New Yorker, he works for an investment banking firm that used to be based in the World Financial Center, just west of the World Trade Center. He witnessed the attacks and the mass exodus from downtown Manhattan mere minutes after the first plane hit the North Tower.

———

I used to work across West Street and I loved working downtown, it felt like you were in the middle of everything. You looked out the office window and right there was the World Trade Center.

My apartment's in Midtown so every morning I'd take the E Train to the World Trade Center station, then walk from the station into the mall underneath. I'd either head out onto the Plaza or walk through the lobby of the North Tower, up an escalator to the bridge which took you to the World Financial Center. My standard morning commute.

I was running a little late on September 11th. I was annoyed that someone had moved my polling place and hadn't bothered to tell me.[3] I got to my initial polling place, but they told me, "You can't vote here" and sent me to the new place. Aggravating. But I got my vote in and hopped the train and made it down to the World Trade Center subway station.

I got off the train and walked through the turnstiles. There was a row of glass doors at the south end of the station which let you into the underground mall, do you remember? As I was approaching those doors, every one of them opened at the same instant and a wall of people came out, talking loudly about a bomb. They were rushing - I wouldn't say it was abject panic with people running for their lives - but they were certainly moving with purpose and if I didn't move with them, I might have gotten trampled.

*   *   *

I've lived in New York City my entire life, lived through bomb threats and scares. I've worked for Jewish agencies and organizations where we had to evacuate our buildings, so it wasn't the first time I'd confronted something like that.

I remained calm, thinking, "Every other time, it's been a false alarm. I'm sure it's a false alarm this time, too. There's enough people moving in one direction. I'll just move along with them." I didn't want to get trapped underground if something was going on.

---

[3]September 11th was the mayoral primary in New York City. Following the attack, the primary was postponed.

As I turned and moved away from those doors, I saw the first possible exit over to my left: a staircase up to the street. I moved toward it. Everyone was being helpful. There was a woman with a baby carriage and two people grabbed the front of her carriage, with the baby inside, and helped lift it up.

I'm sure if anyone knew what was actually going on, we would have told her to take the kid and leave the carriage. But nobody knew yet.

*   *   *

The reality of the situation hit me while I was on that staircase. We were moving slowly, there were a lot of people crowding behind me. But when each person ahead of me got to the top of the stairs, they screamed. Not good.

Some of us started urging people, "Keep moving. Don't stop when you get to the top. We all need to get outta here."

Having no idea of what was at the top of the stairs, we prepared ourselves to run for cover. I got to the top and looked up. I don't remember if I screamed or not, but I know I had that same sentiment. I saw the north Tower on fire; I saw the confetti - for lack of a better word - falling down. I looked closer and saw larger things falling and it became clear quickly that they were people jumping. Or falling.

*   *   *

I moved away from the staircase, east toward the corner. Came up on Vesey Street, which ran along the northern edge of the World Trade Center plaza. I don't know how far down the block I was, but I was closer to Church Street.

My thoughts went back to '93. "Okay," I thought, "a bomb caused this." But it was so high up, it had to be a really big bomb.

I moved to the corner and found a colleague of mine who was looking up in disbelief. We conferred. Near us, there was a payphone with a long line and one of the people said, "No bomb, it was an airplane."

I remembered that an airplane had once hit the Empire State Building but that had been in the middle of a storm. So I asked, "What kind of airplane?"

He said, "A little corporate jet."

I began thinking, "A little corporate jet that must've been packed with explosives to make a hole *that* big." The man said he'd seen the tail of the plane as it entered the building, and this all made sense enough at the time.

We stood there watching more people fall. Luckily, my view of the Plaza itself was blocked by 7 World Trade, so I didn't see the bodies hit the ground. A friend of mine from business school who had been in 7 World Trade later described walking out of that building:

"A meat truck must've overturned on the street because there was hamburger everywhere."

Such a horrifying thought, but I was shielded by the plaza and other buildings. It was horrible to see but it didn't affect me; I was already in shock. I'd worked on an ambulance corps for four years in college. You teach yourself to become immune. I think that instinct kicked in.

*   *   *

My colleague and I still had this fantasy of getting back to our office. But we decided to move away. The first fire trucks were beginning to arrive.

It's odd. I was still able to rationalize: "Okay, there's a big fire up there and that's horrible. But we've all seen building fires and the Fire Department is here, they will take care of it." The situation had not yet progressed to something none of us could fathom.

We started walking north. We were walking in the middle of the street because there were a lot of people moving north. We didn't get very far, maybe not even one or two blocks up Church Street, when there was this explosion behind us.

I turned around and saw a fireball coming out at me. That's the image - more so than the people jumping - that I haven't been able to get rid of: the image of the second tower getting hit. You've seen the video footage of the plane going into the South Tower, I'm sure. The plane was traveling from south to north when it hit. I was just north of that building. All the debris and plume from that explosion shot out over where I was standing. The exit wound of the building, for lack of a better word.

If there was ever a moment of utter pandemonium that was it. Everyone started running. No one knew what was going on. To give you an idea of how close I was, I felt the heat on my face from the fireball coming at us. At first, I thought, "There's no way I could've felt that heat. It's too far away." But my colleague mentioned the same thing later on.

Abby Bullock

I started to run. Didn't know where I was going, but I knew I wanted to move away. A large piece of concrete hit the ground about ten feet in front of me. Larger than a cinderblock. Big enough that if it had hit me, I wouldn't be talking to you right now.

I started feeling, One: angry at myself for standing around looking at things for so long and not moving away. Two: pretty sure there was a good chance I'd get hit by something and die. And Three: pretty sure it was really going to hurt. Nothing noble, like thoughts about my family or anything. It was, "I'm about to die. It's really going to hurt. How do I keep that from happening?"

I saw a car parked on the street, so I crawled under it. It was an old American car, like a Chevy Monte Carlo. Really big and really heavy. I tried to get the engine block over my head. I figured it would protect me.

* * *

I don't know if that was the smartest thing to do or not. I'll tell you, there's a lot less room underneath a car than I'd thought. I really had to flatten myself against the ground to fit under there.

Other people crawled under things, too. Some hit the ground and covered their heads. Pieces of debris hit the street in front of me. I waited for a bit. I don't know how long I stayed, but eventually I decided to come out and put some more distance between me and the Towers.

I slid out. There was a fine white dust falling. I helped one person up to their feet and they started running. The colleague I'd been walking with came around the corner, suddenly. I'm sure he thought I was dead or severely injured since one minute I was running next to him and the next I disappeared. But I joined him around the corner and we regrouped for a moment, noticing only then how people were filing into the lobbies of buildings to off the street.

A woman came running over and pressed herself up against the building next to us. I'll never forget her face.

I said to her, "Are you okay?" She had really wide eyes and she just nodded, didn't say anything. I said, "Let's all try to move north, away from here." She just nodded again and took off at a dead run.

*　　*　　*

Somehow I wound up a block east of Church Street; I have no idea how I got there, I just know I was moving north. My colleague and I ran into another person we knew, and she joined us.

Off-duty emergency services people started showing up. There was an off-duty fireman directing traffic and I asked him if they had evacuated the World Financial Center yet. My stepfather also worked in the World Financial Center and I began to worry about him. The fireman had no idea what was going on, so we kept moving north.

Further on, I asked a cop if they had evacuated the World Financial Center. She said, "I don't know what's going on. Here, you find out." She handed me her two-way radio.

I still can't believe she did that. She was too busy to listen for what was going on and direct traffic at the same time. She said, "If you hear anything, let me know."

I sort of listened for 30 seconds and said, "Thanks, but I'm going to get out of the area."

I don't remember what I heard on the radio. Thank God I don't remember her name, she probably would get into a lot of trouble for doing that.

*　　*　　*

I made a decision to go to a competing investment bank's offices where I have friends. Solomon Smith Barney at 388 Greenwich Street. My cell phone wasn't working, but I felt I had to get word to my family that I was okay. I figured my friends at Solomon would let me into their office to use the phone and Internet. But when we got there, we found out that they had already evacuated.

107

I started moving north again and decided that this time I would go to the Stern School of Business at NYU, where I had graduated a year before. It was going to take me a lot less time to get there than to walk home to Midtown, and there were phones and Internet connections at Stern.

At some point, I stopped next to someone who had their car radio turned up and I learned that the Pentagon had been attacked.

Then I heard the radio announcer scream, "Oh my God," and I heard the people around me scream, too. I turned and saw the south Tower collapsing. I see that image of the Tower collapsing still. Vividly. I was pretty close, but not so close that I was in danger this time.

My first thought was that I just watched 10,000 people die. And then I thought that I probably watched half of the New York City Fire Department die - I had seen the fire trucks and I know how they work. They go in, they go up, they fight fire. That was a very sobering thought.

Now I was really concerned for my colleagues and step-dad. What if they'd decided not to move away? What if they'd been told not to?

I kept moving north.

*　*　*

I knocked on someone's door and a young couple with a little baby opened it.

I said, "I worked down there. I gotta get word to my family. Can I use your telephone?" They invited me in, but their phone line was dead. They had their video camera on until the first Tower collapsed and then they just went inside, shut the door and didn't want to think about it anymore. They wished me luck. And I kept moving north.

We heard another jet engine and people started to get scared again. I recognized the sound, though. Not a commercial aircraft, but a fighter jet. I was able to put things into context again. "Okay, we're at war. The military is here to defend us."

My first thought while I was under the car was, "How could a fire in one Tower cause an explosion in the other and cause it to fall apart? It didn't make any sense." I voiced that and someone near me said, "No, no, it was another airplane."

I couldn't believe that. I thought, "Cruise missiles look like airplanes. We must be under attack by cruise missiles." Each person I talked to tried to rationalize what was going on, to put it into a context they could understand. But it started to dawn on us that this wasn't an accident. We all knew it wasn't.

I moved on again. When I crossed 6th Avenue east to get to school, the north Tower was still standing and I stopped to look at it. But not for long.

When I got to NYU, I walked along the south side of Washington Square Park, past the Catholic Center. They had just put a piece of paper up saying, "THE CATHOLIC CENTER IS OPEN FOR QUIET PRAYER AND CONTEMPLATION." It reminded me of stories I'd heard when Apollo 13 was in trouble.[4] The churches opened their doors for people to pray.

*　　*　　*

I got to the Business School and they had a lot of televisions on with everyone crowding around the screens. I had lost my eyeglasses under the car – I'd realized it at the time but didn't go back for them. I couldn't make out much on the TV.

I looked a mess. I was covered with dirt from when I had laid down. The dean of the school, who had been my professor, saw me in the lobby. He came over and shook my hand, asked how I was doing. The Business School has a lot of connections to Wall Street and the Trade Center so he was trying to take stock.

We chatted a minute. I asked him if the phones were working, he said, "Sometimes yes, sometimes no. Let yourself into any office and do what you need to do."

I managed to get through to my mother's secretary and left a message that I was okay. I also told her that I'd meet her at her apartment later with the rest of the family. My mother, father, stepmother, stepfather, brother - everyone works in the city. Later on, when we compared stories, it turned out my stepfather, father and I had all been within three blocks of each other.

I knew my brother had a two-way Internet pager and I knew they were still working because I'd seen other people using them. I sent him an e-mail.

---

[4]The Apollo 13 lunar landing experienced an equipment malfunction in April of 1970 which placed the lives of astronauts James A. Lovell, John Swigert, Jr., and Fred Haise, Jr. in severe jeopardy, forcing them to return to earth before reaching the moon.

Then I started running into colleagues of mine from school, people who had graduated with me. Like I told my mother later, "We all had the same idea: to go back to school. There were phone lines and Internet and it would be safe.

But my mother balked. She said, "Bullshit. When you're under stress, you go somewhere you feel safe. Like a small community."

I spent at least two hours there. The school ordered pizzas and said we could stay as long as we wanted. Later, one guy came in who'd been on the 69th floor of the south Tower. He was totally covered in white dust. He had run down all the floors and had barely made it across the street when the building came tumbling down. He was . . . well, psychologically, I think he was a mess.

I decided to go home.

*   *   *

Against my family's advice, I went back to my apartment, alone for the first night. I felt a strong need to return all the phone calls I knew would be waiting on my answering machine. I was useless for the first two or three days after that.

The first time I felt normal was when I got a phone call from the office. I knew I still had a job, but there was no place for us to work. So I tried to volunteer. I registered with the Red Cross and city agencies, but they didn't need me. And because of some recent international travel, I wasn't able to give blood. There wasn't anything I was able to do, so I spent time with friends and company.

It turns out that was very important.

*   *   *

When I finally went back to work, it wasn't to do my original job. I got a call from my company to go to New Jersey to unload trucks of computer equipment.

A colleague said something to me that was very inspiring. "Jesse, I'm not a doctor; I couldn't rush to the hospital to put people back together. I'm not a construction worker, so I couldn't dig. I tried to give blood, but the line was four hours long; they said to come back tomorrow. So the way I fight back is to make sure our company is not affected. I can do whatever it takes." I think those of us who are recovering well have taken that to heart.

It's tough. I've been to funerals. I have a very close friend who lost her father, a remarkable man. Another colleague of mine broke her collarbone in the evacuation, she got trampled in a crowd . . .

We gotta keep going. If you let the attack affect you as minimally as possible, that's the best way to fight back.

*   *   *

Look, I grew up in this city. Those Towers were part of my life. I remember when my fourth grade class took a field trip to the observation deck, we were studying the island of Manhattan. I used to go dancing at the Greatest Bar on Earth up near the top floor. I remember. And I take this personally. When the city gets attacked, it's like *you've* been attacked. Hurt physically.

The rest of the world thinks of this as a terrible, tough place. When you live here, you know there are wonderful people, helpful people. Have you seen the way this city has pulled together? I think that's what the rest of the world has learned: what it means to be a New Yorker. ॐ

ALBERTO BONILLA, 28. Originally from Honduras, Alberto moved to Jersey City from Tempe, Arizona to study acting in New York. He is a brightly energetic man.

———

I got a call from *All My Children* and the casting director said they had a role for me and that it would tape on the 11th. I was told to bring a bunch of different clothing for costume options.

So I had the 11th down on my calendar as a day I'd be acting in a soap opera. Imagine that?

*   *   *

I normally leave the house at 7:30 a.m., but I ended up leaving at eight. I had to carry four changes of clothing for the shoot. I take a bus to the PATH station at Grove Street in Jersey City. The PATH shoots me into the World Trade Center. From there, I'd hop a subway to midtown where I temp at Morgan Stanley.

Well, the day started off bad. The bus was 25 minutes late. I was furious and worried. I was carrying all my clothing, so my back hurt. I kept looking at my watch because I was so concerned with time; I had to get to work early so that I could take time off for the *All My Children* shoot. I couldn't afford to lose my temp job. Finally, the bus came at 8:15.

I got to the PATH station and it was mobbed. There were two trains, one to 33rd Street in Manhattan and one to the World Trade Center. I took the Trade Center one because every morning I'd get my breakfast at the Mall underneath at a smoothie place. I'd buy the $3.45 smoothie.

Well, we made it to the World Trade Center. It was 8:42 - like I said, I was sure because I kept checking my watch. There were hordes of people in the mall. I got into this huge line to get a smoothie. Looking back on it all now, I think: how self-involved am I? I don't remember a single face from that line of people. Not one of them.

It's 8:44 or 8:45. I'm still standing in line, I'm frustrated, it's taking forever. I look in my wallet and . . . I don't have any money. That's how it is when you're an actor. Sometimes you have money, sometimes you don't. That week had been financially rough for me. I was literally a starving artist. So now I'm really pissed off and I'm going over my options in my head. I can find an ATM in the middle of the mall. Or I can go without breakfast.

I got depressed. That can happen when you don't have money to eat. So I figure, okay. This morning, I just won't have breakfast. I high-tailed it out of the mall.

* * *

I went to catch the E train uptown and the oddest thing happened. There was nobody waiting on the platform. It went from being utterly crowded to nobody. Maybe it was after the first plane hit. Did I miss people running? I don't know how it makes sense now.

I sat down on the train. It wasn't moving. There were only two people on board. A teenaged Oriental rave girl with headphones, a hip black outfit and a silver purse; she was all the way at the end of the car. And right next to the door was this older black lady wearing a dress. She was knitting and humming to herself.

We wait. And we wait. And we wait. Nobody's coming. The station's empty. And I was a mess. My backpack's falling off my shoulder, I'm holding onto my clothes. I didn't have enough money for a suit bag so my clothes are on hangers in the dry-cleaners' plastic. I'm so involved with myself, I'm shouting in my head: "Why the hell isn't this train moving? I'm gonna be late."

Then all of a sudden, the doors close and the train starts to go. There's still nobody on board except us three. And I'm thinking, "Why is the train operator leaving? There's nobody on board."

* * *

I work for the Data Integrity group at Morgan Stanley on 47th and Broadway. So I got off at my station, 42nd Street, Times Square, and I'm running. I get to work and take the elevator up to the 37th floor, thinking, "I'm late, I'm late." Run to the bathroom, dying to use it. I run back out and . . . everybody's gone. Again. The whole cubicle section is empty. And again, I'm thinking, "What the hell is going *on*?"

That's when I noticed all the computer screens in my department. Showing this picture of the World Trade Center with fire coming out of it. Every single computer was logged onto CNN. "What? What?!" I mean, I'd just come from there . . .

I ran to the corner of the building and, looking downtown, I could see it now, clear as day. Both Towers. From that altitude, they looked really close. I could see the fire, the yellow, the red, the black smoke. A few coworkers came up beside me. Nobody said a word. The TV was turned on, but nobody was watching.

I remember hearing someone crying hysterically. A sound I'd never heard in an office. You know, as an actor, I study things, try to recreate emotions, behavior. I have no idea how to describe this. It was as if God was crying. I looked around to see if somebody else had heard it, but everybody was watching out the window. Then I checked to see if the person crying was me, but it wasn't.

Over the intercom we heard, "Everybody leave." And just like that they evacuated our building.

* * *

Now I'm walking through Times Square. I see all these people who don't seem to know what's going on. People laughing. Tourists taking pictures of the TKTS booth.[5] And then it hits like a wave. This energy. Suddenly everybody starts popping their cell phones on. Suddenly everyone seems frantic. Suddenly the information has rolled over everybody - don't ask me how, but you could see the affect it had on everyone in Times Square. Suddenly everyone's in the know for this terrible secret, and the look on everyone's face is changing.

I grab my cell phone, too, and call my best friend, Rex in Arizona. He's crying on the other end, on the other side of the country. "Oh my God, it's falling," he says. He was watching the whole thing on the TV.

Standing in the middle of the street, I yelled, "The Tower's falling!" And everyone within 50 yards stopped and looked at me, even the people on their phones. The whole world stopped. Right then, my phone died. Everyone's did.

I ran into a New York Sports Club and watched on a video monitor as the second Tower fell.

Then the whole city locked down.

* * *

I called a friend, Nancy, who lives on the Upper West Side. I ended up walking to her place on West 75th Street. Around 70th Street, I saw people running to the Red Cross to give blood right away. Which turned out to be a fine idea, but of no use whatsoever.

I got to Nancy's and she asked, "Are you hungry?" I realized, "Yeah, I'm starving."

---

[5]An outlet for discount theatre tickets.

But I called ABC studios - this is the actor in me not wanting to lose my job. I asked them, "Uh, are we still booked for today?"

The guy on the other end says, "Yeah. Why wouldn't we be?"

I said, "Because we're being attacked by terrorists?"

He says. "Oh. Okay. I'll call you back."

I get a page a little later and call in. A different person, very somber, says, "We've cancelled."

*   *   *

We went out to a Greek place for breakfast and I kept asking myself, "Why am I so hungry?" I sat down and the waiter brought the food. Which is when I realized, "Holy shit. I'm hungry because I didn't have enough money to buy breakfast. And because of that, I didn't have to wait on line. And because of that, I wasn't directly under the Tower when the first plane hit. And all those people, those people. Those faces I can't remember. I missed everything because I didn't have $3.45 to my name."

That was the best breakfast I never had.

But then this feeling started to set in, and it took me a few days to realize what it was. Guilt. Guilt for being alive.

The waiter brought out a mimosa and I downed it quick. Then I drank Nancy's too.

I was happy I was an artist that day. I think my life was spared because I didn't have any money.

*   *   *

Walking away from the restaurant I ran into another friend, Katie. She saw me and burst into tears. She hugged me and told me this:

Katie had an estranged sister who'd just sent her an e-mail. They hadn't talked to each other in years. But the e-mail said, "I don't know where you are. Please contact me. Let me know you're okay. I'm sorry for everything. I'm so sorry."

I looked at her and said, "A lot of people lost their sisters today. You're lucky. You got yours back."

HUSTON STEWART, 24, hails from Jacksonville, Florida and went to school at the University of Alabama, Tuscaloosa. Huston (pronounced like the Texas city) made plans in the fall of 2001 to move to Manhattan to be closer to his girlfriend, Hobby, and his best friend, Whitfield, both of whom lived in New York. Huston's experience of September 11th was one that many people around the country and around the world shared: the tension of waiting for news of a loved one who worked in the Towers.

———

I came to New York August 15th to the 30th of 2001 to apartment-sit for friends of my parents. They were going back to Jacksonville to vacation for two weeks - it worked out perfectly. I had two interviews right away with Doyle Dane Bernbach, one of the largest advertising firms in the world. Then, on the third day I was in New York, I interviewed with Opal Financial They offered me a job on the spot and it wound up being perfect for me – a transfer into finance. I was supposed to start work there on September 17th. So that left me with two weeks to just vacation.

I wound up meeting this girl, Hobby, while I was in New York. We started dating and fell in love. She was like, "So you're gonna move up, huh?"

"Yeah."

I went back to home on August 30th. My plan was to fly to New York from Jacksonville on September 12th and move into an apartment. I had all this stuff set up for the day after the 11th.

*   *   *

On the morning of the 11th, I turned on the computer at about 8:30 in the morning on the 11th at my parent's house in Jacksonville. Walked over, turned on the TV, put on CNN like I do every morning to follow the economy and check the news. The first Tower had already been hit. I thought it was some kind of accident.

I immediately called my girlfriend who was on her way to her job at Sotheby's Auction House. I told her what happened but didn't get it, she hadn't realized the magnitude yet. She was in the stairwell of her building and she said, "I'll call you later."

So I sat down at the computer and logged on. I'm still watching the TV. All of a sudden I see the silhouette of a plane fly behind the second building and *Boom!* Just like that the second Tower exploded.

The first thing that went through my head after that was, "I'm not going up *there*. I don't have a job any more."

*　*　*

Of course, the thought that went through my mind next . . . I started immediately frettin' about my best friend Whit. He was working in the Towers at the time. We grew up six houses down from each other in Jacksonville. He'd been home in Jacksonville two days before the 11th and we'd gone out deep-sea fishing. Man, all I could think about was his parents. But I didn't want to go down to their place because I guess I didn't really want to know.

I sat on my couch in shock until around noon. Finally I went down the street. It turned out Whit's Dad, Dr. Athey, was alone at the house; Whit's Mom was in Connecticut visiting his sister. A few close family friends had gathered and I was welcome, of course. But the front of the house is all glass - you can look right into the living room. As I approached, the first person I saw was a priest and I flipped.

See, I was 50/50 on Whit's chances before I got there. I saw that priest and I was like, "Oh, shit."

I got inside, and they all said, "We're waiting to hear." Which was sort of a relief. But then I thought, they hadn't heard anything for four hours . . .

I don't know how long I hung out there. An hour? It seemed like a long fucking time. Then the phone rang. I don't remember who called, but Whit's Dad picked up the phone and just listened for a second. Whoever was on the other end must have just said, "He's okay."

Dr. Athey fell down on the couch and buried his face in his hands, crying tears of joy and relief.

*　*　*

I'd contacted an old fraternity brother of mine when I visited New York in August. He showed me his apartment and offered for me to move in. It was a beautiful place. Huge, with bay windows that overlooked the Trade Center.

After the attack, I e-mailed him to see if he was okay. Hell, to see if he was alive.

He said, "I'm fine, thanks. You're still coming up, right? You're more than welcome to."

117

So I did. It went perfect. Searching for an apartment in New York City is insanity, but here I got this place with no broker's fee, no lease. Of course, when I moved in, those Towers were gone. I was paying cheap for a huge apartment that didn't have a great view anymore.

We were alive though, that's something to think about. And I didn't lose any friends in the attack, so I figure, "What the hell have I got to complain about?"

*   *   *

On Thursday, September 13th, I called Opal Financial to see if I still had a job and they said, "Well, just come up and see what happens."

So I moved to New York exactly seven days after the 11th.

The economy was a mess right then. The stock market had reopened, but no one knew what was going to happen in the long term. It was a scary time. Whole companies had been wiped off the face of the earth.

The guys at Opal advised me to start sending out resumes. But I was patient. A funny thing - there was this guy who was supposed to start the same day as me? He got really impatient and they told him to back off. His impatience reflected poorly on him.

I started working at Opal three weeks later. So did the other guy. But after a month the other guy was asked to leave.

*   *   *

I let September 11th be a testament to the fact that I was coming to New York regardless of what happened. I was ready to do something with my life, to pursue something. I met a girl worth enough to make me move - which is a big step for me. I made the commitment to go way before September 11th.

Everyone tried to talk me out of it. They didn't think that, being the Southern Boy that I am, New York would be the place for me.

I took that into consideration. But I've done pretty well since. And I've never been happier and I'll never regret it. 𝔰

JARED PAVA, 32, portraiture and reportage photographer for eight years. A tall, lanky man with a charming smile and a lifelong New York accent that creeps in around his vowels.

———

I woke up somewhere near 8:30 in the morning and was walking my pit bull, Rose. My apartment is approximately five blocks away from the Trade Center. I was hungry, so I stopped in my deli on Hudson Street, off North Moore in TriBeCa.

I went to the counter, got a coffee, and asked for a toasted bagel with butter. Then I heard an explosion. I looked at the deli man and said, "That sounded like a bomb."

The deli man kinda craned his neck and listened for a second. Then he turned back and shrugged. "Nah," he said. "That's just a truck."

But immediately, I heard people running across Hudson Street yelling. Gasps and shouts and ahh's. I ran out of the deli, untied my dog, and looked up at this huge hole in the World Trade Center.

Rose was flipping out. Her eyes were really wide and she was jumping all over me. When she gets excited or doesn't understand my behavior she jumps on me for reassurance.

In my chest, I felt a shock like I never felt in my life. Like a weight, very heavy, very intense. Simultaneously, a rush of adrenaline. It made me want to run and that's just what I did.

But before I went, I ran back into the deli and I yelled to them, "The World Trade Center's been hit."

A lot of people from the grocery ran out and looked for themselves. I totally forgot my bagel.

I ran back to my building, about two blocks away. I wanted to take pictures.

*　　*　　*

I told people I met in the lobby of my building what I'd seen happen. A lot of people already knew. Some seemed genuinely surprised. Shocked. Some were more subdued.

Up in my apartment, I picked up my Canon A2, a zoom lens, and grabbed three rolls of Tri-Ec 400 black and white film from the refrigerator. I grabbed some color negative. I looked for an extra battery, took a tripod. My hands were shaking, I was in disarray. I went out and locked the door.

I live on the 33rd floor. I pressed the down button for the elevator but it didn't come for a while. So I ran down 20 floors. I was in such an adrenaline rush, I wasn't tired. The elevator finally came and stopped. This is the first time it hit me that the elevator might not be the keenest idea in the world. You know? I thought, "If there's an explosion in the World Trade Center, I don't know what could be happening in my own building."

I took it anyway for those last few floors.

*   *   *

Outside, I had my tripod over one shoulder and my camera over the other. I ran down Greenwich Street, turned downtown, went all the way to Jay Street, four blocks from Building 7. I could clearly see the Towers and the hole where the plane went in.

Through my lens, I could see offices on fire. Sheets of ordinary 8 x 12 office paper flying all over the place like a blizzard. A blizzard with gray and black smoke. And a fire raging from somewhere deep inside the crater of the building that lit all the windows a deep, deep orange.

The faces all around me . . . people intrigued. Women crying. Masks of disbelief. Everyone dressed in business clothes, ready to go to work.

A group of Asian men to my left were speaking a language I took to be Chinese. One Asian man broke off from that group and came closer to me. He spoke in broken English. He pointed at my lens. "What do you see? Do you mind if I look through your camera?"

I said, "Sure," and let him look.

He looked for a long moment and grunted as if he was satisfied. Then he went back and told his friends what had happened in their own language.

*   *   *

My zoom lens allowed me a very close-up view of what was going on up in the Towers.

I saw people waving a white t-shirt out the window. Then a man waving a yellow bucket, like the kind you see someone washing windows with? Through the lens, it seemed like they were looking toward me. Directly at me. God, I wished I could help them. I felt so helpless.

Then, I started to see people jumping.

It stopped time, that moment. When the first person jumped . . . everybody got upset, wondering out loud, "Why can't anyone help them?"

Another man came over to me. Blond hair, early to mid-thirties. He saw my camera and said, "I would like pictures of this immediately."

I said, "No problem. Gimme your number." I felt that what I was capturing in this moment was something very important. So I thought for a second and said, "Look, would it be possible to get the numbers for the *New York Post* or the *New York Times*? I want to submit my pictures."

He said, "Sure. I'll go upstairs and call them."

I guess he went up to his apartment. While he was there, I snapped off a bunch of shots. When the man came back down, he handed me a card, with his name on it. On the back, he had written the *New York Times'* number.

It was surreal, watching these 10 or 12 people jumping. I knew that those were human lives. And my mind was beginning to play tricks on me. I was far enough away from the Towers, and there was certainly a lot of noise and commotion swirling all around me. But in my head I thought I heard each falling body yell in a real human voice.

I asked myself, "Did I just hear that? Is that . . . did I just hear that?"

I decided later I couldn't have. There was too much noise. I think my mind did that to sensitize me to those people's pain.

*   *   *

I didn't see the second plane hit. By that point I'd grabbed the 1 Train at Franklin Street and was heading uptown to the *New York Post* office. The other people on the train were all subdued, reading their newspapers. I could see by their expressions that some of them couldn't possibly have known the attack had happened.

I was frantically looking for someone holding a copy of the *New York Post* because I wanted to get the paper's address. I noticed people were looking at me very strangely. I think now it was my energy. I didn't care. I worked my way through the cars, looking for a paper.

An African American woman was crying hysterically, saying, "I saw the plane go in. I saw it. My train was going over the bridge and I saw it - oh my God." I thought maybe she had been coming into the city from Brooklyn or Queens, someplace where the subway rides above ground for a stretch. Somebody went over to her and placed their hand on her back, asked if she was okay.

I got to 34th Street and asked a woman if I could see her newspaper. She said, "Keep it." But I couldn't find an address for their offices anywhere. I noticed my hands were still shaking as I shot through the pages.

Then I ran into Macy's, because I knew they had payphones.

*   *   *

I called Information, very impatient, and asked where was the *New York Post*. Again, people were looking at me strangely. A woman standing with her elderly mother said, "What is he *doing*?" I thought my tripod must have looked bizarre and they thought I was going to rob the store. I presumed they didn't know what had happened.

Back out on the streets of Midtown: emergency vehicles, chaotic energy, sirens, people rushing across 34th Street. A black man crying, "Jesus Christ is with you! You see? He is showing that you have to accept Him!"

I ran all the way up to the *Post*, on 6th Avenue.[6] Security wasn't letting anybody into the building. I pushed up to the front desk and said I had pictures. The security guard gave me a queer look and called upstairs. A moment later, he hung up and told me the photo editor had said to come up and give him the film. At that point, I calmed down a bit.

I gave the *Post* some rolls and kept some to bring to a wire service; I happened to remember where Reuters was. So I went down to the subway again, figuring maybe I should call first; I looked for a payphone.

There was a man on the phone down in the station. He was talking to someone, but he looked up and I guess he saw I was intense. He said to whoever he was talking to, "I have to get off." And hung up.

*   *   *

At Reuters, the photo editor came downstairs personally and said, "What do you have?"

---

[6]Between 47th and 48th Streets.

I said, "I have undeveloped rolls. Black and white film and color."

He said, "We don't develop film. You have to get it developed." This was at about noon or so.

I ran from 42nd Street to a lab on 27th Street. I'm running through Times Square. People are sitting on the curbs, walking down the middle of empty streets. There are no cars moving, no traffic; police have blocked off Broadway. Parked cars and vans had their doors and windows open, blasting radios, the air filling with information. And me sprinting past while people just sat there, trying to take make sense of it all.

*　　*　　*

I ran into the lab - adrenaline flowing - slammed my tripod on the counter, said: "Can you develop this?"

The attendant looks at me and says, "We're gonna close soon." He needed to get home because he lived in Queens.

I said, "Look, this is film of the World Trade Center, and I want to get it out over the wire services. Can you. . .? Please?"

I think he picked up on my intensity because he said, "Okay, I'll do it. Two hours at the most." He took the film and disappeared.

*　　*　　*

I ran back up to Reuters where a different photo editor looked at the prints and said, "Do you have any people?"

I said, "I think I have people jumping."

He seemed skeptical. "Show me. I don't see them."
The headquarters of Reuters was in a total uproar. People yelling into phones. The editor commanded his troops while looking at my pictures through an ocular loop.[7]

Someone shouted out, "What street is this building on?"

He switched prints and called over his shoulder. "Liberty Street."

---

[7]A tiny lens used to magnify details in small photographs.

A woman asked him how to enter something on the computer. He shifted to get better light and told her: "Hit F9."

Finally, he worked through all my pictures and said, "Well. It looks like we have a lot of this stuff already."

Then I looked down. He had dust all over his shoes. He was a photographer, too. He'd been there that day, shooting.

He handed the pictures back to me. "Sorry, I don't really think we can use these."

*   *   *

The most important thing to me then? I said to myself, "I really need to see how Rose is." I'd left the windows open in my apartment. I hoped nothing bad had happened to her. You never know. That cloud of dust had traveled everywhere.

No trains were running. So I walked from 42nd Street to TriBeCa.

I took some deep breaths. I was dehydrated; I wanted water. That's when I first noticed that my hip was in pain. Black and blue, from the camera banging against it as I had run. I felt empty and needed to rest. But when I got back to my apartment, I could see that, for some people, the whole ordeal was just beginning.

It didn't hit me that thousands of people had died. It took a week and a half or so. I think my body needed time to cope and to process.

I went to a friend's house upstate about two weeks later and took in some fresh air, which was essential because the air quality in my neighborhood was so bad. Being in the quiet of the woods allowed me to reflect. How different the city had become so suddenly. How different my neighborhood was, how different everything was. And then there was that ultimate contemplation, you know? Thinking of what would happen next. The unknown. ॐ

KIRKE MARSH, 30, grew up in Seattle. After moving to New York to study law at Fordham University, Kirke spent five years doing commercial, corporate, and construction litigation at a small firm. He later set up his own practice. Kirke's wife became stranded in Michigan when her flight was cancelled after September 11th, so he drove from New York City to Detroit to retrieve her.

————

"Let the record reflect." That's a term you hear a lot as a lawyer. So, let the record reflect that the Trade Towers stood four blocks from the back door of my office building on Broadway. The record should also show that my building faced east so that the Towers were behind us. Didn't matter. They dominated our landscape.

Every day I'd get off the subway, for instance - right at Trinity Church. You'd come up the steps from the tunnel and there's this ancient church that's stood there since New York City began. I believe Alexander Hamilton is buried in the cemetery yard. Then – behind you – you had the Trade Towers, which were a built a lot more recently, in 1976 or so? You had the old versus the new.

But the Towers weren't just real estate. They dominated the life downtown. Take the night before the attack, for instance. I was hanging out in a bar called O'Hare's, situated about a half a block away from the base of the southern Tower. I used to go there a lot with a bunch of other lawyers. We were watching football that night, drinking beer, and talking about the World Trade Center.

You'd think that when you worked near a place or in a place like that for very long you'd come to take it for granted. Not so. We were always in awe of it.

We were discussing the Towers even as we got in a cab and pulled away from the Trade Center when the game finished up. That was the last time I saw them in their natural state. Because on the 11th, when I came out of the subway at Trinity Church, I saw the largest holes you could ever imagine had been punched into one of the buildings. Smoke. Fire. Madness.

I stood there watching just as the second plane punched through.

*   *   *

My wife is also an attorney. On the 11th, she had an appearance to make before a judge in Detroit, so she flew out Monday night. She was going to spend Tuesday in Michigan, then fly back.

Monday night was miserable as far as weather goes. My wife's plane sat on the runway for over an hour as the pilots waited for a break in the skies to take off. All this makes it that much more ironic, since Tuesday the 11th turned out to be such a beautiful day.

So on Tuesday, I got to work a little later than usual. Blame that on my wife being out of town and the visit to the bar the night before. I live on 96th Street on the East Side, so I take the 6 train down to 86th Street, then change off for the 4/5 to go express downtown. I was on the subway at the Brooklyn Bridge stop when an announcement was made: there would be no stop at Fulton Street station.

Now from City Hall to Wall Street stations, the only stop between is Fulton. The announcer said that there'd been an *incident* – didn't say anything about a plane, an explosion, nothing of that sort. Just the normal, sterile announcement of, "due to an incident at the Fulton street station . . ."

Very innocuous. I mean, for anybody on that train there was nothing in that announcement which would have led to the belief that something big was happening. There was nothing to lead someone to believe that maybe they shouldn't get off the train, either. That maybe it'd be better to just keep on riding into Brooklyn. Or get off right there, switch tracks and head back north.

I didn't even bother to look up at Fulton Street. I had my nose in one of the Tolkien trilogy books. I couldn't tell you what was happening on that platform, if anything.

I got off by Trinity Church at the Wall Street Station and came up the stairs that face south. Immediately, I could smell the smoke. I thought there must've been a fire, that the fire must've been the incident that shut down Fulton Street. But when I got to the top of the stairs there were all these people gathered in crowds, facing north. I turned around to look.

*   *   *

That's one of those images that burns into your mind. There's not a photograph in the world that can make someone feel or see what it was actually like. High up on the building, the metal exoskeleton of the building was twisted away, bent back and peeling off the façade. Flames gushed from the hole, which was as tall as if you put two semi-trailers together end to end. That hole was much bigger than I've seen any picture do justice to. Smoke poured out . . .

And the faces of the people all around me, staring up at this – masks of horror. I think we were all struck dumb.

The people were blocking the streets. Standing around, looking up at the Towers made it difficult for emergency vehicles to get to where they needed to be. At that point, Broadway runs south. So I'm not sure if the vehicles I saw coming toward us were attempting to get people away from the disaster site, or if they were trying to find another route onto the Trade Center campus. There were a lot of sirens, though. Lots and lots of sirens.

I'm not a rubbernecker. I won't stop to gape at a spectacle. As a matter of fact, it bothered me that so many people had whipped out their cell phones and were calling in a play-by-play to who knows who. I got aggravated. The first thing that went through my mind was that there were people who truly needed to be on a phone line during a time like this. And anybody who's lived in New York for a while knows that you can pick up your cell phone to make a call during normal business hours and all circuits are busy.

So this particular instance of people hanging around Broadway talking on their cell phones bothered me. I thought it was selfish. And I kept moving. In fact, I ran all the way to my office building and ducked inside.

*　　*　　*

Why did I run? I don't know. I guess I had this need to find out if everybody I worked with was okay. A lot of people who worked with me took those subway lines that ran under the Trade Center. But I think I also wanted to gain information about what was going on, and my office seemed the best place to do that with all of its resources. The Internet and 1010 WINS news radio.

Of course, I wondered what had caused all this. I got to my office on the 12th floor and heard immediately that planes had impacted the Trade Towers. But right away that made no sense to me. Because two Towers with holes in them meant two planes. Plus I've flown cross country with my father-in-law in small airplanes. I know enough about aviation to know that visibility for that day was perfect. In fact, it was one of the clearest days of the year.

Altogether, four attorneys worked in our office at that time. One of them was unaccounted for. This had me worried, since I knew he took the subway route under the Towers. As it turns out, for whatever reason, he was just running exceptionally late that day. Lucky him.

So we had a quick meeting with everyone in the office – about ten paralegals who functioned as closers on real estate transactions plus support staff - about 20 people in all. And we agreed that the incident had been terrorism, but we didn't know why it had happened. We also determined it would be best for everyone to stay inside the building for the time being.

First of all, we weren't located too far from the Stock Exchange. We didn't know what events might follow the attack on the Towers. Bombings, maybe? The magnitude of the attack was unclear. It seemed unlikely that terrorists would choose our nondescript office building at 39 Broadway as the next target, so staying put seemed best.

Plus it seemed wise to stay off the streets. We didn't want to present any impediment to the people whom we knew would be working hard to get their jobs done.

*　　*　　*

Shortly after the meeting, I began reaching out to friends and family over the phone. But I couldn't reach my wife. Normally, I get her right away with my cell phone. This time? No connection. And she couldn't get hold of me because there were no incoming calls on our direct dial office phones.

The first person I was able to reach was my father in Seattle. It must have been six or seven a.m. there. He was fully already fully aware of what was going on – he'd been watching it on TV. I told him I was all right and I said, "If Michelle calls, tell her I'm okay."

To which he responded: "Why would Michelle call here?"

"Because you might be the only person she can get hold of, and she would expect me to call you."

Then I called my in-laws who live in Farmingdale, New Jersey. My mother-in-law was very difficult to talk to that day. She was hysterical. She had this incredible fear that something might happen to me.

I ended up calling my in-laws a number of times since they were my only source of real information. I had 1010 WINS on the radio, but they had the TV news. My wife hadn't been able to get hold of them either. As it turns out, she did have the sense to call my father from Michigan, so she learned I was okay through him.

*　　*　　*

My father-in-law and I talked. He brought up the possibility of the buildings coming down. It was the first time I'd thought about it.

I hung up the phone and went to find one of the attorneys I work with, Stan Horowitz. Apparently he was waiting for a borrower who was scheduled to come in and close a loan that day - I believe a closer from another company was coming in as well. I took Stan aside and we went into his office and closed the door. I told him, "What if the buildings come down?"

He said, "No. No way. Did you see the way they were hit? They're not coming down."

But I couldn't get this notion out of my mind. I kept thinking we were only four blocks away from the Towers. If they came down, who knew where they'd fall? Or how? Suppose the buildings toppled. Would we be under them? Granted, we might have been far enough away to escape damage. But trust me, that's not the way you think during a time like that. I was considering the worst case scenario. Perhaps a domino affect with all the buildings in my area toppling each other over? I didn't know.

Given the situation, this all seemed like rational thinking at the time. With all the shock of that morning, there was no such thing as unreasonable fear.

Stan kept insisting that everything would be fine. "No way. They can't come down. Just relax. How are they going to come down? Think about it."

It was at that moment that we began to feel the rumble.

*   *   *

The rumble. The shake. Like an earthquake. My building vibrated. Not a horrible tremor. But if you've ever been in one of those restaurants downtown that's near a subway? When the train goes by the silverware rattles and your water glass shudders. It was that kind of feeling, but there wasn't a lot of time to think about it, because the next thing I heard was screaming from the street.

I ran back into my office and went to the window. Our building happened to be right on the curve in Broadway, just before you reach the statue of the Bull on Wall Street.[8] The angle of my building was such that you could actually look north if you craned your neck and stared back up Broadway.

I did this, and I saw this incredible dust cloud jet forth from a side street about two blocks north of me. It slammed into a building on the west side of Broadway – it might have been 120 Broadway – and the cloud just rolled right up the side of the building. Then it broke right and started blasting toward us down Broadway. I saw all this from 12 stories up.

---

[8] A large bronze statue of a charging bull, the symbol of the Wall Street district, has long been the mascot of traders. The statue is located at the noth tip of Bowling Green where Broadway splits apart.

The cloud? The best way to describe it - think of the ashes you scoop out from a fireplace. Sooty, gray in color. Heavy and clinging in consistency.

I saw the cloud overtake everyone on the ground running away from it. It just swallowed them whole. Then the cloud slammed into my window and everything went pitch black.

*   *   *

This beautiful day plunged into midnight. My window went so dark that I couldn't see the ledge, which is two inches from the glass.

I don't think we got the worst of it. The stuff outside my window seemed fibrous. No pellets or debris. We were too far away from the actual collapse and angled such that so many other buildings blocked out the main blast. But it took about an hour to dissipate.

Everyone gathered in the center of the office to get furthest away from the windows. We wet a bunch of paper towels and handed them out for people to breathe through. Some people took them and some people wouldn't. The air quality in the office was affected. I didn't really notice it that day so much, but when I returned to the office later, I could smell an odor like dust.

I made a few more phone calls to people I knew who were working in the area. We all handled construction issues professionally, and all of us were concerned that at least half of one of the Towers contained asbestos. I made certain that the air conditioner in our office was set to recirculate so that we wouldn't take in air from the outside. We hoped that the filters on the ventilation ducts would keep the worst particles out. Unfortunately, this might have also kept particles that made it inside airborn for a bit longer. But what could you do? It was a no win situation.

*   *   *

By the way, that borrower made it into the office. We didn't really notice him until he came out of the waiting area – this guy in his 50's with an English or Irish accent. He asked, "Well, are we going to close this loan today or not?"

We just looked at him. As if we had to explain to anyone that there were other concerns at that moment.

He said: "If we're not going to do it, I wish somebody would have told me. Why have I been waiting here?" I'm not sure how long he'd been in the waiting room, and he didn't seem angry, really. Just a little irrational and most definitely out of touch.

We said, "Look, there's no one here to close for you. No one made it in. And we're sorry, but we kind of thought you were taking sanctuary here with the rest of us. Which you're more than welcome to do, of course."

"Well!" the man said. "Well!" And he kept going on about his loan.

I looked at the other attorneys and saw that we were all thinking the same thing - a sudden urge to revoke the sanctuary for this gentleman. I mean, I know that people deal with stress in their own way, and I was trying to give this man the benefit of the doubt. But it was difficult since I considered his behavior so inappropriate.

*　　*　　*

Something I'd like to point out:

I mentioned that we were a little strapped for information. We listened to the radio and called people who gave us TV recounts. But I was amazed at what the radio was putting out over the air. No damage reports. No advice. No instructions on emergency procedures, on what you should and shouldn't do. Just pure, unadulterated sensationalism.

One of the stations I flipped to was talking to a father who'd been on the phone with his daughter when the first plane hit her Tower. I think they mentioned that the daughter had been on one of the exact floors where the plane had hit. The father talked about how he'd been on the phone with her, how she'd said something like, "Wait. There's something coming toward us." Then the line disconnected. He hadn't heard back from her.

I don't know the veracity of reports like these. But I remember thinking very clearly that, if I was listening for information at 39 Broadway, there must have been people listening in the Towers, too.

And it was absolutely shocking to me that there was never any emergency broadcast signals. Remember how we spent our childhoods listening to them test the system by bursting into a radio or TV program and playing that long, high-pitched tone from time to time? A day or two later, after things had calmed down a bit, it occurred to me that I'd never heard it. After all those years of rehearsing. And you know, what occasion would have been more fitting?

Information was pretty much impossible to come by. All the friends I called described the television feeding them the same thing. "Fires raging. Panic. Disorder. People jumping from the Towers to their deaths." But nobody telling us what to do. No announcements like: if you're in this area of town, here's what you should do to get out. No announcements to stay put. Nothing.

In fact, if anything? There seemed to be a lot of *dis*information flying around. I remember reports of a fire on the Capital Mall. A bomb report at Pace University. Reports that fire-fighters had been found alive in the rubble. Obviously a lot of these reports can get chalked up to the hopefulness and chaos of those hours. But I'll always remember how disorganized things were on September 11th. We didn't seem to know what to do with ourselves.

When you look at the media response, it's clear to me they were struggling to get a handle on it all. I remember Tom Brokaw had a tough time going on air that night. He was devastated. And maybe that was a better reaction than to go on the air and try to fudge through a broadcast by hitting the sensational points. I much preferred Mr. Brokaw's attitude of "let's figure out how to help people in need. Let's make arrangements."

There were so many people around the world who didn't know what had happened to their loved ones that day. To hear about people jumping to their deaths must have made their waiting unbearable.

*　　*　　*

Eventually, everyone in the office decided it would be okay to leave. The sun had begun to shine through the clouds of particulate matter in bright shafts. When the ashes outside the window had begun to clear out, Stan and I went to the west end of the building where we could get a more northern view of the last Tower standing.

There was a window in a women's restroom that looked north. We'd just made it to the glass and were getting ready to open it so we could crane our necks out when the second dust cloud came blasting through Battery Park City. Stan and I looked at each other. We knew what that meant.

This time the cloud seemed slower but I think that was a matter of perspective. We could see the cloud heave itself up over smaller buildings, slamming against the sides, pushing out and up, blossoming, becoming airborn. Stan and I didn't run away but we walked out of that bathroom pretty hastily.

We got back to the office and told everyone the second Tower had fallen. Disbelief all around. You'd think that the first Tower might have prepared us. Nope. Not at all.

*　　*　　*

You know, it's hard not to take a building for granted. It's not until after it's gone that you realize what a massive part of your life they are. I can't tell you how many times I bought books in the Borders Bookstore in the mall complex beneath the Towers. Or used the ATM machines. Or went to public concerts in the summertime held outdoors in the plaza between the Towers. 110 stories times two. How could you ever think that someone would topple such magnificent structures? We thought they'd live forever.

*   *   *

When the second Tower came down? Again: everything went pitch black. And again, it lasted a long time, maybe another hour. We all decided we'd leave the office together, then, but the elevators weren't working. Our building hadn't evacuated – we later learned that many buildings in the area had. So we walked down the stairs together, snaking in a line down to the bottom.

In the lobby, we stood before the glass front doors to the building and waited. Whenever we tried to open them up, an emergency vehicle came tearing through the street, kicking up the layer of dust which lay six inches deep on the ground. It got in our eyes and our faces. Two people tried to lead the way out of the building several times, but they only made it a few feet before the dust choked them and they were forced to turn back.

There was a Duane Reade at the corner of our building. The gate was down over the storefront, but I found employees inside who were in the same position we were – they couldn't really leave. I dashed in there and bought 12 bottles of water. I bought about seven packages of handkerchiefs, too, so that people could wet them with the water and wear them like bandanas. I knew that some of us had quite a walk ahead of us to get home and there were no cabs in the streets. No busses. The subways had shut down.

We'd confirmed that the Staten Island Ferry was still running, and a large contingent of people from our office were Staten Islanders. We decided to walk to the ferry together. I walked a little ahead because my wife worked at 1 Broadway at the time; even though she was in Michigan, I still knew people in her office. I popped my head in the lobby of that building to see if one friend in particular wanted to join our trek, but I found out he'd already left.

We made it to the Ferry and dropped of the Islanders. It was a strange good-bye. And the rest of us turned around and started north again, following the FDR Drive.

*   *   *

Anybody who's ever driven the FDR? You never think that someday you'll be walking up it like a refugee. There was absolutely no car traffic. And all across the macadam? Like a ticker-tape parade, falling from the sky: banking account statements. Trading account statements. White papers, yellow papers. Stuff that looked like had been readied to go out in the day's mail.

The whole highway was dead save for these straggling lines of somber walkers – tourists dressed in shorts for the weather, office people in suits. Everyone getting covered in a fine layer of soot as we moved along.

In fact, by the time we reached mid-town, that was the way you could tell who had been downtown. The people covered in ash had been there. You didn't even have to look at their faces.

The police and city officials kicked everyone off the FDR as we reached the Brooklyn Bridge. They funneled us onto the off-ramp and we began to snake through the city. So many people, a thick line heading gradually and gradually north. A lot of people walking with their heads down in their dress shoes, sweating through their suits. Still, no one said anything. There was total silence. I think everyone was trying to figure out what was going on.

*　　*　　*

You passed by kitchen-aid stands. Churches with their doors thrown open. People reaching out from the sidewalks, offering things to you.

"Do you need a restroom? Come in here. Do you need a bite to eat? Come in here."

They had mobilized themselves immediately, these people, trying to figure out how to meet people's needs.

I walked up to 36th and 3rd to a friend's apartment where I eventually stayed the night.

*　　*　　*

Now my wife, remember, was in Detroit. She learned about the World Trade Center at a convenience store where she went to buy a pen before appearing in court. The man behind the counter said to her, "You know the World Trade Center's been hit by a plane."

And she said, "Well, that's terrible." Thinking he was talking about the World Trade Center in Detroit. Most cities of size have a World Trade Center, you know. There's one in Baltimore, there's one in Seattle, they're all over the place, although so many people think New York's Trade Center has some sort of proprietary status.

"No, you don't understand," the man said. And he clarified that it was New York. My wife then tried to get as much information as she could. From a television, a radio, from anywhere. She knew then that it was her home that had been attacked. She ended up going to court, but the judge cancelled all appearances for the day. Everyone was in shock, even in Detroit.

The firm my wife was working in association with cared for. They kept her occupied, they extended her hotel room. Remember, she'd only gone out there for one day to make her appearance in court. She had just enough things with her to get by for that one day. I don't think air traffic was allowed again until the Saturday or Sunday following the 11th. She was going to have to sit tight for a while.

But I was out of work. I couldn't get back into my building. I had already set up a number of our employees at different locations throughout the city, but there was very little else for me to do. So I decided to hop in my car, drive out to Michigan, and pick up Michelle.

* * *

I kept a Honda Civic garaged at a space up on 106th and Park. I'd had it eleven years – the seven years since I moved to New York and four years before that. It had 130,000 miles on it from taking trips to Vermont, Maine, and Washington, D.C.

I called on the phone once I found a working line and told her my plan. She thought I was crazy – this was on Thursday. But Friday morning I woke up, got the car, jumped in and drove out there. Nine hours. Not bad.

I listened to a lot of talk radio. There were a couple of dead spots in western Pennsylvania where I couldn't get a signal, but I heard a lot about how local communities were working to send supplies to Ground Zero. Filling up tractor trailers with batteries, flashlights, boots, clothes. Some people were going in to volunteer themselves for the recovery work.

I heard a recording of a piece that moved me. It'd actually been written a number of years ago by a man whose name I think is Gordon Sinclair. It was a short essay about how generous the United States is. How we've contributed so much to so many nations. How our generosity is rarely repaid save with bad-mouthing and dissent. I'd heard the truncated version of the essay before. But here I was listening to a recording of the author reading the piece in its entirety. And then I was reminded that Mr. Sinclair wasn't even American. He's Canadian.[9]

---

[9]This famous essay is called "The Americans," and was indeed written by Gordon Sinclair...Continues onto next page

On the road, there were overpasses draped with American flags. And every once in a while as I drove northwest, I'd see those orange signs that get towed behind trucks, the kind that display messages to warn motorists of roadwork ahead or weather conditions. This time they didn't say, "Caution, Go Slow Ahead." They said, "God Bless America." 𝔰

Continued from previous page...(1900 – 1984), a famous Canadian commentator. The initial broadcast of the essay went out on June 5, 1973 on radio station CFRB Toronto. The essay was prompted by an overseas run on the American dollar, and a report issued the same day that the American Red Cross had run out of money for disaster relief at home. Sinclair points out that, while America-bashing seems fashionable, the United States has helped control flood damage along the Nile River and the Yang-tze in China - and no foreign nation has ever stepped in to help the devastated plains of the Mississippi. While Americans, whom everyone calls "war-mongering," have forgiven billions of dollars of foreign debt, everyone calls them "decadent." Sinclair says that America would be entirely justified to abandon the rest of the world to save itself for a change, citing several incidents where the United States ran to the world's aid in times of dire emergency and received only jeers when they themselves were wounded. Sinclair's essay circulated prolifically during the months after September 11th, reborn in a new grass-roots campaign that put this twenty-eight year old testimonial in a new context: Americans have nothing to be ashamed of.

ELLEN SHAPIRO, 32, owns and operates New World Catering, a burgeoning gourmet shoppe in Maplewood, New Jersey, an affluent metropolitan suburb.

———

Around the corner from me, on James Street and Main, they arrested this Iranian guy for burning his wife. The morning of the 11th, he put out prayer mats and they came and arrested him about two days later. He owned a bookshop called PRINTS OF PEACE. The place is closed down now.

He didn't kill her, he burned her. I don't know how he did it or why or what he used to do it. But on the 11th he set her on fire at the end of my street in South Orange, New Jersey.

I knew this guy. His name was Mohammad. I used to buy cigarettes from his store. He drove around in a Mercedes Benz with New York plates. So the police took him away and now he's gone, don't ask me where.

There were some other people living with him. But after this happened, they all just . . . went away. I think the wife must've known something. In fact, that's what everyone in my neighborhood thinks. We're so close to New York, you never know who lives next door to you.

* * *

My friend, Mark[10] had just got a new job working in the World Trade Center. He's an insurance agent for a big insurance company.[11] He'd literally just started his job a couple weeks ago. His wife just had a baby that's three months old. Mark's . . . let me see. I'm 32, so that makes him. . .34? 34.

Anyway, this is what he tells me. He was going to work. He walked into the building and pressed the button for the elevator. He was standing there, waiting for the elevator doors to open when he heard this loud crash. Which was when the plane hit the first Tower. So he turned around and went outside along with many others. He looked up, and he saw the crash. He said he was looking at this great big burning hole in his building. Everyone started running away.

Mark said he got three blocks, before he turned around to watch what was going on. Which

---

[10]Not his actual name.
[11]Name withheld.

was when he noticed there were a lot of people rushing past him going *toward* the building, to see what they could do to help, you know?

Then the second plane hit the other Tower. He was watching the whole thing. And right at that point, everyone that ran past him to help? They all died. There was a rain of fuel and debris and bodies . . .

And Mark said there was one guy who fell. . .flew. . .out of the second Tower. I don't really know if their eyes met or what happened. But Mark is convinced he made a connection with this gentleman, this falling guy. He said he might've been 50 yards away from the building, said he saw maybe 50 people fall from the building. Maybe seventy-five people in all died right there in front of him.

And he's telling me he definitely can't sleep. He doesn't want to come into the city to work anymore. His psychiatrist told him not to. Basically, my friend is a mess.

*   *   *

I'll tell you why I think this is important. I saw Mark yesterday, on the 23rd of September. So it's been, what? A week and a half since the attack. My boyfriend and I were invited over to visit with the new baby and drink beers.

When we arrived, Mark was outside. He's a big, handy man. His place is rural, he's got two acres of land covered with thick trees. And the first thing we saw, he had put up a 40-foot flagpole in the front yard with this huge American flag.

"Okay," I thought. "That's a bit unusual. Patriotic. But unusual."

So we go inside, he's laughing and joking and everything seems normal. Too normal. Mark gets a video tape and says, "Get a load of this."

He popped in the tape. It was a video of his baby, his three month-old little girl trying to say hello. Real cute. And then it switched to something else. This . . . he had filmed this.

On a tree in his yard he had tied a noose with 12 knots. He had one of those Anatomical Annie dummies from CPR classes, a big plastic doll with a chest cavity. He'd wound a black and white scarf onto the dummy's head in a turban and he'd hung it on this noose. Next to it was a sign painted on a big piece of plywood that said "BIN LADEN MUST DIE."

It was dark outside on the tape. But Mark had put spotlights out. So there's this video of a body hanging by a noose in a spotlight, a body that didn't have any legs from the waist down, which was eerie in itself. And the spotlight fell on the American flag, too; it was very dramatic.

I sat there, watching the tape, stupefied.

This is one of my best friends. He's generally a pretty calm guy. But this behavior. Uhm. He's been married for five years and now he's got this little girl. This was a little scary.

*　　*　　*

Mark's company moved and now he's actually working at an office in Parsippany.[12]

He said he got a phone call from his wife during the week because she wanted to make sure it was okay to take down the doll. The cops had come to visit her and they said, "We don't have a problem with what you're doing. It *is* your freedom of speech. But there are three of four school busses that go by here every day and this is not something for kids to see."

So she said, "Look, I want to make sure it's okay with my husband." She didn't want it up in the first place.

So Mark said, "Take it down." But he still has the dummy in his garage.

I had no idea what to say to him as he showed me this video and told me all this. And I can't even comment on what it must have been like for him to have gone through what he did. What can you say to seeing a hundred people die right in front of you?

I consider myself lucky to not have been a witness. ⑀

---

[12]New Jersey.

DREW NEDERPELT, 34, went downtown to help his girlfriend – a television reporter - cover the news shortly after the second plane hit. They arrive three blocks from the north Tower as it began to fall.

―――

I screamed at her to move but she just stood there. I'm not sure if she was just in awe - it was an unreal sight, this huge gray mountain just falling in on itself. Or maybe she couldn't process what was happening. It didn't matter. We were only three blocks away. If we didn't move, we'd be toast. That's the only thought that was running through my mind.

I grabbed her hand and we ran around a corner about 40 yards down the street. We threw ourselves into a doorway on Murray Street. I guess I expected the debris to file nicely along the avenues and streets like water pouring into the cubicles of an ice tray. But instead it came crashing overtop the 30-story building we were behind. The sound was incredible, just a great big *swooooosh*. And suddenly everything was pitch black - I mean totally, unbelievably black.

I screwed my eyes shut, but when I opened them again, there was no difference. And then I started to cough. Breathing was near impossible.

I thought to myself, "I'm not just going to sit here and die in some dingy doorway." So I backed up and started kicking at the door, which was made of metal and glass. It was an outer door to an apartment building, I think, and it wasn't that strong. On the fourth kick the latch just popped out and the door flung open with a crash.

We both ran inside, thinking we were clear. But there was another door in front of us, a large, sturdy solid metal thing with a thick glass window. And of course, in the blink of an eye, all the debris that was outside just whooshed in after us and there we were, in the same predicament. We were choking in this tiny, confined space and I remember thinking, "so this is it, huh?"

*   *   *

I really didn't have a choice. I believed that if we wanted to live we had to get out of the debris. I had no idea how long the cloud was going to last but I wasn't going to wait until I found out. There was no way I was going to break down that door, it was solid. So I started on the interior glass.

I kicked it, but I had on a pair of rubber-soled sandals and my feet just kept bouncing off.

I remember this very vividly, knowing that my leg was eventually going to punch through the glass and shred my entire calf, being absolutely sure about it. And I've run marathons, I'm a runner, my legs are important to me. But I couldn't have cared less. It was one of those things where you figure a shredded leg is a small price to pay for being alive. So I just kept kicking.

We were both starting to choke pretty badly from the debris in the chamber and I was blindly wailing on this door - 15, maybe 16 kicks. And then, slowly, the glass began to tear away from the sides and the whole pane just folded down and left a hole in the bottom half of the door, which we crawled through.

We found ourselves in a small anteroom staring at an elevator. I hit the button and the elevator door opened with a cheerful *Bing* – like it was saying, "I'm ready for you, thanks, today is business as usual."

I looked inside. It was a bright, clean elevator. Thinking back I can hear peaceful elevator music but I know that isn't possible. I think it just seemed so far removed from what was happening outside - so surreal – that my mind is playing tricks on me.

I made the decision that we weren't going into an elevator in a war zone. So instead I just threw up on the floor.

*   *   *

Then we heard banging.

I looked down the antechamber we'd come through and saw the shadow of a person outside the first door.

I looked at this guy and my first thought was, "You know what? We have our air and we had to fight for it. If we open that door again we'll let all that stuff back in here."

But then, you know, you remember that's a human being out there.

So I ducked through the hole I'd kicked in the second door and opened the latch on the outer door and this cop staggers in. He was completely covered with the soot, like we were. He came in and then he just stood there, panting.

I asked, "Are you OK?"

He didn't say a word, he just barely nodded. He was completely stunned. He stood there in a daze with his shoulders slouched, ghost white from the debris - which was interesting because he was African-American. You could see the word "POLICE" stenciled on his vest. *(Plate 4)*

Then there was another banging, and my girlfriend opened the door. Another man crawled in. He didn't say a word either, he just stood in the corner, grabbed a hanky from his pocket and began wiping himself off in silence.

This guy was covered from head to foot in an inch of crap and he was dusting himself off with a little checkered handkerchief. It was absurd. He reminded me of Lady Macbeth trying to scrub off the "damned spot" - like he was in shock, or denial. He didn't realize he couldn't make a dent in his appearance with his little hanky. Turns out he was a plainclothes policeman.

*   *   *

I took a few pictures with the digital camera I always carry with me, and after about four minutes it looked as if things were getting clearer outside. So we all stepped out and went our separate ways without saying a word. The cops, I guess, went and did what they had to do. We went to report the news.

*   *   *

Every minute or so you heard an explosion from somewhere close by. I thought at the time that they were bombs, but I later found out they were cars exploding from the heat of the fires.

I remember hearing that the Pentagon had been hit. At the time there were all these rumors. The Sears Tower was in flames. The UN had been hit. And I remember thinking very clearly as these explosions were going off around me that, if the news feeds were reporting buildings across the country going up in flames, this must be what it's like to feel under siege. Like London in 1941, or Dresden. To feel like everything that is near and familiar and yours is being destroyed by people who don't know you and don't appreciate you. Who don't care what you do or who you are.

I wanted to grab hold of whoever was responsible for all this and shout, "Don't you understand? You've got the wrong place, the wrong people! There's been some misunderstanding!"
I think that most conflict in history has been about misunderstanding.

*   *   *

Later that night my girlfriend used her media clout and convinced a couple of cops to drive us through Ground Zero. I'll never forget it. The jagged shards of the Towers loomed up into the sky like fangs sprouting from the ground, lit by hundreds of spotlights as thousands of firemen and rescuers climbed over them, picking through what had already become known as The Pile.

We were the only car on the streets. As we picked our way along, the driver gave little bleeps on his horn to move the hazmat units out of the way.

I was bothered that we were disrupting the rescue efforts to indulge in our personal guided tour of the area. But my girlfriend had promised these two cops who were with NYPD Intelligence that she'd put the call out on the air for any video that had been shot in the hours before the attacks if they'd give her a tour of Ground Zero.

The media exists for quid pro quo.

*　　*　　*

At one point a cop with a gasmask banged on the window and yelled, "What the hell are you doing?" He peered in at the two of us in the back of the car.

"We're with Intel," the driver said, and showed him a badge.

The cop looked at the badge, looked at the driver, and said, "You're a fucking asshole." And he walked off. But we didn't turn back, I guess because my girlfriend didn't offer to and these cops felt they owed her - like a deal was a deal.

Not one minute later another cop runs up to the car. I mean this literally when I say we were the only car moving on the streets. Every other vehicle was pulled off to the side of the road and here we were in a white Crown Victoria driving around the middle of Ground Zero at nine o'clock at night. This second cop bangs on the window, screaming, "What the fuck are you doing!?"

Our driver rolls down his window and starts to explain, "We're with Intel and…"

But this new cop screams at the top of his lungs, "I don't care who the fuck you are, turn this fucking thing around and get the fuck out of here! Now!"

And with that we did a six-point turn in the middle of the road, sending all the poor rescuers that we had just beeped, scrambling for the sidewalks again.

We left Ground Zero. My partner managed to do a live phone report on network television calling what she had just seen, "the face of hell."

* * *

Here's my bottom-line assessment:

In a lot of ways the media did some great things that day. They provided a lot of value, and often acted heroically. But there was a lot of terrible stuff too.

For instance, several journalists managed to 'acquire' a few hazmat suits and helmets and snuck into Ground Zero and video-taped for hours. The network didn't bother to use any of the footage. They knew they'd have to answer for how their reporters managed to get footage from inside Ground Zero.

Then I remember how my girlfriend and the host from a popular network morning show had a screaming match about using some ex-NYPD big-wig for a guided tour of The Pile. They went toe-to-toe, right there in front of two hundred people, tearing at each other about who had the right to tell the story while 300 yards away there were thousands of missing people buried. It ended up with the morning host being shown 'the hand.'

And there were all these Assistant Producers crawling all over the place who'd been dispatched to help out their TV stations. Without many exceptions, assistant producers in TV are all young twenty-something's trying to get their start in the business. On 9/11 and the days after, their idea of getting an interview with a rescue worker was to walk out from the bullpen where reporters were kept tethered, grab a subject, and literally hang onto their sleeves, physically dragging them to the sidelines. It was really unbelievable.

I remember seeing dozens of firemen shaking their arms while these AP's hung off them like rabid schnauzers. All these girls and boys had never been out of a studio in their professional lives and their idea of convincing someone to interview with them was to scour lower Manhattan for anyone in uniform and forcefully yank them aside. It was sad.

And several on-camera reporters who'd been caught under the debris refused to have anyone brush them off. On September 11th, my girlfriend physically fought off a dozen people - producers, friends, bystanders, anyone who walked up to her and tried to dust her off. She was proud of the fact that she had been there from the beginning. That debris was her badge of courage.

Drew Nederpelt

I remember seeing tape of one news anchor who'd been under the north Tower when it collapsed. Reporting from the studio two hours later, he still had the dust in his hair and all over his shoulders. The make-up department must have gone to extremes to do his face without disturbing the soot that covered him.

*   *   *

But there were a lot of bright spots too. I remember two cops who asked me to take a picture of them. They were smiling and so proud to be together, to have survived, to be helping. I saw so many examples of utter selflessness, too.

The owners of The Square diner opened their doors to everyone and gave out all their food for free. They literally refused to take any money - even from the expense account-laden media. I managed to hide 20 bucks under a cake-stand on my way out that they hopefully found long after we had all gone.

I befriended a firefighter from Connecticut, and I was able to get some media for a 100-mile bike rally to Ground Zero to benefit the victims a few months later. I became close to the camera and sound guy that I worked with at Ground Zero, and when I ran into them unexpectedly several months later, I was so happy to see them, we hugged. It was great. They told me they still worked as a team. In retrospect, when I think back to all that happened, I prefer to remember these other things.

These bright spots. I think they tell me so much more about what that day could potentially mean for our future.

* * *

I remember I didn't cry that day. I think I shook for most of the morning though. I went all day on a Powerbar. Food was nothing. I was flat out on the go from the moment I got up that morning for a run in the Park until I hitched a ride home on the back of a fire truck after midnight.

I didn't cry until I was standing in my shower at one a.m. on September 12th. All alone, in the silence, I watched the black and the soot and god knows what stream off my body and down the drain. ℸ

THE TURNER FAMILY: JAKE, 48; his wife, SEAN, 45; their daughter MADELINE, 11; and their new boy, JAMES, 18 months. By sheer luck, the Turners moved from an apartment on Warren Street[13] to a space further on Greenwich Street on the 1st of September, 2001. The shift in location spared them from being directly beneath the Towers during the attack and the collapse of the buildings.

Jake: The Greenwich Street location was as an empty warehouse when we bought it. The process of moving took over two years of planning. We gutted the location and converted it to a living space from scratch. We had to install everything: heating, ventilation, plumbing, electric, the works. The Byzantine city bureaucracy held us up for a long time. We had to get permits and papers, there were codes and statutes. We had moved into the space on the 11th, but it was far from finished. We still had workmen going full tilt every day.

I was shaving in the bathroom when a Chinese workman came in. He can't speak much English but he said, "Come out here. Come, come, come!" He took me out into the street and we looked up at this big, gaping hole in the Tower. The first thought I had was, "Well. We can fix that." You know? "That can be fixed."

*   *   *

Jake: It's amazing to me when I think back. I keep going over the sequence of events, 'cause I want to remember everything. I think in my old age I'm going to forget the minutia.

Sean: I knew right away. I said, "That's terrorism."

Jake: Sean yells, "Go get the camera." And I'm out there on the street videotaping this gaping hole when the second plane hit. This explosion shoots out fire that covers blocks. Which is when I dropped the camera and said, "Shit. This is terrorism. I'd better get Madeline." She was at her school which is about two blocks north of the Towers.

Sean: It was her fourth day at a brand new school in Battery Park. IS-89,[14] right next to Stuyvesant High School. She'd just started middle school. 6th grade.

Jake: We had actually gone through this whole process. In New York, to enroll a child in a city school, you have to go through an interview. You have to pick your place and you have

---

[13]Three blocks from the Trade Center.
[14]IS stands for 'Intermediate School.'

to be accepted at the school. Some of her friends went to a place up on the East Side but we thought, "Well, we're in this neighborhood now and IS-89 is a brand new school, it's beautiful. The facilities are great and she can walk there."

So after the second plane hit, I grabbed my bicycle and jumped on. I'm riding down West Street, going south. Meanwhile, people are streaming in the opposite direction. They're running, they're walking - it's hard to ride the bike there's so many people coming north. Plus sirens are wailing and trucks are going south.

I get to the school and everything's very calm. I didn't have a clue as to where Madeline was - she was new there. I didn't know her homeroom or anything. So I ran through the school, sprinting up floors, looking in doors.

Finally I ran into a teacher who said, "They're all down in the cafeteria."

*　　*　　*

Jake: I went down and sure enough, the students were all massing. They didn't know what was going on. Some of them had heard the explosions but none of them had actually seen it, I don't think.

I found Madeline and grabbed her. She said, "What's going on?"

And this is where it started to fall apart for me because I said, "Oh. Well. . ." And I didn't know what to tell her. I just looked at her.

All I could think was, "I'm so sorry you have to experience this. I'm so sorry I have to tell you what's going on." I mean, *I* had never experienced this. *Nobody's* ever experienced this. And here she is, 11 years old and she's got to go through it, fumbling, like the rest of us.

I said, "It's okay, honey. A plane's run into the World Trade Center. Come on." We went outside.

*　　*　　*

Jake: Her school's right there. When you walk out the door, you looked up and you could see the blizzard coming down, you could see people jumping out the windows. I don't think she saw anything because there was paper and debris flying everywhere. I *hope* she didn't see anything. We walked north. By this time it was too crowded to even consider using the bicycle.

148

There was this van parked in the middle of the street with the doors wide open and the radio's blaring out. The President's on and he's telling the nation about what's going on in New York City. He's describing for the whole country what was going on right where we were and *that* was surreal. In the middle of everything, this huge crowd of people had massed around this van, quiet, trying to listen, trying to figure out what happened while this chaos exploded all around.

To me, it was one of those moments in history you only read about. That's when I realized this was big. This was huge.

*　*　*

Jake: We got home and I picked up the camera again. I was standing out on the street, filming, when the first building collapsed.

Sean: We're 15 blocks away. You could see everything.

Jake: The first building collapsed and I thought back to '93. We were here when the first bomb went off. Nobody expected a collapse to happen then, nobody expected one to happen now. A little while later, the second Tower came down.

Our apartment is on the street level, and this steady crowd of people kept streaming past our windows. Suddenly this guy who's totally covered in dust presses himself against the glass of our living room. He's all white from the dust, you can only make out his eyes. He had a badge and he pressed it up against the window, said he's from the FBI.

I wouldn't know an FBI badge from anything, but I let the guy in. He wanted to use our bathroom to wash off and we say, "Sure. It's over there."

As he's walking toward the bathroom, he says, "This is the saddest day in American history." And he goes into the bathroom and closes the door.

We're waiting out here, like, five minutes for him to finish up. He took a long time. We stood here and listened to him. He was weeping in the bathroom.

*　*　*

Jake: I later found out there were lots of FBI guys in town that day for some sort of UN conference. When the guy came out of the bathroom, I said to him: "Do you want to use the phone? I don't think it's working, but you're welcome to try."

He looked at me and said, "My office was in the Tower. It's gone. It's all gone. I don't know who to call."

The poor guy didn't know what to do. And he was, you know, a federal officer. Eventually he decided to go back to his hotel, which was someplace in Midtown, I think. He said, "I guess I'll just go back to the hotel and see who shows up." He didn't know what had happened to his colleagues. He had no idea what became of them.

*   *   *

Jake: Sean's a real estate broker. Later that afternoon, she walked down towards the Towers for an apartment showing, thinking that her clients would keep their time slot.

Sean: I was supposed to be closing an apartment at one o'clock on Broadway and Warren Street. That was supposed to be our final walk-through before signing the papers.

When Jake left to get Madeline, I started heading down Greenwich. As you're walking down Greenwich, the first thing you come upon is the Smith Barney Traveler's Building, which is the tall building about three blocks down with the neon umbrella logo. Everyone who worked in that building had spilled out on the street. Everyone practically 30 or 40 years old. Every ear had a cell phone jammed in it and every head had turned in the direction of the Towers, talking. And I thought, "Oh, my God. They're talking to people in the buildings. They're talking to their friends who work up there." It was frightening.

I cut over to Hudson Street. These are blocks that I walk every day of my life, but this was so different from any other day. I don't know if anyone else described this to you, but you'd be walking along, things would seem normal. Then, all of a sudden, for an unexplained reason a group of people would just panic and start running. But nothing new had happened. You felt this electric fear that worked itself through whole crowds on a whim.

Jake: Right. For instance, at 5:30 p.m. that afternoon, when 7 World Trade collapsed, there was all this panic. People were screaming, "The building's collapsing! The building's collapsing!" We were sitting here, having watched the Towers collapse, thinking, "Why are you panicking *now*?" I think people react in different ways.

Sean: We weren't filled with panic when we saw the planes hit. We thought, "Okay, life is gonna go on, those Towers are gonna burn, but life is gonna go on." As I walked closer and closer to the scene, I started feeling those little pockets of panic hit. But when I got down to the building where I was to show the apartment on Warren Street, the super[15] was there sweeping out the lobby as if it were any other day.

I didn't see my client anywhere. I thought, "Well, she may not show. I'd better go up and check the apartment so that, at the closing, I can vouch for the fact that it was in good shape." This is how you're thinking!

So I go up to the apartment, I lower the shades, everything looks fine, everything works. I go back down, the client's still not there, I wait a little longer. Then I think, "I'm gonna find a phone." But every pay phone had huge lines of people.

That's when I felt the air change. You felt little particles. Then I heard a roar. I looked down Broadway and saw the brown cloud with people running full tilt up the street in front of it.

My first thought was bio-terrorism because of the brown quality of the air. When I first heard the noise, I thought they had hit something else, like the Woolworth building. I was surrounded by so many buildings directly in front of me, I couldn't see the Trade Center.

Jake: On the videotape I shot, I have the aftermath of walking down there. There was like a . . . snow everywhere. The army vehicles driving by. People covering their faces with handkerchiefs, napkins, shirts, anything. When the Towers collapsed, everything was like living in a dream. A dream where you kept thinking, "We're going to wake up. Any moment now, we're going to wake up."

*　*　*

Sean: So I decided to head north and get back home. My biggest concern, strangely enough, was that I not get trampled to death. I went down a side street to get away from the crowd. I thought, "I know this area really well, I used to live here. I'll be smarter than them, I'll go down Thomas Street. No one's gonna go onto Thomas." Which is when I saw the McDonald's.

There were two sets of workers: the workers outside and the workers inside. The workers outside were hollering, "Come on! Go!" Like they were in the path of a bomb or something. And the workers inside were just as adamant. "We can't leave, we can't just *leave*!" Their friends screaming, "Get out of there!" But these few guys were hanging in. They wanted to stay. I guess they were going to work that day no matter what.

Jake: That was just like the guys who were working on our place. They're Chinese, they don't speak any English. Lew, the Taiwanese foreman, was crying. They were all in

---

[15]Building superintendent.

such shock.

We all huddled in this empty room where we had a TV and nothing else. We all sat on the floor.

Sean: Yeah, how come our cable continued to work? We never lost our cable throughout the whole thing.

Jake: I don't know, ask the cable company. But we all sat in there and Sean went out to get sandwiches.

Sean: I thought, "The only thing I can do for people is feed them." So I took Lew with me to this cruddy little deli a block away and said, "We'd better get supplies." We loaded up with anything I could think of. Things we might have to eat for the next three or four days.

Jake: We didn't know what was going to happen next, you know? For a long time, part of the stress was, "When is the other shoe going to drop?" So we stocked up and there we were, all of us in that room. Five or six Chinese guys -

Sean: No. More than that.

Jake: Maybe. Five, six guys and Lew - who spoke a little English, the only one of all of them who did, really. Everybody was stunned. They didn't eat anything.

Sean: They only ate potato chips.

Jake: They didn't *want* to eat. We all watched the news. Nobody knew what to do.

Sean: We were getting ready to have them stay with us, if that was what needed to happen. For all we knew they would live with us. We didn't know where people would go.

Jake: That was sort of an error in translation. For a while, they thought they *had* to stay. Those guys are so used to their jobs. Eventually, we just told them to go home. We weren't kicking them out, you understand. But we made it clear to them, "You certainly don't have to work today. Go home to your families. Make sure everyone's okay."

*　　*　　*

Sean: Our neighbor had a double whammy. She found out she had brain cancer. They live on Warren Street, so they were eventually displaced from their home. She had to deal with brain cancer and being a refugee.

Jake: What are the chances?

Sean: Their skylight began to leak a day before the World Trade Center. So by the time they got anyone in to fix it, like a month later, their whole floor was warped. Everything was ruined. Water just came pouring in. She had surgery, she's fine now. But. Wow.

Jake: Our other neighbors, Marcella and Foster - a couple who used to live above us when we were on Warren Street. We took them in right after the attack, they needed a place to stay. Foster's suffering from severe colon cancer. While they were staying with us, he had to walk north nearly every day to get his chemo treatments. They stopped him every time going in and out past the checkpoint. He had to keep explaining to the authorities who he was, where he was staying, why he was staying there, what he was going to do. Talk about determination, the poor guy.

*   *   *

Madeline: When I first heard the noise, it was a loud boom and there was a whirling sound outside the schoolroom. I was in my math class, the windows were facing out toward the West Side highway. We couldn't see the Towers, but we saw people running with their hands over their heads. Then teachers started running into the classroom.

The first teacher said that a car had hit the World Trade Center. But we all thought that was strange. A car had made all this noise? Then another teacher came in and said that no, it was a plane that had hit. That seemed a little weird, too, but it seemed right. Finally, our Principal's voice came on the overhead loudspeaker. She said that we should stay calm.

Our teacher tried to get us back to work on adding, subtracting, multiplying and dividing fractions. It was really easy because it was only the fourth day of school.

But then parents started running into the classroom. The gym teacher came on over the loudspeaker and told everyone to go down to the cafeteria. So we did. Everyone was just waiting for their parents to come. A lot of kids couldn't get in touch with their parents at the office, so they went home with their friends and their friends' parents. My Dad was already in the cafeteria when we got there and he took me home.

When we got back to my house and were standing in the door, I saw my old fifth grade teacher walking with some of the students from her class. She was holding onto their little hands walking north.

I said, "Hi."

She said, "Hi," but she kept walking. I guess she had a lot on her mind.

*　　*　　*

Jake: Were you scared?

Madeline: [pause] Yeah.

Jake: You were?

Madeline: Yeah.

Jake: What do you think about the move to the new school. To where you are now?

Madeline: [shrugs] I was only in the other school for four days, anyway. We didn't really get used to it. It's still my school at the new place because the building's not the school, the people are, and they're all the same. The teachers and the students. Except that some students never came back. Like this one kid got so scared he never came back.

Jake: But all of your textbooks are still in the old school, right?

Madeline: Except for the math ones. We had those with us when we left.

Jake: They've been working on Spanish without textbooks.

Madeline: Some kids that day had stuffed things into their lockers for the afternoon. Like, our lunches were in there. I think I heard that they broke open our lockers to get the lunches out.

Sean: I hope so.

Madeline: I had one of my favorite books in there, too. I had my writing notebook, which I had all decorated nicely. But then I had to use another one that they gave us. Some of my friends had cell phones in their lockers, but the company gave them new ones.

Sean: Do you guys talk about all this much at school now?

Madeline: No. We got to go see a free performance of "Beauty and the Beast" and we got to go see a lot of old silent films where a live band plays along with the film. We used to go to Chelsea Piers Amusement Park about every week and a half to do rock climbing, soccer, basketball, and the batting cages. I don't think about it much anymore.

* * *

Jake: From what I've seen, there are two camps of people, parents, and teachers in the neighborhood. There's the people who want to move ahead and the people who want to dwell on the incident. A lot of people want to get back in the school, get back into things, get back into living life. Other people are panicked for any number of reasons. They focus on the schools not being safe because the air quality's not good. I think, "Well, this *is* New York City. How good was the air quality *before* all this happened?"

You can worry about the air quality – there's an argument there. But at the same time, during this crisis, you're sitting there watching other things happen to your children that are just as detrimental. We kind of feel that it's more important, psychologically, for people - certainly for the kids - to get back into some sort of normal routine.

You want to acknowledge what happened. You have to - how can you not? But at the same time, you don't want to dwell on it. Because really, in the end of it: what can you do?

Madeline: I do want to go back to my school because the school we're at is scary. We're sharing space with teenagers and high schoolers and some kids were mugged across the street in a park. Plus, I play the clarinet. Right now in music class we have to be taught alongside the saxophones and flutes. The class is split in half, so we only get 20 minutes to work on something. When we go back, we'll be able to have our own time.

Jake: When do you go back?

Sean: The 22nd of January.

Madeline: We missed a lot of school days, the week after the attack happened. And while they're moving stuff back into the school, we're going to miss another, like, three days – that's what they tell us. I don't know whether we're going to make up the time at the end.

Sean: I'm sure they'll figure something out.

Jake: Maybe they'll just say, "Okay. We can forget about it." Would that be all right with you?

Sean: [smiling] Yeah.

MIKE X has worked on the floor of the New York Stock Exchange for 15 years. He was in the World Trade Center immediately before the attack on September 11th. He walked to work at the Exchange in a state of shock, and witnessed the shut down of the American economy. This interview was conducted in a popular Wall Street area bar.

———

My name's Mike. No, I'm not giving you my fucking last name. That's it. Just Mike. Alright?

I'm a trader on the floor of the Exchange. I'm not going to tell you what company I work for. Suffice it to say we're the two-dollar broker on the floor of the New York Stock Exchange.

You know what? Turn that thing off 'til I get good and drunk.[16]

*   *   *

Okay. I live in Jersey and I'd take the PATH train into the Trade Center everyday, walk through the stores and the galleries underground. Every day I went into the Trinity Church cemetery walking my regular route from the Trade Center to the Stock Exchange. So. This day, the 11th. I heard a noise and looked up.

Couldn't see 'cause there was buildings on Broadway. Thought maybe it was just another transformer blew. So I kept walking. Came down Wall Street. Saw people pointing and I looked up. "Holy shit." There's this big plume of smoke. I said, "What the Hell's goin' on now?"

Kept walkin' down Wall Street. The plume's getting closer. I'm on Broad and Wall. Turned around. Paper started comin' down outta the air. You know, papers from the World Trade Center, papers woulda been on someone's desk. Spit out of computers. They're all burned round the edges. Again, I think: "Holy Shit. This ain't . . . this ain't normal."

Three minutes. Three fucking minutes earlier, I would have been right under it all.

Everybody ran into the Exchange.

*   *   *

I get in there, first thing I hear is some guy sayin', "Yeah, some twin engine plane hit the

---

[16]He indicates the audio recorder.

Trade Center."

Everybody's gathering around the TVs they got on the trading floor. I'm, like, "No. That's not a twin-engine plane. A Cessna would have just bounced off those buildings." Jesus Christ. . .

Confusion. Mayhem and confusion. The market never opened. The head of the Exchange announced, "Trading will be delayed until we can figure out what's going on." Then, as things developed they said, "We're not opening at all."

I'm on my floor, got nothing to do, so I call my parents and friends. Everybody. Tell 'em I'm all right. Then the first Tower came down.

*   *   *

The Exchange building started shaking. There's these huge glass windows all around the Stock Exchange - they started rattling. Lights started flickering. That's when I thought, "Wow. This is it. They got us, too." Everybody tried running out, but you couldn't get out. No matter how many fire drills you have. Nobody could get out.

The foreign markets had opened. England. Europe was still open. But after the second plane hit, all the news services stopped broadcasting. A lot of them were in the Trade Center.

After that, we got all our news from the TVs on the floor. We got it from the networks just like the rest of yous.

*   *   *

That whole week we didn't open. There wasn't a lot – nothing to . . . you know? No work. So you sit at home with all this news. The TV's always on in my apartment. Phone's ringing. I'm getting the damage report little by little from friends. Not about damage to the Towers, that stuff was pretty obvious - you could see the smoke plume real clear in Hoboken. And not damage to the nation - who cares about that? I don't mean it like that.

What I mean is – as it turns out - I lost six buddies in all. Six good buddies. They were in there when the buildings came down. That, to me, is damage.

That whole week. Fuck it. Where's that bartender?

*   *   *

We went back the first day of trading which was last Monday, September 17th, 2001. It was.

I don't know. Somber. You know? After all the adrenaline you usually feel in the Exchange. Now nobody wanted to be there.

All sell orders that day. It was expected.

I'm a phone clerk. I take orders from the outside customers, give it to a broker to execute. That day? Ninety percent sell orders. And anything that had to do with recreation got crushed: Disney. Kodak. Travel stocks. Crushed. It made sense to me. The airlines? Jesus, who wants to fly after what happened? Who wants to take a cruise? Hotel stocks? Crushed.

Second day went pretty much same as the first. So did the third day. And the fourth. That whole week we all just watched. Numb. The market plummeted. Then it held. Plummeted again. Rallied a little. Plummeted further, and rallied once more. But it was definitely a downward slide. It just kept slipping down. Fighting like a wounded animal. But we handled it.

Give you an example, I get this chain e-mail circulated on October 2, 2001. Pretty much says it all, you know? It says:

> "If you bought $1000 worth of Nortel stock one year ago, it would now be worth $49.
>
> If you bought $1000 worth of Budweiser (the beer, not the stock) one year ago, drank all the beer, and traded in the cans for the nickel deposit, you would have $79.
>
> It's time to start drinking heavily."

*　　*　　*

It turned around first time last Friday, it tried to rally. That's what we wanted. Rallied 'em a little bit. Then this week. We rallied 'em up 400 points. Down about 16 percent overall by then.

These experts on the news – they *call* themselves experts, I got other names for them. They say this is the worst slip since the Depression. Well, yes and no.

A lot of stocks are undervalued right now. Shouldn't be tradin' where they are. But nobody has the confidence to step up and buy 'em. Middle America isn't going to do it. Not yet. No, no.

As a point of perspective? I saw the crash of '87. Let me tell you: '87 was a panic. This was lot more orderly. Unless you work down there, I don't know how to explain it to you. People were just more . . . prepared.

For instance. We didn't have the computers, the electronic capability back then that we have now. Nowadays, the computers stop the market before it slips too far down. Cooler heads prevail. You don't want a mob mentality out there on the floor, let me tell you. You gotta let people digest the news, you know? Disseminate the news. Cooler heads. That's what happened this time. In my opinion, the Exchange acted exactly perfect.

*   *   *

Sure, trading'll be back up. I know it will. How long will it take? Shit, if I knew that I'd be a billionaire. It's all about consumer confidence. And if I knew what *that* was, I'd be a billionaire. Right now, I wouldn't say it's business as usual, though. It's still very tough.

Grab that guy. I want another beer.

*   *   *

I saw a lot of people lose their shit that day. Old guys on the Exchange with their heads in their hands, crying. I got scared.

And now? I don't take the PATH train no more. I take the ferry out from Hoboken. Still. Twice a day I gotta walk past those Towers. Twice a day. It'll never be business as usual again. And it's sickening. Seeing what happened. Sickening.

I personally lost six buddies. Maybe another 30 people I knew from, "Hey, how you doin'?" You deal with that. You go on. Do what you can do. Like, I'm a big New York sports fan, so I got Rangers season tickets, Giants season tickets. I go to those games. Try to live my life as much as normal.

But no, I won't ever forget this and I don't want to. You forget and you know what happens? It happens again. ⚡

DR. WALTER GERASIMOWICZ, 49, has worked as the director of Advisory Services for Lehman Brothers since the autumn of 1995.

———

I have bone disease. Albright's Syndrome, which is also called Polyosthotic Fibrous Displasia. It's a very rare bone condition which most physician's never even see; as a matter of fact, it's so rare that it's not even funded as an orphaned disease by the government for research purposes. What it amounts to is that I have portions of normal bone and portions of bone which are somewhat fibrous, non-crystalline. They bend, they deform, they break. I'm most impacted on my left side, particularly in my left femur, hip, and back. I'm permanently on crutches.

On that morning, I had come into work and into my office on the 28th floor of 1 World Financial Center, directly across the street from the World Trade Center. My office faces onto West Street with a direct view of the Towers. I'd say the distance is 50 meters at most, maybe 30.

When I heard the first impact, people started to rush toward the east side of our building to watch the Towers burn. We were uncertain as to what had initially happened. Whether it was a bomb or some other explosion. Then we were told, by word of mouth, that a plane had struck the building. We were told by security people to stay put. At this point, there were quite a few people in the offices watching what was occurring. In addition, some of us had televisions in our offices on which we would watch the financial news networks. We were listening to the news as it broke.

I was surprised because there was a great deal of chaos in my office. People running, people screaming, people horrified. No one knew exactly what had occurred - I think that many people thought that perhaps a pilot had gotten sick or had a heart attack. But we were all watching this . . . and then the real horror began as people began to leap from the Towers to their deaths.

You could see them as they climbed out of the windows and onto the ledges. Then falling or leaping. It wasn't one or two, it was scores of people. I was literally in a state of shock for the next two weeks.

*   *   *

I got on the phone to one of my colleagues, Doreen Benson. She was traveling in Florida. I told her to turn on the television and we were speaking and watching the coverage on the television simultaneously.

She said, "Walter leave. Leave now!"

And I immediately did. People were screaming and running past my office in tears. Then we saw the next plane fly in and hit, exploding. At that point, we knew this was no accident and pandemonium broke lose. Everyone headed for the stairwells. It was obviously too dangerous to get on elevators. We didn't know, by the way, if our own building was under attack.

* * *

Now, I'm on crutches. As I started to head toward the stairwell, I was feeling mixed emotions. Do I wait? There were hundreds of people trying to run past me. Do I hold them up or do I begin the process of getting down those stairs?

As I got there, people came to me with assistance. I'll give you their names, because it's something I'll never forget: Mark Stevenson, Steve Campbell, Richard Feldman, Richard Cuomo, Alan Reichman.

These men. Despite not knowing what was going on, they refused to leave me at any point.

I said, "Go. I'll get down. Go."

But they refused.

I was using one crutch and the banister of the stairwell to descend. I gave my other crutch to another colleague who was going down the steps, Mark Soloman. I told him, "Leave it at the bottom of the staircase."

* * *

So I'm going down the steps and meantime people are rushing by. We're trying to tell everyone, "Go around! Go around!" Obviously, it's taking me a lot longer to use the stairs.

The men I mentioned to you all stayed with me, and when we got to the main level - the street level - there were two paths to take, two stairwells. The gentleman who had taken my crutch took one of those paths but I didn't know which way he'd gone. We just chose one, and we never found the crutch that day. So I guess we chose the stairwell that Mark didn't.

Thus, I ended up with one stick.

What's kind of interesting about that crutch - the one that I'd given up to Mark? It was used to hold the door open in the other stairwell. It allowed everyone who passed that way to run right out of the building. My colleagues found it there, still propping open that door three weeks later when they we were allowed back into the building to inspect the damages. It served a noble purpose, I think.

*   *   *

Once we got down to the street level, we turned and I put my arm on the shoulder of Mark Stevenson. Mark is the manager for the New York office. So I had my crutch under my left shoulder and Mark under my right. We turned and headed west toward the Hudson River, passing the Gateway building. We were basically between 2 World and 1 World.

We had walked about a hundred meters or so to where there were some benches and I sat down on them temporarily. Pandemonium ensued all around us: emergency people rushing in, thousands of people rushing out. Boats were coming in from the Hudson River to make rescue stops. We were facing the World Trade Center, only two to three hundred yards west of them, watching both of them burn. Absolutely horrible. At the same time watching more and more people jump from both Towers. Time was more or less surreal. But at some point the first Tower went down. It just went down.

Everyone started to run but in my case, with my mobility so limited, I continued to walk toward the river. Alan and others flagged down emergency personnel who pulled up in this sort of golf cart - like a flatbed electric cart. Alan and Richard Cuomo and I got into that cart. We were taken down to the Hudson River to one of the boats and the other men in my company were left in that area.

*   *   *

The boat area was pandemonium as well because, as the boats were coming in, they weren't level with the ground. There were people trying to jump onto the decks from the dockside; they broke their legs as they landed. Some fell into the water. I didn't know how I would be able to get aboard, but luckily one boat had a platform that folded out from the back and became flush with the ground. With Alan's help, I was able to begin boarding.

Rich Cuomo went back to find our colleagues and tell them there was a boat available. Unbeknownst to me, the rest of the men from my company had begun to head north, walking up the West Side in order to get away from the disaster.

*   *   *

As they opened up that back platform, there were hundreds of people trying to stampede onto the boat. Alan stood more or less in front of me, acting as a buffer. I was holding onto the rail with all my might because I would have been knocked down otherwise. We waited for everyone to pass. There were people covered from head to foot with ash, many in a state of shock. People crying, people running, people panicking. Others filed past with absolutely no expression, as if in a trance.

After the melee had passed me, Alan helped me onto the main body of the boat so I could sit down.

As I was standing there facing the Towers, the second one went down. Within seconds, all of us and all of lower Manhattan were consumed by an opaque black cloud of ash, dust, and soot. You couldn't see the Battery[17] at all.

One of the rescue workers on the boat was standing next to me and crying. He said, "My God. I'm here trying to help everyone else and my family is down there. I live there."

We all tried to call loved ones on our cell phones. But, of course, we couldn't get through for hours.

*   *   *

Ultimately, the boat left and crossed the river. It was like a war zone evacuation. The people of Lower Manhattan were ferried across the river and dumped in different places. In my case, we ended up in Hoboken. Alan Reichman was still with me and he helped me off the boat; now I was using him as my crutch.

We ended up getting on a train that took us to the most northerly point in New Jersey and then crossed over into New York State where Alan's home is. From there, we were able to grab a taxi. There was no way for me to get back into Manhattan for a number of days. All the bridges, the tunnels, everything was shut down.

I stayed with Alan's family. Then he brought me back into New York once the George Washington Bridge opened and delivered me to my home on the Upper East Side. I received hundreds of phone calls from family and friends, people from around the world. It was all very moving.

---

[17]An area at the base of Manhattan below the financial district, now the sight of Battery Park which is visited by thousands of people daily. The Battery gets its name from the fort that was built there during the War of 1812, later named Castle Clinton in 1817 after DeWitt Clinton, who was Mayor of New York City at that time. After the army left the site, it served as an entertainment center, an opera house, and an immigration landing depot. It even served as the NYC Aquarium until the site was closed in 1941. The Battery currently serves as a dock site for boats to Ellis Island and the Statue of Liberty.

*   *   *

In the days afterward, a friend called and we talked about the state that the city was in.

He said, "Walter, we've got to do something about this. We can't just sit back." So we went out to some of the local pet stores and bought up all the dog food and supplies that we could. We thought that so many items had been donated for humans, food and so forth. But no one had really thought about the rescue dogs who were being used to sniff for survivors at Ground Zero.

Roger Smyth

We loaded up the car with everything we could carry and I drove. We made it all the way downtown, stopping at various checkpoints. The officers would wave us on for the most part when they saw that we were carrying supplies. We basically made it to the base of the site, which, by that point, had been sealed off rather heavily. The food we were carrying was sorely needed, as were the dog 'shoes' that we had. Many of the rescue animals had gravely injured themselves by walking over shrapnel and debris to look for people.

*   *   *

One thing I'd like to point out: New Yorkers became a far gentler group of people to one another during the time of the attack. Unfortunately, it didn't last long.

Those men who stayed with me? They did so at the risk of their own life and limb. And these people have families themselves. To me, that was most important.

I'd like to get those men together and take a snapshot of all of us together as a remembrance. Just a simple shot with all of us in one picture together. I will never forget what they did for me that day and I'd like to keep that as a reminder. 🦂

NELL MOONEY, 23, lives in Astoria, Queens. Picture a strawberry blonde spitfire with a pixie grin as big as the moon. She sometimes gets so involved with what she's saying that she hops up and down in her seat.

———

I hated that job on Wall Street! I worked in the Check Processing Department with a woman who was the most miserable human being on the face of the planet. All the other women were great - I loved them. My boss, for instance, was fantastic - she was the Buddha, one of those strong women who have their college degrees and their Master's, but was happy to be in the Check Processing Department.

But that one woman made it Hell. She would come to work in the morning and everyone would say in a sing-songy voice: "Good mooooorrrrnnnnnning, Rosaria!"

And she'd say, "Hrrrum! What's good about it?" And she was serious.

She was a diabetic, but she'd bring in Krispy Kreme donuts and Italian pastries. She was just *not* a happy woman. She was the *epitome* of *un*happy. The devil was her playmate. And on that job, we weren't at desks, we were all in bullpens.[18] And I had to share my bullpen with guess who? Right. Rosaria.

Some temp jobs are perfectly fine, but that Wall Street job was a temp job where I actually had to work, which I found unacceptable. Jot that down as a historical note on the state of the economy in 2001. All these people hanging around and getting paid to do nothing while waiting for other pursuits in their lives to take root.

When somebody from the temp agency called and said, "We have a different job for you," I said, "I'll take it."

I left on Friday and started the new job on Monday September 10th.

I wonder how many temp workers with dumb luck were in the Towers that day.

*   *   *

The new job was at Reader's Digest on 35th and 5th. I was helping them move office locations. It was kind of a lousy job, but at least there was no Rosaria.

---

[18]Office cubicles.

I actually saw the first Tower on fire as I took the subway in from Queens. Nobody knew what had happened. Everybody kept saying, "What stupid ass set the World Trade Center on fire?" Nobody knew it was a plane.

We were in a train and everybody was talking about it. The usual boundaries between people fell away in an instant and everyone was openly discussing. "Must've been a kitchen fire in Windows on the World. What jerk could have done that?"

My Mom called just before the train went into the tunnel[19] and said, "Are you all right?"

I said, "I'm fine. How are you?"

She said, "The World Trade Center's on fire."

"I know, I can see it."

Then she said, "A plane flew into it."

I got off my cell phone and looked at everyone in the subway car and said out loud, "A plane flew into it!"

Everyone was like, "Oh my God."

And the train went into the tunnel.

*　　*　　*

I got to work about 9:30 a.m. and watched the second plane hit the second Tower. I watched the first Tower fall as it was happening on the office TV. Next thought: "Forget this, I'm getting out of here."

I waited around Manhattan longer than most because I was waiting for my boyfriend. He was working a temp job, too, at 47th and Madison. We met on a street corner and he took the time to go get the new Bob Dylan album which had just come out that day. I remember saying, "The world is crumbling, the world is in fetters, and you're buying the new Bob Dylan album? Okay."

---

[19]Many subway trains that run to the outer boroughs do so above ground at certain intervals, which makes cell phone reception possible.

He was guilt-ridden over that afterwards. "I can't believe the world was dying and I had to go get Bob."

We ended up listening to that album all day while watching the news. I don't think I'll ever listen to it again.

*   *   *

The subways weren't working so we walked along the streets. People were on their cell phones giving us the news. "The second Tower just fell. There are still planes in the air. They bombed the Pentagon."

And then a bunch of other things. Rumors. "The Capital was hit. The Supreme Court was hit." We could see the F-16s overhead, you could hear their screech as they tore through the air, and there was mad panic in the streets.

We live in Queens, so we had to walk over the 59th Street Bridge. As we walked, we saw a man give another guy $100 to take him home on his motor bike. We were seeing things like this all over the place.

*   *   *

It was a long walk, but we finally got to the bridge. At this point, we didn't know whether we were trapped in the city or not. Whether we'd be allowed to cross out of Manhattan.

I said, "Okay, if we're trapped, we're going to go get brunch in style with champagne. If we're gonna die, I'm gonna get drunk. Either that or we'll have sex in an alley." But the bridge was open. So we started walking across.

It was really hot, I remember. And there was this mass exodus of people. It looked like the New York Marathon, where the 59th Street Bridge is littered with people, so many that they look like a colorful torrent of ants. There was one lane open for cars that were going back to Queens, and one lane for pedestrians. No cars were allowed into the city.

But we kept seeing these dump trucks rolling by full of people. The truck drivers were letting people climb up and ride. There was an empty one cruising past us and this guy about two or three lengths ahead of us said, in this heavy New York accent: "Hey! Why wonchoo let *us* on?"

The truck had some lumber and debris in it. But it stopped. I made a run for it, jumping the lane island, while my boyfriend was like, "Ah . . . sweetheart? Ah . . . I don't think we should do that . . ."[20]

Well. We hopped in the back of the dump truck. And I swear to you, it was like the demographic from *The Stand*.[21] It could have been a Showtime movie: "*Back to Queens: The Long Walk Home*." There was a social rainbow of escapees from New York. We had the nice, white couple. There was a little Korean girl. The driver of the truck was Latino. There was this black woman, a construction worker who must have been the size of Hulk Hogan . . . she reached down and lifted this skinny Chinese man into the back compartment of the truck.

I remember the construction lady laughing, saying, "You guys just aren't used to this, are you?" We were all in our business casual outfits. I was wearing a skirt; she was wearing heavy-duty overalls.

The construction worker woman was lifting everyone into the back of the truck. She was massively strong. And we all sat there in the back of this truck going over the Queens Borough Bridge. Talking about what had happened. Trying to believe it. And what normally would have been the boundaries between black and white; Asian and Hispanic, economic distinctions, gender distinctions . . . it was all gone. There was nothing left between us.

*   *   *

We got off the truck at the end of the bridge. We live at least five miles from the bridge in Astoria Park. Geographically, Astoria runs parallel to the beginning of the Bronx. So, if you think about that: we walked from 34th street in Manhattan, over the bridge, and then all the way up to the Bronx. The whole thing took us about four hours. We got home around two p.m.

People had their radios on outside as we walked, so we would stop every once in a while to listen. It was a pretty amazing day.

But what was so upsetting to me is that thought that there were artists temping in the World Trade Center that day. People who weren't there doing the thing they loved, they were there working to *finance* it. And they died. All that sacrifice they had made for their art and it came to naught. The whole thing disturbs me, of course. But that aspect strikes me as a special tragedy.

---

[20]She waves her hand dismissively here.

[21]A novel by Stephen King. In the story, a government-manufactured biochemical weapon is accidentally released, destroying most of the earth's population save for a small group of survivors who come from all walks of life.

I think any type of huge upheaval makes you reevaluate what you're doing with your life and how you're living it. I decided right then that there were other ways I could find for financial supplement without compromising my artistic integrity. My job ended and I went on unemployment. I haven't been back to the temp office. But then I landed this great job; I'm training to be certified to teach ballroom dancing in New York public schools.

I love to dance. It leaves me enough time to audition for acting roles and it pays well. I'm just training right now - I haven't been in to teach a class yet and the thought terrifies me! But at least I'm doing something for a living now that doesn't suck my soul. 🎵

"JOSEPH" AFSE, 36, from Bombay, India is proud to be an American citizen after emigrating to the United States 26 years ago. His parents have owned and operated a small luggage and leather goods outlet[22] called India Bazaar on Church Street for many years. Joseph has worked there nearly every day of his life, greeting customers and getting to know the unique world that thrived four blocks from the World Trade Center. Joseph's shop operated beneath the massive shadow cast by the Towers when they stood. Now it still operates, but the neighborhood has changed forever.

———

The business is dead now. September 10th was a great day. I earned a whole month's rent on a Monday! Then the 11th came. And now everything is gone.

*   *   *

September 11th, I saw on the news that everything was gonna be sunshine so I came to the store early. Opened up, like 7:30 a.m. and fixed everything up. It was a beautiful day, a lot of people walking. At 8:45 I heard too much sound, like a plane was landing right here. When I looked up, I could see the plane coming. It hit the building. I see the flames, I see the windows shatter. All the people walking here thought it was an accident. A lot of us thought the pilot is a drunk.

Then the ambulances coming, police running. People are scared, watching the Twin Towers like we was all in a movie theater. Two news people from Channel 7 came out fast and set up a movie camera right here, taking pictures.

Then? After 15 minutes, I hear the next one. *Boom!* That looked like a big bomb. Smoke. The police came by and told all the merchants on this street, "Close up, close up, close up."

I called 911 and said, "This looks like an attack on the United States. This is like war starting."

*   *   *

So I'm trying to close up. Almost, I'm done. I put the shutter down over the storefront, I put the lock on. I was putting on the second lock when I saw this thing, like a hurricane coming. Darkness. Suddenly, you can't see nothing. Everything is gone.

———

[22]Joseph's shop is typical of many small industries in that district. Backpacks and suitcases are laid out on display in front of the shop. You can walk inside the tiny store to view more wares: wallets, belts, handbags and the like. Joseph will greet you with an instant 'hello' and a warm smile beaming from the dusky moon of his face. He speaks with the frankness and honesty of a merchant who spends his life talking to people and getting to know them for who they are rather than who he wants them to be.

Smoke gets in your eyes, your hair. You're like a blind person, can't see nothing. I try to run. On Warren Street, everything is a dark cloud.

When I was running, I hit the fire bumper[23] since I couldn't see and I fell down. And this is a natural, human thing: when I fell down, I put out both hands. See what happens to both hands? I rip it up. Knees, too. Rip it up.[24]

I thought maybe I was gone. I thought maybe I should just lie down and go to sleep. Then I thought of my wife, my daughters, my sons. I have seven children. My mother is too old to have me die. At that time, I called God and said, "I don't want to die now. If I'm going to die, my mother is going to die too from a heart attack."

I stood up after two or three minutes - too much pain, but I had no choice - and I walked up to the Municipal Building.

*   *   *

I saw a lot of fire officers, police officers. They put me in an ambulance. I told them I had too much pain in my foot, so they cut my pants and checked. The doctor is expert, so he moved my leg and said it was good, not broken. He looked at my hands. This

one? He said it had too much crystals in the wound. Like dirt and glass and whatever. He washed them out.

The doctors dropped me off at my house and told my wife what medicine I should take. They gave me tablets, capsules, liquid medicines. Too much medicine.

See how they are now?[25] The skin has come back seven times and they still look like this. It hurts. The blood comes back in and the skin cracks open again. But it's still much better than it was.

*   *   *

My business! My business was covered in dirt. And I lost a lot of merchandise. I tried to clean it off, but some of it is ruined. A lot of business I lost.

---

[23]The curb.

[24]Joseph shows his hands, the palms of which have been ground up into raw purple wounds. He shows his knees which are the same.

[25]He holds up his hands once again.

You know, 90 percent of my business was from the Twin Towers. A lot of my customers worked there, coming in from all over New York, Connecticut, Long Island, New Jersey, Brooklyn, Queens. They all died. Their bodies burned inside the Towers. Or they're missing. Or they don't want to come around here now.

*   *   *

The Red Cross people! God bless these Red Cross people! The Salvation Army. FEMA. Safe Horizons. They have helped with my home apartment rent. I went to Pier 94 on October 1st. So many people there - so many people were affected. I saw store owners, limousine drivers, taxi drivers . . . everyone who suffered stood all in a line and they were being helped. All of them.

The agencies gave out coupons according to how many family members you have. They take down everybody's social security number so they can find out how much help the person needs, how much food they need - and they write a coupon. Safe Horizons gave everybody a two-week paycheck. At that time, I made $200 a week; they gave me a check for $440. Some woman standing in front of me in line worked in a bank in the World Trade Center and she made $750 a week after taxes. I saw them give her a check for $1500. If you made $500 a week, you got $1000.

I tell you! The Red Cross is number one! The government - all agencies. Trying to help those people who are injured. Suffered. Big problems. Lose business. They helped me and many people in this neighborhood. I have many Chinese friends with stores along Canal Street. They're getting help, too. Anybody! Everybody who needs it.

*   *   *

Are things getting back to normal? No. Business has picked up to only 20 percent of previous earnings.

But a lot of people have no jobs. There's no money to spend, so how are they gonna go shopping?

We're trying to keep the store. We're talking with the landlord and we tell him, "This is not a tragedy, this is war," you know? I tell the landlord, "We need your support."

He says he's thinking about giving a break to everybody on this row. Even for the people who live in the apartments above the store. He owns this building, a nice gentleman. He came personally to every store and every apartment; he talked to everybody.

He's gonna give us a break for January, February, and March of 2002. Then he says, "After that, let's see how the business picks up." He comes by every two weeks to check for himself. When things get back to normal, everybody will pay what they used to pay.

*   *   *

See this restaurant next door? It used to be open 24 hours. Now they close at 6:30 every night. No customers.

Before? On this street? Too much traffic! You come out here at two o'clock in the morning, four o'clock in the morning? It looked like daytime at 12 o'clock. People walking everywhere. Limousine drivers, yellow cab drivers parking all over the place waiting to pick people up. All for the World Trade Center, which was open 24 hours.

They had a lot of big companies there. Lots of international banks. They had a Hilton Hotel inside. A lot of restaurants. The shopping mall underneath. It was a good life.

Now, there's nothing. It's all gone. Now it's . . . how do you call that? Too much 'headache'.

*   *   *

One thing I saw, this announcement two weeks ago on Channel 7. The government asked, "Who lost their loved ones?"

In Washington D.C., the director of this charity office says he will give $1.5 million to people who lost their loved ones. And this is a good thing. Because you know, loved ones cannot come back. You lose a son, who in turn has a daughter four or five years old; it affects everyone, everyone in the family. Money should go to help these families because that son helped the family with what he earned, you see? ʒ

GROUND ZERO
& THE VOLUNTEERS

ROGER SMYTH, 35, New York City 911 Paramedic.[1] *Roger moved from Belfast, Ireland to New York City because he wanted to be a paramedic. "It's work that suits me," he says. "It's never predictable." When he speaks, his voice rolls out in a clear, lyrical northern Irish drawl.*

September 11ᵗʰ was supposed to be Roger's day off. This is how he spent it:

———

It was like Vietnam going over the Brooklyn Bridge. You see all these refugees spilling over the Bridge, the smoke billowing out behind them. And then I heard . . .you know how you're driving near an airport? That sound? "Hwwwwaaaaaaaaaaaaahhhhh!" It was a jet. You know how jets sound when they land?

I'm thinking, "Wait a minute, that's too low."

But let me backtrack a bit.

*   *   *

My girlfriend woke me up about a quarter to nine. She said, "The Trade Tower's been hit by a plane."

We went up to my rooftop in Brooklyn and you could see the Tower smoking. I took pictures of it. There was a call over the television set for anyone who could help, people with skills - a state of emergency. I work at NYU Downtown Hospital.[2] Ten minutes after I got up, I was going in to Manhattan.

I took my car. I've got lights and sirens. I drove across the Brooklyn Bridge. It was pandemonium running through Park Slope, Brooklyn. There was an orchestra of sirens goin' off. The police had everything cordoned off well, though; I had free passage from my house to the hospital, literally ten minutes from door to door. They respected the sirens; I was in uniform in an official car.

---

[1] A Paramedic's job covers all the basics of emergency care: oxygen, splinting, long boarding. They give the same emergency care in the field as would be given in an ER. They carry drugs; intubate; perform cardiac procedure; and administer IVs. The City system (911 dispatcher) is under the jurisdiction of the New York Fire Department. Calls from dispatch are routed to independent hospitals and paramedic staffs. A common shift for Roger lasts 8, 12 or 16 hours maximum. How many calls come in on a 16-hour shift in New York City? "One," says Roger. "Or 20. You just don't know. There's no such thing as a typical day. You might treat some kid for asthma or you might have three cardiac arrests, a couple of shootings, a few very bad car accidents . . . or the World Trade Center."

[2] Three blocks from the World Trade Center at 170 William Street.

The first plane had already hit and I'm driving over the Bridge, looking, when I heard the second plane come in. "Hwwwwwaaaaaaaaaaahhhhhh!" I couldn't see it hit, but I saw the explosion. 9:03 am.

I thought, "Oh shit. That's another one." The people on the Bridge heard it and they seen it, too, I think, 'cause before? The crowd had some sense of calmness. They'd been walking over the bridge. Now they started running. A big cloud of smoke covered the Brooklyn Bridge, totally engulfed it. And here I was driving right into it.

*   *   *

I went to NYU first of all and picked up an ambulance. I grabbed my bags. The two main bags you carry in a paramedic ambulance - everything for life and death emergencies - you have your trauma bag and a medical bag. In the trauma bag you carry an intubation kit, fluids, IV setups, drip administration, trauma bandages. We'll also carry some equipment for crichs[3] so if you have a crushed airway you cut into the neck.

In the medical bag? We carry about 60 different drugs for cardiac arrests, diabetic emergencies, respiratory emergencies. Morphine, Valium, Versed, Ativan. Narcan, which is a reversal agent for heroin overdose. Vasopressin. Benadryl. Lasix, for removing fluid from the lungs. Adrenaline. Lidocaine. Atropine. Magnesium Sulfate. Sodium Bicarbonate. Different types of cardiac drugs. Calcium channel blockers. For cardiogenic shock, we carry Dopamine.

There's a whole slew of other drugs, too, but what's the point? None of that came in handy that day.

*   *   *

We parked at the base of the World Trade Center while the Towers were still standing. Pandemonium. Things strewn everywhere. Everything from bits of bodies, to bodies, to furniture - office furniture. Luggage. Shoes. Handbags. Mementos. Personal items. Scattered everywhere from the impact and the explosion, the debris and everything blowing everywhere. Bodies falling out of the sky. People scattering in every direction. Emergency workers trying to get people out.

This was no such thing as a structured call like you'd get on a regular day over the radio dispatch. You can't imagine what it was like. Thinking back on it, it's hard to comprehend

---

[3]Stands for Needle Cricothyrotomy, which is making a puncture in the cricothyroid membrane and creating an airway tube. It's a similar procedure to a tracheotomy.

the amount of people swirling around. For our first patient, we had a young girl approximately 25 years of age. She was burned from head to toe, third degree burns across her entire body.

These people just called to us, "You've got to help this girl, she's badly burned," and they thrust her toward us. We intubated her; passed a tube down past her vocal cords to her lungs so she could breathe. That way she could receive oxygen and medications.

We took this girl to NYU Downtown along with a couple of walking wounded. She was stabilized there. Then we brought her up to Cornell Burn Center. And on our way back down the FDR, the South Tower crumbled right in front of us as we were driving. That was at 9:50 am.

Nobody believed . . . you know, you used to hear so much hype about those buildings. You didn't think they were ever gonna fall. But when the first one came down, you pretty much knew that the other was gonna go too.

*   *   *

NYU Hospital was pandemonium. And in the midst of it all, I lost my partner. There was another girl I knew, a Fire Department EMT from Brooklyn - she had lost her partner, too, and her ambulance when that Tower'd come down. So I couldn't find my partner, she couldn't find hers - we teamed up in the ambulance and started to drive down Broadway, heading back into the thick of it.

At that stage, the visibility was down to around ten feet from the debris. Flames everywhere. It was like a nuclear snow. Hard to believe it was New York City.

We went back down to within a couple hundred yards from the base of the Towers and set up a triage area. Quite close. There had been ambulances closer than us but they had been wiped out in the collapse of the first building.

We were starting to dispense treatment when they started shouting, "It's gonna collapse, it's gonna collapse," and everyone scattered. Concrete falling everywhere. We ran under an overhang. And then this huge engulfing cloud of smoke. 10:29 in the morning.

As soon as it settled, you could hear voices. Screaming. Shouting. People not knowing what direction was what because the smoke was so dense. The Fire Department guys, they wear motion trackers. If they stand still for more than 30 seconds, their motion tracker goes off. So you heard all these high-pitched, whining electrical screams. "*Reeeeee Reeeeee Reeeeee*

Reeeeee." Those were the sounds of the boys who were trapped in the rubble.
As soon as the smoke started to clear, I saw people getting up and going toward the rubble
to get whoever they could out. *(Plate 5)*

*   *   *

We stayed there the rest of the day. But after the buildings came down, there were no
survivors. The treatment we administered was for emergency and fire personnel.

One guy in particular was a firefighter in his early to mid-forties. He was burned around
the side of his neck and his head and his back. Could have been caused by a hot metal
hitting him. Fuel. Burning debris. I honestly don't know.

His blood pressure was very low and we tried to get an IV started. And he's wrestling with
me to get back up, to get back into the rubble. I said, "No, no, man. It's over for you, now.
You're job's done."

And he says, "My whole company's in there, my whole battalion. I need to get back in."
I ended up literally having to wrestle with this guy.

I didn't even take him into the ambulance. He was just sitting on the edge off the back. And
then he disappeared. He just got up and he left.

I told him not to go. But what can you do? If I was in his position? If I had come out with
maybe 14 of my buddies still in there? I probably would have gone back in, too.

There was a camaraderie and a selflessness that I had never experienced before.

*   *   *

This guy here in this photo?
That's Ronnie. I told you I
teamed up with another girl
who had lost her partner?
That's him showing up five
hours later. If you see us
smiling, it's not because we
were having a good time. It's
because we thought he was
dead.

Roger Smyth

179

You would bump into different people throughout the day. You didn't know who had come down and who hadn't made it out. There were a lot of different rumors floating around about; different people missing. Nothing was verified. You just worked and worked and hoped for the best.

* * *

After the second Tower came down, we didn't transport any more patients to the hospital. We treated people for inhalation, respiratory heat emergencies. A lot of the treatment was irrigation of the eyes. Oxygen treatment. You see in some of the photos I took where the Fire Department guys are sucking on the oxygen.

Those particle masks that people were using? They didn't work, so I didn't use one. We kept wet cloths over our faces. Breathing the air was pretty horrible. You weren't suffocating but just in the force of the blast coming toward you. You didn't know what was in it.

One thing I seen, it was a bit bizarre. It looked like a Halloween mask lying on the ground. But it was somebody's skull with all the skin fried off it. It looked like a joke mask, you know? Like one you'd see in a window? Doesn't look real? But it was.

The body parts. It was hard to see anything clearly. If you got a big lump of meat and threw it on the ground, covered it with dirt . . . is that a body part? Is it not? Obviously if it was a torso or an arm . . . you'd go up to it. Look at it. Ooop. It is.

But you didn't do anything about it. It wasn't our concern. At that point, it wasn't a priority. At that point we were still looking for survivors.

* * *

There were a lot of people who weren't part of any special structure down there. For instance, there was a cop from New Jersey; he just came down with his search dog. Like: "Right. I've got a dog. I'm ready to go. What do you need?"

There was organization initially, in response to the planes hitting the buildings. But it all got wiped out when the Towers came down. So you had a lot of fire crews and paramedic crews who were freelancing, going in, search and rescue. There was no tabs on them.

And a lot of boys were very emotional, you know? They'd lost friends and brothers. You know they're not gonna listen. If you're my boss and I've lost two of my best pals in there, I'm gonna go, "Fuck you," and go back in. I mean, you can see from these photographs. These boys are really fried. (*Plate 6*)

Around noon, these firemen came out of the rubble and just threw themselves down against my ambulance. Wrecked. Dog tired. They just fought their way out. There's another photo of an ambulance there. Crushed.

*   *   *

Our ambulance was right beside those boys who were raising the flag.[4]

There was smoldering rubble everywhere. Smoke and chaos. We were all waiting for something to do. So I seen these three Fire Department guys climbing up on top one of those broken buildings. With a flag post they'd set up, near Vesey Street and the West Side Highway. The three guys get up and you see the Stars and Stripes come out and they started to raise it. (*Plate 7*)

I'm not into any form of patriotism. But I was very moved by what was going on, this symbol of defiance in the midst all the rubble. It was very reminiscent of Iwo Jima. Even as I took the photo I was struck by it. And there was total silence. You might think, looking at the pictures, that there was this massive noise and chaos going on all around. But they were raising that flag in this very eerie silence.

*   *   *

I didn't come down emotionally until I got home that night. I'd gotten to Ground Zero at around nine o'clock a.m.; I got back to my apartment around one o'clock in the morning. I came back with two friends from the site, Robbie and Trin and we met with a couple of friends who live downstairs from me. My friends set us up with a couple beers and we sat down to chat. But we all just sat there with the thousand-yard stare.

It's . . . you felt something but you couldn't describe it. There was a numbness going on in your body. We were still very hyped-up when we got back, not quite sure what to think. And then we put on the news. And we hadn't seen it, you know? We hadn't seen the media coverage. So all of a sudden, we're looking at the destruction through a camera lens, the buildings, the chaos. We're going, "Jesus Christ."

---

[4]Firemen Dan McWilliams, George Johnson, and Billy Eisengrein raised a U.S. flag amid the rubble of Ground Zero on the afternoon of 9/11. The act created an instant media sensation, a moment of inspiration in the wake of the attack. Many people couldn't help but notice a similarity between the image of the three firmen and the one depicted in the United States Marine Memorial – commonly referred to as the Iwo Jima Memorial near Arlington National Cemetery. The incident eventually sparked controversy, however. A bronze memorial statue was commissioned from photographs of the firemen raising the flag. McWilliams, Johnson, and Eisengrein – all white men – were replaced in the sculpture by a white man, an African-American, and a Hispanic. Fire Department spokesman Frank Gribbon stated that, "given that those who died were of all races and ethnicities, and that the statue was to be symbolic of those sacrifices, ultimately a decision was made to honor no one in particular." Opponents to the statue claimed that politics should play no part in a historic memorial.

181

Then one of the Fire Department guys came round and picked up Robbie and Trin. I was sitting with my friends Mark and Tara, the Scottish couple downstairs. Sat there watching the news. Then I felt this well of emotion brewing inside and I broke down. I couldn't contain myself. I cried like a baby for 20 minutes. Uncontrollable sobbing.

When we were down there all that day, our spirits had held up. We were working, we were joking with each other a bit, keeping morale up. But the enormity . . . when I actually came home and sat down, away from the work area. You realized what had actually happened. And then the emotion set in.

*   *   *

If the Towers hadn't have fallen, we'd have been busy, busy, busy. But they fell and they crushed everybody and that was it. That's the long and short of it. If 110 stories of concrete and steel is coming down, what's it gonna do to you? I mean, you're only human.

The thing I had the most problem with was finding the personal stuff. A shoe. A handbag. That sort of stuff still sticks in my head, not the body parts.

A shoe would turn your imagination around a little bit. "Well, where did that shoe come from? Where did that person go? Is that from luggage? Is that from a person on the plane, is that from a person that fell, was that person burned?" Whereas if you look at a body or a body part, it's like, "Well, that's a body part, they're dead." Maybe it's the paramedic viewpoint. We're so used to seeing the gore that it becomes more about the intimate things.

*   *   *

I treated this firefighter guy, Sal; he works for Ladder 7, Engine 16 and I met him on the first day. He was suffering from heat exhaustion, badly dehydrated with muscle cramping, feeling a bit dizzy. We started a couple of IVs for him, gave him some fluid therapy to get him going again.

I kept bumping into him on that first day and I thought, "You know, it's quite uncanny that, in the midst of all this, I keep bumping into the same person."

Then on the fourth day, September 15th, we did Search and Rescue and I kept bumping into Sal again. And I thought, "There *must* be something in this." And I told Sal, "Wherever you guys go today, I'm going, too. I'll be your paramedic." I was down there on me own time, wasn't getting paid for it. I had my trauma bag and all me equipment. So I went Search and Rescue with their company, right into the rubble of the Towers.

*　　*　　*

After 13 hours of searching, all we found was a rag doll and a bag with a journal in it. That's when it started to hit home that we weren't gonna find anybody. It's done. It's over.

The journal? It was a little notepad and it had these words written in it: "Flirting is just an innocent way of getting to know somebody." I found it in the rubble and I remember thinking, "Huh?" That weird sense of, "Did he write that just before it happened?" I believe it was a he. There were bills in the bag with a man's name on them. Personal stuff. Damp and wet. I didn't bother flicking through. I picked it up and thought, "Well, that's somebody's personal stuff."

After I checked the journal, I put it back in the bag, and then handed it back. If you found any personal items, you passed them back down the line to where people were collecting them. Probably the Red Cross, the Fire Department. There was so many agencies there, I don't know.

A couple other things I seen. Like a big glass paperweight, a solid ball paperweight that would be on somebody's office desk. You didn't know where it came from and you certainly didn't know how it didn't shatter. But there it was.

There was an unbelievable amount of paper lying around, paper and luggage from the fuselage of the plane, charred, broken, but intact. Everything was there in every possible stage. There was such an influx of the senses; your smell, what you're seeing . . .

It was demoralizing. I realized that, as a paramedic, there was nothing more for me to do. I was just an extra set of hands down there. If I stayed on, all I'd be doing was collecting rubble. There's nothing for me to do as a skilled paramedic.

*　　*　　*

The day I found the journal and the rag doll was the day that the President came, September 15th. The rubble of the Towers was still smoking very badly and you know where the gold ball[5] was? We were like, 20 feet away from that. I found myself looking around and, in some strange way; it was like being on a movie set. The surroundings didn't seem real. I was waiting for somebody to say, "Cut! That's it! Action!" But maybe that was just a coping mechanism.

---

[5]Sculpture: "The Sphere" by Fritz Koenig in the plaza at the base of the Towers.

Then the next thing we heard was the "*Whhoooopp, whhooooopp, whhooooopp.*" The big Chinooks, two big helicopters coming toward us. Then, out of the smoke, the Tomcat jets banking in. "*Hwwwwwwaaaaaaaaaaaahhh.*" And I'm standing there in the rubble of the World Trade Center, in the middle of New York City, watching these war planes swoop down. It was too surreal. You know that scene from *The Terminator*? When those big robots are coming in and blasting everything from the sky? Post-Apocalyptic. That's what it reminded me of. And here I was standing right there in the middle of it.

*   *   *

I was probably down there for about 70 hours total. About 13, 14 hours the first day; seven hours on the second. Third day? Maybe seven or eight. I had my normal shifts at the hospital and I went to those, as well. But in between I went down to help. I couldn't sleep anwyay.

After the day we found the doll and the bag with the journal, I didn't go down anymore. My skills as a paramedic could be utilized elsewhere. People still have heart attacks in other areas of the city. People still slipped and fell and needed attention. The world moves on, after all.

14 total EMS workers were lost. I had this mix of emotions. "Shit, I'm glad to be alive." But also this feeling of guilt: "How come them, and not me?" How come there's guys in there with families are in the rubble and here I am, a single guy, I have basically no ties? But I understand that's a normal grief reaction. Survivor guilt. To be able to identify with that? It's a normal grief to have.

*   *   *

When I was walking around in the rubble, I bumped into this fireman who took one look at me and said, "Are you fuckin' kidding me?"

I said, "What?"

He says: "Take a look at your shield number."

My number is 9110. And here I was at Ground Zero. The coincidence of it. I felt that, in some strange way, when I was given that shield number, I was meant to be there. 🟊

SALVATORE S. TORCIVIA, 35, New York City Firefighter. Sal served as a New York City Police officer for nine and half years before switching to NYFD. "I wound up with the Fire Department because it was more of a brotherhood. I was slotted to work the September 10th/11th Monday night shift, the 24 hour overtime tour from six p.m. to nine a.m. I gave it up to George Cain, may he rest in peace."

A total of nine firefighters were lost from Sal's ladder company.

Sal coughs frequently as he talks, turning his head to one side and hacking from deep within his chest.

———

I dropped my sons off to school that morning and took my daughter to the YMCA for her first preschool class. One of my best friends had his son in her class and he said, "Sal, I just heard. A plane hit the Twin Towers." I'm thinking he meant a two-seater.

I says, "Do you know what size?" He said no.

So I get in my pickup truck and I'm heading back home. I had Q104[6] on. I hear the announcer say that another plane has hit and I say to myself, "What do you *mean*, 'another one hit?'"

I go home, put the TV on, I'm looking at it and I'm in shock. I called my father and told him, "Dad, I just want to let you know, I'm heading into work. If you don't hear from me, don't worry. They might need me."

My father told me he was on the phone with my sister who was outside the Towers at that moment. She works in one of the banks opposite the complex. "She said people are jumping, things are falling. Thank God you didn't go into work."

I said, "Tell her to get out of there now."

*　　*　　*

I went to the YMCA to tell my wife, Adrienne, I was leaving, she was waiting for my daughter to get out of class. I searched the whole place but I couldn't find her. I didn't want to leave without telling her, but I had no choice. I told my friends, "Tell Adrienne I had to

---

[6]Radio station

185

go into work.

Then I grabbed some clothes. I knew I'd be there for a while. Just by seeing the devastation of the Towers on the TV *before* they came down, I packed enough clothes for a week.

I started driving. I put my four-way flashers on and tucked in right behind a police escort in Staten Island. They weren't about to do any car stops, they had to get some place fast and I wasn't causing any problem. We ducked in and out of streets. Everything was a ghost town.

They took me right to the Verranzano Bridge. Somebody checked my ID and let me through. But when I got to the Battery Tunnel they stopped me and said, "Everything's closed off. No getting in or out of the city."

*　　*　　*

A bunch of firemen were waiting in fire trucks, getting ready to get through the tunnel. They had a temporary command post set up; I think they were Battalion 32 from Red Hook.[7] I was looking around, seeing what I could do to help, and I ran into a police captain from the 76th Precinct in Red Hook who used to be my Captain from the 60th Precinct when I was in Brooklyn.

He says, "Sal, I could use you right now. Help people get out of the tunnel."

We were taking care of who'd run from the Trade Towers through the Battery Tunnel on foot. We took them aside, gave them water, soaked their faces. Checked to see if they were okay. We pointed out ambulances if they needed them.

After being there half an hour, someone told me the Brooklyn Bridge was open so I hopped back in my truck. I grabbed another off-duty fireman and drove him to his firehouse in Manhattan at 24 Truck, on the west side. Then I went back to my firehouse; 16 Engine, 7 Truck on 29th Street between 2nd and 3rd and proceeded to get my gear.

I ran into the Captain of my engine and a lieutenant from the truck. We loaded up my truck with guys and equipment and drove down to the Trade Center.

*　　*　　*

The Fire Department had told everyone to stay at their firehouses and wait to be called. But we knew both our companies were already down there. We weren't going to sit around. We

---

[7] In Brooklyn.

didn't have any fire apparatuses but we didn't care. We just wanted to get down there to help.

I loaded up my truck with a few guys and we had a Chevrolet Suburban from the Fire Department that we commandeered as someone was passing by - we loaded up guys in that. We drove as close to the Trade Center as we could, I'd say about six blocks away from the Towers off the West Side Highway. We parked and walked the rest of the way down.

We'd heard that the Trade Center had collapsed. But I was still, in my mind, thinking that just the top part had come down, the upper stories where the planes had hit. I couldn't believe the whole building came down. We were walking, trying to find where the new temporary headquarters for the Fire Department was . . . we couldn't believe the amount of rubble there. No Towers standing. Either one. We were in shock.

We went up to one of the Battalion Chiefs and said, "What do you want us to do?"

He said: "Find whatever tools you can. Start digging."

*   *   *

We found an area and started working.

We searched the rubble the first day trying to find survivors, anybody. Just looking at the pile, my first opinion was, "No one could have survived."

They told us where the Command Post had been: off the West Side Highway by Battery Park City. We figured we'd have a chance to find survivors there.

We kept coming up with bodies of the deceased and body parts.

*   *   *

They pulled us off the main pile when they thought a section of the building was coming down. We moved back in and started finding more civilian bodies.

It was hard to keep track of where you were. You lost your bearing. You couldn't remember what street you were on, what building was here, what building had stood there. Everything looked like a pile of rubble.

I'd say I started that first morning around 9:30, helping out on the Brooklyn side of the tunnel. By the time I got down to the Trade Center itself, it had to be around 10:30. I worked from 10:30 to 6 o'clock at night.

I did as much as I could until I became dehydrated, cramping up bad. I said, "Let me go to one of the ambulances to get an IV, something for the cramping." I hoped to continue working. I ran into a gentleman named Roger Smyth, a paramedic from NYU Downtown hospital. He hooked me up with a couple IVs, gave me a few bananas and got me going enough for me to continue until 11:30 at night.

That first day while I was getting the IV, another building, a hotel started rumbling. It was scary . . . I was still so cramped I couldn't get the needle out of my arm. My IV was done, blood started coming out of it. A fireman from my house had to help me pull it out as we ran for cover. The building came down. After that, they moved everyone out.

You heard nothing but explosions all day. The fires, the jet fuel burning. The nearby buildings had air conditioning and refrigerator units - they were all exploding from the super heat. It sounded like bombs going off. I believe the Secret Service had their armory in one of the Towers. That stuff ordinance was going off. You didn't know where to turn.

*   *   *

Then the Department called off whoever had been there all day. They said, "Take a break. We'll get a night crew in here. Come back in the morning."

They'd called us off numerous times by that point. A lot of the guys who were physically spent . . . we felt we were no good if we couldn't keep on working. We had a fresh bunch of guys waiting, so we figured, "Let them jump in, we'll be back in a few hours."

*   *   *

That night, around midnight, we found our truck from Ladder 7. It was abandoned, parked a few blocks away from the Trade Center.

I went back to pick up my own truck and the other guys drove the fire truck back to the firehouse. We proceeded to clean the debris off our fire truck until around five o'clock in the morning. It was covered from head to toe with pieces of cement, paper, lots of dust, lots of rubble. We moved 14 bags of garbage off that rig.

It's a tower ladder truck; it has a bucket where three guys can stand and operate a nozzle to control a fire or get to a window for a rescue. There were problems with the tower ladder and the truck's radiator was clogged with about two inches of soot and garbage. But it was still running. (*Plate 8*)

*   *   *

A friend of mine who has a business in Coney Island said, "Papers were falling into Coney Island from the Trade Center. When I saw them, I thought buildings in Coney Island were burning." They found inches and inches of soot on cars all over Brooklyn.

What I'm saying is, Coney Island's a nice distance from Manhattan. 15 miles or so.

Debris landed all over the place. It was unbelievable.

*   *   *

When the Trade Center collapsed, the Fire Department did what they call a recall. Anyone off-duty, on vacation, or out sick had to report into work, no matter what their condition was. I continued going back down to Ground Zero every day for two weeks straight until they called us off.

That first day, we worked around the clock. The second day, too - so that was 48 hours straight combined. Then they broke us into two shifts. You work a 24, you're off 24.

*   *   *

There was so much fire - you kept dousing water on it hoping you could keep it at bay. One of the buildings we were covering had to be 30 stories and I'd say 90 percent of the floors were on fire. We didn't know if it was going to come down on us or not. The fire was burning for a day and a half but the building was still standing. So, while you're try-ing to pull bodies from the rubble, you have all this stuff going on around you.

How do you fight a fire like that? You just try and hope for the best.

You're in a reaction mode. Your fellow members of the Fire Department, your close friends, are missing. You're doing whatever it takes to find them, putting yourself in harm's way. Myself and this other fireman, Jerry Bonner - also from my firehouse - we stayed together almost the whole two weeks. A lot of guys were doing the bucket brigade - we did that in the down time.[8] But most of the time we were searching in the voids and tunnels of the debris field.

---

[8]During the first few days after the collapse of the Towers, rescue workers and volunteers formed lines going into the debris field. The man at the head of the line scooped debris into plastic buckets and passed the buckets back for dumping. Some of these lines reportedly ran as long as 50 people.

It was such a large area, there weren't enough radios to go around. You couldn't report, "Okay, I'm searching over here or there . . . ." We had a can of spray paint to mark what we found or didn't find. If we found something, we would start digging - get guys to start a bucket brigade. We found a cop from the police academy photo unit this way. Half his torso, and one of his legs was missing.

*   *   *

At times, you *knew* there were remains where you were digging, but you couldn't find anything. There was just a smell. The bodies are totally decomposed from being crushed. They'd been ground into the dirt and the rubble and that's what you were smelling.

I was a cop for ten years and I saw a lot. Sometimes you got a DOA call.[9] You'd get to the location - an apartment, maybe - and the body's been sitting for two or three weeks in the apartment. The deceased had no family. The body's decomposed but you hade to wait until the medical examiner gets there to remove it.

But this. This was like nothing I'd ever experienced. Nothing prepared me for this. Even when you found the remains of someone, nothing was recognizable. And that was so very sad.

How many thousands of people? That's a lot of bodies in one place decomposing. The smell got to you after awhile. By the second or third day it was raw down there. I was gagging. You're just shoveling up the bodies you found into a body bag - there's no other way to pick them up. You hoped that they'd be able to ID them through DNA down at the medical examiners' office,

*   *   *

It wasn't til the fourth day that I found intact bodies, but everyone was naked. I'm like, "Why do these people have no clothes on?"

I was talking to other firemen who were there that first day when the buildings crumbled and I got an answer of sorts. As the Towers came down, firemen were running from the area; the force of the blast created a wind tunnel. It ripped their bottles, the packs we wear for breathing, off their backs - lifted their jackets up and threw them aside like dolls. This stuff is heavy equipment and it's strapped on. So if the blast could rip that stuff off, business suits and regular clothes would be nothing. Like blowing bubbles away. (*Plate 9*)

*   *   *

---

[9]Dead on arrival.

You couldn't find any glass or office furniture. No office equipment. I think there was so much steel and cement coming down in the collapse that everything was made into powder and rubble from the force.

Everyone was like, "Where did all this dirt come from?" Everything was destroyed from the force of all that heavy steel and cement coming down. The largest piece of cement you could find, you could pick up in your hand. Everything was powder.

You had every type of material in the powder that you could imagine. You had a lot of glass. Both Towers had transformers which carried PCBs[10] to keep them cool. That stuff causes cancer. We lost quite a few firemen back in the '70s in a telephone building fire – they were exposed to PCBs when all the transformers in that building burned and they didn't have the proper equipment to protect themselves. Numerous guys died the first year from cancer. Over the next five to 20 years, all the guys from that job died, the majority went within the first ten years from cancer.

There's gonna be a lot of people sick from this. And not just firemen.

I wasn't wearing a mask the whole time for the first two weeks. They issued us these paper masks used for painting but they don't stop anything. So I wore the hood that we wear around our heads when we go into fires. It reminds me of the headgear that a knight wears to protect himself in battle. It keeps the heat from our head. When we have our face piece on, it seals our forehead down to our chin and ears and keeps us from getting burned.

That was my respirator, that's what I found worked the best. I used it to cover my nose and I tucked it into my shirt. I didn't feel like I was getting exposed to the dust in the air . . . but the way that I feel now, I don't think that it did very much. It kept me going at the time, and I guess that was the most important.

*　*　*

From day one, everyone was complaining of the cough and the sore throats. We thought it was from inhaling the dust. We didn't think of contaminants.

But the second day or third day I was getting told by private test groups at the site that the contaminants in the air were off the charts, they were so high, they couldn't register them. But we were also being told by the city and the State that everything was within the range

---

[10]PCBs - polychlorinated biphenyls; chemical liquids used as insulation in electrical equipment until they were banned in the 1970's for being highly toxic.

where it's not gonna harm anyone. That just wasn't so - it wasn't possible.

We knew deep down that stuff was gonna harm us. But we were out there to find our brothers and civilians. That's what we get paid for and that's what we wanted to do. You wanted to bring your family home. (*Plate 10*)

But as time went on, the sore throats and coughing got worse. I noticed around three weeks after September 11th, I was starting to get very easily winded.

*　　*　　*

I was back in the firehouse the second week after the Trade Center. They wouldn't let anyone from the 1st, 3rd, or 11th divisions go back down. Two thirds of the men we lost were from those divisions; we were all working on our days off because of the loss.

Then, going on the normal runs, we noticed that a lot of us were getting winded more easily. Some guys less, some guys more. On regular walk-ups,[11] where I never had a problem before, I thought I was gonna have a heart attack. I couldn't catch my breath. But because we had so many memorials going on, I figured the sleep patterns we were having? The way we were eating? I was out of shape, not doing my regular fitness routine. I chalked it up to that.

But it was getting to the point where every call we went on, I didn't know if I was gonna make it or not, the way my heart was beating. I was gasping for breath.

I really started feeling the problem around four weeks after. We could go down to the medical office and get it checked out, but I didn't want to be out of work. If they put me on the sick list, they wouldn't let me help out at the Trade Center.

*　　*　　*

Losing nine members in a firehouse is very hard. We had nine families we had to look after. We wanted to wait until most of the services were done before getting ourselves checked out.

We lost a lot of guys with over 20 years. They could've retired. There was a guy - September 11th was his last day working. He had 40 years on. I think he was in Rescue Company 1. His son was in the Fire Department, too. That man's wife lost her husband and her son that day.

---

[11]Climbing stairs in buildings while on call.

I couldn't tell you how many memorials we've been to. On our days off, you get a printout that tells you all the services going on. You go to as many as you can, sometimes you try to make two in a day. I think Staten Island's lost close to a 100 guys out of the 300 or so total firemen lost.

You want to show the families support. That they're being thought of and that the person is remembered. Before this happened, a line-of-duty funeral would have anywhere from five to 10,000 guys showing up for a funeral. Now? You're lucky if you get a 100 because there's so many services going on. We're spread thin. You've got guys being laid out upstate, in Queens, Brooklyn, the Bronx.

*   *   *

Finally, a little over two months after September 11th, it was like four o'clock in the morning. We were walking up the FDR Drive, responding to a car fire, walking because we couldn't get through traffic, there were too many cars blocking the roadway. After walking about ten blocks with all my gear and equipment, I thought I was gonna pass out.

I went to my officer and told him, "Boss, there's something wrong. I don't know if I'm having a heart attack or asthma." I never had asthma before.

They got some paramedics to check me out and everything showed okay on my EKG. Nothing wrong with my heart. My lungs were clear. But they said, "Definitely follow up with a pulmonary doctor."

*   *   *

I went to my regular doctor who's a pulmonary doctor. He gave me a breathing test. I had just taken one back in August, but this one came in dramatically low. There's a certain volume you push out when you breathe, it's measured in liters. A normal person my size and weight should be pushing out four-point-five to five liters of air. I was pushing out a little over three. And I'm in shape. So I decided to go for more tests.

I went to the Fire Department surgeon and *they* gave me a breathing test. The Department usually gives you a full medical every six months to a year to make sure your heart's okay, your lungs are clear, you get a blood workup. This time they found out that I've dropped around 40 to 45 percent of my breathing capacity since the last time I was tested.

They said, "Let's put you on some inhalers and see if that helps. Maybe you developed work-induced asthma from all the stuff down there."

193

I was on the inhaler for a week, but it wasn't helping so I went to see a specialist. He explained to me that all the stuff that got into my body down at Ground Zero - wood, glass, metal, cement, and who knows what other chemicals combined in the dust - I didn't just inhale it into my lungs and bronchial tubes. I *ingested* it. I got it into my stomach and the nasal passageways in my head. And everything working together is keeping it constantly inflamed and infected.

So for the past four weeks I've been on three types of inhalers and three different kinds of steroids. Nothing seems to be helping.

*　*　*

Sometimes it's worse than others. I'm the type of person who enjoys getting four hours of sleep. That gives me plenty of rest. Now? I can't get enough sleep, I feel I'm always tired. They say it's a form of depression. I'm sure that's part of it . . . but the physical fatigue is crippling sometimes. The doctors told me, "Since you're not breathing enough air, you're breathing in more frequently and it's making you tired."

Normally, I'm just buzzing along. I like to food shop. I cook, I clean, I do things around the house. My wife labeled me "Mr. Mom" but I do these things because I *like* doing them. They used to call me the Energizer Bunny. "When are you going to sleep? When are you going to stop?" Now I get winded just pushing a shopping cart along.

*　*　*

There's four to five hundred guys with breathing problems. I heard that from the medical officers down at the Bureau of Health Services and from other members of the Fire Department with similar problems.

There's about four guys with severe lung damage that shows up on a chest x-ray – without even going for an MRI or a CAT scan; it's showing up on a regular chest x-ray, which is very bad.

There's guys who went for the blood work-up and it comes back with three or four different viruses. Guys that had a scope stuck down their throat, the doctors saying there's a bunch of crap down there that you can actually see with the camera. But they don't know how to get it out yet.

That's why they're treating us with the inhalers. Hopefully the bruising and inflammation on the bronchial tubes will soothe and the body will heal itself.

Yeah, I'm a little angry. But what am I gonna do? I'm happy I'm alive. The one guy who took my spot working that day, George Cain, is gone. I'd only been there a year, I felt close to him. A really great guy. We were always around each other. We lost a lot of guys . . . but I was pretty close to George. It hurts.

*   *   *

That first night, when I got to close my eyes? I had my one and only dream.

I was hanging out in the firehouse. George and I were on a fire truck, in the engine, just driving around. We came upon a car accident which another fire company was at. The car was on fire and we were able to rescue the kid inside. It felt good. We did the EMS stuff and we got the fire out.

I woke up, I'm looking for George. Everyone looked at me funny: "He's not here." It was so painful. We knew at that point that he was missing. It was so unreal for the first two weeks to know that he's not coming back.

This guy was a marathon runner. He was a rock climber, an avid skier. He traveled all around the country. He was a health food nut. The guy was in phenomenal shape. He lived for being a fireman. He was waiting to get transferred to a busy company up in Harlem because he just loved going on calls, no matter how dangerous it was. Like most of us.

People ask us, "Aren't you scared to go on a call?" No. That's what we're waiting for. We've got a job. We get to do something. Whether it's a car accident, someone's stuck, someone's sick. It makes us feel useful. It's a good feeling to help someone.

Why do we do what we do? It's hard to say, unless you're a fireman. People say, "Why do you run into a burning building?" It's about helping people in need. It's as simple as that. When I heard about the plane crashes, I knew that guys in my company would be on their way down there . . . these guys love what they do and they do a great job. Always. ꙮ

NICOLE BLACKMAN, 33. Like many hardcore Manhattanites, Nicole dropped everything when the Towers fell - her entire life of work, friends, home, and habit - to pull the city from the grip of tragedy. Her story is a love letter to volunteerism, the ethic that impressed the world with the tenacity of the Big Apple and its citizens.

Nicole is a tiny, raven-haired woman with a striking voice. It can climb through multiple-octave ranges of expression with startling ease and grace.

———

I think it was the day after. I was on the phone with a friend of mine, Sue, who lives down in TriBeCa. I checked on her because she's one of the only people I know who lived in that area. She said she was spending time in a volunteer center that was providing an information clearinghouse: what to do if your power was out, what to do if you couldn't get back into your building. Everything was changing so quickly that the community started organizing on its own.

She said that relief services were setting up to help the rescue workers coming down the West Side Highway, handing out sandwiches, masks, and bottles of water.

I said, "Well, do they need anything?"

She said, "They needed sandwiches. They have nothing to give these guys."

"Great."

I immediately started e-mailing and calling friends. We put together a big production line. We had five or six of us; someone had the bread, someone else had the cheese, someone had the turkey and we started making sandwiches. Wrapped them all up and printed out labels so everyone knew what they were. No mayonnaise, we didn't want them to go bad.

We didn't really know where to bring them, though. We tried bringing them down to St. Vincent's hospital, but they weren't accepting food donations. Finally, we were walking around downtown and we found this restaurant called Fiddlesticks. They said, "We're doing food storage for the hospitals because they can't store all their stuff, they don't have room."

On the 12th of September, we all still thought there would be tons of survivors from the Towers. We thought they would need the supplies.

*   *   *

People throughout the city didn't know where to bring stuff and the people at Fiddlesticks said, "Store it here for as long as you can." They had this giant cold storage in their basement.

You wondered, "Who's organizing this? Who's in charge?" But there really wasn't anyone. We had to make it all up as we went along.

So they offered to store our stuff and I thought, "Okay, at least the sandwiches are going to go to someplace useful."

*   *   *

I started walking across town to the West Side Highway and I ran into a friend of mine who had spent a lot of time in Paris. He was sitting in an outdoor café, smiling, having a cigarette with his dog.

He asked me what I was up to and I explained to him about the sandwiches. He gave me this look. Then he said, "Listen, girl. This kind of stuff happens all the time in the rest of the world. You can't get yourself all crazy about it."

I wanted to strangle him. He hadn't seen any of the missing posters outside of St. Vincent's. The news vans covered with flyers. The people holding up signs that said, "Thank you" to any cop or fire truck that drove past.

I was like, "You really don't get this, do you?"

And I knew that I couldn't convince him, so I thought, "This is someone who's just trying to distract me." I said, "Thanks. Good to see you. I'm gonna go."

*   *   *

There were tents set up along the West Side Highway where people were handing things out. I asked, "Hey, who's in charge?"

"That girl over there in the baseball cap." It was very organic, a real grass roots operation. Not like she had an official hat on, and a sign that said, "Me In Charge."

So I said, "Who needs a hand? What can I help with?"

We basically had a stock of bottled water, respirator masks, and sandwiches. And there were people lined up at tables making more sandwiches. I said, "Hold on a second. Do you guys know about Fiddlesticks?"

"What's a 'Fiddlesticks'?"

I said: "Who's got a truck?"

Someone said, "Get a truck, someone go with this girl. She's got a source."

They flagged down some guy in a van who was driving along the West Side Highway. The driver - from Connecticut or Massachusetts or something - had gone to a Home Depot and bought all the boots and respirators he could find, a couple thousand dollars worth of stuff. He threw it all in the van and drove down to Ground Zero thinking, "This is what they're gonna need." Then he spent the rest of the day driving around town going, "Who needs help moving stuff?"

Somebody flagged him down and said, "This girl needs to go someplace to pick up food. Go with her." So I'm sitting in the van with a perfect stranger. Loveliest guy. We drove over to Fiddlesticks and I walked in.

I said, "I've got a van here to take some food over to the West Side Highway."

"Great. What do you need?"

The bartenders were hopping over the bars to help. The waitresses were putting down their checks, saying to their customers, "Dude, you're gonna have to wait for your sandwich, I've got something else to do." Everyone laid down their aprons and we formed a daisy chain, 20 of us. The dishwashers, too, the guys who didn't speak English. There was a door from the downstairs storage up to the sidewalk and crates kept coming up. Water and juice; Power Bars, sandwiches, cans of soda, bags of ice. If it was portable, it went into the chain. People thankfully hadn't donated things like deli platters; only individually packaged items like candy bars and potato chips.

We filled up the van. I thanked the guys at Fiddlesticks, and they were like, "Hey. Great. Glad it's all going someplace you can use it."

And I'm thinking, "What would have happened if I hadn't been there at Fiddlesticks and known all this stuff was there?"

Do you see? That chance circumstance set the tone for everything else that happened.

*　　*　　*

You were a pinball that made the connection between two points. "You guys need ice? I know somebody who has some." That's how the network developed, little by little. No one said, "If you need coffee, you call here. If you need this, you call the Red Cross." It was more like, "Okay, I need 500 pounds of coffee in an hour. Who do I call?" This fragile little network started building itself.

We unloaded everything at the West Side Highway and the people in charge said, "Oh my God! And the sandwiches are *labeled*!"

Trucks were coming down the West Side Highway. A lot of the guys on board were reporting to the Ground Zero site for the first time.[12] They didn't know what services were available. We would rush up to a truck and say, "How many guys do you have and what do you need?" You learned sign language.[13] *Water. Eat. Mask.* You didn't want them to roll down their

Sheperd Sherbell

windows if they didn't have to. The air was bad and we wanted to protect them. A lot of volunteers were wearing masks.

Someone might sign back to us: *Four masks. Three waters. Two sandwiches.* We would collect everything in an armload and tap on the window. They'd roll down the window, we'd throw in the supplies, they'd roll it back up.

*　　*　　*

After a couple of hours, someone said, "There's another pick-up at this location. We've got more stuff over here than we can use." We had things we weren't going to be able to use

---

[12]The West Side Highway became the main conduit to shuttle rescue and recovery workers in and out of Ground Zero for months after September 11th.

[13]She mimes:

199

that night because we weren't going to be able to refrigerate it.

The guy in the van was still driving around so I corralled him and said, "Let's bring some of our food over to the Armory."[14] Which was where they were starting to bring relatives of the missing to get them processed and collect DNA samples.

It was a nightmare over there, security was thick as thieves and the cops weren't letting anyone in.

They asked, "Do you have identification?"

I said, "Yeah."

"Who are you with?"

And I had to say, "I'm a New Yorker. Look in the back of the van. Sandwiches. Here's what we have."

Basically, they had to take it all on good faith. And they did. I couldn't get angry at anyone, I knew they were just trying to do their job in a situation that changed every ten minutes: "Let volunteers in. No! Don't let volunteers in. Check them. Only let them in Red Cross or Salvation Army." I understood, it was a very difficult situation.

So I just said, "Okay. Tell me what *you* need and then I'll give it to you." I was trying to be patient, but it was really frustrating. The traffic, for instance. To go two city blocks, it sometimes took half an hour.

*   *   *

At the Armory we said, "We've got food, supplies, and bottled water." And they said, "Okay! Great!"

Some of the workers came outside and started grabbing things but I said, "It actually works faster if we make a daisy chain and hand things off. You guys know where the supplies should go, I don't know where you want it." This way it made it easier on security, because less unauthorized people would be inside the building.

---

[14]On 26th and Lexington Avenue. The Armory became the site where thousands of desperate family members filled out a detailed nine-page missing persons report to assist in the search for survivors. Lexington Avenue became wallpapered with home-made posters showing the faces of missing persons with heart-breaking descriptions.

So we set up the daisy chain. I remember there were three or four Japanese tourists standing outside. They had obviously been in town during the attack. At one point, they started taking pictures. I stopped for a second and looked at them. I said, "You can take pictures or you can put your cameras down and help."

Someone had to translate for them, but when they understood what I'd said, they put their cameras down and moved in to lend a hand.

That was the attitude I had: you can gawk at this and you can say, "Wow, shit's fucked up, man! Look at what's happened to the city. It's crazy, man! Isn't it weird?" People were walking around on the streets with cell phones talking like this, trying to give their friends eyewitness accounts. Or you can be a part of it instead of watching it happen to other people. You can say, "Here's how I got to know someone who I'd never spoken to before, here's how I pitched in." Because then, wouldn't you have a more extraordinary story to tell?

It was shocking to me how some people couldn't understand that attitude or elected to take the other stance. I thought, "My God. Look at how this one event has brought out the best and the strangest in people." Not the worst, I think. But just some really strange responses.

*　　*　　*

This is all still on Wednesday or maybe Thursday. I lost track of time. After the Armory, we were driving past one of the blockades on 14th Street which, at that point, was still the official DMZ.[15] We were trying to get back to the West Side Highway but got detoured. On 14th Street, there were all these people standing by stockpiles of donations. They didn't have any idea where to bring them, so they brought them as far south as they could before running into security.

Piles of fruit, batteries, bottled water, and junk food 12 feet high. All sorts of nonperishable goods stacked in blocks. Blankets, flashlights, pick-axes, helmets, goggles, saline solution, band-aids, medical supplies. Stuff that people had obviously donated from their jobs, but also stuff that people had literally gone around their building and collected. "Does anyone have any socks? I'm putting together a basket of socks." There was factory-fresh stuff, but there were also used items.

We drove past this and were like, "Oh. My. God."

A state trooper stopped us and asked us if we needed to go below. I tried to explain to him

---

[15]Demilitarized Zone.

that we had just brought stuff over to the Armory, we didn't have official ID, but we were just trying to get back to the West Side Highway so we could do more food shipments.

I said, "What's going to happen to all of this stuff?"

The trooper said, "I don't know. We need someone to bring it down to Ground Zero, but no one has clearance."

"Well, what do you need to get it down there?" There's nothing I hate more than waste. I'm looking at all this stuff piled up and I'm thinking, "We have a van, we don't have clearance. What do we need to make this equation work?"

The trooper, Tim, came from upstate New York. He was this big, heavy-set guy. He said, "I'll drive down with you. I can get anywhere, I'll just show my badge."

"You would do that?"

"They don't really need me here. They have enough guys guarding this place."

So I said, "All right. Load her up."

We opened up the back doors and I stood in the back of the van because it was the only way I could talk over everybody. "Can I have everybody's attention? We can get all of this stuff down to the site."

And you heard: "Yeah! Great! Excellent!"

I said, "What we're gonna do is try to put all the items in together to make it clear and easy to dispense when we get down there." I didn't know what kind of mess it was going to be at the site. "We're gonna do shoes and boots first. Find all your shoes and boots and we'll put those in the far corners of the van. All the clothing items go in the back, medical items go in the front. Bottled water and emergency medical supplies toward the end so we can unload it in order."

This way, if someone else had to help us unpack, at least there was a layout to the van. Boots are here, helmets are there, pick-axes here, gloves and da da da da *da*. If you needed something right away, you could get to it faster.

We started announcing, "Now we're doing batteries. Now we're doing flashlights." And there were 20 people or so who looked through everything and started calling out, "I've got batteries. Do you have batteries? Okay. All the batteries are done. Now we're doing helmets."

We loaded it all up and I was sitting up on top of the equipment in the back. Tim and the driver were up front.

*   *   *

It took us a long time to get down there because we had to stop at every checkpoint. Tim had to show his badge each time and say, "I'm bringing them down. We've got all this stuff." We'd have to open the doors so security personnel could take a look. As we got further and further down Manhattan island, there were less people but more checkpoints and more smoke. It got blacker as we went down. It was as if, little by little, everyone said, "Okay, on this block, ten people: turn out your lights. On this block: 20 people. On the next block: 50 people turn out your lights." We were literally sucked into a black hole.

We weren't getting stopped at red lights, because there were no red lights. There was no traffic at all. There might be a fire engine parked across the street and we might have to wait for that to move or we would wait for rescue services to go through.

I would say, "Do we have 30 seconds?" And when I heard, "Yeah," I would hop out with my respirator on, a big plastic full-face mask, and I would run along the line of fire trucks and ambulances. These people - they had obviously been down there since the beginning. They had holes for eyes. They were smoking inside the cars and trucks and a couple guys would be asleep in the back, holding onto each other as they slept.

I would run up and again I'd tap on the window. I'd mime: *Water? Face masks? Food?* They would nod and I'd do the sign for how many? The numbers: one, two, three. At this point, you could feel the dust and I was wiping stuff out of my eyes. I was only wearing a tank top and jeans. I never thought I would get that far south. I was completely unprepared.

I grabbed what I needed from the van and threw it through their windows. Same routine: roll down the window, throw it all in, roll it back up. I worked the line. I would do about a dozen cars and trucks at every stop and then go back to the van. We'd start moving and I'd load myself up again. We'd stop and I'd be off up the streets again. At the fire trucks, same thing. *Food? Water? Masks? Eye drops?* We developed hand signals for everything.

At one point, someone said, "Do you have any aspirin?"

---

[16]She holds her head.

I mimed like this:[16] *Headache?*
I was like a flight attendant. Whatever they needed.

*   *   *

The thing that struck me most, though, is how I would hand somebody something and they'd say, "thank you" and I would say, "thank you," back. No one in three weeks ever said, "You're welcome." None of us felt worthy of what the other person was doing. The firefighters were like, "Listen, we have to be here. But you don't. You're giving up your lives and your families to be here. Thank you for that."

But I was like, "I'm handing out medical supplies and sandwiches. I'm not doing anything. You're down on your knees picking up bodies. You're picking up hands. I hand you a cup of coffee and you say, 'thank you' to me?"

That was when I realized we were in a different culture. Nothing was normal. The usual manners didn't apply. The situation would bring out things in you that you never knew were there, both good and bad things. A lack of patience or an extreme reserve of patience. Or ingenuity. Or organizational ability.

It was astonishing to see what came out of me and what came out of other people. Especially when we got down to the Pit.

*   *   *

Huge bales of smoke. Shit everywhere. It was so dark you couldn't see despite the emergency lights they had hung. All of lower Manhattan was painted black. No light except for flashlights or the headlights of your car. No televisions heard all along the street. No salsa music on somebody's car stereo. There was none of that. It was as if someone had literally burned up New York and painted it all black and people were walking around with candles.

Down there, it was all pretty much rescue and relief workers with badges and walkie-talkies. Everyone with big boots on. I thought, "I'm gonna get thrown out of here really quickly. I better do my job fast. I'm obviously not supposed to be here."

We pulled the van up. I can't tell you where we were because I wasn't really looking. They had supplies lined up on the sidewalk. Boots in size order, helmets and axes. They had it set up so that, if you needed stuff, you didn't need to go in a building. You just dropped your old gear, picked up what you needed, and went right back down the line.

We started unloading and a couple of people came over and asked Tim, since he was a state

trooper. "Who's in charge here?"
He points at me and says, "This little girl right over here."

I'm like, "I am?" My mask was covering my face and I felt really funny. I think I said something like, "Hi." The looks they were giving me weren't very supportive.

But I thought, "I have to show them I can do this." So I said, "Okay. Here's what we have." And I ticked through the list of supplies in the van. "How do you want me to unload it?"

"We'll get you some help." And they brought over a bunch of guys.

That was when I realized that it was really all men down at the site. So few women, except for a handful of rescue workers, ambulance drivers, police officers. At least from what I saw, it was a very different dynamic. It was the Planet of No Women. Some sort of sci-fi movie where everyone had been bombed out of Manhattan and only the men were left.

* * *

We unloaded everything and Tim said he had to get back up to 14th Street. The van driver said he had to get back home but he'd bring me back to the West Side Highway or wherever I wanted. I said I'd like to have a moment to quietly pay my respects.

Of course, everyone's seen the site on television. But there's very few people who have actually been that close. I stood at the base of Ground Zero, ten feet away from where the rubble began. The remains of the building, the façade, jutted up like big Pick-up Sticks. There was so much activity going on around it, like a noisy beehive. And yet there was a sense of quiet, sort of like a drone. A sound that drowns everything else out. (*Plate 11*)

I stood there for a good, long moment because I knew that, in a little while, it wouldn't look like that anymore. I kept trying to understand the weight of it, what it meant. It was the kind of thing you can't really write down or explain to someone else. I wanted to take a mental picture, which is what I do in situations when I know a photograph will never capture a moment. I literally look at something for a couple of seconds and then close my eyes.

I did this, and before I left, I asked Tim if I could take a picture with him. Not a celebratory picture: "This is us at Ground Zero." He'd been showing me pictures of his wife and his kids and I wanted him to have something to show his family when he returned.

I took a picture of the two of us standing by a fire truck. There was already the sense that "you don't take pictures down here," I got that unspoken vibe very quickly. For some people, though, snapping pictures was like going after big game. I explained to Tim that I didn't want a picture of the site. "I want a picture of you. Because I want to remember your face and what you did."

I took the photo, very low-key, and then I put my camera away.

*   *   *

We drove back to the West Side Highway and I checked in with everyone, told them that their deliveries had gotten where they needed to go. They had shifts of people working for a couple of hours through the evening, by that point. I said to myself, "Okay. I need to go home and absorb this." So I walked from 8th Avenue all the way over to 1st Avenue to catch the L train back to Brooklyn.

I called my friend, Sue, and told her what I'd done the day before. She said, "Well, I understand that relief services further over on Chambers Street could use some help. Why don't we get together tomorrow and go over together."

"Fine."

Understanding that my clothes were going to get destroyed, I didn't wear anything that I cared about the next day. I wore a crappy watch - I didn't care if it got scuffed up. I brought a cell phone. Didn't bring a bag, but I wore a pair of camouflage pants that had pockets where I could put identification, cash, an ATM card, my house keys, eye drops. And I think that, because I was wearing those camouflage pants, when we got over to Chambers Street, the military saw me and waved me in.

Sue is a model. She's tall and blonde. She always gets in.

*   *   *

We walked over to Stuyvesant High School where most of the relief services were. A school crossing guard was doing security at the front door, stopping everyone and asking for ID. She wasn't doing a very good job because we walked right on in and she started chasing us. We went and hid until she gave up.

Stuyvesant had basically become base command for non-medical relief services. By the time we arrived that morning, they had already determined that medical supplies would be on the first floor; chiropractors, beds and massage tables on the balcony; second floor was clothing and a canteen area for food in a triangular-shaped locker area and more cots for short-term sleep. The next floor had classrooms where you could go in, close a door and get long-term sleep. And then the locker rooms and showers where we kept the grooming supplies: towels, soap, shampoo.

Basically, it was like this: you could come in, swap out all your gear; get a chiropractic adjustment; talk to a counselor; eat; grab a cup of coffee; and take a nap. We set it up like, "We'll put the counseling center over here so they can get coffee and eat . . . then go talk to someone and take a nap. Put all that on one floor." We had to set it up that way because if the relief workers had to walk up a flight of stairs, they wouldn't do it. They were exhausted. We only wished we could change where the showers were, they were on one of the higher floors. We put everything else down as low as possible to make it easy.

When Sue and I walked in, we looked at the list of where everything was. It wasn't an official menu, by any means - more like a paper plate on which someone had written, "FOOD ON 2". Really haphazard. I went up to the second floor and found piles of boxes, garbage bags, shopping bags and crates jumbled all over the place. I had no idea where they had come from. There were a couple of tables in the middle of the room and a couple of round picnic tables off in one corner. It looked like a ramshackle AA meeting-slash-tornado relief camp. This woman was taking a break at one of the tables. She looked as if she'd been working for a couple of hours.

I said, "Hi, I'm here in case you need help."

She said, "Well, workers basically come in and get what they need to eat and then they go back down."

I saw these aluminum-and-steel shelving racks that had probably been rolled up from the cafeteria. "Uhm, how 'bout if I organize this for you?" I figured we could use the racks to store things so that, at a glance, we could see what we were almost out of. "I could make this look nice."

She said, "Hey, if you want to do that? Yeah. Great."

Basically, I'd given myself a job.

*　*　*

In two hours, the place looked like D'Agostino's.[17] I organized things according to categories

---

[17] A popular upscale market in Manhattan.

in case we needed to put together shipments for Ground Zero: this many of this thing, this many of that thing. When the supervisor's shift ended, she said, "Okay, I'm going home. How long are you staying?"

I said, "I don't know, I thought I'd work for about six hours. I'm not really tired yet, I'll just keep working."

"All right."

"Oh. Ah. Who's the next, you know? Supervisor in charge."

She said, "Well, I don't know. But they should be here shortly."

"All right. I'll just try to keep everything rolling."

It was kind of quiet now, around 11 o'clock. I thought, "How difficult could this be?"

No one ever came. Seventy-two hours later, I was running the place, in charge of the food service.

*   *   *

I had volunteers showing up asking me, "Do you need help?"

"Yeah, start over there."

The Guardian Angels showed up and we put them on duty in the pantry.[18] We stored all the stuff we would need during the next four hours on the ground floor, but the long-term storage was upstairs with the walk-in coolers in the cafeteria. We had no power on the lower floors so, in order to keep drinks cold, we had to get big garbage cans and fill them with ice. I put one of the Angels in charge of making coffee because they had to boil these huge vats individually and each one took four hours to boil. I had them doing four vats constantly so that one was ready every hour.

Sue worked with me for a while that evening and then she went home. She came back the next day for a few hours and said, "You're still here?"

"Yeah. Listen. I need . . ." And I rattled off my wish list.

---

[18]The Guardian Angels are a volunteer urban watch patrol.

All the stuff getting shipped down to us was coming from the Chelsea Foods Market - that was one of the main drop sites for donations. Chelsea Piers, the Javits Center, and Pier 40, all donation drop sites with volunteer crews working there trying to figure out how to get their supplies to Ground Zero. In the first couple of days after the attack, a sort of hourglass pattern started developing. Distribution sites from all over the city were trying to move stuff down to Ground Zero; it all filtered to us at Stuyvesant High School. Then we'd redistribute it to satellite areas directly around the perimeter of the site because a lot of workers couldn't make it uptown to Stuyvesant.

These volunteers would come up on Gators - those little military golf carts? They'd come up and say, "Hey, I'm from this church" or "I'm from this site and I need 30 sandwiches, 30 bottles of Gatorade, eye drops and gloves."

We were like, "Okay." And I'd assign them a volunteer and say, "Take them to shop." Whatever you needed, you came to Stuyvesant.

Now I was in charge of food and this girl, Karen, who is a very well-known fashion stylist - she was in charge of clothing. Bags and bales of clothing came to Stuyvesant and she started putting together teams. They took over individual classrooms. T-shirts here, sweatshirts there, sweatpants and underwear in the next room, everything organized in size order. Shoes set out in rows with size numbers taped on the bottom and laces tied together. It was the Wal-mart of tragedy.

*   *   *

I remember walking one firefighter through. I was outside getting some air and he approached Stuyvesant, covered in debris, totally shell-shocked. I could see in his eyes that he couldn't make sense of anything. I took his hand and said, "Hi. I'm Nicole. You've never been to Stuyvesant, have you?"

"No."

"Okay. We have these services available to you. Why don't we get you a change of clothes, take you upstairs to the showers and get you clean so you can get some rest. How much time do you have on your break?"

I had to help him make decisions because he was long past that.

We got him up to Clothing where workers undressed and threw their old clothes into garbage bags because those old clothes were considered Haz-mat. We got him into sweat-pants and got him a stack of brand new gear. Karen and her volunteer assistants had the routine down so pat they could just ask you, "Size? Extra-large? Long-sleeve? You want jeans? How are your socks doing? Do you want something to sleep in? High boots, low boots, how do you like your boots? Underwear: briefs, boxers, boxer-briefs?" The girls would run off and fill the order while the relief workers just stood there, dumbfounded.

The showers were laid out the same way. Shampoos, soaps, washcloths, towels, eye drops, deodorant. A garbage can for when you were finished - you could just dump it all and move on. The supplies were lined up like a drugstore, like Genovese,[19] and I sent a volunteer up there every hour to straighten up. I said, "I don't want anyone to look at the way this place is set up and frown. I want this to look like the Happy Delicatessen of Plenty. There is never to be one of any item left. If we only have one of something, take it off the table and hand it to someone. Because if this is the last soup spoon, no one will take it. Everyone thinks someone else deserves it more than they do." I saw this happen more than once.

So there was never one toothbrush. Never one sandwich. Never one Power Bar. As soon as we saw six of anything, we replenished the stock.

*   *   *

I would say, "Do you have time for a nap? Can you sleep for a couple of hours?" For the volunteers who slept in the short-term sleep bay, I would write post-it notes over their heads reminding me what time to wake them up. Then I would set the timer on my cell phone. 20 minutes, 25 minutes, an hour and a half. The timer would go off and I would go down the line. "Barry, you said you wanted me to wake you up. Do you want to sleep a little more?"

Usually, they would say, "No, no. I have to - I have to get up."

Sometimes I convinced them. "Look. Sleep for half an hour more. I'll come wake you up. Trust me."

In half an hour, these guys were so deep in dreams, it was hard to pull them out. I didn't want to wake them. And yet I knew they'd be upset. They wouldn't trust me anymore if I didn't.

I would wake them up like my mom used to wake me up, really gently. A lot of times, they

---

[19]Drugstore chain.

wouldn't know where they were when they came to. It was strange to have them look at me like they did. It broke my heart every time that they would open their eyes and realize it wasn't a dream. Sleep had been their escape. But now I had to bring them back. It was so hard to do that.

*   *   *

The Board of Education came in and said, "Do you want our lunch ladies to help you out?"

I said, "Why, yes. We would love to have your lunch ladies help us out."

It was absurd, all of these people asking me what to do. It was crazy. But of course, the only people I ever mentioned that to were people like Sue. To everyone else it was, "We need 600 pound of ice a day, three times a day, I have no refrigeration." I was serving between 3000 to 6000 meals a day.

I realized I had really gotten the system down when a police captain came up to me at one point about two weeks into it and said, "'Scuse me, who's in charge here?"

I thought, "Oh, Jeez. That's it. I'm screwed."

I raised my hand. "Me. I'm in charge."

He said, "Ma'am, my name is Captain So-and-So. I want to bring in some of my officers for breakfast. They haven't been down to the site before, they're relieving a number of officers who have been here a few weeks. I wanted to find out what your system was here. How many people can you handle all at once? How would you like us to stagger their meal shifts?"

I was stunned. But instead of going, "Holy shit! He's asking me!" I thought, "Bluff! Bluff!"

I said, "We can handle 100 to 120 comfortably at a time. If we give them 20 minute shifts, I think we can handle that."

He said, "All right. We've got about 600, we'll take up six of your shifts."

Just like that. Breakfast for 600.

*   *   *

We didn't have vitamins at first at Ground Zero so I started buying them on my own. I would go into GNC and say, "What do you have?" I would buy the biggest Centrum maxi container you could find, the $180 one; I would get six of them. I would tell the people running the distribution sites what we needed and they would say, "Okay, let me see if we have that." But they never did.

I made sure that I went to all the tables to give the workers their vitamins. A lot of guys didn't want to take their pill, so I would walk from table to table and make a game of it. "Okay. Who hasn't taken their vitamin today?"

"Well, I don't need one."

"I don't take those."

"Well," I'd say. "Centrum is complete from A to Z. Complete with Vitamin V: Viagra!"

"Oh, I don't need that."

"Oh, buddy. That's not what your wife said."

And everybody would go, "Ooooooooh!" But they would take their vitamins. After three days of this, they'd see me coming and go, "C'mon, Nicole. Gimme my vitamin, gimme my vitamin." And no one got sick on any of my shifts. I made sure they got their anti-oxidants; I made sure we had milk thistle, which is very helpful for clearing out lungs and for liver toxicity. There was so much crap in the air, it became a matter of doing anything we could to try and help the workers clear their lungs.

Eventually, I talked to a friend of mind who said, "Well, what do you mean, you're buying your own vitamins?"

I said: "I don't have time to spend running all over the city lobbying for multi-vitamins at supply distribution centers. I have to get back down to the site.

So my friend looked on some web sites. And he found Whitehall Robbins, which manufactures Centrum. He called them and forwarded them the e-mails I'd been sending out which described what I was doing. A representative called me and said, "I understand you need some vitamins. We've been trying to figure out how to make donations, we didn't now who to go through. What do you need?"

"A truckload of Centrum. Right now."

"What have you been doing?"

"Buying the big jugs. I don't know if you have the individual packets, but those would be a lot cheaper to hand out."

She said, "No problem. How many do you need?"

"Well, we're doing between three and six thousand meals a day. Probably two and a half thousand people for breakfast. I don't know how long we'll be at Stuyvesant, but if you send me 10,000 tablets, I'll tell you how long it lasts."

"Fine. No problem. What else do you need?"

". . . I don't know. What other products do you represent?"

"Oh. Well, we do Chapstick. We do this and we do that . . ."

God bless Whitehall Robbins. The next day, a truck came and I had a pallet of vitamins.

Then the word went out to Dr. Scholl's that we had all these boots but no in-soles and they sent a truckload. Corporate America would send us anything; they just didn't know where. They didn't know who to contact. It wasn't like, "Call Ground Zero Incorporated at this number to contribute." Volunteers would see where the real need was and say, "Okay, I need Immodium."

That's when I started calling ABC News and putting things on the little zipper tape that runs across the bottom of the TV screen, "We no longer need bottled water and we no longer need dog food." People thought the search and rescue dogs were starving. Let me tell you - those dogs ate better than a lot of people do. And they don't eat normal dog food anyway, they eat specialized vitamin stuff - not Alpo off the shelves. We had, like, 5000 pounds of dog food.

*   *   *

The canteen upstairs at Stuyvesant started looking like Costco.[20] We had cans of fruit and vegetables; bottled water; cans of coffee; bales of rice; boxes of stuff. I thought, "What are we gonna do with all this?" We had it stacked up in boxes so that you could walk through with a hand-truck trolley and off-load whatever you needed.

---

[20]Wholesale store.

We'd get a food donation from Pier 40 and the driver would say, "Where do you want it?"

"4ᵗʰ floor, please."

The Guardian Angels upstairs knew where we needed everything and they'd take care of it.

It got to the point where we were self-sufficient. The things that got frustrating were that we couldn't necessarily get what we needed when we needed it. We never knew where things were coming from. Also, the distribution centers started to get shut down. Chelsea Piers Market was shut down first, and then I think Chelsea Piers, and then Javits. Pier 40 was last, I think.

These sites would take all their donations and bring them down to the rest center before they shut down. Chelsea Food Markets needed to get back to business; Chelsea Piers, too. As these sites got shut down, we had less and less opportunities to get resources. Because the people at one site were gone, I didn't have a source for coffee anymore. Or it'd be like, "This place is gone. Now I don't have a source for medical supplies."

They would come down to Stuyvesant and swap phone numbers. We had phone lists ten pages long that read: "Bob: Coffee Guy" or "Mark: Soda Guy". "Rick: Ice Guy." If we could figure out a person's specialty? We didn't need their last name, we had a phone number.

I'd call them: "Hey, it's Nicole at Stuyvesant."

"Right. What do you need?"

It was all done in shorthand, like CB handles. You didn't know any normal things about people on the list. Like: "Oh, Bob? Sure. He works in advertising. Five, nine. Dark hair. tennis player." Nothing like that. He was Coffee Bob. It was Leo the Driver.

But as sites kept getting shut down, we had to find ways to figure out getting supplies in from the outside. That's when a lot of our friends would say, "We brought donations to this site, but there was no one there to receive it. Javits got rid of their receiving area - they needed space to house the National Guard, they're sleeping on the floor." At that point, the DMZ had moved from 14th Street to Canal - later on it was moved further south to Chambers Street. Closer to us, but people still couldn't get through the gates.

* * *

People took up collections at their offices. They donated medical supplies, boots, clothing, backpacks. A friend of a friend passed along my e-mails to everyone he knew. "They have enough of this, they need more boots and in smaller sizes." More women were starting to work at the site but they had no sizes for women, everything was in double-XL. Old sweatshirts, T-shirts, sweatpants, anything like that. Anything that no one would be too upset about throwing away at the end of the day. Clean underwear and clean socks. People were sending us old, used stuff and it's not that the thought wasn't appreciated, but if the underwear had skid marks we had to say, "No."

*   *   *

People started bringing supplies to the Church of Scientology in midtown. There were Scientology members all over the place at Stuyvesant. They all had these bright yellow T-shirts on. We called them "The Chickadees." The shirts said, "Church of Scientology" and they had their address and phone number on the back. Someone explained to me that one of the tenets of Scientology is that you help in a disaster, everyone pitches in. They're apparently very well known for lending a hand at disaster sites. I didn't know this.

But if a toilet was backed up? I could find a yellow T-shirt, hand them a plunger, and say, "Listen, I'm really sorry. The toilet's backed up."

They'd be like, "I'd be happy to."

No job was too dirty or weird. It was just, "I'd be honored." And not in a rote-robotic, zoned-out religious way. "I-would-love-to-clean-up-the-toilet-for-you-thank-you." Just honestly feeling privileged to pitch in. I found that 98 percent of them were a real pleasure to work with. They were so even-tempered and gracious, so calm and soothing to be around. Even at the height of craziness . . . of "Oh, my God! We don't have this item in supply!" . . . they would say, "Okay. Relax. I'll find out about it."

I owe them a lot. They had some pamphlets and some books with them, but they weren't pushing anything. They did a lot of nerve assists, which is where someone lies on a bed and a Scientologist traces the nerve endings across your back, arms, and legs. Just tracing through the nervous system to help soothe, calm, and relax someone. They would do this for five to ten minutes for folks who were jittery. It was all really very helpful and they would sit and talk to you if you needed someone to talk to. Anything that needed to be done.

They were the ones who solved the drop site problem by saying, "Why don't you have donations dropped at the Church of Scientology? It's a secure location. When stuff comes in with your name, we'll call you. We'll send a driver to pick it up." So that's what we started doing.

*   *   *

When everyone down at the site started asking for cigarettes, we started calling cigarette manufacturers. I had started to buy them myself and I asked friends to donate them. Finally, I called Phillip Morris, but since the lawsuit settlement, they're not allowed to give away cigarettes anymore, even for disaster sites.

I was like, "Guys. I understand you're not allowed to give away cigarettes in bars or at high schools. Look, this is a disaster site. Come in and back up a fucking unmarked truck full of cigarettes. Who's gonna know?"

"Oh, no. We can't really. We really can't. . ."

"I won't tell anyone where they came from, I promise. I'll hand them out and say they were donated. I'll say I paid for them myself. Just bring them down here, what's it gonna cost you?"

They couldn't or wouldn't do it and neither would any of the other cigarette companies. However, a friend of mine orders cigarettes from Tobacco By Mail, a website catalog where you can order cigarettes in bulk - exotic brands, things you can't get at your local metropolitan chain stores. She called me and said, "I understand you need cigarettes?"

I said: "The workers are requesting these three or four brands the most."

"How much do you need?"

"We're going through ten or 15 cartons a day. I can't tell you what to do. If you want to donate, I'll let you know how long it lasts. If you want to donate again, I'll call you in a few days and let you know. It's entirely up to you."

She sent me a crate of all different brands, something like a 100 to 150 cartons. Tobacco By Mail could donate because they're a catalog company, a reseller, not a manufacturer.

Friends of mine were saying, "I want to pitch in. I want to donate something but I can't take time off from work. I have nothing that could be of use - what can I do?"

So I said, "Can you pitch in five bucks for a pack of cigarettes?" Everybody could do that. I e-mailed everyone: "Ask all your friends who smoke if they can buy a carton of cigarettes.

Put them in a duffle bag or a milk crate and give me a call when it's full and we'll send someone over to pick it up."

*　　*　　*

Martha Stewart Living. A couple of gals who worked in the art department put together
backpacks because they knew we needed them to transport stuff. We had to have thick bags
to keep things inside clean. Open bags gathered too much contamination.

They asked every staffer to bring in their old duffle bags to the office. They packed the bags
with clothes, toiletries - Martha has raised these girls well. They had little American ribbons
on every bag. They had notes in them: "Good luck. We're with you, Martha Stewart
Living." I wept. I don't even think Martha knew that her art department did that.

Cleopatra Records send down a big duffle bag full of CDs. They said, "We don't know what
else we can donate, but if some of those guys might need something to listen to . . ." They
sent major labels. So I was handing out John Cougar Mellencamp CDs and P.O.D. An
awful lot of Bon Jovi. If you were from Jersey, you got a Jon Bon Jovi CD.

No one knew what to bring down, see? They surprised us with variety.

*　　*　　*

I tried to make sure I got out to get some fresh air at least twice a day. At Stuyvesant,
during that first 72-hour shift, I had hardly stepped foot outside. But after 72-hours, I was
afraid to leave the site. I didn't know if I would get back in. Security changed so quickly,
so constantly. Even if you knew the cops at a checkpoint or the Army or whoever it was -
even if you recognized them by sight . . . six hours later it's now the Air Force in charge. I
think the head of FEMA told me at one point that there were 17 different government
agencies involved at Ground Zero; all branches of the military, the police, OEM, FEMA,
the works.

Communication within these organizations is difficult enough. But imagine having basically
every American security relief volunteer and military outfit on active duty at once. It was
amazing anything happened at all.

It was frustrating for us because we heard: "No, you don't have clearance. I don't know who
you are. No." I would send runners down to the site where the food deliveries were coming
in and they would never come back. We were hemorrhaging volunteers, it's one of the
reasons we all ended up sleeping at the site. We didn't have passes and if we left the building
we wouldn't be able to get back in. We were down to a skeleton crew after three weeks.

Outside there was this little smoking area where everyone would hang out on their breaks. We'd chat and drink a bottle of water. I remember I was starting to hallucinate at one point, looking at my watch, "Three o'clock", and thinking, "Wow, the lunch rush was kind of quiet today. Huh." Not feeling too bad about going out for a break. It was pitch black.

It wasn't three o'clock in the afternoon, it was three o'clock in the morning. Working at Stuyvesant was like working in a casino. No windows, bad lighting, the clocks had stopped.

*   *   *

I looked at this young volunteer and said, "I need a break, can you keep things going?"

I was standing outside on Chambers Street at one point and I started shaking, I broke down crying. A couple of the guys I had become close to - I was feeding them three times a day - came up to me and said, "What's going on?"

My brain wanted to keep working, but my body was seceding. I was way past whatever my limit was. I knew what had to be done and my brain wanted to do it, my heart wanted to do it, but the body couldn't, so the triangle broke down, totally exhausted. But there was nobody to hand everything off to.

Sergeant Gaita from the Marine Corps was in charge of passes and they had set up in this little war room tent across the street from the school. They had it all laid out with maps and secure phone lines, the works. These friends of mine who saw me break down escorted me into the tent. I had totally dissolved. I'm weeping, thinking, "This is not good. I've lost my shit and they're not gonna let me back in. Get a grip!" It was like when you come home drunk to your parents and you try to sober up really quick.

This soldier looks at me and says, "What do you need?"

I said, "I need to get my people back on the site. I need to put together viable shifts so that we can have humane, sensible conditions for the volunteers. I've been here so long because I can't find anyone to hand this off to. You're taking all my good people."

He said, "Our first concern is you. We don't want you messed up. We want you to go home and rest up."

He started talking to me a little patronizingly, like you would talk to a crazy person. And I guess I could understand. From their point of view I was just this crazy civilian who was working too hard. But the NYPD and the Fire Department guys told them, "You don't understand. If she's not here, we don't eat. Give her whatever she needs. These girls . . . if it wasn't for them . . . please . . ."

They handed me 40 all-access numbered passes. I had to give them the names, phone numbers and social security numbers of the volunteers I handed them out to. They would have to show the passes as they came into the site, and if their name didn't match the list, they'd be taken away and it was my ass. I gave them out to the most trusted workers we had, whoever was in charge of a department at Stuyvesant got a couple of passes. I said, "If you smuggle someone in, we all lose our passes. Do you understand this?" It was going to work out.

They handed me the 40 colored passes and said, "You have 20 minutes to hand these out and then we're escorting you home. You can't come back for eight hours. Get some rest."

"What are you talking about?" They were treating me like a crazy person again.

Sergeant Gaita said, "Look. We need you here. If you break down, there's no one else to keep the machine going. You have to sleep."

That's when I realized that they understood what I was doing. I was a very important idiot savant.

I walked back across the street to Stuyvesant with the passes and some friends of mine there were like, "Hey, Nicole. How's it going?"

The police officers on either side of me said, "She can't talk to you right now, she's got to get some paperwork done and we're escorting her home." They wouldn't let me carry my bags, my backpack. "No, ma'am. We've got it." They escorted me to the Ladies Room and stood outside the door. They put me into a squad car and drove me back to Brooklyn. One of the cops knew the neighborhood and said, "We'll drop you off on the corner. We don't want your parents to get worried."

"How old do you think I am?" I didn't have any make-up on or anything. They thought I was 19.

I took a shower and really slept. And then I went back down to the site. I spent many more overnight shifts there, 24 and 48 hour shifts. It's what needed to be done.

*   *   *

One of the things I learned at the site? What was essential and what wasn't.

Some things became unimportant. Laundry and getting your hair cut. Cleaning your house or cooking. Shopping, reading, watching television. Keeping up on your e-mail. Going out to museums, going out to shows. Seeing your friends, putting on make-up.

Every morning I would go back down, reassessing things as I got dressed. Rings? Unimportant. A watch? Important. Nail polish? Not important. Nail file? Important - I don't have particularly long nails, but if they got in the way, you'd cut them off. Hair beret or a rubber band, get the hair out of the way, pull the bangs back. Is this jacket important? Yes, it warms me and protects me. A notebook? Not really. A cell phone? Yes. Everything had to earn a place in my pockets or my bag. It became an exercise in "What can I lose?"

Must call my mother every other day. Must put quarters in my pocket in case I needed change for a pay phone. Must have eye drops. Must carry Vasoline for my cut-up hands.

We were running out of pens yesterday - let me grab some of those. Ziploc baggies for people who went through the food lines and didn't know when they'd be back. "Take some more. Take some for one of your pals who doesn't have the energy to walk up to Stuyvesant and give it to them."

I started opening up the different pockets on their uniforms and shoving Power Bars, eye drops, vitamins, Immodium, sun block, candy bars, anything I could get in there so they'd have it down at the site. The rescue workers would protest and say, "No, no. I don't need it. Really." But they'd come back later on saying, "I handed everything out, do you have any more?"

I found myself getting very frustrated with people who weren't at the site. People who were doing things that now seemed trivial to me. "I'm gonna do brunch. I'm gonna go to the library. I'm gonna go walk the dog."

Walk the dog? You're kidding, right? Hold the dog out the window and squeeze it's ass. Figure out a better system for walking the dog and that's half an hour you can use to feed someone.

I had to learn to recognize that not everyone functioned the way I did. Not everyone thought that it was important to help. At one point, I saw a young family going out to a restaurant on a Sunday morning in lower Manhattan and I thought, "My God. That's what a person *should* be doing." But I honestly didn't know how they did it.

Plate 1 – "The Winter Garden was an indoor atrium which houses very tall palm trees. It could almost be described as an indoor version of the Austin J. Tobin Plaza." - Photo by R. Andrew Lepley

Plate 2 – "I turned around and I couldn't believe we were so close to the commuter ferryboats going over the Hudson River to New Jersey. We were right next to the railing leading down to the docks. . .I looked to my right and saw masses of people pushing their way onto the dock. I found an opening at the railing and thought that, if we just continued to move forward and stayed right where we were next to the railing, we'd be able to board easily." - Photo by Roger Smyth

Plate 3 – "The other firefighter said, "Let me try to find a way out." And he climbed up on this mountain of debris and went over to the other side until we couldn't see him anymore. We kept calling out, "Are you okay?" and he would holler back, "Yeah." But he found out there was no way to get out – the debris just kept rolling on and on forever - and he came back." - Photo by Roger Smyth

Plate 4 – "He didn't say a word, he just barely nodded. He was completely stunned. He stood there in a daze with his shoulders slouched, ghost white from the debris - which was interesting because he was African-American. You could see the word "POLICE" stenciled on his vest." - Photo by Drew Nederpelt

Plate 5 – "As soon as it settled, you could hear voices. Screaming. Shouting. People not knowing what direction was what because the smoke was so dense. The Fire Department guys, they wear motion trackers. If they stand still for more than 30 seconds, their motion tracker goes off. So you heard all these high-pitched, whining electrical screams. "Reeeeee Reeeeee Reeeeee Reeeeee." Those were the sounds of the boys who were trapped in the rubble. . . As soon as the smoke started to clear, I saw people getting up and going toward the rubble to get whoever they could out." -Photo by Frank Cutler

Plate 6 – "These boys are really fried. Around noon, these firemen came out of the rubble and just threw themselves down against my ambulance. Wrecked. Dog tired. They just fought their way out." - Photo by Roger Smyth

Plate 7 – "So I seen these three Fire Department guys climbing up on top one of those broken buildings. With a flag post they'd set up, near Vesey Street and the West Side Highway. The three guys get up and you see the Stars and Stripes come out and they started to raise it. I'm not into any form of patriotism. But I was very moved by what was going on, this symbol of defiance in the midst all the rubble. It was very reminiscent of Iwo Jima. Even as I took the photo I was struck by it. And there was total silence. You might think, looking at the pictures, that there was this massive noise and chaos going on all around. But they were raising that flag in this very eerie silence." - Photo by Roger Smyth

Plate 8 – Top – "It was covered from head to toe with pieces of cement, paper, lots of dust, lots of rubble. We moved 14 bags of garbage off that rig . . . There were problems with the tower ladder and the truck's radiator was clogged with about two inches of soot and garbage. But it was still running." - Photo by Roger Smyth

Plate 10 – Bottom – "We knew deep down that stuff was gonna harm us. But we were out there to find our brothers and civilians. That's what we get paid for and that's what we wanted to do. You wanted to bring your family home." – Photo by Roger Smyth

Plate 9 – "As the Towers came down, firemen were running from the area; the force of the blast created a wind tunnel. It ripped their bottles, the packs we wear for breathing, off their backs - lifted their jackets up and threw them aside like dolls. This stuff is heavy equipment and it's strapped on. So if the blast could rip that stuff off, business suits and regular clothes would be nothing. Like blowing bubbles away." - Photos by Rob Epstein

Plate 11 – "I stood at the base of Ground Zero, ten feet away from where the rubble began. The remains of the building, the façade, jutted up like big Pick-up Sticks. There was so much activity going on around it, like a noisy beehive. And yet there was a sense of quiet, sort of like a drone. A sound that drowns everything else out." - Photo by Steve Olsen

Plate 12 – "There's a shadow history on this city and it might never go away." - Photo by Roger Smyth

Plate 13 – "I was so proud of my city. This is my home. The way everybody stood up. There wasn't any crying, there wasn't any weeping, there wasn't any pulling of hair. It was just, 'We're gonna deal with this.' And nothing was gonna stop anybody." - Photo by Andrew Walker

Plate 14 – "I took it as a sign that God was there . . . . These two beams, one horizontal and one vertical, that were riveted together in the perfect shape of a cross. It was sticking out of the ground - you've seen this on the news. It was brown, rust colored. There was a firefighter's jacket hanging off one of the spars. I would guess it was probably 12 feet high from the ground to the crosspiece; maybe another six feet tall above that to the top. It stood down in the pit, about three stories high." - Photo by Bobbie-Jo Randolph

Plate 15 – Top – "We can piece this together from calls made by fire marshals. It was a bad situation up there. People trapped in elevators. Firemen rushing up, trying to find those elevator cars. No clue as to what was about to happen." Photo by Roger Smyth

Plate 16 – Bottom – "You know the video clips of the planes hitting the Towers? The ones they played over and over and over again? We found that the young kids - kindergarten and first grade - couldn't distinguish that it was one event played over and over again on the television. They thought it was happening anew each time. So some of them thought that all of Manhattan had been destroyed." – Photo by Bob London

Plate 17 – "When I first heard a plane had hit, I thought it was a Cessna. When you worked in the Trade Center, you always saw Cessnas and other little planes flying below you. I figured some idiot had lost control and flown into the building. In retrospect, I guess that was a little naïve. A Cessna would just bounce off those buildings like a bug." - Photo by Bob London

Plate 18 – "You could see the whole city skyline. From where I was standing, you were looking out towards Queens, northeast, toward LaGuardia airport. You could see the planes coming in and taking off; from as high up as we were, the planes were actually below us. Turn your head just a little? You could see Central Park. And it's crazy: geographically those Towers were pretty far away from the Upper West Side and the Upper East Side. But you could see it all laid out before you from up there. Like the whole city was painted on the ground in miniature." - Photo by Robert Ripps

And friends from all over the country would call me, the only person in Manhattan they knew; they were trolling me for experience. They wanted to pick out the pearls. Live vicariously. That way they could call their own friends and say, "Did you hear about Nicole working at Ground Zero? Did you hear about the guy who came into her place to eat after picking up human hands?" Like it was the biggest party of the year and, since they couldn't get in, they wanted to say they knew someone who was there. It infuriated me, so I stopped talking to them.

I feel the same way when people go down to Ground Zero now as tourist attraction. I can understand how people want to go down to see it, to understand it, to pay their respects. But then I heard from a friend of mine in California who was coming to town. I said, "What are you gonna do while you're here?"

"Oh, it's gonna be great. I'm gonna get my hair cut, I'm gonna go do yoga, I'm gonna go to Ground Zero, I'm going to the MOMA,[21] I'm having dinner with so-and-so. . ."

Great. You've just dismissed one of the most profound experiences this country has ever seen. I just hope that they go down there glib and get the shit scared out of them by the words still etched in the dust of the buildings all around the site.

"God help us."

"Pray for us."

"This way to the Morgue."

There's a shadow history on this city and it might never go away. (*Plate 12*)

*   *   *

We were finally running efficiently and we still hadn't seen anyone from FEMA or OEM. No one had ever popped in and said, "How can we help?" I had taken to staying inside again. Why not? We had our own little floating city with clothes, beds, showers, food, a radio with batteries, everything you needed. If you brought your cell phone charger down with you to the site, you could basically run the country from there. It was easier, psychologically to stay there rather than get distracted by the outside world. You got more done.

We never knew how long it would go on. A campaign of Chinese whispers began, "I heard

---

[21] Museum of Modern Art.

we're gonna get ousted today. No, I heard tomorrow. Should we order more coffee? Should we order more water? They're changing the color of the passes again. Yellow, then red. Then I hear they're moving into blue."

Finally they ordered a shut down at Stuyvesant. Rumor had it that one of our Senators had a daughter who was a student there and didn't like being bussed to another location. They wanted to turn the school back into a school and move all the relief services to a big cruise ship over on the waterfront. But we had millions of dollars worth of supplies in there and I wanted to know what was going to be done with it.

"Sanitation's coming tomorrow and will throw it all out."

"No, no, no. Give me three days. We'll find people to take it."

They gave us the three days. We called every homeless shelter and church, every volunteer organization, soup kitchen and volunteer ambulance corps we could think of and told them, "Make an appointment, come on down, bring your vans, and shop. Take whatever you want." We gave the food supplies to the school as thanks for hosting us. We found homes for about 95 percent of the stuff we had.

We were packing everything up and the head of FEMA finally came in, a huge man with huge hands, a very sweet man. He stopped by with the head of the Police and Fire Departments.

He said: "Wow, you guys really filled a gap. You've done an amazing job." It turned out that no one had ever stopped in on us because they thought we were an organization. They thought we were the Red Cross. They thought we were official.

"Well," I said, "I'd like to take you on a tour so we can show you what we've been doing."

I started doing a walk-and-talk. "And here we have the Beverage Center. You can get a trolley here and take what you like. Just sign here because we need to know your name and phone number so we know which deliveries went where. Now, if you'll follow me downstairs. . ."

I wasn't looking, but Karen, who had run the clothing department, said, "I wish you could have seen the look on the FEMA Director's face. He couldn't believe it." Apparently, he had run the Oklahoma City operation and he couldn't believe how we'd organized the Clothing Center, the kitchen, the sleeping bays, the Massage Floor.

When we were finished, he turned to us and said, "This is the most impressive volunteer operation I've ever seen. I have to thank you and the Mayor will be congratulating you, trust me."

I never heard from him again. But in all honesty, that doesn't matter one bit. ◊

TONY RASEMUS, 54, served two years as a marine in Vietnam. A lifelong resident of New York City, Tony has learned many skills over the years; he trained in iron working and construction and volunteered his skills at Ground Zero the day after the attack on September 11th.[22] Tony is a wiry man with a bristling reddish mustache and unstoppable energy, frequently leaping to his feet to reenact the scenes he describes. He pantomimes how he lifted rubble with his hands and illustrates the proper posture for crawling into a debris cavity.

———

That first day, I went to volunteer at the Javits Center and nothing was organized.[23] There must have been 10,000 people from all walks of life. People wearing shorts and sandals . . . I don't know what they were thinking. Totally inappropriate clothes for rescue work.

They had various tables set up for construction workers, ironworkers, riggers.

I said: "Where do you want me to go?"

"Go over there. They're taking names."

I saw a couple of guys hanging around with tool belts; I had my Carhartts[24] with me. So I went toward them.

My wife had gone down with me; she was trying to find a place to give blood. She said, "Do you want me to hang out with you for a while?" I said, "Nah, I don't know. This might take a while." So we said good-bye. She wasn't gone five minutes before we got loaded onto a bus, a variety of guys, and it was zip! Right into Ground Zero.

*   *   *

There was all kinds of people on that bus but mostly construction workers and ironworkers. They let us off a few blocks away. Don't ask me exactly where we were, I didn't know the geography of that area when it was functional. I'd been in Windows on the World and I think at one time I knew somebody who had an office in one of the Towers. So my knowledge of the geography basically consists of the subway tunnels and the PATH trains.

---

[22]Iron and construction workers came into high demand because of all the metal debris that had to be cut away in order to check for survivors.

[23]The Jacob K. Javtis Convention Center, called the "Marketplace for the World", located at 34th Street and the West Side highway. A positively mammoth center which can be adapted to fit any sort of gathering imaginable.

[24]Heavy duty work pants.

We couldn't go directly into the rubble. We had to move west and swing around. They took us down the West Side Highway. People cheering with signs up on the sides of the road.

I can tell you one thing that you should probably note in your thing there:[25] as my wife and I went down to the Javits Center, I was looking at the various construction sites around the city. I noticed that all the cranes were at a rest position. Right? There was no ironwork being done. You want to find heroes from the rescue workers; those ironworkers are the guys to talk to.

I'm telling you right now: outside the EMS people and the firemen, there was nobody in this city stood taller than the ironworkers. They shut down every construction site in New York City. I heard some of them talking to each other and they said, "This is the only job we got now." And I'm telling you, you could tell. You saw nobody climbing the iron all over the city. Nobody up there riveting. Nobody doing bolt-ups. I think they did an across-the-board union call. They shut down and headed in.

The second group I saw the most of down there was the electrical workers. Lots and lots of IBEW.[26] They had apparently lost some people.

*　　*　　*

Firemen were still suppressing fires in the rubble. We had a couple of cutters, a couple of burners, some small pieces of heavy equipment. I don't know which Tower I was working in. You couldn't tell anything from what you were standing on, I can tell you that.

We were all on the bucket brigade that first day. A whole bunch of guys would go up, pick up a piece of debris, stick it in a bucket, and pass it back down the line. Empty it out and pass

Fred George

---

[25]He points to the recorder.
[26]International Brotherhood of Electrical Workers.

the empty bucket forward. Buckets. Whatever you could pick up with your hands went into the buckets.

You'd create a cavity in the debris. Then you'd hear somebody say, "Stop! Bring the dogs, bring the dogs!" The rescue dogs would come up; mostly German Shepherds but I saw one Golden Retriever. They'd get in there and sniff around. Next word you'd hear: "Bring the body bag up." The rescue workers would go in and drag out whatever they could by hand.

We didn't find anybody alive.

Twice I heard rumors that they'd brought people out alive. I think the last group was on the 13th, which was Thursday. A fire truck had been buried and I heard at first that they'd found five guys, but later I heard it was two. All I know is this: no one I personally saw was alive. And I never saw a whole body, either. Just parts, everywhere. Everywhere. Pieces strewn in with the rubble, not readily apparent until you got right up to it.

And construction workers didn't touch anything. The protocol was to call for the EMS people and they'd come up to handle it. Then you'd go right back to the Pile. You'd leap back in and get to work again.

* * *

There was one section that had been a bridge between two buildings and the dogs were going crazy over there, right? Me and the ironworkers went over to it and some battalion chief, some fire guy, said, "No, you can't get in here, this is unstable."

Sheperd Sherbell

And we were like, "Yeah, we know, but the dogs. There's something in there, let us go in." The guy kept telling us it's dangerous but the ironworkers were like, "We walk around 30 stories in the air on bare beams, okay? Trust us. We can do this."

So about two hours pass by and they finally let us in. We brought out 12 bodies. Later on, I talked to a fireman and

I learned that the location had been one of their command posts.

See, when the firemen showed up at the Towers - because of the immensity of the disaster - they set up command posts so they could say, "This company goes here, this company goes there." We brought out nothing but firemen from under that bridge. Damn thing must've dropped right on top of them.

*　*　*

The second day, Thursday, I went down to the Javits Center, same as before. It was now a lot more organized. But it was also taking a lot longer to get people dispatched. They were trying to segregate people by skills and, this time, they said, "We need acetylene burners."

There was a bunch of us who stuck up our hands. "Yeah, that's us."

They said, "C'mon," and they moved us to the front of this long line. There was, like, 18 or 20 of us and everybody had to sign up: what your skills were, your phone number, your address, all this and that. But after we did the paper, we stood around and waited. And we waited. And we waited. And we waited, for whatever vehicle was supposed to take us down.

*　*　*

This stake bed truck pulled up and a crew of guys, ironworkers, got off. They were wearing dark blue T-shirts that said, "Ironworker Local, Mackinaw City, Michigan."

I went up to one guy, I said: "Are you really from Michigan?"

He says, "Yeah. A bunch of us came down. Five of us."

I said, "Not for nothing, but how'd you get here?"

He looks at me, he grins real big, and he says, "Drove all night."

Right then we're standing there, and the guys in charge, the foremen - they called out, they wanted a burn crew. Like I said, there were, like, 20 of us and these guys are ready to go. These guys are like Marines, man, I mean ready to freakin' God-damned go. But they sent another crew, instead, so we had to wait again.

After about two hours, we got sick and tired of waiting. Some of the local guys from New York City and Jersey? They just started walking down the West Side Highway. I mean, you could see where the smoke column was above Ground Zero, so we started out. A group of

20 guys straggling down the road with equipment.

*   *   *

At one point a truck goin' north on the West Side Highway stopped and we talked to the people inside. It was this pickup truck with a young couple in it.

"Yeah," they're saying to my guys. "We love you. Thank you. Way to go."

Next thing I heard was one of my burners say: "Can you drive us down there?"

I have no idea who this couple was. They were in a brand new pick-up truck and they thought about it and said, "Yeah. We can get you down there." So 14 or 16 of us jump up on the flatbed - boom boom boom – of this regular old-fashioned American pickup truck.

I'm sitting squashed in next to the tailgate. There's an ironworker to my right who's French Canadian, must weigh at least 250 pounds. I got him around the neck and if he falls off the truck, he's gonna take my arm with him. His neck was the size of my thigh. Another guy was holding on to me, right? Everybody's just grabbing on. All we needed was a little olive oil on us. We were in that truck like sardines.

And these guys were going into Ground Zero for the first time so everybody's like, "We gotta come up with a story to get through the blockade."

See, we weren't officially cleared 'cause we just walked away from the Javits Center. We didn't want to wait. But I told the guys, "Look. We don't have to come up with a story. I was there yesterday. The firemen and the policemen ain't gonna stop you. They got too many brothers buried underneath. The only problem we're gonna have is the military."

My crew had all sorts of battle gear. Tools and pry bars and the like. And this couple with the pickup, all we heard out of them was, "Watch the paint! Watch the paint! Watch the paint!"

*   *   *

So we got down there and I'm trying to lead the guys back to where I was the day before. But by this time they had the whole thing barricaded off, we couldn't go in.

Then all of a sudden this group of guys, there was about a dozen of them wearing those orange reflective road crew vests that say, "CONTRACTOR" on the back? They had some kind of pass. I think they were being brought in to adjust for safety, they looked like engineering types. But the orange vests were being let through, so this crew I was with, we immediately piled in behind them to get through the barricades.

This national guardsman stops us and says, "Wait a minute, what's going on here?"

We said: "We're the burn crew, we're with the contractors! We're supposed to go through with the contractors!"

The guard's standing there about to give us a hard time when the contractor turns around and realizes, all of a sudden, that he's got a lot more guys than he came with.

He grins and says, "Oh yeah. They're with us. Let them through.

The guard's like, "Yeah. Uh – okay. Sure. Bring them through." And that's how we got in the second day.

*   *   *

I took over an acetylene torch from a fireman crew. These firemen were not leaving, right? Their battalion chief would tell them, "Go home. Get some sleep." They would stand up and shuffle off to somewhere until the battalion chief left. Then they would go back in.

They were bringing in trucks from welding suppliers because nobody had proper acetylene gear. And there was this one fireman who I found slumped up against a wall, wearing his burn clothes.

I went up to him and said, "Listen, I'm here with a burn crew but I don't got the appropriate stuff. Can I . . .?"

The guy started to get up, he said, "I'll go, I'll go back in."

So I said, "Look. I'm an ironworker. Let me take care of this for you. Get some sleep."

So the guy gave me his stuff and I wore his gear and went back out into the Pile. A leather jacket so the sparks don't bother you. The goggles. Heavy-duty gloves that don't burn. And my Carhartts.

See, you couldn't burn a hole through a 20-foot I-beam, whatever the dimension is, and jerk it out with a crane. There might be somebody trapped underneath. So you cut it off here, cut it off there, have three or four guys lift it out and put it on something, haul it away.

Build another cavity, start all over again. I put in 12 hours on Thursday September 13th.

* * *

I didn't go back down on Friday because I knew it was gonna be ridiculous getting back through security. We got lucky those two days. But late Saturday night the Javits Center called me, saying they needed more burn people. Because I'd filled in that form on Thursday, they said, "We gotcha down as a torch guy. Can you come in?"

"Yeah," I said. "Sure."

I was back down at Javits by six on Sunday morning. And it was the same thing all over again.

* * *

I was so proud of my city. This is my home. The way everybody stood up. There wasn't any crying, there wasn't any weeping, there wasn't any pulling of hair. It was just, "We're gonna deal with this." And nothing was gonna stop anybody. If anybody wanted to see what this city is truly all about, it was down there. (*Plate 13*)

My wife's manicurist is from Russia; she's lived here about eight years. She says to me just the other day, "I've never seen Americans be like this. I never knew this is how Americans could be. Especially in New York."

I think that's what a lot of people think. And that's a shame. ℥

CASSANDRA MEDLEY has been a staff writer for an ABC soap opera, a Walt Disney screen-writing fellow, and an award-winning playwright. Her work has garnered her an Outer Critics Drama Circle Desk Award, a New York Foundation for the Arts Fellowship, and a playwriting grant from the National Endowment for the Arts. Like many other New Yorkers, Cassandra refused to be denied the chance to help at Ground Zero.

———

For the record, here, let me set the tone:

I'm in Union Square last week – this is a week after the attack. And I overhear two men talking.

One of them said: "My office is down on 20th and there's this hotdog vendor who I always buy lunch from. He looks like one of them."

The other guy goes, "I knew it, they're everywhere."

The first guy says, "Just two days before the attack this vendor says to me, 'You know what? Saddam Hussein does not like America.'"

The other guys says, "You're kidding me."

And the first guy says, "Nope. That's what he said, that's just what he said. So. Think I should call the FBI and report him?"

Blind, unreasonable, paranoid fear. Or is it?

*   *   *

I went down to visit a very close friend who lives on Laight Street in TriBeCa on September 12th. She had been evacuated the day before and she'd just got back into her apartment. I went so we could comfort each other.

I got down to 8th Street by train, but then you had to walk further down since the subways weren't running in the aftermath of the attack. I walked as far as Houston Street where I ran into a total blockade.

The police had set up those blue sawhorses. You couldn't go further south unless you lived there or you were an aid worker. You had to show ID. Now I was stuck. I didn't fit the qualifications. But ironically I ran into somebody I hadn't seen in years: Pat, a painter who lived on the next block.

We hugged and I said "Would you say that I'm visiting you so I can get through?"

We're in line and this one policeman—this big, big guy - he knows I'd been on line before to no avail. I approach him and say, "I'm visiting her." I point to Pat.

He kinda looks at me. Then at Pat. Then at me. He shrugs and he lets us through.

*　　*　　*

After you cross Houston and Canal? The smell? It was like tire rubber combined with bitter tobacco. A sickening sweetness. My friend had a mask for me to wear because it was overpowering.

So I walked up to Canal Street and my friend lives right on the next block. I go to her place and we hang out.

Across the street from her, a gourmet caterer had opened up his shop, taken all the food he had and was cooking these huge meals. We joined the owner's two teenage daughters and a couple of neighbors in this troop of people volunteering to deliver food. There was a police station and a triage center a short block away. We had to cross the blockade again. Same burly guys, same strict faces. But as soon as they saw food, no problem.

We had to stop at a deli to get some other provisions. And here were these tall teenage boys on the corner, I'd say 17 or 18 years old. Watching.

One of them says to me: "Hey. How're you doing? You all delivering food? And they let you through, is that right?"

I said that yes, that was the case.

"Well, *we* want to get through," he says. "We want to help pick up the bodies."

"Why on earth would you want to do that?"

"We want to get some training. You know how graveyard workers get paid really well? So we want to get some training and put that on our résumés…that we helped pick up bodies."

We recommended that they go further down Canal Street.

After we'd passed them by, my friend said to me, "There's some things you just can't write, can't make up."

*   *   *

We got closer to Chambers Street and it became more and more like a war zone. You could see smoke and rubble. We were surrounded by army jeeps and soldiers and national guardsmen. Sniffing dogs. Doctors and medics, standing around. Waiting. Volunteering. All these spaces with IV stands. Personnel in blue hospital scrubs. Hundreds of empty beds with white sheets, waiting for people.

But nobody was there. The place was set up for survivors they couldn't find.

I heard somebody on the phone saying: "No, I couldn't get their name. I just told them to keep breathing. I think they're at Roosevelt or Beth Israel Hospital but I didn't get their name. I told them to relax." It sounded like someone had been rescued and they'd had trouble identifying that person.

At this triage center? Efficiency and silence at the same time. Now rescue workers were coming in, firemen and policemen. They were dusty and sweaty. Beleaguered. Men and women. They were asking for sandwiches and lots of ice because it was a hot day. We got ice in large plastic bags from area restaurants with their doors open.

For us, it was all catch as catch can. We were just wandering the streets, creating jobs for ourselves. Helping out whomever and wherever we could.

*   *   *

We got back to the gourmet place and they were already making sandwiches - some vegetarian, some cold cuts. We were wrapping them together.

It felt so good to be doing something. Through all these checkpoints, all the security, if you had food, you were waived on. All you had to do was appear with a cake or something.

Later on that day, we were making our rounds again and everyone started yelling, "Get down!" Additional parts of 7 World Trade Center were falling down.

It was like a war zone. I'm telling you. A battlefield after the battle.

*   *   *

I think what moved me the most. . .see, I've always had an ambivalent attitude toward the police.

As a black woman, I have relatives and friends who have had racial incidents. You've heard about them on the news? Well, I've lived through them. It changes your attitude. But what I saw that day was a complete change.

We were delivering food and there would be neighbors who would come up to us and say, "You know what? The policemen and firemen around the corner? They don't have anything to eat."

Sheperd Sherbell

There was a phalanx of uniforms all along North Moore Street. Policemen - women and men, both white and black - running in and out in shifts, standing guard. We would gather up some food and come around to them. And their faces! Such glowing appreciation. "Oh, thank you! *Thank* you!" Personal, eye to eye contact.

People came out from the back of the station house. "Oh, this is so great! *Wonderful*! Thank you!" It was so important to have that human contact. And to feel that change in my experience. For me, it was that mutual empathy and sympathy that let us know we were all in this together. Huge perception shifts when a person said, "Oh my God! A *salad*! Thank you!"

See, everyone was broken. Everyone was tired. Overwhelmed. It was the day after and the folks in uniform were still in shock, having been down there so long, round the clock since it had happened. We all were.

*   *   *

I feel that such a time calls for us to look at our collective humanity. This is the reason why some of the current flag-waving disturbs me.

The way that public figures are speaking about the attack on America, the attack on *this* country. They're going on without empathic acknowledgement that we're *all* in this. The whole world. Every nation has been wounded.

I would prefer, myself. . .well. If there were an international flag? If there were a Planet Earth flag? I would be waving it. ✝

In the wake of the attack on the Trade Towers, Canal Street turned into a highly-organized, bustling refugee camp overnight. Restaurant owners like ANTONIO "NINO" VENDOME scrambled to feed thousands of hungry rescue workers, police and firemen from their kitchens. Nino's, a neighborhood favorite at 431 Canal Street covered the initial expenses, estimated in the millions of dollars, from its own pockets. Nino is a square-shouldered, barrel-chested man in his 50s with spiky, steel-gray hair.

———

Why did I open my restaurant to these people?[27] The way I figure it, it's not a birthright to have people risk their lives and their families and not be appreciated.

Let me tell you something. My family came here from Italy in 1955 with four suitcases and $40 to get started. I started off in real estate and ended up doing pretty well. I established myself in business when I was 21. I put a key in the door of my office at four a.m. one morning and I turned it. I knew there were risks being out on these streets. But I also knew there were men in blue there to protect me. I could never have established anything if these men in uniform weren't out there putting their lives on the line.

*　　*　　*

The attack happened on Tuesday morning and I organized the restaurant on Wednesday so that we were up and running as a relief shelter on Thursday. We've been going 24/7 ever since and we've been here a month already. When we started, it was obviously an emergency situation; none of us knew whether we'd be operating for one day, two days, three. But as long as I'm around, we'll stay open. We'll stay open as long as we're needed.

Our location is ideal - we're about 15 blocks from Ground Zero, a distance where the air quality is acceptable. And I'd say we're feeding between five to seven thousand people a day, which includes everyone involved in the rescue efforts - policemen, national guardsmen, Con Edison power company workers, sanitation workers, utility company workers - everyone working in the rubble right now. We don't ask questions. Our doors are open, whether you want to come in and cook for yourself, or you want a meal prepared. Maybe you just need a place to sit and take a nap. That happens a lot.

We've served maybe 100,000 meals, thousands of different people coming in here. Bone tired. Exhausted. They come in from different situations. But I have yet to hear one of them complain.

---

[27] The rescue workers.

*   *   *

I set my own staff of about 10 to 15 people to work. Then I hired 50 more and took in at least a 100 volunteers to round out the ranks.

We're handling an incredible volume right now. We prepare 2700 eggs a day; 400 pounds of potatoes; 350 pounds of meat; 180 pounds of bacon and 150 pounds of sausage; 125 loaves of bread.

We're going to need more bodies as we become more organized. Volunteers have been coming in from around the country. We have no idea where they're staying, all I know is they're coming here selflessly to do what they can.

For instance, across the street there's a barbeque truck run by a church that drove up from Texas. They're cooking ribs and chicken in this submarine-like oven. This thing must be 30 feet long and it's cooking 24 hours a day, seven days a week. There's a tractor-trailer behind it full of chopped wood to keep the grill fires going.

And this is what Americans are doing. We're very resourceful people.

*   *   *

We were originally producing all the food we serve here, but the volume grew so rapidly. My place can only handle 150 people at a time. So the question became: how do you serve 7000? It's a game of logistics.

I've recruited other restaurants in the community to help prepare food. Immediately, we were looking for products with nutritional value. Carbohydrates and proteins; lots of pastas and chicken. The mainstay is Italian, but we have French food, all different types of vegetarian cuisine. We've asked suppliers for donations of stews, chickens, frozen pizzas. Romaine and mesculin lettuce. Sports drinks and sodas. Kitchen stuff,too: garbage cans, paper napkins, folding chairs and toilet paper. There's a list outside that specifies who's contributed everything.

And people have astounded us with their generosity. Right after this whole thing happened, we had survivors from Windows on the World working with us. One of their managers was working here one night. His name was Steve - I forgot his last name. After all he went through, here he is, laughing and joking to keep people's spirits up, serving chicken and salad. A great guy to be around.[28]

He was working with us night and day. Then they had a memorial for some of his co-workers and he just fell apart. He hasn't been back since.

We're just letting him be, for now. What else can you do? He's been through a lot, he *gave* us a lot. We'll reach out to him in time.

For some of these people . . . what can I say? It's going to take a lot of time.

* * *

I started my business right around the corner from here about 30 years ago. I've been involved in restaurants for well over 12 years.

In all that time, I've seen the selflessness of people and I've seen the selfishness. This situation has brought out the worst in some people.

At one point early on, I needed more refrigeration. So I went to a local distributor and he drops off a refrigerator. The thing is worth $500 and he wants to charge me a thousand a month rent for it. I agreed because I needed it right away to do the job. I knew I was getting robbed.

So I explain to this guy that he's a thief and a crook and that this is not the time to be doing this sort of thing. Then I cut the check for a thousand. He comes to the restaurant and says, "What about another thousand for the deposit?"

I said, "You know what? Do I look like a fucking idiot to you? Get out of here before I decide to do something stupid."

So I've experienced that kind of idiocy. It doesn't matter. I've experienced some unbelievable unity as well.

* * *

There's a big sign out front that reads, "Feel free to share your thoughts with our nation during this tragic time." People have taken us up on the offer. The walls and windows of buildings up and down Canal Street are covered with stickers as far as the eye can see. And

---

[28]Windows on the World, the famous 30,000 square foot restaurant located high atop the north Tower, 73 employees were lost.

each sticker bears a unique message from a rescue worker:

"Love like your life depends on it."

"From the ashes, we will rise and become even stronger."

"It's time for America to bless God."

"Dennis is gone, a wonderful spirit."

"Life is good even when it's bad."

"How much foreign oil are you using? It's now our war."

"New York: May we never forget how close we've become. Let's stay this way."

There are drawings made by children. Crayon-on-oak tag images of Captain America and Superman. The cartoon hero, Wolverine slashing through Osama bin Laden with his razor-sharp claws. Inscriptions from representatives of many religions and countries. The Baha'I B'rith, the Jews for Jesus. The Virgin Islands, Argentina, and the Dominican Republic.

I read these notes and I was blown away.

They started out as a way to help the rescue workers with their mental fatigue and stress. We issued them papers to express themselves, whatever their thoughts may be. The terror, their families, the war, whatever. It started small. People would write a note and stick it to the wall. Now the entire block's covered. We've encapsulated them under plastic to protect them from the elements.

I've been talking to the New York Historical Society and the Museum of Modern Art. This is something that needs to be documented for the world to reflect on in perpetuity. A thousand years from now, people will want to know. People will want to read what our reactions were.

*   *   *

All these fellas, these uniformed officers. We serve them a meal and they're so grateful. "Thank you, thank you, thank you." That's all I keep hearing.

These are the guys who were running into the buildings as they were collapsing and everybody else was running out. They've lost their dear friends, but they still stop to say thank you when someone hands them a bottle of water.

We want to make a statement here that identifies unsung heroes. I am so grateful for this privilege.

*   *   *

I'm no one special, write that in your story. I'm like everyone else. We're all constantly working to keep a roof over our heads, working to nurture our children.

These people we're feeding? None of them live in three and four-garage homes. None of them is secure with their children's educations. They're just men and women whose families live with the idea that every day they go to work, they might not be coming back. In the '60's we used to call them pigs and God knows what. But it's time we stopped cursing at them and spitting at them and taking them for granted. It's time to take a step back and appreciate what these uniformed people do.

So you plant the seed of knowledge. You plant a vision. Maybe now some coffee shop in Utah will look at that uniformed individual a little differently. And maybe they can't afford to give him a free meal, but they can afford to treat him with the respect that he deserves.

That's our goal. To protect these people who are the mainstay of this country. ⚡

BOBBIE-JO RANDOLPH, 27, a volunteer firefighter and on-call EMT from Hermiston, Oregon. Bobbie-Jo is a member of DMAT, the Disaster Medical Assistance Team,[29] a branch of FEMA. She was one of several rescue workers who responded to the call for assistance at Ground Zero from all corners of the nation.

––––––

A few years ago I met a pediatric emergency physician in Portland named Dr. Helen Miller. She works for Oregon Health Science University. She had moved to Oregon from Seattle, where she had been on the DMAT team. There was no DMAT team in Oregon and she had really enjoyed working on it. So she decided to put one together. I went to an emergency medical conference in Sun River outside of Bend and met her. She was recruiting people.

Initially, there weren't more than 20 members so we had to get more people interested. The 20 of us went out into our communities and said, "This is what we do. If you're interested, come talk to us and we'll try to get your applications through." That was in 1999.

At first, we did some local events with the Seattle county team. In Oregon, they have what's called the Gorge Games, a large athletic event where they do everything from windsurfing to running to biking. It's a televised event, a week long, and we provided the medical care. But mostly what we'd done over the past two years was drill ourselves for upcoming disasters that may or may not occur.

When New York happened, we thought we were ready. Ground Zero was the first time the federal government deployed us.

*　*　*

When a national disaster is declared, DMAT teams from around the country send their rosters to the head honcho at FEMA. We were one of the first teams to get our roster in. We said, "Look, we have an entire team ready to go."

Normally there are different team levels: One, Two, and Three. Level One is the highest priority with teams that have more people and more equipment. Oregon is currently at Level Two, so we're not normally the first people to get called. But having our rosters together helped. There were several other teams that were closer, like Ohio and North

---

[29]DMAT is usually a regional group of volunteer medical professionals and support personnel with the ability to quickly move into a disaster area and provide medical care. DMAT's can rapidly deploy for any type of disaster that requires an immediate medial response.

Carolina; those teams were deployed first. Each team went to Ground Zero for a two-week period before getting rotated out and replaced by another team. Oregon team members were asked to go in mid-October.

We sent a first team out, then the government asked for more. I was on the second team. I think I left the 1st of November, 2001.

* * *

I was in bed when I heard about the attack. Someone called me and said, "Turn on your TV right now," and I did. It was still before the second plane had hit. It must have been 5 or 5:30 in the morning on the West Coast.

I was watching when the second plane hit and at first I thought it was a replay of the first plane's impact. Then I realized: that's a different building - there are *two* buildings on fire. I'd never been to New York before. I'd never seen the Trade Towers except on TV or in photos.

Honestly, the first thing that came to my mind was that I wanted to jump on a plane, get over there and help. That, and my concern for the safety of the people in the buildings. Before the buildings collapsed, I wondered what the chance for that was. These are things that go through your mind when you're a firefighter.

I remember thinking, "Those buildings are huge. A few floors might collapse, but nothing else." It was never in my mind that the entire building could fall. But when it did, I remember thinking, "There hasn't been enough time for the firefighters to get out." Wondering if there were people still in there . . . did they evacuate? The news wasn't coming as fast as my mind was going.

I remember sitting there, watching everything and wondering if this was real. It seemed more like a movie. I guess everybody says that, huh?

* * *

After the buildings fell and we knew that it was definitely going to be a disaster site, I called my team leader. Dr. Miller had been inundated with phone calls. She told me what she'd told everyone else: that already called FEMA and told them we were available if anyone needed us. At that point, nothing was set up yet. It was too soon. This was the day of the attack.

She asked us to just keep a watch on our e-mail rather than keep calling her. She wanted the phone lines open in case. Every day we'd get an update: "We're still on the list. Keep your bags packed, we don't know when we'll go."

Usually you have anywhere from 12 to 24 hours from getting the call to leaving for a disaster location. DMAT wants to know that you can be on a plane immediately after they call. That makes it difficult in Oregon, which is a huge state. I live three hours from the nearest major airport. Plus I had my kids to think about. I do different things with them on different occasions. When I left for New York, my mom, my ex-mother-in-law, and the boys' father took turns watching them.

*   *   *

I remember getting the call. Helen didn't do it, because she was already here in New York with the first Oregon team sent out. But with Helen in New York, Steve Myron was the acting team leader in Oregon. He happens to live 20 minutes from me - we were the only two people from our team living in Eastern Oregon - and we're good friends of six years. He's a police officer, an EMT, a firefighter, and he does HazMat.[30] A King of All Trades, an awesome guy.

Steve and I were involved in something called the Hometown Heroes Ball, which was sponsored by our local country radio station. It was a huge dance with a few famous singers - New Yorkers probably don't know them because they're country singers. But the dance was to thank all the local heroes, the firefighters, policemen, EMTs, even servicemen, anyone with a badge. They all got in for free and their guests paid a nominal fee and all of that money plus money from a silent auction went to the charity funds in New York.

I'd been listening to the radio and planning on going to the Ball. Steve had put together a PowerPoint[31] program about September 11th, a very moving presentation with music under it, about three songs long. We'd shown it to a few people and everyone cried when they watched it. But he hadn't done anything else with it. I thought, "Wouldn't it be great if we could do the PowerPoint show at the fund raiser?" So I called up the radio station.

I told them we had a team that was working in New York right then and that we'd love to show the presentation and talk about what we do. They said, "Awesome. We'd like to see it."

*   *   *

We went to the dance and showed the PowerPoint program. About halfway through the slide show, there are pictures of the firefighters, paramedics and police who died, 15 or 20

---

[30]Hazardous Materials
[31]A Microsoft computer program popular for designing graphic presentations.

243

slides with 15 or 20 people on each slide. People started clapping as the pictures came up. They offered a standing ovation and continued clapping until the images of the people were done and the show went back to slides of the site. I looked around the room and there wasn't a table where people weren't crying openly.

We were sitting at our table when Helen called us on Steve's cell phone.

"Put a second team together," she said. "You're coming out here on Monday." Just like that we were being deployed.

We got right up from the table, left the dance and went home to pack.

*   *   *

We have such a large team now that I wasn't positive they'd have a spot for me.

Steve left that dance and drove the two and a half hours to Boardman, where he lives. He found out he needed to have two doctors, two nurses, two paramedics, a team leader, a logistics officer, and an administrative officer.

Steve called and said, "I can't use you as an EMT, but I need an Administrative Officer. You're it." Our regular AO was in Maryland. I could fill in during a pinch.

The Ball was Saturday night and Steve called me at about two o'clock in the morning on Sunday. We left that Monday morning, the 5th of November on Delta airlines. We landed in LaGuardia airport.

*   *   *

Getting on the plane was difficult for some of the team members. Some of them were pretty nervous about the previous hijackings. I was anxious only during the take-off and landing, but I was fine once we were in the air.

Normally we wear uniforms on the plane, but this time we didn't. We were told by our team leader that DMAT didn't want people in uniforms on the aircraft.

I'd been fairly quiet, into myself during most of the flight. I was sitting next to three women. I heard them talking as we were flying over New York. They asked me what I did. I told them that I was coming to help with recovery and to provide medical care for the workers. They were very excited about that.

I asked them, "What do you do?"

They said, "We work for Martha Stewart. We're her aides."

"That's great," I said. "I love Martha Stewart." I'm looking out the plane's window and, since I figured they lived in New York, I asked them to start pointing out the buildings.

They pointed out the Empire State Building. Then we saw lights and smoke – you could see it real clear from the plane, and one of the girls said, "That's it. That's Ground Zero."

One of the girls had a hard time talking. She turned away.

*　　*　　*

We landed and went into the airport. Most of us were carrying these enormous hiking back packs since we'd often been deployed to places where there was no running water, no bathrooms, no anything. Even though we found out at the last minute that we'd be staying at a hotel, we still brought the bags. Normally, I carry cooking utensils. Salt and pepper. Dehydrated meals that you can buy in camping stores; the kind that you can make by opening, adding water, or clicking to heat. But we took all that out. We waited in line for a van that picked us up and took us to the Sheraton New Yorker.[32]

That van ride? I thought I was going to die. It was the worst driving I'd ever seen, my first taste of New York traffic. But our driver was from Maryland – some kind of volunteer. He'd been here since Day Two, picking people up and dropping them off at the airport, shuttling them back and forth between the hotel and Ground Zero. I guess he'd learned a lot about driving fast 'cause he drove as badly as I thought the New York cabbies were supposed to.

I think we went over two or three of those concrete lane dividers? We went the wrong way down one-way streets. I had a middle seat in the front of the van with nothing to hold onto. I was literally grabbing the bottom of the seat. My knuckles had to have been white.

*　　*　　*

I wasn't expecting to stay at one of the nicer hotels in New York, either. The first night we were there, Mayor Giuliani was holding some sort of event. So I remember having my pack on as we walked up . . . looking up and seeing all these video cameras and photographers lined up behind red velvet ropes, flashbulbs going off. I guess they were there to take

---

[32] On 47th and 7th.

pictures of celebrities, but when they saw us, it was some kind of photo opportunity.

I was overwhelmed. I couldn't understand how anyone would have any interest whatsoever in taking our pictures. I was there to do relief work. I felt it wasn't about pictures of me, it was about the policemen, the firemen, and the rescue workers who had been there since Day One. They were doing the work, not me.

*   *   *

We were debriefed that evening for 15 minutes in a room where FEMA was stationed - they had the whole top floor of the Sheraton. We sat down in the debriefing area and were told that at seven o'clock the next morning, we would be meeting in the hotel lobby in uniform. Our first shift would start at eight. They didn't tell us what we'd be doing or what we'd see. We had a rough idea: running a medical tent at the site. And we had already talked to Helen, who had been here for some time and had told us a little about her experiences.

We knew we'd be caring for construction workers and firefighters. We knew that mostly the medical teams were handling foreign bodies in the eyes, respiratory problems, lacerations, things like that. As administrative officer, I would be keeping track of everyone's hours, getting everyone's social security number correct, paycheck administration, that sort of thing. Essentially, we weren't told much. Just when and where to meet, plus hospitality things like where we could do laundry, where to get food, and so on.

We had our ID pictures taken. We needed two cards with us at all times in order to get through the Ground Zero security checkpoints; we wore them on lanyards around our necks. The first card was from the Mayor's Office of Emergency Management. The second was our National Disaster Medical Systems ID issued by FEMA; it had a logo of the Trade Towers in the background and an American flag. At the bottom it said, "September 11th" and listed our team designation as Oregon 2 DMAT.

*   *   *

After the debriefing, we got a 15 minute break. Then they took us down for a quick tour of Ground Zero.

We took the van over. Again I was sitting in that middle seat. I'm looking forward through the windshield and the first things I saw as we came down the West Side Highway were the cranes and smoke. We went through a few security checkpoints.

Then, to my left, I saw a building with computers hanging out of it by their cords. I don't know why that was, although it's not an odd thing to happen during a fire. Maybe the firefighters had gone in spraying water and blown the equipment out the window. Or the wind from the blast did it – I don't know. This was nearly two months after the disaster, so who knows? But the building was charred on the outside. All the windows and most of the wall structures were gone; you could look right inside and see the offices. Everything was so burned, it was hard to tell what was what.

Then I saw the Cross[33] and, personally? I took it as a sign that God was there.

These two beams, one horizontal and one vertical, that were riveted together in the perfect shape of a cross. It was sticking out of the ground - you've seen this on the news. It was brown, rust colored. There was a firefighter's jacket hanging off one of the spars. I would guess it was probably 12 feet high from the ground to the crosspiece; maybe another six feet tall above that to the top. It stood down in the pit, about three stories high. (*Plate 14*)

I got a little teary-eyed when I saw it. Then came the realization that I didn't have a right to cry.

It wasn't my turf. It hadn't been my family and friends who'd perished. It's not my town, it's not my state. I had no right to grieve as the other people did. Understand that right next to the Cross was a small makeshift building where the firefighters were stationed. There were firefighters walking across the dirt road to and from the site; sitting along the road. They looked like soldiers come in off a battlefield. Dirty. Exhausted. Changed. Some of them would nod their heads and wave as we went by. I realized they couldn't see me in the van but it didn't seem right to let those people see me cry when this was their site, not mine.

*   *   *

After passing the Cross, we continued down the West Side Highway until we came to our tent. We were relieving two teams that were on duty at the time: Seattle, King County DMAT 1 and another that was, I think, from Oklahoma.

Our medical tent was positioned under the walkway that used to connect 1 World Financial Center to the Marriott Hotel. But the bridge had collapsed. All that was left was the stubble of the walkway jutting out from the building. We entrusted ourselves to the firemen who told us that this was the safest place from falling debris.

---

[33] The Cross Bobbie-Jo's referring to, one of several found at the disaster site, was a crucifix-shaped hunk of I-Beam which was more than likely recovered from the wreckage of the U.S. Customhouse at 6 World Trade Center. It drew the attention of the international media when clergy blessed it in a solemn ceremony held outside the building on October 4th, 2001.

When I say *our tent* I should clarify: there were actually three. The first tent was our treatment center. A tent behind that one held our medical supplies and the tent closest to 1 World Financial served as our command tent. There was one doctor, one nurse, and one paramedic in each tent.

When we got out of the van, you got hit by the smell. It depended on the wind but sometimes you'd smell nothing and sometimes it was very bad. Contrary to popular belief, it wasn't so much decay and the smell of death by the time I got there as it was the smell of ground cement and sulfur and burning rubble. But it definitely stunk. We were issued heavy industrial respirators a couple days after we arrived.

Inside the command tent I found two team leaders, two logistics officers and two administrative officers; one from each of the two teams we were replacing. They were downgrading the site; our one team would replace two. When we arrived, there were 20 people on the site in two teams, ten and ten. After the downgrade, the ten from my team would provide the care that 20 people had offered before us.

I'm assuming that the downgrade happened because the site wasn't as busy medically as it had been. And we knew that sometime in the near future, DMAT would be pulling out their medical tents completely.

*   *   *

We didn't bring our own medical equipment. Everything from gauze to defibrillators was provided for us. We had a full running mini-ER in each tent, like a MASH[34] unit. We had a huge Ryder truck stocked with pharmaceuticals. Our team pharmacist kept track of everything from narcotics to ibuprofen.

I had to learn the administrative system as I went along each day. The paperwork system, the computer system, tracking information . . . we had laptops in our tents connected to the city, the Mayor's Office and our own command center at the Sheraton. Everyone needed to know how many people we treated, who we treated, what we had treated them for, whether or not they were transported to a hospital, whether or not they were transported by paramedics or had walked in on their own. What medications they had been given - everything needed to be tracked. That was my job.

*   *   *

---

[34]Mobile Army Surgical Hospital.

I did meander to the treatment tents once in a while to get an idea of what was going on. I normally work as an EMT so, of course, I had curiosities. For me, if there was anything difficult about being at Ground Zero, it's that I wasn't able to really treat anyone. Instead, I helped the team leader arrange to clean out the outhouses that hadn't been emptied by the Sanitation Department when the site was closed on Veteran's Day. I was needed for different purposes.

So we were orientated. Most of us were pretty tired after that. We went back to the hotel and spent $30 on one meal at TGI Fridays. Welcome to New York.

At seven the next morning, we reported to the lobby. At eight o'clock the teams we were relieving left, and we were on our own to take care of everything.

*   *   *

I was in the command tent when I first saw them pull a fireman out of the Pit.

The paramedics were stationed right next to our tent, their ambulances were parked there, and they would come in and chit-chat with us. While I was talking to one, another guy came in and said, "They just found another body."

The paramedic I was with said, "All right, let's go."

He walked out. I talked to my team leader, told him where I was at with my job. He gave me permission to go on outside. One of our paramedics, Christie Wells, wanted to go with me. So she and I walked down the ramp that led to the site, down into the Pit with its 30-story cranes.

An ambulance had already backed in with its rear toward the Trade Center. Its lights were on. They were waiting for the remains. People lined up along either side of the ramp. There were stairs going down into the Pit; someone had shored them into the ground. There were people at the top of the stairwell, plus paramedics, firefighters, construction workers, and a fireman with Chaplain written across his helmet. There were several Red Cross volunteers. We all waited – no more than ten or 15 minutes, but it seemed like a long time.

They knew this body belonged to a firefighter because they had found a jacket. When the procession passed me firefighters went by with a Stokes Basket, which is a metal mesh basket used to extricate bodies from wherever they're found, beneath a cliff or under some rubble. The basket was draped with a white sheet. They stopped at the top of the stairs and put the American flag over the body. The priest said a few words that I couldn't hear, a prayer of some sort. All activity had stopped in the Pit. When the priest finished, I saw people make the sign of the cross.

Then everyone stood at attention. Someone told us to salute. They got the basket into position and it went by all of us toward the ambulance. They put the body in the ambulance and gave the basket to the paramedics. A couple of firefighters got in the ambulance and closed the doors. The sirens were turned on and they drove out of the site, north along the West Side Highway. There was a point where someone said it was okay to take your hand down from the salute.

When the ambulance was gone and people were starting to disperse, Christie and I walked back toward our tent. I didn't run, but I walked really fast because it was all I could do to keep my tears from flowing. I got into the tent, I took a deep breath, and immediately started crying.

I wanted to wait until I was hiding. I still didn't feel I had the right to cry.

*   *   *

On the two month anniversary of September 11th, it was also President's Day and my son's birthday. He had a dinosaur birthday cake at the same time Hillary Clinton, the Mayor, and the Governor signed my helmet. I met the President of the United States; he talked to me while walking by.

He was shaking everyone's hand and he shook mine. We were wearing different uniforms than everyone else and he noticed that.

He said, "Who do you work for and where are you from?"

I said, "I'm from Oregon DMAT."

"That's a long way to come. Thank you for coming. We appreciate you."

What I felt then and what I still feel is that he had no idea that, by saying that, he would make me very happy. I live in a town of 13,000 people. I'm just a small-town girl, who never thought that she'd meet the President of the United States, let alone hear that she was appreciated by him. I shook his hand and in two seconds he made me feel like I made a difference.

*   *   *

The next day an aircraft crashed in the Rockaways.[35] It was a tough time. To be standing at Ground Zero and hear the calls for the airplane downed. To see everything stopping; they evacuated the Pit. I could hear what sounded like every siren in New York going toward Queens. I remember what an eerie feeling that was, thinking, "This must be just a tiny taste of what it must have been like for some of those other firefighters and paramedics on September 11th.

We went back to the hotel, back to the Living Room Area, as I called it. They had put out about 50 recliners in an old ballroom with a couple of big screen TVs. Everyone was silent, glued to the television, watching everything happen. Trying to figure out why it had happened again.

I remember looking in some of the rescue workers' eyes and seeing them relive what had happened before. Some had fears and some had utter disbelief. It was one of the only times in my life that I was truly scared.

Drew Nederpelt

*   *   *

I had four T-shirts, one for each of my children. All the guys and women that I worked with

---

[35]American Airlines Flight 587 crashed shortly after 9 a.m. on 11/12/01 while taking off from John F. Kennedy International Airport bound for Santo Domingo. 260 people aboard were killed. While the crash was inevitably attributed to an accident rather than sabotage, the emotional impact on New Yorkers was especially harsh. The city was still reeling from a similarly horrifying wake-up call on a beautiful work day morning not two months before. The public was still justifiably anxious about additional terrorist attacks.

signed them. The writing says everything from, "Thank you for letting your Mom come," to "Always remember that she is a hero." To this day, I can't pick up those T-shirts and not cry.

It helped me to remember that other people actually thought I helped and that other people thought of me as a hero. And I never did anything heroic. I don't feel like a hero. I'm *not* a hero. I don't feel like I should be in a book. And yet that's what these inscriptions say.

I wasn't home two months when my son's teacher asked me to come visit in his class. I went, I took the helmet and the T-shirt that had been made for Brandon. There must have been 20 to 25 children in this classroom and they were glued. They wanted autographs, they touched my helmet, they looked at the pictures. What a great feeling to go to your child's classroom and have all your friends think that you're a hero.

I've been enjoying the kids a lot more lately. Mostly because, between my divorce and being here in New York . . . well, it was an enlightening experience in a lot of ways. It made me realize pretty much what everyone else thinks: that life is short and there are only a few things that are important enough to focus on. Unfortunately, we focus on things that aren't as important. But I don't want to be 30 years down the road now saying, "Why didn't I do this? Why didn't I do that?"

I want to say, "I did all the things I wanted to do. My life was great, I lived it the best I could and I'm happy with what I did."

*   *   *

Now I feel I have the right to grieve. After being there, the firefighters, the policemen and the paramedics all made it clear to me that they not only appreciated me coming, but that I had just as much right to be there as anyone. ৎ

The firm of Leslie E. Robertson Associates[36] has designed some of the preeminent buildings of our time, including the Bank of China Tower in Hong Kong; the Continental Airlines Arena in East Rutherford, New Jersey; the International Trade Center in Barcelona, Spain; the Crystal Cathedral in Garden Grove, California; and the World Trade Center. LERA also serves as a consultant for many of the world's current architectural marvels.[37]

RICK ZOTTOLA has been the LERA partner in charge of the World Trade Center for several years. He rushed to the Towers in 1993 to spearhead damage assessments after a terrorist bomb exploded in the basement. He knows the World Trade Center complex as well as any person alive. In his calm, soft-spoken manner, Rick describes the unique role LERA has taken in the Ground Zero clean-up. He also details his firm's love for an architectural miracle that will never again command the New York skyline.

———

After the disaster, we all had great hopes that there would be significant rescues. But it quickly became apparent that wasn't going to be the case. The collapse, the devastation was so horrible that very few people survived. So the rescue effort is over. Now there's two different efforts going on: clean-up and recovery.

The DDC[38] is responsible for clean-up. We've been retained by them because we knew every nuance of the facility. It was a magnificent structure, we loved it. So we consult with the DDC and demolition crews on the structural integrity of the buildings. It's a big job.

Recovery, on the other hand, is retrieving remains. The Fire Department and the Police Department - plus other emergency workers - are responsible for that.

*   *   *

We designed the structures of the Towers. We were consultants to the Port Authority and to the architect, Minora Yamasaki and Associates. It was a big project. Some last details were still being implemented, but the Towers were pretty much completed before 1976.

---

[36]LERA
[37]LERA founder Leslie Robertson is credited with designing the Twin Towers' innovative tubular steel frame. A week before the hijacked planes struck the Towers, he addressed his colleagues at a conference in Germany. Robertson noted that the Towers were strong enough to take a direct hit from an aircraft [Philadelphia Enquirer, 9/12/2001]. No one can fault him for underestimating terrorism's resources. The destruction brought to bear upon the Towers on September 11th was beyond the scope of anyone's imagination.
[38]Department of Design and Construction, a New York City agency.

Dick Duane

Buildings are living organisms, they're not static things. They age, they wear out, there's maintenance and capital improvements to the property. You improve them as office tenants and technologies advance. We had an ongoing contract with the Port Authority to provide maintenance and services over the last 30 years since the original design.

For example, a tenant might move into many contiguous floors, and they may want to put in their own interconnecting stairs. This would require a structural cut in the slabs. We've been involved in that sort of work.

The Port Authority really takes care of their property well - much better than private organizations. So our work centered around a continuous structural integrity inspection program. We inspected columns, slabs, and structural things throughout the complex. External and internal - wherever you can physically access and visually see.

Some places . . . well, the layperson can't see them. For instance, to see some of the columns inside the central core, we'd climb on top of an elevator and ride inside the shaft. We could inspect the structure much better from that vantage point.

*   *   *

The footprint of each Tower is an acre square - the two Towers make up just two of the 16 total acres of the World Trade Center. The 16 acres comprised six buildings: World Trade 1 and 2 the Towers. The Marriott Hotel, which is 3 World Trade Center, though no one ever called it that. Then 4 and 5 which are low-rise buildings. And 6 World Trade Center, which was the old Customs House.

7 World Trade Center was actually across the street. We didn't do the original design for it; I think we may have worked on some of the early foundations. The Port Authority owned the property, but it was developed, built and operated by a private developer. Six months

ago, Silverstein[39] took over a 99-year lease on World Trade 7 and the entire 16 acre World Trade Center complex.

The site is huge. The Towers, of course, came down but every single square foot of the structure wasn't destroyed. Over that 16 acres are two distinct sections of basement. You may have read in the papers about something called The Bathtub, which is surrounded by the slurry wall. It's being stabilized by tie-dash back anchors to keep the river out. A parcel of property on the eastern edge of the complex incorporates remnant levels of an old railroad station. The Hudson Manhattan Railroad Station was an underground rail 40 to 50 feet below street level that was demolished to build the World Trade complex. At its lowest part, the basement runs seven levels deep to include parking, mechanical space, storage space, FBI and CIA parking.

The vault, which you've heard so much about, was in that old H & M basement facility. Built around the turn of the century, it held gold and silver for the Bank of Nova Scotia. Following the attack, it was a huge security issue. The bank needed our assistance because they didn't know how to get their trucks in there. The New York City and Port Authority police got a lot of precious metals out under . . . we're talking not the greatest of circumstances. But considering the security risk those metals posed, they were happy to get that stuff out.

*　　*　　*

So much of the basement structure was damaged, but – as I say - parts of it weren't. Just luck, really. These were big buildings, but they fell as they were designed to, more or less straight down. When we were poking around the rubble, we found three different levels of damage, crudely-speaking:

First, you had the parts that weren't really damaged. Second, you had parts that were damaged, but accessible; slabs, for instance, that broke away from their columns that you could still move through crawling on your hands on knees. The third condition is total collapse – that is: just a big pile of debris. Those are crude increments, of course; you have many gradations in between.

---

[39]On April 26th, 2001, Silverstein Properties in partnership with Westfield America gained control over the World Trade Center by signing a 99-year lease worth $3.2 billion. This deal put control of the largest U.S. office complex in private hands for the first time. Previously, the Trade Center had been managed by the Port Authority of New York and New Jersey. The destruction of the Towers did not release Silverstein from having to make approximately $100 million a year in payment to the Port Authority. Silverstein filed an insurance claim for $7.2 billion, which became a hotly debated topic. 9/11 dealt a devastating blow to the American and international insurance trade, which were strained by unprecedented payments.

We're still doing condition assessments for the DDC underground. This means suiting up in hardhats, respirators, flashlights, knee pads, elbow pads, and a good pair of waterproof boots; there's a lot of water down there. You've got to get down on your hands and knees and crawl around.

Unfortunately, we have significant experience with this after the 1993 bombing. It's all visual work. I've got a team working with me to gauge the beams, the slabs.

How do you know if you're safe? Ah . . . you don't, really. Things are horribly wrecked and precarious. The weight of all that damaged stuff is tremendous. A square foot concrete slab weighs much more than I do. But the good news is that a person walking through the rubble is not adding any significant load. That's why rescue workers, right after the Towers came down and there was the frantic urge to get survivors out . . . they were literally able to jump right on top of the pile.

But machinery can weigh tons. That's important to know because if you have heavy equipment treading around, you need to know where there are voids below. Areas for potential collapse.

*　　*　　*

We know that rescue workers looking for survivors were able to get everywhere that you could imagine. As they went in, they would spray-paint the walls fluorescent orange and yellow. As we were doing condition assessments, we didn't find anyplace that wasn't marked. It's remarkable. They would identify their emergency unit, like "ESU INDIANA" or "ESU NEW JERSEY" and they'd log the date.

It's like walking down into a coal mine. It's not a straight path, you have to meander down stairs, negotiate over a rubble pile, maybe go down another set of stairs. And it's dangerous; it's not humanly possible to remember how you got in there. So the rescuers would paint arrows on the wall showing the way out. That's what they do. These guys are trained.

We found their markings going down all six levels, all the way to the bottom. They left no stone unturned. They did a wonderful job.

*　　*　　*

Or role differed compared to other engineering firms that were down there. No one could get around underground like we could — we know that place so well. So we worked with the firemen to help them with the recovery.

They had a uniquely difficult situation. The disaster not only destroyed the buildings, it destroyed the management systems. Those systems, and the people with knowledge of those systems from the Port Authority just disappeared. Blown to the four winds within seconds.

So there was no one for the firemen to turn to. They didn't know where the fire stairs were, for instance. 350 lost firemen were in fire stairs and places of egress so they wanted to know where those stairways were. We needed to show them the access points. And they'd say, "Under that pile of debris? Okay, let's dig there."

Keep in mind that the World Trade Center is one of the most complicated complexes in the world. *Without* there being a disaster, it was incredibly complicated. Main basement, shallow basement, the old basement. . . it's a subterranean city with buildings on top as big as cities themselves. The firemen had to struggle with no information, no drawings.

So one of the services we provided, we appraised dangerous areas and hanging debris. We advised whether it's safe or not to go in, how far to go in, how much digging they should do, what tools they should use, whether it's safe for machinery. We'd say things like, "There should be a stairwell over here. There's a corridor down there. Straight down about 10 feet."

And there's a lot of camaraderie that makes it all work. It wasn't a mandated activity. We just saw the need and began to assist the Port Authority employees on an ad hoc basis. For us, it's been important, therapeutic work.

*   *   *

30 years ago, I was playing Little League baseball, so I wasn't part of the design process. I've been with the company for 20 years now, and for the past six, I've been the partner in charge of our efforts for the Trade Center. I've gotten to know the Towers really well.

On the morning of September 11th, I was sitting with another engineer, hunched over some drawings, talking in our offices eight blocks from the Trade Center. All of a sudden this blizzard of paper - snowflake-sized particles - flew by the window. We're only eight blocks away, but we didn't hear anything, I don't know why. So the first thing I thought of was a ticker-tape parade. But it was coming from too high up. I got up and looked out the window.

We have this wonderful view from immediately south-east of the complex. We saw smoke coming out of the north Tower, but we didn't know what it was. We thought someone's floor had caught fire.

Within five minutes, I got a call from Frank DeMartini, one of our colleagues at the Port

Authority. He helped us with reconstruction after the 1993 bombing. A very good friend.

He said: "Rick! There's been a massive explosion in Tower One. Grab a few engineers and some drawings. Come right over."

He didn't know what had happened. His office was on the 88th Floor, the plane hit on the 92nd floor. His wife, an employee of ours, was with him. She was stationed at a small ERA office in Tower Two. But that morning, she was over having coffee with Frank. She was getting up to leave when the plane hit.

We were all thinking of the 1993, a terrorist bomb. We thought, "Here we go again." We got our gear and left.

*　　*　　*

People were running in the opposite direction as we were hustling over in the street. We heard them say that a plane had hit. We figured it was a commuter plane. We had no idea how big that hole was.

We were just two minutes away from south Tower and we were about to go up to our office when we heard this roar overhead, we looked up and there it was. Flying low over the city. We saw the second plane impact the south Tower and watched the explosion from the street, completely dumbfounded.

I don't know how to explain it, that feeling you get just before you go into shock. Everything drains out of your consciousness; everything unique about you is drained out. I'm convinced that everyone standing in the street looking up at the Towers was the same. It didn't matter who you were or what your life experience was. At that moment, all of that stuff was drained out of you. And you're just looking up.

*　　*　　*

Our first inclination was to keep going. Then our senses came back to us. We realized the north Tower had been attacked, the south Tower'd been attacked. We needed to turn around. There was nothing that a structural engineer could do in an attack situation. Who knew what else was going to happen? We returned, and our goal became about attending to the safety of our employees and formulating an evacuation plan.

We stayed here the whole time and encouraged people not to leave. We didn't know if more planes were going to come. Fortunately or unfortunately, the people here had to witness the south Tower falling. After that we couldn't see anything. The wind was blowing in our direction and lower Manhattan was engulfed in a cloud like nuclear winter.

* * *

Everyone who normally reported to our office in the south Tower survived. Nicole DeMartini, Frank's wife, got out safely. By happenstance, the other engineers from that office reported to the central office that day. One of them had been scheduled for outside scans of the building that day. He was supposed to ride the window-washing maintenance platforms from top to bottom. Obviously, he was very fortunate.

Frank DeMartini didn't make it out. He stayed with a few colleagues from the Port Authority, assisting and ushering people out. We can piece this together from calls made by fire marshals. It was a bad situation up there. People trapped in elevators. Firemen rushing up, trying to find those elevator cars. No clue as to what was about to happen.[40] (*Plate 15*)

Frank loved the facility, he knew it like no one else. He had his walkie-talkie and was talking to people trapped in elevators. The last anyone heard from him, he was in one of the elevator rooms saying that the elevator equipment was ready to collapse.

"Send some engineers up right away. We've got to get these people out of here."

* * *

Before the World Trade Center was built, that side of lower Manhattan was a bunch of low-rise, three to 20-story brick buildings. Even though it was private development, the Trade Center was an urban renewal project. It cleared out a lot of the old buildings, including the H & M train station. And when it was built, it looked stupid. These huge Towers with nothing else around them.

As you get toward central downtown and the Wall Street basin, you can still find your pre-War buildings, but the West Side grew up around the Towers. It's probably safe to say that this city grew up around the Trade Center. And now they're gone. You'll never see that panoramic view again.

Southern Manhattan has grown out into the bay over the century. That area was muck. The H&M station was built around 1920 and, essentially, the basement had to be sea wall; it's constructed with eight-foot thick concrete. That wonderful old piece of construction was incorporated into the World Trade Center. It's an intact piece of history that we're hoping

---

[40]Tom Haddad (see his story in the AT THE TOWERS section) later saw a picture of Frank DeMartini on a television special and recalled that Frank had been one of the men who'd come to rescue him after the first plane impacted.

will continue into the next development.

*   *   *

We're already involved with the rebuilding process on a consulting level. It's very early, though. The city says that they'll be cleaning up until the late Spring of 2002. They're stabilizing the site so they can turn it over to whoever develops it. And that gets complicated.

The Port Authority owns the land, but Silverstein owns the 99-year lease. The government has pledged billions of dollars to reconstruction. With insurance companies involved, it's an economic as well as a political decision. All you can hope is that the right things happen and something important gets built on the skyline.

We're unique in our sensitivities to the project. We have little actual influence, but our dream is that portions of the structure built in the 60's will remain so you'll have three tiers of history: the 1920's, the 1960's and the new construction. We also think that the salvaged structure has a technical use. It protects a portion of the PATH station in the lowest basement. If retained, it should help speed up the return of PATH service.

*   *   *

An organization called the American Society of Civil Engineers is undertaking a structural study trying to understand the collapse mechanism. Keeping in mind that people above the impact zones had no way out, they hope to improve the design of buildings in the future.

I'm not sure how much good that'll do. What you learn about the World Trade Center applies to the World Trade Center. How that translates to other buildings is a little unclear since the World Trade Center was unique.

But what saddens me most is that no one is going to remember all the wonderful intricacies of the complex because of the thorough destruction.

Our structural assessments went way beyond just looking at the columns. We crawled through tiny spaces in the old H&M basement and saw the building's mechanical systems first hand, which were tremendous, like no other because of the size and magnitude. Six stations, each the size of small houses, controlled air-conditioning, heating, electricity and emergency generators. River water was pumped in through two pairs of pipes five feet in diameter to cool the air-conditioning systems. Our inspections took us to all these places and more.

We rode the tops of elevators looking at the guts of this building. How many people can say that? We rode in mid-air on window-washing platforms two feet wide. The north Tower was close to 1400 feet tall, the TV antenna added another 360.

We inspected that antenna, too, you know. You had to climb up a ladder inside it until you reached the tippy-top where the flashing light was. At that point, you weren't inside anymore. You were climbing outside, 1750 feet in the air.

There aren't many chances in the world to get that high. ƻ

MIKE POTASSO, 33. Paramedic. A strong back and a crushing handshake. He has jet-black hair cut close on top and shaved to a buzz on the sides. Small, round spectacles accentuate an intelligent, sincere face.

On the ride to Ground Zero, Mike steeled himself for what he thought would be the hardest day of his professional life. Instead, he found himself confronted with the frustration that many emergency workers felt that day, waiting on the front lines for survivors who never arrived.

———

You see a lot of strange things on this job. Some real characters. I've picked up Elvis a few times, picked up Jesus. I had one woman who thought she'd dislocated her Fallopian Tubes. You can't make this stuff up.

Three weeks ago, for instance, I responded to a call: "Pedestrian struck. Someone hit by a car, resulting in cardiac arrest."

We got to the scene. It was a long street with a car up on the sidewalk. We hollered to one of the cops, "Where's the cardiac arrest?"

The cop says, "No, no. This guy isn't under arrest. We're just giving him a ticket."

"There's no one here in cardiac arrest?"

The cop says, "Not that I know of."

Whatever, right? "Okay, see you later."

We see another ambulance at the end of the block and go to check it out, see if they need help. This other cop comes up to us and says, "Where you goin'? We got a cardiac arrest in the back of the bus."

Aha. "Where'd he come from?"

It was the pedestrian. The car ran up on the sidewalk and knocked over a street sign which struck him and killed him instantly, just some guy walking by.

The irony is this: the pedestrian was killed by a "No Standing" sign.

We laughed. You have to. It may seem a bit callous to look at something that way. But when you're constantly exposed to this stuff, you tend to separate yourself from the situation to protect your own well-being.

* * *

Medic school was rough. I'd work my regular 40 hours, plus one to two tours of overtime a week. Then I'd have to go to class three days a week for four hours, and eight hours on alternating Saturdays. Plus, I had rotations to do: 150 hours in the ambulance; 150 in the ER; 40 hours ICU; 40 hours OB/GYN; 40 hours geriatric care; 24 hours pediatric; 24 hours OR; 24 hours Psych; 40 hours of internship. This went on for 11 months. When you get out, you're ready for anything.

As a medic, you learn basic pharmacology and cardiology, respiratory and metabolic emergencies. Along with anatomy and physiology, we're also responsible for 26 different medications and the performance of certain skills such as synchronized cardio-verting, cardio-pacing, EKG interpretation, the starting and maintenance of IVs, endotrachial intubation, needle decompression, and drug therapy.

None of it helped one bit on the 11th. Not one bit.

* * *

I work FDNY*EMS, Battalion 31, Cumberland Station, downtown Brooklyn. We're on the Brooklyn side of the Manhattan and Brooklyn Bridges, a stone's throw from downtown Manhattan. I was working the evening shift, three p.m. to 11 p.m. the night before September 11th. When my partner and I got off work, our lieutenant told us there was overtime available in the morning. My partner was trying to talk me into working it, but I was already working a double the following day. He took the overtime and I went home.

A friend of mine called me at about 9:30 the next morning. "You're never gonna guess what happened," she says, and she tells me that someone just bombed the World Trade Center and the Pentagon.

"Okay. You're full of shit. I'm tired. I had a really busy tour last night, stop playing games."

She says, "Shut up and turn on the TV."

I put it on. I'm just watching. Can't believe it. Both Towers. And I thought, "I gotta go."

My mom called me just then. She said, "Where are you going?"

263

I said, "I'm going into work."

"What do you mean? Don't go. Please."

But you see something like that happen? You don't even think. You just start going through the process:

How am I going to get to work? If I take my car, I'm never gonna get in there - it's bedlam down there. Rosedale doesn't have a subway, it's the most south-easterly part of Queens, the last town in Queens on the south shore. We have the Long Island Railroad, but I wasn't about to wait on that. So I grabbed my bike. It's only about 18 miles from home to my station house.

*　　*　　*

I strapped my tech bag on the back of my bike. I didn't have any uniforms in my locker at the station, but, I always keep one spare uniform at home, so I packed it with my boots. My helmet and my utility belt was in the station locker, thank God. The utility belt's got my shears, my catheters, a clip for my radio, my narcotics, etcetera.

I'd biked to the station before during nice weather. Normally, it takes me an hour, but I didn't think about the time or the distance. I was just pedaling. It was harder than usual because I was laden down with equipment; the 15-pound tech bag and another ten pounds or so on my back.

I took the Conduit to Atlantic Avenue, then Atlantic all the way down to Carlton Avenue, which I cut across to get up to my station. Nobody was on the road. Normally, you could see the Towers clearly from the Belt Parkway. But all I saw was smoke. It was after 10:30 in the morning and I think they had collapsed already.

*　　*　　*

As soon as I got to Bedford Avenue, I noticed more congestion, more people. A mosque in that area was chanting over their PA system. Their daily prayers seemed to resonate and echo over the gridlock on Bedford. Nobody was moving anywhere. So many things going on at once. People coming out of Manhattan, people trying to get into Manhattan, everybody stuck. Everything locked down.

I got to my station around 11:30 and there was a lot of confusion. Nobody knew what was going on. Everybody was running around getting extra equipment ready. It's like you're going into battle; you go through your checklist. Trauma dressings, blood pressure cuffs, narcotics, goggles. Bandages, shears, stethoscopes. The bigger stuff was already down at the site: longboards, collars, oxygen, IV bags, and intubation equipment.

A city bus was coming to take us into Manhattan. The overnight crew was mandated to cover the day tour while the rest of us went to Ground Zero. NYC EMS handles an average of 3000 to 3500 calls every day, so some of us had to stay behind.

We were just getting ready to go when one of our ambulances came back covered in rubble. We treated a couple of our own guys who were overwhelmed. They were there before the Towers collapsed and described what they'd seen. People jumping out of buildings. The debris, the explosions. The Towers coming down.

We gave them oxygen and started IVs. One guy came in covered in debris with a separated shoulder - don't ask me how that happened. We took a spare ambulance and ran them over to Brooklyn Hospital, two blocks away.

They were in shock. They kept repeating, "We did our best, we did our best."

*   *   *

That's when I learned that my partner, Gary, was missing. Initially, there were six guys from my station missing. Our unit was one of the first to respond to emergencies in Manhattan from Brooklyn.

All I heard was: "They can't find Gary. They can't find Danny. Where's Gary?"

The worst possibilities resonated in my head. Gary's missing. He took the overtime from me so I could get some sleep. We'd been talking about it, I'd been making all sorts of excuses. "I'm working the night shift instead . . ."

He'd looked at me and said, "Listen. Why don't you just tell me you don't want to work the overtime, champ?" For all I know, things could have happened differently. I could have been right where he was.

*   *   *

They got us all on the busses and that emergency mentality set in. "Okay, shit's going down." And you separate everything, block it out." You just focus on the job. You're running on automatic pilot, reviewing the protocols.

What do you do first with patients?

We use the "START System." Simple Triage And Rapid Treatment. You quickly assess life-threatening injuries and stabilize them as best you can. Is the patient breathing? No. Try to establish an airway. Still not breathing? Try again. Still not breathing? Black tag. There's nothing you can do for him. Move on to the next patient.

Patient bleeding heavy? Stop it as best you can. Red tag him and move on. The walking wounded get green tags and everyone in between gets a yellow.

Once your initial triage is done, you sort your patients. Do they need immediate transport to the hospital? Can they be treated and released at the scene? Or do they go to the morgue?

It's an archaic way of looking at things, but when you're overwhelmed by the amount of patients, you have to do the greatest good for the most amount of people.

I've been in situations where you have 10, 15 patients at the same time. Like car accidents. I worked in the Bronx one time and a livery cab ran up the sidewalk and plowed down six people. I'd only been on the job for a week. We were the third or fourth unit on the scene. One woman had her leg completely amputated. Another woman had bi-lateral mid-shaft femur fractures. There was a kid pinned under a car. The driver had a broken arm. The whole area was cordoned off. The Fire Department was on the scene, extricating people from vehicles. There were copters overhead and spectators.

This is what I expected to find at Ground Zero.

*   *   *

By the time we got down there, we found that the command structure had already collapsed at the site. For a while, we just stood there. Then they finally deployed us over to Stuyvessant High School on West Street where we set up a triage center in the hallway.

For a while, we were just standing in this dark room and I felt weird. Teams were rotating in and out, lots of EMS teams on the perimeter. I wanted to be helping people, but there was nothing to do except stand there.

*   *   *

One my best friends, a guy I've known for 15 years, is a firefighter for 16 Truck from the Upper East Side. I knew he was working that day and wondered where he was.

I happened to run into him in the midst of everything.

"Are you all right?" I said.

"Fine," he said. "I'm okay."

He didn't have his cell phone with him, so I called his wife. "Freida. I'm here with Joe. He's okay." I called his brother and let everyone know that we were together. I saw that happened a lot, this makeshift method of communication.

* * *

So. Standing in a dark room. Waiting and waiting to go in.

It got so frustrating. I kept thinking, "This is what I came here to do. To get my hands dirty, treat whoever I gotta treat." But I also felt like a spectator. It was horrible. And this went on for hours.

I had two people on my team who'd just got their EMT cards two weeks before. This was their first big job. I tried to help them stay focused. They were so eager, like: "We *have* to go in, we *have* to go in." I understood. It's what happens on a job. You're pumped.

But you have to restrain yourself. We couldn't all go because we'd just get in the way. EMS is not designed to work in a pit like that. You're there to treat people. If you get injured yourself, you can't really help someone if you're hurt.

There were more people helping at Ground Zero than anyone knew what to do with. They came pouring in from all over throughout the day. A fire department from Nova Scotia, Canada – where the hell had they come from? Teams from Boston; from Pennsylvania. They just came - you'd be surprised how fast. The Red Cross was already organized, handing out water bottles. Hatzolah, the volunteer Jewish ambulance company was making kugel.[41] You had a lot of people helping out.

An auditorium at the school became the main staging area for the rescue efforts. NYPD, K-9, and ESU had their command post there and we had a makeshift command post as well. ESU is the Police Department's Emergency Services Unit - Special Ops, tactical. They respond to things like barricaded patients, hostage situations, rescues, subway jobs. They're trained as EMTs, but they're paramilitary; these guys are like a SWAT team.

---

[41]An eastern European baked pudding, often made with noodles or grains and usually featuring a sweet element such as raisins or apples.

So what? We just sat there watching people go back and forth. I felt so useless. Like I didn't even belong there. And I kept wondering what had happened to Gary.

Block it out, block it out, block it out.

* * *

I didn't feel like I was contributing at all.

Not to sound jaded, but EMS is a job where you're dealing with people on a very intimate level. It's a very personal thing, a unique field.

I mean, consider this: people can relate to a fire emergency. They can see the flames as they come toward them. Same thing with a police emergency: you can see what's going on. But with EMS, you're not plunging into a fire, you're not in danger of getting shot. Our enemy is often airborne or blood-borne. You may not see it until it's too late. You're more worried about contracting HIV, TB, or Hepatitis. You hope you don't bring it home to your family.

It's a more cerebral job. You're directly involved, one-on-one with people in need. You deal with people when they're vulnerable, really hurt. And since you can't fix everything, you try to make them as comfortable as you can, often as they're dying in your arms.

It's not all miserable. You get to know your patients sometimes. You might go to their house three, four or five times. You get to know their families. Like I said, it's a very intimate job.

I remember when I delivered my first baby. So far I've done six. You walk home thinking, "This is what I did today."

* * *

The chain of command was quickly re-established. The OEM's office was in 7 World Trade Center, but they had to evacuate before the building collapsed. They had to completely restructure from the bottom up.[42]

You saw people dragging equipment to a forward triage in the American Express building at 3 World Financial Center - a forward is your initial casualty center. If you have an MCI - a multiple casualty incident - the forward triage becomes the safe zone out of harm's way.

---

[42]The Mayor of New York's Office of Emergency Management. When 7 World Trade showed signs of collapsing early on the afternoon of the 11th, the OEM was forced to abandon its crisis headquarters (see: KEN LONGERT and FRED HORNE in THE AFTERMATH section.)

It's where you treat incoming patients. From there, they get stabilized and shipped to one of the triage centers where they're further examined. Then, we decide whether they're going home or to the hospital.

EMS will set up a staging sector where ambulances come in; a transportation office, which tells you, "You have to take *this* patient to *that* hospital." The transportation office is important because if all the patients went to the same hospital, then that hospital would be overwhelmed and wouldn't be able to treat anybody.

New York City has certain hospitals that do specialty referrals. Montefiore is a replantation center; you take your amputees there because they have surgeons who've been specially trained to reattach limbs.

Jacobi is an antidote hospital; snakebites go to Jacobi because the Bronx Zoo is right next to it.

You have special trauma teams at Bellevue, St. Vincent's, Jacobi again. Depending on what your patient needs and depending on their stability, you take them to a specialty referral hospital.

When no bodies were found, we just waited. And waited. I remembered an earthquake in India where they pulled survivors out 30 days later. You hoped for the best.

*　　*　　*

I remember it had just gotten dark. Eerie silence, maybe eight o'clock at night. A few rescue workers stumbled into our area; we washed out their eyes and treated them for minor lacerations. Nothing serious. People were still going up to the site, coming back. Going up, coming back.

I took a walk with one my lieutenants. The neighborhood was all shut down, there was no electricity or plumbing in all of lower Manhattan. The only lights were from generator-powered halogen lights; the reflections bounced off burnt cars and crushed fire-trucks; the only sound, the generators in the background, like sitting down on your porch and hearing a lawnmower in the distance on a quiet Sunday afternoon. Two blocks from Ground Zero, you're walking through memos from people's offices.

I picked up papers and read them. Someone's shopping list. Reports for that day. There were pieces of a coffee mug, and personal effects of people who had been sitting at their desks one day and then *bam!* It's over. This was quite a ways from the actual site of the Towers, too. The debris had scattered far and wide.

At one point, we came to a clearing in the buildings. You could see where Towers 1 and 2 used to be. In the background, a building was still burning inside, like a scene from a movie. *The Terminator*. Firefighters were scurrying to put it out; they'd been at it for hours, they were dead tired.

*   *   *

We walked back down to the site and over to the high school. I realized, "I can't stand here and watch this anymore. There's nobody coming out. There are people in there who haven't had relief all day."

There was a stretcher full of equipment going down there, masks and boots mostly. So I grabbed my team and said, "Come on. We're going."

I didn't care anymore if I was going to get in trouble. I couldn't take standing there doing nothing anymore.

We went into forward triage and I said, "Where do you need us?"

The looks on their faces. You knew right away they weren't going to turn down any helpers. I kicked myself for having waited so long.

*   *   *

Down there, all they were pulling out was body parts. I think we only retrieved one whole body. I'm looking at the faces of some of these new guys on my team. They're like, "What do we do?"

I just looked away and kept digging.

The triage had turned into a morgue. There was a woman's severed hand. You could still see the engagement ring on her finger. A torso. The constant smell of burnt flesh.

At one point we saw a rope sticking up from the ash. You saw everyone running toward it; they thought it was a firefighter. Ten of us jumped onto that pile and started moving shit out of the way, hoping it was something. Well, it wasn't. It was a piece of rope, alright. But there was nobody connected to it.

You tried to keep your emotions in check. But it was tough.

*　　*　　*

At one point, we got word they were shutting down the forward triage. NYPD had taken over and made it officially a morgue. So we went right back to our triage area and continued helping rescue workers and construction workers with minor injuries. We slept a few hours upstairs on the third floor of the high school. And like I said, there was no power, so one of the firemen brought his bolt-cutters and ran upstairs to the cafeteria. Clipped all the locks on the freezers. We were hungry. We ate cold chicken patties.

After I was there for 24 hours, they ordered us home to get some rest. I went home, got six hours of sleep, and went back to work at midnight on the 12th, expecting to go back down to Ground Zero, but no. The orders were: "Just go down to your regular line unit."

I felt horrible. But I knew what they were doing. A person that has a chest pain in some other part of the city needs us just as much as anybody else.

Luckily, everyone from my group had made it out okay. I learned that Gary was alive. He had been hospitalized, but went back to the site and started treating people. He'd been right there in the thick of things all along.

*　　*　　*

I remember coming home that night after Ground Zero and walking down my block. Everyone was honking and yelling this pro-USA stuff. People were shaking my hand. And I felt guilty. Someone called me a hero. I didn't feel like one. What did I do? What had I accomplished? I didn't help anybody out, I didn't make one bit of difference. This, more than anything else, was the thought that stayed with me. So as days went by, I kept going back there.

I worked my regular shift and, on days off, I worked overtime at Ground Zero. Or I attended a memorial service. I did that up until November when my father passed away and I didn't

Andrew Walker

have time to spend down there anymore.

Still, part of me wonders if there was something else I should have done. Maybe I should have worked overtime that morning. Maybe I should have just gone down earlier on my own, not waited for my station. You know, so many people went down there on their own.

I'm thankful I'm alive. And I try not to feel guilty about it. But the truth is I do. ƨ

THE AFTERMATH

The heart of Morris dancing is unadulterated joy. It is art too blissful for soldiers. Still, Morris dancers die in war. Take the case of Steven Adams. Steven danced the Morris his whole life. He died in the World Trade Center on September 11th.

JESSICA MURROW, 51, tells the story of the marriage she shared with a rare and wonderful man.

———

Steve was a very different kind of man. He was quiet, reserved. An incredibly gentle man. I thought, "Wow. What a relief from the other men I've known." Steven wasn't New York City fast-lane. He was country. Simpler. And here he was, a single, good-looking guy. He was fun, and he was available! I mean, how many men in their forties in this world are *available*?

Jessica Murrow

Morris dancing[1] is a huge community and I've played the Morris for years, I'm a musician. The Marlboro team started coming to New York to dance on Easter – Steve and I met twenty years ago – we would bump into each other. Morris dancing is all about tradition and it became a tradition that Steve and his friends would come down from Vermont[2] and stay with me each spring. We rented a house together one summer near Amherst and our relationship just started working.

I had my eyes set on him. I was 44 and I'd had a lot of relationships, not really successful. I'd never gotten married the whole time and I really wanted to make something work.

*   *   *

---

[1]The ancient art form of Morris Dancing arose from the primeval mists of England as a form of harvest celebration and agrarian ritual. Over the centuries, participation in the dance dwindled until it found a home on academic campuses in England, Canada, and America. Morris dancers are a colorful sight with their bells and waving hankies; they move to simple tunes played on fiddles, pipe-n-tabors or melodeons.

[2]Steven joined the Vermont-based Marlboro Morris team in 1980. His friend, Christoffer Carstanjen, danced with the team for ten years. The two friends were strangely reunited by the tragedy of 9/11. Shortly before nine a.m., United Airlines Flight 175 flying from Boston to Los Angeles, struck the South Tower with Christoffer on board. Within half an hour, the North Tower was struck by a second hijacked plane. Sadly, Steven was working on the 107th floor. Neither man was seen alive again.

He had problems making a success of his life. I thought, "Well, I'm good at that, I can fix this in a heartbeat." He applied to law school but he didn't get in. He was in debt; he had to return his car because he couldn't make the payments, and then he owed money on it just the same. He had huge tuition payments to Marlboro College where he'd put himself through and graduated at age 34.

Steve had a real blue-collar background. His father and mother were cooks. They never earned a lot and Steve never learned how to deal with money.

In fact, he struggled all his life to make ends meet. He would claim it wasn't that he didn't know how to handle money, it was that he never made enough. Always robbing Peter to pay Paul. It's a whole way of being when you're broke all the time.

I come from an upper middle-class background, so I didn't have that experience. I've never had trouble with money, I've always made enough. Never spent a dime if I'm *not* making money. You know, I just knew how to do it. Steve didn't.

As years went by I realized this was a major problem. We were getting together and I was really getting pissed off. Steve was living in Massachusetts at the time and it was winter. He would ride his bike 15 miles each way to earn six bucks an hour as a meat cutter. The worst job at the worst pay – he was badly in debt and threatening his life every day to keep it going. I would visit and he would come home from work with icicles hanging off his moustache. It was pathetic.

I cared so much about him, I said, "You can't do this anymore. You're going to get killed."

*   *   *

He let me take over. He came to New York and moved in with me. He ended up staying for six months without ever getting a job. But I couldn't get angry with him because he was the most humane person I'd ever met.

Like we had this great Christmas which I've never had because I'm Jewish. I was so excited. Steve: my first Catholic boyfriend. We had a wreath and a tree. He got me presents, things I really needed though I'd never said a word. It was hard to not be happy with Steve.

He got a paralegal job and started making real money. Things got better. We both said, "We're gonna live together two years and then either gonna get married or bag it." I've lived with people for five years or seven years. I know that if you don't make the commitment, you never will.

And we were older. I wanted a kid. Although, I was having serious doubts about a kid with Steve. But I said, "*I'm* not gonna end it, so yeah. Let's get married." Not a great way to get married, but there are worse ways, I suppose.

*   *   *

The night before the wedding I was in a state of terror. I almost bagged it.

That morning, Steve and I had a long talk. Typical Steve. He said, "I know you're afraid. You think I'm not gonna get myself together. Don't worry about it. If it doesn't work, we'll just say forget it." That sounded pretty good to me.

We went to France on our honeymoon, and for the first three days, I was gonna leave him. I thought, "This is the most horrible thing I've ever done in my life." I'm fast-lane. I speak French. And Steve's lost. A country bumpkin. I had to apologize for my husband.

I thought we were doomed.

*   *   *

The next years were interesting. He kept working at the law office and I lucked out. I got a job mixing sound for an off-Broadway show. That sent me off on a career I had no idea was coming. I wound up mixing *Smokey Joe's Café* on Broadway, and suddenly everything was feeling pretty good. I began to feel like I didn't need this guy I was married to anymore.

I met someone at the show who knocked me out. Fast-lane. Jazz guy. Gorgeous. And I didn't resist. Physical things in my marriage had deteriorated. I ended up with this other guy and Steve was heartbroken. He went back to Massachusetts two years into the marriage.

Steve had been such a sweet man. I remember him standing in our living room, saying, "You are making a huge mistake. We're meant to be. This is a good thing for both of us."

I was a fucking flake. I hadn't grown up. So Steve took off.

I filed papers. Steve and I were separated. I hung out with this other guy, but it fell apart after two years. Mark dumped me in a pretty hard way; I freaked.

And Steve? He was right there. He came back, stood by me, and saved my life. And we rode that out.

*   *   *

I have a cousin who's very practical. One time, I was pining away over Steve, not knowing what to do. I kept saying, "I *want* a good marriage. Why can't I *have* a good marriage?"

She said, "You've *got* one."

I mean, what *is* marriage?! You make the commitment. You say, "Okay, we get along, we like each other, let's do it." I don't know any couple that doesn't struggle in one way or the other.

*   *   *

Well, Steve loved to cook. Back when we were still married, I'd come home to these great meals and I'd go off to work with my little lunch bag. He'd have made me tapenade. People would stare at me while I was eating. I'd smile and say, "Oh, it's nothing. My husband made this for me."

My parents said they would pay for Steve to go to French Culinary School. They could see what he was interested in, it was written all over him. So they sent him and Steve was in heaven. He was on a roll. We thought, "He'll get a job as a chef and he'll rise quickly."

Well, Steve was a great cook at home. But in a fast kitchen with a million people running in and out and a chef screaming and ten guys chopping celery? Steve was *not* a fast person. He *hates* people who multi-task. He thinks that's rude.

So he quit the chef's job and got a job as a steward. He did all the ordering. He was put in charge of hiring and the chef really liked him, but he was really failing. I'd come back home, to find him sitting on the couch drinking beer. He couldn't take it.

One day he said, "That's it. I'm through. I'm going back to Massachusetts and I'm gonna write about food and wine."

I had never seen him write anything, not so much as a letter. I said: "Steve, what are you talking about?"

He said, "This is not working, this is not my thing."

So I said, "Fine. Go up there. Get a job. Make money. Buy a house. Make payments. When you do that - call me."

So he went.

*   *   *

He had a couple jobs where they treated him like a dog. He was making eight bucks an hour. Meanwhile, he'd taught himself about wine. But his employers thought he was lazy. He worked in a huge store - thousands of labels. But they put two Burgundies together because they looked the same.

Steve would say to them, "Look, this is a $25 bottle and this is an $8.99 bottle. They don't go together."

The boss just said, "You know what the trouble is with you? You don't put enough bottles on the shelves every day." They wouldn't give him a raise.

Steve and I were seeing each other again. I loved driving up to visit but we weren't making enough money to do both - to live in New York and have a place up there. That's when he started to apply for jobs in the city again.

*   *   *

He wrote to the French Culinary Institute and they immediately hooked him up with Windows on the World. They were looking for a Wine Cellar Master and hired him the next day. After all the shit he'd been through, *me* treating him like shit . . . life suddenly made sense for Steven. These guys went, "We love you! You're *exactly* what we're looking for!" He was ecstatic. Within two months, he was sommelier once a week at Wild Blue, their smaller restaurant. Then he was made the Beverage Manager.

Things were going well for us all around. I went off to a summer music camp to fall back in love with the oboe and I remember Steve called me with such joy in his voice. "Can you believe it? After two months?"

I said, "Does this mean we're gonna open one of those special bottles of champagne when I get home?"

He said, "You bet!"

We were so happy. When I came home, he cooked something great. He seemed like a different person, the way he walked, the way he talked.

And that was September 4th. We had seven days like that.

*   *   *

Our anniversary was September 10th. I was going to cook a meal for Steve but I got really sick. I could tell he was disappointed. But he said, "Oh, don't worry about it."

It started pouring sheets of rain outside. He was wearing these nice, new shoes that I'd bought him. I said in this little girl voice, "Steve, you can't go out. You'll ruin your shoooos."

And he wheeled around and said, "I'm not going to ruin my shoes! I mean: shooooos'!"

And we both just cracked up. So stupid and silly. He went out to buy a steak but I knew he'd be disappointed because he was always going on about how there's no good cuts of meat available at eight p.m. Sure enough, he comes back moaning, explaining to me, "This one's not *so* bad. The fat is in the meat so you can cook it slowly and it'll melt in. Bad cuts of meat you have to sear really fast. The fat's on the outside and it won't permeate the texture, you won't get the flavor."

I'm sitting there thinking, "This guy really knows his stuff." It was the first time I'd really understood that.

See, all these years I'd been admiring other people who I thought were fancy, bright, or talented. Good at what they did. I felt that that's what I wanted all along. Then it hit me: he's been right here in my own backyard all the time.

We weren't wearing our wedding rings that night. I remember wanting to say, "Let's put our rings on." But I felt so sick. I said, "I'll put it on tomorrow," and I went to bed. He was gone the next morning when I woke up to the ringing phone.

*   *   *

It was Steve's mother. She had seen everything happen on the news while I was still asleep. "Did Steve go to work today?"

"Yeah. Why?"

"Oh no."

I turned on the TV and saw what was happening. I said, "I'll call you back."

*　　*　　*

I called my brother who lives four blocks away. He knew. He said, "I'll be there in two minutes." He came over, and we sat here watching as Steve's Tower fell.

I'm not sure how it happened for him. If he was knocked out right away. If he survived the impact of the plane. Sometimes I imagine it was the smoke that got him before the building collapsed. But I don't know. I'll never know.

One of the general managers at Windows got a call on his answering machine at home. A woman said, "There's been a huge explosion. All the windows have blown out, there's tons of smoke. The fire marshal told us to wait. We don't know what to do." That's the only clue I have to what they all went through up there.

I replay it a hundred million thousand times in my head. Did he try to call me? Did he try to make it to the roof? Did he suffer? I've never seen Steve afraid. He was a rock.

I'm the crazy one. I'm the one who weird things happen to. Not him. Not my husband.

*　　*　　*

I used to say, "Promise me I'll die first."

He always just shrugged. "Okay."

When we first broke up, I'll never forget how he screamed at me. "Do you still have to die first?"

*　　*　　*

It turns out that the FBI or FEMA comes to your door to tell you. "He's been identified."

I went down to Pier 94 where the morgue is set up to get Steve's remains. But they said, "You're not allowed to take them." I was angry. They explained: "You have to call a funeral director who will get the remains. This is a homicide. There's no other process."

I said, "I'm not religious. I don't want to do a ceremony." But they were adamant. So I got out the yellow pages and picked someone that seemed innocuous and went down there with a friend the next day. The guy wrote out a bill. The maximum allowance was $6000, I didn't have the money to pay that. I'm not sure which agency paid for it - they gave me a check.

It said: "For the Victims of the World Trade Center."

I've gotten two other checks, one to help pay rent and one for cash to get by. The funny thing is, I'm still working. I was always the money-maker. I know the money's there.

In the end, what difference does money make? ꙅ

VINCENT FALIVENE, 28. On the evening of September 14ᵗʰ, feeling disconsolate and under-utilized, Vincent walked 70 blocks from his job at the Metropolitan Museum of Art to Union Square Park.[3] That night, a candlelight vigil had been scheduled and all of New York was invited. As he walked down Fifth Avenue, he took in the lampposts papered with color computer print-outs of missing persons. "You'd often see copies of the same image. There was a guy I went to college and his picture was up. There was one poster with twins and both of them were lost. It was overwhelming." When he arrived, Union Square was covered with mourners.

————

It was starting to get dark. Coming down, the closer I got to the Square, I started noticing the smell of - smelled like burning hair to me.[4]

There was a line of Buddhists walking through the park with candles. The orange robes, the shaved heads. Some people regularly dressed . . . jeans, T-shirts. Predominantly Asian. Everyone was chanting. The words weren't in English, so I have no idea what they were saying. But you got the idea from their mood. I didn't jump in the line, but I did follow them through the crowd and into the park.

I kind of expected a lot of disjointed people, this wasn't the case. These Buddhists, they'd had only a day to organize their whole congregation and they generated this huge gathering in such a short amount of time. I thought it was pretty amazing. See, I'm not talking about a short line of people. There were tons. It was like being at a party. Kinda like a Conga line.

There were all these placards and posters, you know, people leaving messages of peace. Images of missing people. Several quotes. There was one long one from Gandhi . . . I mean it was *long*. Written on a white bed sheet with black acrylic paint. It was difficult to stop and read them all. I'm telling you, it was like being in a crowded party, being shoulder to shoulder.

You got to the center of the Square and there were three Buddhist monks handing out candles, lighting them for people going by. Just simple long white candles. The silent monks in orange and yellow or red sashes. They had their eyes down, somber. It was like the whole park was a funeral and the monks were trying to be deferential to the people who were hurting. There were no smiles. There was no laughing and there was no conversation.

---

[3]Union Square: a large, popular plaza between 14th and 17th Streets lined with restaurants, bars, stores, and subways stations.
[4]The smell of the burning Towers laced the air of downtown Manhattan for months after the 11th.

*   *   *

A number of people sat in drum circles on the south side of the Square. Three or four people playing bongo drums and everybody outside singing, "Give Peace a Chance." Guys in the center were dancing. If you go to a Grateful Dead concert, they were dancing like that. Spastic. Reaching up toward the sky, looking up, looking tripped out, singing very loudly, like they were in church.

This one girl in particular I remember was singing between the pauses. They were singing "Give Peace a Chance", she was singing "One Love" by Bob Marley. She was quite bad, but you know. The words. It was a point well taken.

The next circle I got to, there was a couple people sitting with guitars, and another bongo drum, singing "Kumbaya" over and over and over again. That's kinda when I got a little distracted. Because I heard a lot of people arguing –

"You're fucking crazy! We should bomb these people! There's no other response."

Other people shouting back: "There's gotta be a peaceful response to this. There's gotta be another way to go about it. We can't let them goad us into this violent response!"

I could feel tension building. One argument broke out between this African-American guy, tall with dreadlocks and this young girl, probably an NYU college student, wearing a red, white and blue bandana and an American flag shirt. He called her a bimbo and she lost it. She's calling him "a fuckin' asshole."

People chiming in from all sides. People shouting flack. A couple guys got involved, defending the Young Girl's honor. "You shouldn't talk to her like that, man . . ."

Sheperd Sherbell

The Dreadlock Dude retorts, "Hey! She called me stupid . . ."

I started to get nervous. This gathering had started out peaceful and now it was turning into a mob.

With that, Dreadlock Dude stands up and apologizes to the Young Girl. "Look, I'm sorry. I shouldn't have called you a bimbo. But you shouldn't have called me stupid. Obviously we have different views on this."

A guy thanked Dreadlock Dude: "That was very big of you to say, man."

The Young Girl was silent. Then she called Dreadlock Dude 'a fuckin' asshole' and walked away.

*　　*　　*

A Latino standing nearby, said: "How could you say that America has done things that pushed these people to the point where they're willing to lay down their lives to kill us? How could you *say* that?"

Then it all broke open. People started talking over each other.

Dreadlock Dude said, "Okay. Hold it! There has to be some kind of forum here."

He had this piece of poster board rolled into a baton and he held it up. "Whoever wants to speak should come up here and hold up the poster board to signify you are the speaker."

Now he's got the attention of the people in this area. There's people yelling behind me: "Speak up! Speak up!" The first person grabs the baton and starts talking, people yelled. They all spoke over him.

So Dreadlock Dude says "Whoever's speaking should be able to speak. I don't know about all of you, but I don't have anywhere to go tonight. Everyone will get their chance."

So another Latino guy comes up and starts talking. He says, "We should all love one another." Which doesn't get the best reception.

Then this other guy came up and *he* asked for the baton. A big dude. Over six feet tall. His head was shaved bald like a Neo-Nazi. Skin tight T-shirt. Suspenders. Tight jeans and tattoos on his arms. Real *thick* arms. He says: "Listen. In 1983, I lost 18 of my friends in the terrorist bombing in Beirut. Really *close* friends of mine. After that America did bad things. But my philosophy in life is peace through superior firepower. And that's all I'm gonna say." He gave back the baton.

This woman in African garb started yelling at him. She said she had lived in Jamaica and used to tour as a backup singer for Bob Marley. She kept calling him Bob Marley "the prophet." As in: "The prophet Bob Marley said we should all live as one. We need to change our view of the world. It has to be done by loving each other." Then she broke into "One Love" while holding the baton and everyone started singing along with her. It's kinda funny now, but it was very powerful at the time.

I thought this was all wonderful, the kind of discourse that people should be engaged in *all* the time. Obviously, this won't occur on a daily basis. To really sit back and challenge your own belief system, or to try to bring about change . . . for some people, talking that evening? That was as far as they'd ever gone with it.

*   *   *

It was getting dark quickly. The air quality was getting poor. The wind had shifted north, and the smoke from the Towers was blowing into the park. You could hear it in people's voices, they started to get raspy. People were wearing those surgical masks now.

Michael Raab

285

Then, the people who were singing "Kumbaya" started singing "New York, New York" over and over again. There was like a Rockette's[5] line of people from all walks of life linked arm-in-arm doing this absurd version of a kick line. It was insane, but it made me smile.

One more thing. As I left, two sculptors were at work, sitting on the ground, a man and a woman working on a gold and silver plating - an American flag, four-feet wide, a few feet high, two-dimensional, made to look fluid, like it was blowing in the breeze. Each plate alternated gold and silver. As they fashioned it, they were inscribing names from the posters of missing people, putting names on them, very intricate stuff. And as they worked, people were silent, watching them.

These artists. They were very absorbed in their work. I saw it two days later - they auctioned off the piece.

Mostly though, people were singing or listening. Or quiet. It was like a funeral in a way. A funeral for the entire city. ℥

---

[5] Radio City Music Hall Chorus Line

PATRICK CHARLES WELSH, 44. Patrick is a man of tall carriage with salt-and-pepper hair, and ruddy cheeks. He exudes a natural charm. His story begins as an American fable. How it ends is open to interpretation.

———

I'm amazed that I actually survived the '80s in New York.

I struggled when I came here in 1981. I got caught up in the bartending scene. Back then, everybody was riding the wave of Republican funny money. Father Reagan was protecting us all from the Evil Empire and everything was, "Ain't life great? Gimme another line of cocaine! America's Number One!"

New York is a great place to live, but it's a love/hate relationship. If you're not financially independent, it can be extremely difficult. The guy who takes a Town Car and rides an elevator up to his penthouse isn't seeing the homeless person who vomits on his steps. But that's the daily reality and you get a little numb to it after awhile. You find your niche.

*   *   *

I was going through different bartending jobs and I found a new one at Boxer's down in the Village. It was St. Patrick's Day in '87 or '88 and the following day, I met this new waitress named Debbie.

You couldn't miss her. She lit up the room like a psychedelic Auntie Mame. When she walked in, everyone knew she was there. We hit it off right away, driving each other insane across the service bar like Diane and Sam Malone from *Cheers*.

For our first date we went out and saw *The Adventures of Baron Von Munchausen.* Then we polished off a fifth of tequila at a bar I used to work at called the *You're It.* It was a hell of a first date. Debbie was wild. She had this incredible zest for life. She embraced it fully. We hit it off and never looked back.

Four or five years later, I proposed on New Year's Eve.

*   *   *

We lived in a studio on Bleeker Street between Charles and Perry Streets. We got a Dalmatian named Dylan that was like our kid and Debbie found this coat in a thrift store window - a black and white spotted coat that was awful, just awful. I used to imagine how every other customer in the thrift store had gone by that coat on the rack and said, "I wouldn't go near that thing with a ten foot pole." But Debbie said, "Oh my God! That's *perfect!*" Of course.

She was ecstatic about this treasure. She brought it home and showed it off for me and what else could I say? "Baby, it's you."

A black and white spotted coat for when she walked our black and white spotted dog. Deb had a great appreciation for the ridiculous and the absurd; she was unafraid to talk to anybody. I called her The Mayor back then because she knew everyone in the neighborhood.

*　　*　　*

As we spent our lives together, I learned so much more about her.

She couldn't read music, so she'd taught herself how to play the piano by ear. She could play *Rhapsody in Blue* like a professional - it was amazing. I would say, "How did you learn that?"

"I just banged it out on my own." She played the keys by memory and guitar this way, too.

She was older than me. She was born in Darby, Pennsylvania right outside of Philadelphia and went to Notre Dame High School. For a brief time, she was a Flyerette for the Philadelphia Flyers - not really a cheerleader, but there for promotional things, in the press box at the games. She was very *rah rah rah*, so it was perfect for her. Shortly after that, she got a job with Eastern Airlines and did that for a very long time.

Prior to my meeting Debbie, Eastern went on strike which is when she got the job waiting tables at Boxer's. If it weren't for that strike, she would have still been flying and I would never have met her. I think about that sometimes.

Well, the airline industry eventually became a big part of my life because it was such a big part of hers. Debbie was very pro-union. She was a people person. She had no tolerance for financial or political tyrants. In fact, she had a tremendous vehemence for Frank Lorenzo, the guy who tried to dismantle Eastern Airlines, cut it up and sell it off to Continental.[6] The guy was a real bastard. He ruined the lives of people who worked for that company for years according to Deb.

She was based in New York, but traveled the world on her time off. She went to Peru and learned the customs and the language; she hiked the Inca trail all the way up to Machu

---

[6]The movie Wall Street was loosely based on what Lorenzo tried to do to Eastern.

Picchu. She went to Bali where she survived a near-fatal bout of pneumonia. She went to Hong Kong and Malaysia, Germany and Greece using only a Fodor's book.

She always traveled by herself. She was that fearless, a person who embraced different cultures. And in terms of her demise, this was the most ironic thing, to me. She wasn't isolationist, she was a worldly person, always down to earth. Lots of humor, no stuffiness. She was a beautiful and accepting American, quite the opposite of what a lot of the world thinks of our people.

*   *   *

When she met me at Boxers, she'd worked her way through a series of different restaurants. She didn't know if she was ready to go back to the airlines. They had broken her heart. She took work at the Amazon Club over by Chelsea Piers, where part of their proceeds went to save the rain forests - it was a famous place in the late '80s. But for the sake of better benefits, she decided to go back to work as a flight attendant.

Some former Eastern Airlines people had put together Kiwi International Airline, a small company based in New York, which would fly the East Coast to Chicago. It was a fledgling airline so they named it after a flightless bird. The people who started it felt that their wings had been clipped by Eastern. It was a tight-knit group and she loved the notion of it.

Deb explained to me that, when a flight attendant leaves a company, she loses all seniority. Even though you may have years of experience, if you change companies you have to start back at zero as a buck private and go through the whole process again. Seniority is what you leverage to arrange your work schedule. But despite all this, Debbie was thrilled to get back to work.

I remember going to her graduation from Kiwi's training program. I was so proud. Each graduating class would put this skit together. Her class took the music from Criss-Cross' *Jump!* and changed the words. I helped her write it. She coordinated this whole hip-hop dance routine and it was hysterical to see these flight attendants break-dancing in their uniforms.

*   *   *

Well, Kiwi fell under bad times when the airline industry struggled through the early '90s. The company was going into a burn-out phase and Debbie began to get overscheduled because the airline was losing people. It's like having a pitcher in baseball throw every night; you just can't do it. She found out United was hiring and said, "I think I'm gonna make a move. My benefits and schedule will be a lot better, even though I'm starting all over again."

And that's what she did. She started training with United and was truly happy.

Both of our lives started to take off. I started to have great success as a commercial actor. Finally, I didn't have to take any more bartending jobs – in fact, I said I'd never set foot behind a bar again unless it was for a friend. Debbie and I had some time together and we got to travel a little. We were starting to get payoff from all our struggles in New York.

*   *   *

Her mother once told me, "You know, I have tremendous admiration for your marriage. You two just laugh from your heels."

The night prior to the 11th, we had gone to a comedy club where a client of my manager was performing. I thank God for that because our last moments together, we were laughing uproariously like we did through most of our marriage.

The 11th wasn't a normally scheduled day for Deb to work. She had gotten an e-mail from another flight attendant that said, "Would you cover this shift for me? I have a special event I'd like to attend."

Debbie said, "Fine. You can take this shift for me." It was a normal swap.

The woman actually e-mailed her back later, saying, "My plans fell through, if you want to switch back . . ."

But Debbie said, "No, that's fine. Take the day off. I'll cover it."

In a lot of ways - to her friends, her family and me . . . we figure it was destiny. The way Deb was, I know she would have been doing her best to comfort the people on board that plane. She would have been inspirational to a great many people. I know it for a fact.

*   *   *

Normally, when she flew we would exchange information about where she was going. But I didn't know she was going to San Francisco on the 11th. She just said, "I'll be back in two days, I'll cook a great dinner for us, and we'll go see a movie."

"Perfect. Give me a call when you get in." This was normal enough.

Ever since I got a computer, my routine is to get up early in the morning - like five o'clock - to work. She had to be out of the house at about 5:30 to get to Newark airport. I made some coffee and took it to her. She was like Dagwood Bumstead getting out the door that day, papers flying all around her, a real mess. I helped her carry her bag downstairs, kissed her good-bye, and off she went.

*   *   *

I had a couple auditions scheduled for that morning. The first one was for an industrial film and I was getting ready to go out the door when I turned on New York 1.[7] The sound was off. The first plane had already hit and I thought, "My God, what the hell is that?" I was already running late. The news wasn't even sure what had happened. And then the second plane hit.

My first thought was, "I have to think of something to say because Debbie will be so upset when she calls." Any type of air disaster affected her deeply.

I went to the audition. On the streets, people were gathering in front of TVs, in front of shops and diners. I gleaned information little by little along the way to my destination. By the time I got to the casting office, I knew it was a terrorist attack and I was filled with rage.

It was absolutely unfathomable to me, this deliberate mayhem of biblical proportions. It was like Genghis Khan coming through and decapitating children in a village. It was unthinkable that anybody could be so maligned, so full of fear and hatred.

Everybody I met at the audition was the same way, inflamed that anybody could do this to fellow human beings. To call it troglodyte or Neanderthal behavior is insulting to the Neanderthals and troglodytes. Here were people who were so miserable in their lives, so full of fear, which I believe is the basis of hatred. Fear of freedom or the fear of women being intelligent and non-submissive. People so lost in their Byzantine, perverse mindset . . . so enraged that the world won't conform to their oppressive way of life that they would lash out in this fashion.

But at no time did I think my wife was involved. I was still thinking of things to say when she called. I knew that she would not only be upset, but furious.

*   *   *

The auditions were cancelled. I went straight home knowing that such a huge event would stop the world. I immediately turned on CNN. The report came in that another plane had hit the Pentagon. I felt fear for all of us because those actions looked like the prelude to

---

[7]The local New York City news channel.

nuclear Armageddon.

I thought, "This is the day. The horns are blowing, the Seventh Seal is broken, the Four Horseman of the Apocalypse are let loose." And that was the first real glimmer of fear that passed through my mind for Debbie's sake. But I ignored it. I was in denial the whole day.

I had already heard that United planes were involved. I'd heard that one originating from Newark bound for San Francisco had switched directions and gone down outside Shanksville, Pennsylvania. My mind was racing, unable to compute all the information. The cell phones were down. It was mass mayhem.

Then the phone calls started coming in from friends and family asking about Deb. This cemented my denial as the day wore on.

"She's fine," I said. "She's fine. She hasn't called me because they probably told her to keep the airwaves clear. They probably redirected her plane to someplace, I bet they're already in the process of landing - "

I didn't know she was going to San Francisco.

*　　*　　*

A dear friend called whom we had run into the night before outside the comedy club. A bunch of us had stopped and chatted on the street. This woman called and said, "Have you heard from Deb?"

I said, "No. I'm sure she's gonna call me soon."

"Patrick. I'm really worried. Last night she said she was going to San Francisco. That plane that crashed in Shanksville was bound from Newark to San Francisco . . . "[8]

I swear to God, I felt like somebody hit me in the bridge of my nose with an 80-pound bat.

---

[8] Four planes were hijacked and crashed on September 11th, 2001. American Airlines Flight 11 bound from Boston to Los Angeles, which crashed into the North Tower of the Trade Center at 8:45 a.m. United Airlines Flight 175 bound from Boston to Los Angeles, which crashed into the South Tower of the Trade Center at 9:06 a.m. American Airlines Flight 77, bound from Washington, D.C. to Los Angeles, which crashed into the Pentagon at 9:45 a.m. And United Flight 93, bound from Newark, New Jersey to San Francisco, which crashed inexplicably in Shanksville, Pennsylvania at 10:10 a.m. Cell phone calls from the Shanksville plane confirm that the passengers staged some sort of revolt against the hijackers shortly before the plane spun out of control and crashed. Experts theorize that Flight 93 may have been heading toward Washington D.C. to attack either the Capital Building or the White House.

I snapped. "There are many flights from Newark to San Francisco," I said. "She's fine. She'll call me as soon as she gets an opportunity. Debbie's a professional. She's got people to take care of, she's fine . . . "

To me? The odds were unfathomable. It was like I was really saying to this poor woman, "I'm sorry. You've got me confused with someone else. Things like this don't happen to *me*. It's just something somebody like *me* would only ever read about."

*   *   *

But, of course, the day went on. I was becoming more and more unraveled, fighting my own mind. I was bug-eyed, glued to the television, pacing. A wreck of a man spiraling downward. By late afternoon, all planes were ordered to the ground and I had yet to hear from her.

People were calling left and right. Debbie's sister called, her mother called. "No," I kept repeating, "I haven't heard." Realizing I was in denial. Realizing I was in this incredible ghost of gloom that drifted around me like a nightmare. One that I couldn't wake up from.

My mom was trying to comfort me. "Maybe she's all right. The cell phones are still out of whack. She'll call as soon as she can - "

It was right then that I got a call from a United Airlines representative.

"Hello, Mr. Welsh?" I can't remember the woman's name on the other end. My mind was reeling.

"I'm so, so sorry to inform you that your wife, Deborah, was on the manifest for Flight 93 that went down in Shanksville."

I can't imagine what that person had to go through to tell me. That job? I wouldn't give it to my worst enemy.

*   *   *

Time stopped. I can't tell you. I was so devastated from this unheard cry of souls from all the people who had been killed that morning. This moan of humanity going up to heaven. I was already shaken, but when this woman told me Deb was gone, I fell to my knees and dropped the phone.

It was no accident that my mother was on call waiting.

I was down on my knees, weeping uncontrollably. I don't know how long the woman from United was on the phone. Finally, I said, "I'm so sorry. I can't talk right now. My mother's on the phone . . ." I don't know what else I said.

"I understand," the woman said, "I'm so sorry. . ."

I clicked back to the other line and said, "Mom, they just told me that Deb was on that flight in Pennsylvania . . . "

I didn't know who I was. Everything about life lost meaning. I felt like the shell of a person; I felt like somebody had scraped out my insides. I couldn't stop weeping. I couldn't talk. The phone started ringing mercilessly. I took a few calls. Then the pastor from our church called, Father Brett Hoover from St. Paul the Apostle. And I told him.

He said, "Patrick, I'm coming right over."

I said, "I'll meet you downstairs."

I dragged him to a bar and threw down one drink after another. I didn't know what else to do.

He understood perfectly. He said, "I'm right here with you."

* * *

People still remembered her in the old neighborhood. After September 11th, people put memorials in their windows. There were flowers everywhere on Bleeker Street. Dear friends of ours, Pam Moss and her husband Tim, had taken this beautiful picture of Debbie when we first got together. They framed it in black with an American flag that said, "In Loving Memorial."

She would have been 50 this July 20th. We would have been married for eleven years.

Two weeks later, I delivered my wife's eulogy at a memorial in her honor. I didn't think I would be capable of it, but I think she was there to help me. I knew I had a responsibility to my wife, that she needed a wonderful, lasting tribute and I made sure she had it.

"The world has been transformed," I said. "The transformation isn't in the malevolence of these madmen. It isn't found in the scarred skyline of our great city. It isn't in the broken walls of our proud Pentagon. It's not in the charred crater of courage in the gentle fields of

Pennsylvania. The true transformation is how all these people – our countrymen and the world - came together. That's what we must take away from this. That transformation is the divine rescue of God among man."

I remember it was near sunset and so many friends had come. We had a lovely Irish wake up on the roof of our building. We'd had lots of parties there over the years, gatherings of very creative people. Now we grabbed hands and said the Lord's Prayer. Each person had a moment to impart something about how Debbie had touched their lives. It was incredible. People were weeping incessantly. I was just barely holding myself together. I thought it was my duty to do that.

I looked around and saw how Debbie had touched the lives of all these people. And once again, she had touched my life from beyond her own. She's forever a part of me, forever a part of my life.

For two months after that, I was . . . I was not good.

*   *   *

I'm a different person than I was. I'm not just Patrick anymore. I feel like I'm Patrick and Debbie and a lot of these other people. That's the person I am now, the person who's going to mold my new life in whatever direction God has chosen for me. I struggled for a long period with this. But you have choices to make in life and life is very hard.

M. Scott Peck started off his book "The Road Less Traveled" with "Life *is* difficult." When we finally understand that life is hard and that anything that's easy is the gravy, then it's actually not so hard anymore. But if you think that the world owes you a living and everything should be a silver spoon in your mouth, you're gonna have a hard time.

Editor's note: Patrick wanted to be sure to thank Greg Wolfe, Madeline Klinkova and her sister Vanessa, Barbara Sinaris, and many other dear friends for their remarkable friendship and support during his grief. "They came to my rescue," he said. "Please make sure to mention them." ℈

LAUREN ALBERT, 35, describes a situation that thousands of families throughout the New York area were forced to participate in following the attack: the search for a missing family member or friend. Lauren went down to the Red Cross the day after the attack to register her friend KAROL KEASLER as missing.

———

Abby Bullock

I was here in my Murray Hill apartment on Tuesday. I made some coffee and watched the first plane hit on TV. I called my mother up in Maine and said, "Oh, my God, you're not gonna believe what fucking happened." Then the second plane hit. I thought I was seeing things. My hand went to my mouth and I kept saying this, involuntarily: "Oh my God. Oh my God. Oh my God."

I was in shock. Who wasn't? The phone went out, so I got on-line immediately, I have a cable modem, and there was this flurry of e-mails. A tight-knit group of my friends – we rent a house together every summer out on Fire Island - everyone was asking each other to check-in. "Please! Reply to All."

And everything seemed fine, everyone seemed accounted for. Until we remembered Karol. And Mike, another friend who worked for the same company - no one had heard from him, either. Karol worked on the 89th floor, Mike on the 88th. Which I guess is what eventually made a difference.

*   *   *

We were all frenzied. No one had heard from them. I called the offices of Keefe, Bruyette, and Woods in Chicago to find out if they had any information. I told the woman in Chicago Mike and Karol's names. She was really helpful. She said, "Oh, I *know* Karol. We know some specific departments escaped entirely and have already checked in. But we don't have any information about Karol or Mike."

I thought, "Well, okay. So some people as high as the 88th and 89th floor got out. There's a good chance for both of them, then."

So I called the Boston offices and I got a guy who also knew Karol. He said he used to sit right across from her when he'd worked in New York. He said, "We haven't heard anything. All I can tell you is to keep calling. And pray." He was definitely not as optimistic.

I thought, "Well, he's just being emotional. People *did* get out. It's probably okay. It's just really hard to get in touch with people right now since the phones aren't working."

Well, when the phones started working again at three or four o'clock that day, I got word from my friends that Mike had checked in. He had gotten out of the second Tower and called Rhonda who got in touch with all of us.

Mike had worked in the Towers for years and was there when the first bombing happened in '93. He's an ex-Marine who worked in a small department. He said when the first plane hit, they all heard it. They felt it. The folks in his department had looked at each other and said, "Let's get the fuck out of here." So they left.

He found his girlfriend who worked at the World Financial Center. She'd had pretty bad smoke inhalation. They took the ferry to Staten Island where she lived and he'd finally called in from there.

But four or five that afternoon, no one had heard from Karol.

The Chicago office was nice enough to call me back to say they hadn't heard from Karol but had heard from Mike. I said, "Yeah. Okay. I got that. I know."

I was numb. It was starting to sink in.

*   *   *

I'd known Karol four years. She was Vice President of Events and Communications for KBW, a securities broker and investment bank on the 88th and 89th floor of Tower 2. She coordinated events and road shows for her company.

Early Wednesday morning, I talked to my friend Elizabeth. She said: "I have some upsetting news."

"What is it?"

She said, "Karol's fiancé, Michael, has been living in Moscow. . ."

"Right," I thought. Karol was gonna move there. Michael had been calling frantically from Moscow. He'd obviously heard, but he couldn't get in touch with anyone. Karol's Mom had been in touch with somebody and it ultimately got back to Elizabeth. This is the way it happened for a lot of people, I later learned. This round-robin of diluted information that went on for days.

Elizabeth said, "After the first plane hit the first Tower, Karol called her Mom. She told her, 'Mom, I'm okay. We know what happened. I'm all right.' But then the phone went dead."

When Elizabeth told me the phone had cut off, I knew. I just knew she was gone.

*   *   *

That afternoon, my friend Jason called and said that the Red Cross was opening up a Missing Persons Center at Bellevue Hospital on 1st Avenue. I was closest to Karol out of our group of friends. And maybe I was the most equipped to handle it. Everybody was in a state of shock.

I had a bunch of pictures of Karol from this Luau party we threw the summer before. She was gorgeous. Really short platinum blonde hair. In the picture, she was wearing a sarong and a coconut shell bra and hugging another friend. That was the best picture any of us had of her face. I took it to Kinko's, made a bunch of color photocopies and went down the Red Cross to wait on line.

*   *   *

When I got there, the line was three blocks long. All these people. Everyone with photos. It was very organized. The line was very quiet. Some volunteers were giving out boxes of sandwiches and coffee and cookies and bottled water.

There was a guy walking up and down the side of the line with a list. A white guy about 30 years old. Tall and thin. Like a Mid-Western farm boy with strawberry blonde hair. He had the most recently updated casualty list and he was going person-to-person to see if anyone's missing person had been found in the hospital.

He didn't find anyone.

I asked if he could check to see if Karol was on his list. He came over to me and I could tell that he was exhausted. By now it was four o'clock in the afternoon on Wednesday

September 12ᵗʰ. He looked overwhelmed. I had to give him Karol's name five times. His hands were shaking.

I saw an older man with white hair and a chaplain's collar call out to a little ten-year old girl who was standing on line with her mother. He said, "Come here, honey. Come here. What was your Daddy's name again?" The mother started crying.

There was a group of four or five girls my own age. I figured out by overhearing their conversation that they were there on behalf of their friend. They were saying things like, "How's she gonna get through this? She hasn't even written the thank-you notes. She hasn't gone through the wedding pictures yet."

I just sat there thinking, Karol was going to get married. She'd just gone to Quebec City with her Mom a few weeks before to buy a wedding dress.

*   *   *

At the end of the line and they handed me a questionnaire to fill out. I couldn't answer a lot of the questions. I could do the basic descriptions. HAIR COLOR. SKIN COLOR. WEIGHT. APPEARANCE. But, the rest? I wanted to make sure, you know? I wanted to make absolutely sure she had, like, blue eyes and not green.

Suddenly, I'm standing there in that line and I didn't know *anything* for sure anymore. Like, I couldn't remember if Karol had pierced ears or not. I couldn't remember exactly what her engagement ring looked like.

I guess that's when I realized I was in shock. I realized the importance of the little things you've seen a million times that don't quite register. Questions like: HOW LONG WERE HER FINGERNAILS? HOW LONG WERE HER TOENAILS? DOES SHE HAVE ANY SCARS, BIRTHMARKS, OR TATTOOS?

I'd seen Karol practically naked. We spent summers together out at the beach in little bathing suits. I was almost certain she didn't have any tattoos . . . but stuff like BROKEN BONES? and WHAT WAS SHE WEARING THAT DAY? I had no idea, I hadn't seen her that day.

WAS SHE RIGHT HANDED OR LEFT HANDED? I just wanted my friend back.

I had to call a lot of friends on my cell phone to fill out that form. "Do you know *this* about Karol? Do you know *that* about Karol? Can you call her mother? I need her dentist's name, do you have that information?"

*   *   *

Then they brought us into an auditorium to get a case number for the person we were declaring missing. I was sitting in a row next to a woman about my age. At one point she just broke down and started crying. So I started crying. Not for her. But because I had to.

The young woman kept repeating things like, "Well, we checked his answering machine. Employees are calling in to see if he's okay. We checked his answering machine."

I started looking around. I felt like I wanted to just . . . bear witness. I looked directly into people's faces. I saw a lot of people staring into space. Shock. Expressionless. People with tears in their eyes. Quietly crying on their own. I made it a point to look at their faces because I wanted to remember that.

I got a case number: 759. I assume that meant that, at that point, they had that many people. It must have been early in the process.[9]

*   *   *

A friend mentioned to me that she'd been walking home on Tuesday evening. She lives in Stuyvesant Town and she saw something on Avenue A right below 14th Street - somebody had painted a huge mural on the side of a building in the time between the planes hitting the buildings and that same evening.

The mural showed the New York City skyline with the Towers on fire. And they had written, IN LOVING MEMORY OF OUR FAMILIES AND FRIENDS. Then the date, and the inscription REST IN PEACE. Already, there were candles and flowers and offerings in front of this mural.

I went there on my way back from Bellevue. I decided to bring some flowers for Karol. Pink star lilies because those were her favorite. When we used to go out to the beach on the weekends, she always brought star lilies. Before she even put her bags in her room, she would cut them and arrange them in a vase on the table.

The sky in the mural was orange and the buildings were gray. I put the flowers down and just stood there. I thought of Karol. And I guess I stood there a really long time.

---

[9]It quickly became apparent that over 3000 people were missing.
[10]Early October of 2001.

*　*　*

We've already had a memorial service for Karol.[10] Michael, her fiancé, flew in from Moscow. At first her family was fixated on things like going to the morgue. But then they just made a decision that she was gone based on information they heard.

For instance, a guy who worked on the same floor as Karol apparently called his wife after the second plane hit Karol's tower. Nobody knows how his call got through. That wife eventually got in touch with Karol's Mom.

This guy told his wife: "There's smoke. The heat is really bad. I'm not going to make it out. People are dying around me of smoke inhalation. It's bad."

And another person who was running to evacuate after the first plane hit said she saw Karol and said, "Aren't you coming? Why don't you come? We've got to get out of here."

Karol said, "No. I'm staying right where I am."

That's about all we know. Just those two things.

There's dust all over the city now. In the past two weeks I've breathed it in. I've breathed in Karol. I think it's better to think that she was incinerated and I'm breathing in her dust that's being sprinkled over the city that she loved.

I've been numb, pretty much, that feeling you get when you've slept on your arm all night. But when you wake up, all the blood comes rushing back in. The feeling's coming back to me now, and I wish it wouldn't.

I know she's gone. But now I just want to believe that she didn't die in vain. I can't feel hate for anybody. I just want her death to have meant something.

I'm waiting to see what this meant. ▓

KEVIN KILLIAN, 43. Chief Information Officer for Verizon, in charge of support and direction for all the systems, needs, and strategies for the Enterprise Solutions Group, which supports large business customers: commercial, city and federal. Kevin recounts how he and Verizon labored to resurrect one of America's greatest institutions – the New York Stock Exchange – as quickly as possible in the wake of the attack.

———

I had a meeting the morning of the 11th, at 1095 Avenue of the Americas. When I got there at around nine o'clock, they had a large-screen TV off the elevator that showed a big picture of the Trade Center with smoke coming out of it. Underneath the picture, the caption said a plane was believed to have hit the building.

At that point, the media was still thinking that the aircraft had been a small twin-engine plane or something of that nature. But the next thing I knew I was watching the second explosion. From the TV camera's view, you couldn't see the other plane as it hit the building but you could sure see the fire coming out the other side.

We moved quickly to the windows. We were watching from the 23rd Floor. We started to hold our meeting, but then we heard about the Pentagon and realized the situation was getting bigger and worse. A bunch of us went to the windows again and witnessed the buildings collapse.

I used to work in the brokerage industry for nine years. I worked downtown everyday for nine years, so the situation hit close to home.

I couldn't get out of the city that night. Part of me wanted to leave, sure. But another part wanted to stay and see what I could do to help. It turns out I'd have my hands full.

*　　*　　*

People who tried to use their phones in New York on September 11th may have gotten what's called a "fast busy" signal. Maybe even for a few days after. This was due to the sheer volume of calls. We had to reroute so many of them. And people whose service rode over the cables that were severed didn't have service at all until we installed the temporary, what we call "bypass cables." High speed Internet was affected, too. It runs on those central office cables.

But like a lot of telecommunications networks, Verizon's network is built with a lot of automatic, diverse routing. The network is designed to provide alternate ways to go. If, for instance, a cable gets cut - if a backhoe digs up a cable, the network automatically reroutes traffic to different facilities.

So a lot of the service throughout Manhattan was rerouted. For example, we never lost 9-1-1 emergency service in New York. It automatically rerouted to alternate facilities and networks despite all the damage.

*   *   *

The next morning, Wednesday, I reported back into 1095 Headquarters to get together with my group and see what we could do. I met with some of the senior executives in the crisis center and listened to the things that needed to be done.

Basically, we had to reconstruct two million circuits and reroute 1.5 million lines. More circuits, a tremendous amount, had to be rerouted through different offices in order to bypass the ones that were down. We had to rebuild 18 sonic networks. And then there was the big problem of the network management platform that supported the Stock Exchange and the member brokerage firms.

We had to totally rebuild the network in preparation for the Stock Exchange's proposed opening on September 17th.

*   *   *

The main systems supporting this platform were located on the 23rd floor of one of our central circuit hubs in the city, at 140 West Street. A brief item on how they're set up:

Each of the brokerage firms in the Exchange has dedicated facilities in this network and gives Verizon the ability to manage the system. If, for instance, a brokerage firm wants a private line, or a voice ring-down line to call their representatives on the stock exchange floor - or if they want a line between one member firm and another - we already have the facilities for that. Through the network management platform, we just connect a circuit in one location to a circuit in another. Normally, we can set it up in a matter of hours. But a lot of damage was sustained. A whole lot of damage.

*   *   *

Further complications developed:

We weren't even able to get into 140 West Street. The building stood adjacent to the Trade Center and, by Wednesday morning, our next door neighbor, 7 World Trade, had collapsed. The steel structure of 7 World Trade was about 49 floors high - when it collapsed, it literally slid into our building, peeling it open like a can opener. The bottom six or eight floors of 140 West were exposed. A steel beam had shot out one of the Towers and pierced the left side of 140 West Street around the 15th or 20th floor, taking out two floors. The damage was heavy.

Personnel had been evacuated and power had been shut off. Despite the trauma, the building was still standing, so this appeared promising. But we had no idea what condition our equipment was in after being exposed to the dust and the smoke. There was internal damage to the building, obviously. We just didn't know how much.

And there were other considerations. The fires that raged around 7 World Trade were being suppressed by the fire department. So there was a tremendous amount of water pouring into all the buildings in that area. The water had flooded into the cable vaults of 140 West Street - these are the basement vaults where all the cables come in. If you can imagine cables running underground, in all the manholes, connecting to different office buildings and switching centers, they ultimately connect at the cable vault.

The first ten floors of 140 West constituted one of the largest central offices for switching equipment we had in the city. All the cables from the surrounding buildings connected there, as well as all the facilities connected to other central offices in downtown. Basically, it was a hub for the whole Manhattan area.

And all of these circuits were compromised from the water. The cables were shorted out. You couldn't get conductivity.

This was going to be a very big job.

*   *   *

We started scrambling on Wednesday to rebuild the network management platform from scratch. We got vendors like Cisco Systems involved. We contacted groups within Verizon, like corporate IT[11] and gave them our grocery list. We needed routers, we need servers, we needed all sorts of equipment.

We started plans to locate all this equipment on Wednesday morning. We sent people down to the DC area, locating servers we could use. We had Alcatel helping, a vendor with parts that support the network management platform. We had parts coming in from everywhere, down from the New England area, from Canada. By midnight, we had people all over the

---

[11] Information Technologies.

country shutting down equipment that wasn't considered vital to their operation and putting it on trucks to bring in overnight for Thursday. With all the restricted access around Ground Zero, we had to work very closely with the police and Emergency Management people.

We had open lines to four or five different command centers who were all working on a different piece of the network: the facilities, the systems, the connectivity within the cables, verifying all the circuits one by one. Imagine the blizzard of conference calls we had with all these command centers, "Okay. Where are you on *this*? Where are you on *that*?"

On Thursday, we started to rebuild the platform at our Pearl Street location, where many people who supported the network were based. As we started to put it together, we realized that, not only did we need all this hardware to rebuild, we'd also need the databases that resided on the existing platform . . . and these resided at 140 West Street.

To manually rebuild all that data - populating the field tables, entering the information, plotting connections to all these circuits - we felt that to do that manually would take about ten days. We didn't have that long. The stock market had to go back up and we had to shoot for Monday, September 17th.

*   *   *

From our point of view, there was more damage from 7 World Trade collapsing than from the Towers. When 7 World Trade came down, it crushed a lot of underground cables. We realized it would take months and months, if not years to rebuild - obviously not an acceptable time frame in an emergency situation. So we went for the quickest fix. We connected cables to the switches on those upper floors of 140 West Street and threw the cables out the windows, running them like spider webs to various other points downtown, splicing them in wherever we found cables that hadn't been destroyed.

Over the next couple of days, Verizon employees ran cables outside the building from the 6th and 7th floors, draping them across the streets to provide local service for the disaster recovery efforts. The city, the police and all sorts of people had lost service and communication, as you can probably imagine, was paramount in the aftermath of the attack.

They strung cables over streets, from building to building, whatever they could do at the time. Over on Pearl Street, next to Police Headquarters, we had cables running out windows. In some cases, they snaked out the front door of our headquarters.

*   *   *

On Thursday afternoon, I went to the crisis center with the senior management team. I indicated that we had done all we could at that point. Now we needed to get into the 23rd floor of 140 West Street and grab equipment out to rebuild the Stock Exchange platform. People had already gone into the lower floors to assess the damage to the structural stability of the building.

I obtained authorization. But there was still a lot going on down in that area. Smoke. Fire. Chaos. The military, the firemen, the police, and just about every government agency you can think of. There was the fear of all the toxins in the air. Management wanted us trained in the use of respirators and "moon suits"[12] before entering the building.

On Friday morning, I left with five people. We were up in Midtown and had to take a subway as far downtown as we could, which turned out to be 14th Street. From there, we walked down to Canal. We picked up some flashlights and tools from one of our central offices along the way. And we decided that, if we were going to bring these servers down from the top floors, we were going to need something to protect them from the dust and dirt. So we picked up a bunch of garbage bags, too.

We'd walked about a mile from the last subway stop when I was able to stop a police van which drove us the rest of the way down to West Street. They dropped us off a block from the building.

*　*　*

I'd prearranged it with some of the facilities people so they knew we were coming. When we got to 140 West Street, there were a lot of folks doing cleaning and abatement of the building. We asked eight of the cleaners to help us carry the equipment down, this way we wouldn't have to make multiple trips. This was early Friday afternoon..

We got into our environmental equipment and went up to the 23rd floor with flashlights, tools and the garbage bags. At this point, no one had been above the 10th floor; the cleaning crew had mostly focused on the physical equipment in the central office. We were told point blank that we couldn't go on one side of the building because, structurally, they weren't sure it was sound.

We didn't stop to scrutinize the damage on the lower floors, we were in the stairwells in the center of the building. The damage was obvious anyway. There was a lot of dust on those lower floors. A lot of exposed steel beams and concrete. The ceilings were falling down, the

---

[12]Environmental protection suits

floors were cracked. Desks, cubicles and switching equipment were strewn all over the place. A tremendous amount of devastation.

We went up slowly and carefully. We didn't have too many flashlights so we tried to stay together. On the upper floors, things didn't look too bad. It was dark and dusty, but other than that, there wasn't a lot of devastation. The data center was in a more controlled environment - there were several doors in place there. We broke a window into one of the rooms because we didn't have a key.

We cut the cables that connected the servers to make them easier to get out. We unscrewed them from their racks, put them into the garbage bags and secured the bags to keep them dust-free.

In all, we were carrying ten Sun servers that were the main databases; size wise, they were each the size of a PC - not the huge-sized, heavy servers. But heavy enough.

We trucked them downstairs to the lobby.

*   *   *

We had a truck on stand-by to pick us up but President Bush was in the city. As you recall, he spoke to the crowd at Ground Zero and he was standing right outside our building at the corner of 140 West Street.

You know how it is when the President comes to town. They shut everything down. There's no traffic, there's no movement at all. We couldn't get the truck in. I made phone calls to our folks who dealt with the police to see if we could get a police van to come pick us up, but we couldn't get through. So we ended up sitting there for a few hours until the President finished and only then were we able to get the truck in and take the equipment out.

I stood outside, waiting, listening to the President's speech. It was an emotional moment. When he finished, he went through the crowd shaking hands and I happened to be standing next to the truck he was coming back to. I got to shake the President's hand and then Governor Pataki's.

*   *   *

We took the equipment to the 375 Pearl Street location and started to rebuild. We worked that whole weekend, coordinating with different groups all through the nights. To pull the data out, we had to rebuild the entire system and bring the platform up gradually. We had it up by Saturday, but to bring the network fully back on-line, one of our corporate planes had to go to Texas to bring back some additional equipment. All this while equipment from other places around the country kept arriving in the middle of the night after which it was shuttled to different central offices who'd develop different aspects of the new network.

On Sunday night, I walked downtown to one of the NYSE offices. I was trying to get conductivity so that NYSE had access the network management platform and could make changes. I was there until the middle of the night trying to get that aspect up, then I went back to working with different people until dawn. At five o'clock a.m., I was still wondering if we'd be able to pull it all together. Certain things were working but we still didn't have full conductivity.

But in that last hour between five and six o'clock in the morning, everything started to click. All the last pieces fell into place. At six o'clock we finally had the ability to access the network and make immediate changes. We had the folks at NYSE come over and sit in our Pearl Street office. From there, we tackled everything on a priority basis according to what the businesses and the Stock Exchange needed. We worked right up until the point the Stock Exchange was opened at nine a.m.

*   *   *

Was I short of breath? Well, at 8:59 am, I'd been holding my breath all night. I think one of our executives described the situation as 'a diving catch in the bottom of the ninth.' The opening bell sounded at the Exchange and everything went pretty flawlessly. Obviously certain firms weren't fully operational and others were scrambling to have people work at different facilities because they couldn't work from their regular offices. But the network worked and it was a record day of trading volume.

Chairman Grasso from the Stock Exchange was very happy. We got a tremendous amount of recognition from the government and the Stock Exchange and from all the member firms who were elated we'd been able to pull it off.

*   *   *

The teamwork within Verizon was incredible. Everyone, all the different groups, focused on getting things done. People had been working hard since Tuesday the 11th. I can't tell you how many hundreds - maybe thousands - of people within Verizon never went home from the 11th 'till a week later. They lived in their offices. They slept on floors and sofas. They got an hour's sleep here, an hour's sleep there. Just kept doing what they had to do. Some went out and got new underwear and shirts when they had to, but they didn't go home.

You know, one of the first things you think about when something traumatic happens is the desire to be with your family. These people stuck it out. They were very emotional about their jobs.

There was never any feeling that we wouldn't get it done. Everyone knew we would. The attitude was: "The President of the United States wants this to happen. The Governor, the Mayor, the President of the Stock Exchange. This is critical to our country, to get this up and running. To show terrorists that they can't stop us and keep us down."

I get choked up thinking about it. The dedication and commitment, the teamwork within Verizon and all the other businesses that assisted us. An incredible, incredible effort. I've never seen anything like it.

And I am proud. Very proud. §

CHRISTOPHER CASS, 43, grew up on Long Island in Cold Spring Harbor, a Yankee fan from the day he was born. He lived in Manhattan for many years before moving to Los Angeles.

I had purchased a ticket weeks before to fly on September 13th from LA to New York on the red-eye. Well, the 11th happened. My sister, Nancy, was in the World Trade Center on the 44th floor. All air travel shut down for three or four days across America and my flight was cancelled.

I called the airlines and was unable to get through, but I live close enough to a hotel in Beverly Hills that had a satellite office for United Airlines. So I walked in, took a number and waited in line. It was a big crowd. Everybody was saying the same thing. "I was supposed to be on a flight - what's happening? When can I get outta here?" Finally, I met with the travel agent and she switched my flight to Monday night, the 17th.

*　　*　　*

LAX is a messy airport - it's self-contained with all the terminals in this large horseshoe. Because of 9/11, authorities said, "Get here early for your flight. Two hours minimum for domestic, three hours for International." For the first time, they actually meant it. I had a ten o'clock flight, so I made sure to get there well before eight.

Unfortunately, no one was allowed to drive into LAX, even to drop off or pick up passengers. Authorities were telling everyone to park in, like, "Parking Lot Z" which was nowhere near LAX; it was, like, in Long Beach. So, my wife drove me out there and I joined this amazingly long line of people with luggage queuing up to get on shuttle busses that would take us to the terminals. I could tell then that I was in for a strange evening.

I get on the shuttle bus. I throw all my luggage on, we're packed in like sardines. The driver's on the microphone with that insanely pleasant voice saying, "Terminal One," and a few people get off. "Terminal Two," a few more people get off. "Terminal Three," one or two get off. And then: "Terminal Four," which is the international flight terminal. *Everybody* got off the shuttle! It was a mass exodus, except for me and one other guy. Everybody who got off at Terminal Four looked like foreigners and I got the distinct impression that they were all eager as hell to get out of America.

*　　*　　*

Now fast forward a bit: I'm in the United terminal to check in. I go up to the counter, hand over my ticket and passport. I ask the woman if there's any way I can get a window seat.

She rapidly strikes her keyboard, glances at the screen, and says, "Everything's all booked up, but ask the attendant at the gate, there'll probably be cancellations. We might be able to fit you in."

That day, I was concerned with security - obviously. So while I'm at the counter, I ask the woman specifically, "Look, I've got this laptop I'm gonna carry on. Is that okay? Should I put it in my bags?" She says, "No, don't worry about it." And I think, "Fine, fine." I leave the United counter and head toward the security checkpoint.

I queue into the metal detector line which is long and slow. Everyone's going through one security checkpoint; there's only one conveyor belt for luggage, one metal detector. I'm fidgeting; I can sense that everyone's getting antsy. There's an Arab-looking man in line and it's impossible not to notice him under the circumstances. And this woman with a baby stroller turns to me and decides at that moment to say, for whatever reason, in a voice loud enough to carry four or five people in front, "I'm going to Baltimore and I hope *that* guy's not on my flight!"

She made no bones about it, she didn't even try to clean it up. Didn't whisper it under her breath, it was like, "To hell with being PC,[13] this is how I feel, so this is what I'm saying." I ignored her. Chose not to engage in conversation, pretended I was distracted with my own thoughts. Doing the half-polite, Gee-I'd-rather-not-talk-to-you-right-now sort of airport body language. I didn't know how to deal with her and I didn't want to. What she said made me sad. Ugh! The Ugly American.

*   *   *

Then I get to the security checkpoint. I throw my laptop, backpack and fanny pack up on the belt. I usually carry a little Swiss Army knife on my key chain, but I'd already taken that off because I'd heard that nothing even vaguely sharp would be allowed on board. Not wanting to get hassled over a two-inch pocket knife, I packed it in my luggage.

I noticed that every item going through the x-ray machine stopped, backed up, and then went on through again. Everybody's stuff: forwards, backwards, forwards again. More security people than I'd ever seen at an airport checkpoint, too. U.S. Marshals in blue windbreakers with yellow, bold lettering on the back. LAPD. LA Airport Transit Cops. National Guardsmen. The works. A police state.

---

[13]PC - "Politically Correct", a modern sociological phenomena whereby people phrase their responses to certain situations in a way that could not possibly offend any societal group.

My laptop went through and I was prepared to deal with some questions. The *sir-could-you-step-over-here, turn-your-computer-on-please* deal. What did I have in that case? The computer. Lots of phone cord for the modem. An extra battery for my cell phone. A tiny travel alarm clock. Couple of camera lenses, film canisters. What I supposed would look like the makings of a small bomb through an x-ray machine.

But the security guys slipped the computer case through the machine once. Twice. The attendant nodded to me, I grabbed the case and was on my way. I took about three steps past all these men wearing uniforms and guns, and I thought, "Are we really any safer than we were a week ago?"

I was struck with this insane urge to just call one of these armed guards and say, "Look, I just breezed on through here and nobody checked anything. What the hell is going on?"

*   *   *

It's nine o'clock now and I walk up to the gate counter because I wanted to get that window seat. This woman, whom I'll call United Employee Number One, takes my boarding pass and types my name into the computer. I tell her how I'd prefer the window. She says, "We're gonna start boarding in about 25 minutes. Why don't you come back and I'll see what I can do for you then? I'll hold onto your boarding pass in the meantime."

25 minutes later, I'm back at my gate and United Employee Number One is nowhere to be seen. So I go up to the counter, now manned by United Employee Number Two, and I explain how Number One has my boarding pass, and I want a window seat and blah blah blah blah. Says Number Two, "We're not boarding just yet. She'll be back. I'll keep an eye out for you."

Off I go to find a chair and sit down amidst this crowd of people who are all . . . watching everyone else. Everyone sizing each other up. Who are you? Why are *you* flying on this flight? *My* flight? This sense of vigilance. We had been in shock all week. We were all a little paranoid.

I *did* notice at that point that there were two or three Arab-looking guys. And I *noticed* that I noticed them, you know? I thought, God, now I'm like that woman with the stroller. But I just couldn't help it. I noticed and I felt bad for it. But I noticed just the same.

Then, the announcement comes over the speakers. "Sorry, we're experiencing a slight delay. The pilot is having a staff meeting with the crew. There are five flight attendants on this flight. Three of them have checked in and two are still going through the security checkpoint and they're on the way up. We apologize."

I thought, "That's the most information I've ever heard an airline disclose about a flight delay ever."

When the two flight attendants came rushing down the concourse, it was a validation. Ah! They were telling the truth. It's a nice feeling when the airlines tell the truth.

*   *   *

Now the passengers are starting to line up at the gate, I go back up to the counter to meet with United Employee Number Three, an older woman with a nicer uniform and a bright red scarf. She appeared to be some sort of senior United official. And I strike up a conversation with her, "I gave my boarding pass to a woman who used to be here, she told me not to worry. I was trying to get a window seat."

Number Three finds my boarding pass and says, "Yes, there will be a window seat available. I'll change it for you." By now, we are over 40 minutes late. It's ten o'clock and we haven't even gotten on the plane. More PA announcements: "We're sorry, we're sorry."

Finally, they call my chunk of rows and I get on the plane with my laptop and my backpack.

Now prior to going to the airport, I had - for whatever reason - pulled a note card out of my drawer at home and scribbled a few lines to the crew of the flight I was going to be on. "Dear Crew, I know we've all had this horrendous week and I just wanted to share my sympathies with you, your company and your fellow workers. This is a tragedy of epic proportions, blah blah blah . . . ." Just a sympathy note to let them know that some passengers care about them and what they do for a living.

I had never written a note like that before in my life. I just wanted them to know that they're appreciated. We don't know what happened to that one plane that crashed in Pennsylvania but it could very well have been that the crew and passengers worked together to stop any further disaster from happening.

I'm walking down through the gangway to get on and as soon as I hit the threshold of the airplane, here are these two flight attendants who are all smiles. "Welcome! Welcome! Hello!" And the first one I saw, I just reached in my pocket and shoved the envelope into her hands. I barely even made eye contact with her, I just mumbled, "This is for you." And then I hiked my bag up on my shoulder and walked off down the aisle. Didn't want to make a big production out of it.

I go to my seat, look down the fuselage of the plane and there is, well, for lack of a better word, there's "Abdul" sitting in an aisle seat.

*   *   *

I don't even know what the proper phrase is. *A Middle Eastern man? An Arab-looking guy?* He had olive skin, brown eyes, black hair, and a moustache. Fairly nondescript, but most definitely of Mediterranean or Middle Eastern origin.

I did the *airplane nod* the one that says, "Hi, I'm going to be living in that seat right there, you need to get out so that I can get in." He understood. He stood up right away, I threw my laptop in the overhead, scrooched into the row, and put my bag under the seat. I pulled my newspaper out and I thanked him and he sat back down, started futzing with the seat belt, and there's elbows flying, and I'm folding the paper, but before I begin to even read the paper . . .

. . . And I never do this. I mean I *don't talk to anyone on airplanes.* But I thought about it for a long moment and said, "So. How was *your* week?"

*   *   *

This thought hit me a few days after the flight: I was doing something that people were frightened to do. Fly to New York. Go to Ground Zero.

I had to admit I'd been making calculations in my head, like, "okay, if I'm taking a redeye flight and we're loaded with 60,000 pounds of jet fuel and were leaving Los Angeles, the terrorists are not going to crash us in New York because there's not going to be any fuel on the plane by the time we get there. No fuel means no explosion, so they're going to crash here in L.A. They obviously would want a flight they knew had less passengers so there wouldn't be any more Shanksville incidents. But hang on a minute. My flight is *full* . . ."

This was the kind of shit floating through my head.

*   *   *

"So. How was your week?"

He looks at me and says, "Fine."

It was just one word. A cold delivery. It felt like after the word *fine* left his mouth a big white sheet of cardboard came up that read, THAT'S IT. THAT'S DONE. Then I thought, "Cut the guy some slack, huh? If it wasn't this particular week, if anyone had asked me the same question two weeks earlier, I would have said, 'fine' too." So I put my newspaper up in front of me and went about my business.

But then I had this thought right after that. How can you just say "fine?" How can anyone just say "fine" after the week that just happened? September 11th was . . . it was a Kennedy moment. Where were you when JFK was shot? Everyone knows where they were when John Lennon was killed. Everyone knows where they were when the Space Shuttle blew. It's a Kennedy moment, a Pearl Harbor moment.

I just didn't expect to get *fine* and then have him drop it so suddenly. So I *pretended* to read my paper. But now I can't help but preoccupy myself, "Why did he say 'fine?' What does he *really* want to say?" And now I'm looking out of the corner of my eye, thinking, "Wow, he really *does* look like an Arab."

I noticed that there weren't any airline magazines in the front pocket of my seat. I found out later there'd been a picture inside the magazine showing the World Trade Center so United had decided to pull them.

* * *

Now it's 20 minutes after ten and we're still at the gate. The flight attendants have run down the aisles, taken the head count, and whacked down the doors to the overhead compartments. We're all ready to go, but now I'm having these crazy thoughts:

"If this guy *is* a terrorist, what do I do? I've just put my rinky-dink, little Swiss Army knife in my bag, it's packed up and stowed below. I've got this copy of the LA Times, I could roll it up and hit him with the Sports Section. I've got a blanket and a pillow. I could throw the blanket over his head."

And then I'm thinking, "Why am I having these thoughts? He's just a passenger on a plane. No different from me."

But for these 10 or 15 minutes that we're waiting, I got a little wigged out. Abdul crossed his leg and he had the right-foot-leg-tap going. His right leg crossed over his left, just barely sticking out in the aisle. This was all registering.

* * *

About another five or ten minutes went by. Then, I saw a flight attendant come down my aisle. She stops right in front of where Abdul and I are sitting. She hunkers down, looks at us and says, "I'm sorry to do this, gentlemen, but you fit a profile and the captain would like to see you both."

My mouth is wide open. "Me?" I say, almost audibly choking on the idea.

And she's smiling. Still smiling the whole time. "Yes, if you could just follow me?"

Neither one of us did anything for a dramatic beat. Then, I unbuckled my seat belt and Abdul unbuckled his. He stood up. He wasn't in any hurry to go. I, on the other hand, can't wait to find out what's going on. *I* fit a profile?[14] I've got my American passport out -

I thought, "What is it? My goatee?" But then I thought: "Aha! The card! Someone gave the flight attendant my card and they must have thought, 'He's out of his head! He's the good cop, Abdul's the bad cop! He's too nice. Why did you give us this *card*, sir!? Let's question him!'"

Well, I got up. Abdul got up. He's walking in front of me, right up ahead of me, and every head on the plane is looking at us. I have my passport and I have my California driver's license, gathering it all out of my little fanny pack. I'm thinking, "Okay, I know I'm not in any kind of trouble. If nothing else, I will have a good story to tell when I get off the plane." But I was insanely curious. And it wasn't even an option to protest.

I thought we were going to the cockpit. We didn't. We deboarded the plane on the gangway. I'm thinking, "Oh, wow. I didn't expect to leave the actual airplane. Now aren't there some sort of merchant marine laws that go into affect when you get on and off a plane?" I had this little moment of "what-are-my-rights?" I step out and there's a small crowd of United employees standing around.

There's the captain and a U.S. Marshal. Other United security guys with their blue blazers and then there's the two flight attendants, hovering by the door, but still inside the plane. And the two other Arab guys are out there. Three Arab-looking gentlemen, and me.

*   *   *

The captain is engaged with the other two Arab guys. His posture is rigid. He's shaking his head back and forth and back and forth, holding passports in his hand. It's not a pleasant look on his face. It's like he's got bad gas. He's breathing a couple of deep breaths. I saw him

---

[14]At this point it's probably important to describe Christopher Cass as a Caucasian male with brown hair, blue eyes who was, at the time, wearing a goatee. On the day of the flight, he was dressed casually in a jacket, denim shirt, tie, and khaki pants.

hand the documents back to the two Arab guys. Then he turns to Abdul and says, "You've probably been getting this all week and I apologize, but I need to see some identification."

Abdul pulled out a driver's license-looking piece of ID. I started getting tunnel vision, I couldn't focus on anything but my pounding heart. I started getting sweaty. What am *I* nervous about? Why is *my* adrenaline running?

I remember hearing one of the blue coats say, "Do you have anything else? Where are you from? Where are you going?" The captain was now rolling his eyes, and shaking his head. I kept repeating this inner monologue of, "I don't want to be here. I don't want to have anything to do with this." Meantime, everyone else is just watching.

The pilot, looking like he's finished with Abdul, looks up at me. I look at him - then past his shoulder. And I see another person who's been standing there the whole time. It's the Senior United Woman with the red scarf, standing behind him five feet away. I make eye contact with her, her eyes bug wide open, her mouth drops, and she mouths, "What are *you* doing here?"

I shrugged my shoulders and mouthed back, "I don't know." And the captain starts to walk toward me, but the Senior United Woman intercepts him. She grabbed him by the bicep, grabbed me by the bicep and huddled the three of us off to the side. Our heads were really close together and she said to the captain, "Steve, this is Mister Cass. He's fine. We talked a little while back. His sister was in the World Trade Center and he's going to New York to see her. I put him in that seat 20 minutes ago."

The captain looks at my passport, then at me, and says, "Well, aren't you traveling with this guy?"

"Nooooooo," I guffaw.

He looks back at Abdul and asks, "Are you traveling with him?" Abdul looks at me, then back at the Captain, and shakes his head, "no".

The captain says to me, "I'm really very sorry. I assumed you were traveling with him. These other two gentlemen are traveling together. I'm very, very sorry. Please accept my apologies. You can go back to your seat."

My pulse rate is peaking by now. The lovely United employee is holding onto me with both arms saying, "I'm sorry. So sorry. Please. Enjoy your flight."

I'm genuinely sincere when I look at both of them and say, "It's fine. Really." And I walked back into the plane.

*　　*　　*

The first person I saw was the flight attendant whom I'd handed the card to. I looked at her and said, "Is this because I gave you a card?"

She gasped, "Oh, *you're* Mister Cass. I'm so sorry. We loved your card! I've passed it around to the entire crew - we've all read it. So-and-so cried when she read it. They took *you* off the plane? Oh my God, please!" She grabbed her co-flight attendant and said, "This is the guy that wrote us the card." Suddenly everyone wanted to kiss me.

Well, I walked back down the long aisle and again, every head is watching me, everyone's eyes saying, "What happened?" I'm not in my seat for one beat when two heads, the people sitting in front of me, pop up over the chair. And the guy behind me sticks his head up over my seat. And it's like an E.F. Hutton commercial. The guy down the aisle is sticking his ear out trying to hear what I'm going to say. I abbreviate my experience to them by saying, "I'm not sure, but it's pretty serious."

About 10 or 15 more minutes go by. Two flight attendants come down and sit in Abdul's vacant seat and put their hands on my arm. "We're sorry, please accept our apologies, we're all under a lot of pressure."

Two other flight attendants walk quickly down both aisles. One stops at my seat, the other stops where the other two Arab guys were sitting toward the back of the plane. I see the overhead bin open up over me; I see the other two flight attendants on the other side open the compartment over the other guys' seats. They're rummaging through stuff, then *whoosh*, she takes the bags right off the plane.

We're past 11 o'clock now, over an hour late. The pilot gets on the PA and says, "We're taking off in a few minutes. We're just removing some luggage from down below."

And then? Applause. Not a standing ovation, but there was quite a reaction.

My emotions were mixed. I'm as angry as the next person about what happened on the 11th, but want to run around killing all Arabs, all Muslims, because that's not what it's about. But clearly what had just happened was a "let's-intern-the-Japanese" move. It was clear we were gonna pigeonhole these people, at least this week we were. The political and moral machinery inside my head was grinding and not grinding easily. It was confusing, it was awkward.

*   *   *

We took off. And by the time we'd been in the air an hour, every single flight attendant on the plane had come by my seat to apologize.

There was a young black woman sitting one row behind me in the center section. She was clearly in view of what had happened, but not within earshot. At some point in the flight she got out of her seat and sat down next to me.

"Hey, what happened?" she asked.

There was an older black couple sitting nearby who looked to be in their seventies, at least. Very nicely dressed, middle class, knowledgeable. You didn't have to say what we were all feeling, you could feel it. After the 11th, there was this sort of unspoken communal pain among people. We were all in tune with some sort of human wavelength that allowed us all to communicate, practically telepathy. Everyone and everything was heightened.

The young black woman said, "Boy, I'm so relieved they took those guys off the plane." And she got up and walked away.

A split-second later I wondered: would she have been saying that 40 years ago if a black person had been escorted off? This woman who was barely in her thirties had missed the hardcore civil rights movement, but here she was, certainly benefiting from it.

I kept trying to looking at the older black couple trying to read what they were thinking of all this. But they kept to themselves and never looked over. I just wanted to get a feeling, some sort of expression. But they didn't share it with me. I know this: a black man in his seventies has felt discrimination in this country. I was just hoping that there would be some wisdom in that man's face that I could learn from. But nothing came. ဒ

SCOTT SLATER, 30, a New Yorker...

Scott Slater

After the attack, I holed up in my apartment, compulsively watching the news for two days. But then I felt the need to get out, to do something. I grabbed my camera and started walking, visiting every site in New York I could possibly think of. Lincoln Center. Union Square. Canal Street. The Empire State Building. The Armory. I walked all around the city.

Then, at Rockefeller Center, I was struck by an image.

Normally, there are flags flying from all different nations. On September 13th there was a single American flag flying at half-staff. The other poles were bare. It was a pronounced statement of sorrow. Our flag was still there.

A few days later, I happened back in the area with my camera. The single flag had been replaced with more American flags than you can imagine. One for every single pole, all flying full staff, a tremendous show of strength. On that second visit, I looked at the flags and thought, "We have risen again." 🥢

Scott Slater

If you follow the music scene in Manhattan, you've surely heard of The Bogmen. In the mid-1990's the band was the toast of the town playing rock music they smirkingly described as: "Hi-Fi/Lowbrow Super-charged Lounge Fodder." BRENDAN RYAN, 30, helped found the band with his brother Bill and their friend, Bill Campion.

Brendan's wife KRISTIN IRVINE RYAN co-founded a charity called Secret Smiles which, in the wake of September 11th, has taken on a mission its founders could not have possibly imagined. Brendan tells us his story: about music that plays again, charity that finds new purpose, and a love that refuses to die.

———

When the first plane hit, Kristy called me and said, "Put the news on."

I saw what was going on and said, "Are you guys going to evacuate?"

She thought the explosion was in her building at first. But I was watching it all on TV. I said, "No, no. You're the Tower without the antennae, right?" Just to be clear. "No, it's in the other building. Are you evacuating?"

". . . No." Still very poised. Kristy had nerves of steel.

"Why aren't you evacuating?"

She didn't know. But then she told me that an announcement came on saying that everybody should relax. The fire was in the other building and it was being contained, the announcement said.

I thought, *contained?*

She said, "I'll call you back." She wanted to wait for more instructions and she wanted to called her dad to let him know she was OK.

* * *

I'd known Kristy since I was twelve. We grew up together. At the time we met, she went to Catholic school and I went to public school in Huntington, Long Island. We became very good friends. Like best friends.

We talked about getting married and having kids when we were in ninth grade. We went to proms and dances together, but we weren't 'boyfriend and girlfriend'. Kristy always thought that if we got together too young, we would never last.

She always said, "After college." As if she had a crystal ball. "After college, we'll get serious."

We went to college and wrote letters to each other. We called each other; she was in Dayton and I was in Providence. It was a . . . you know, it was a healthy relationship.

After college, we were together a long time. Eight years. Engaged for a year. Then married last June, 2001.

Ninety-four days. That was the duration of our marriage.

*   *   *

Kristy had worked at the Equities desk of Sandler O'Neill and Partners since '93, after she graduated from college. She loved that job, she loved the people there. A draw back to a job in investment banking is that you spend a *lot* of time with your colleagues; the people at Sandler were together all the time. But they were like a family. There was very little privacy. If Kristy had a doctor's appointment, she couldn't hide it. Everyone was right there, everyone knew about it.

They were all so close, such a special group. They really enjoyed each other's company and got along well. When you work that closely with people, tensions are bound to get high and relationships get strained. But Kristy's equities group remained close friends throughout.

How often do you see people stay at the same job on Wall Street? Kristy was there for eight years and she never wanted to leave.

When we were preparing for our wedding last June, we reviewed the guest list and I said, "Wow, there's a lot of Sandler O'Neill people here. We've got to cut it down." We ended up inviting ten.

*   *   *

When she called back, I said, "I'm watching this on the news. When you go downstairs, don't go outside. I can see debris falling off the first Tower."

I didn't imagine another plane coming in. Who did? I was hoping Kristy and her group would leave soon. I looked at the fire in the north Tower and got concerned. I had just watched a TV special two weeks before where a fire in a Californian suburb had spread too rapidly to be stopped.

"When you get downstairs, stay low," I said. "Go into the subway and call me. Call me when you get down there. What does it look like up there?"

She said, "All we can see is black smoke."

I was on the phone with her, watching the TV when I saw the second plane hit the south Tower. Kristy was working on the 104th floor.

The phone went *ssssshhhhhhhh*. Then it came back in.

She said, "We're going down now."

I said, "I love you. Call me when you get downstairs."

But the phone went dead. And that was it.

*   *   *

The night before, on the 10th of September, we went for a walk. We talked about . . . everything. I guess it's kind of strange to have that kind of talk the night before she passed away. The subject of her job came up.

She mentioned how a lot of our friends who work on Wall Street were struggling and looking for new opportunities. But Kristy said she felt fortunate. Sandler O'Neill was a great place to work.

"It's secure," she said. "I love everybody I work with." She told me this on *that* Monday night.

Also that night the subject of Sandler O'Neill's lease came up. Kristy told me that the firm might move out of the Trade Center in January or February.

I hadn't heard Kristy say anything about it until that night. I said to her, "you never told me this."

"Oh, yeah," she said. "No big deal." Which was a typical response from Kristy because she took everything in stride.

"Well, what do you think about it?"

She said, "Well, to tell you the truth, I'm sick of the whole Trade Towers thing. The elevator systems are inadequate. Like once you're up in the office, you're up there. You can't go down."

I said, "What other 110 story buildings do you have to compare the elevator systems to?"

She said, "Well, anyway, I wouldn't mind moving."

So there was talk of them moving to mid-town. But not fast enough, I guess.

*　*　*

I'm a musician and I've always traveled a lot. But Kristy was very patient. She held on to our relationship saying, "I have no choice. You're the one I want to marry."

Music was something I did in junior high school, high school and college. Early on, The Bogmen had interest from a manager who managed Miles Davis and Cyndi Lauper. He said, "Look, I'll pay your rent, I'll get you guys a studio. We'll get a record deal with Warner Brothers." So we signed a full-time contract with him, but it didn't work out. We toured around the East Coast without representation. We played here in New York City a lot. Within that year, we became the biggest unsigned band in the city.

Then we signed a deal with Arista records in 1994 and ended up having a long four or five year relationship with them. We put out two albums and a live album. Did a little bit of MTV, toured some, had some success. Then the group broke up about two and half years ago.

It just got old. It wasn't fun anymore for us. It's so hard to keep a band together.

But here I had this relationship with Kristy that was so easy. She encouraged me to keep going, to work through it. She wanted me to do whatever made me happy.

The last year I was with The Bogmen was not a good year for me. I was pretty miserable. But she supported me emotionally through it all.

*　*　*

It didn't register to me right away, what had happened. I thought that the fuel tank had exploded from the first plane and spread to Tower Two - that's how it looked at first, from the angle of the news camera. That's what the commentator said had happened.

So, thinking that the explosion had only hit the edge of Tower Two, I tried to convince myself that she was okay. I kept thinking, "She can get below that."

But when they replayed the second plane's attack from different angles, and it began to sink in. I kept dialing her number, but the line was dead.

That's when I realized there was no chance. Nobody who was up that high could have gotten out.

I knew early that day that it was over. I just hope and pray, like all family members, that it was painless and quick.

Whichever version of an afterlife you believe in, you have to believe these people are in a special place. I believe Kristy is because she, as much as anyone, deserves to be.

*   *   *

Let me tell you a little about Secret Smiles.

It began with Kristy's best friend, Meredith O'Neill Hasset, who's a school teacher in Harlem. Her father is Tom O'Neill - that's how Kristy got her interview at Sandler right out of college.[15]

In '98, Meredith felt really bad for one of her outstanding students. The boy's mother was a single parent on Welfare who didn't have a refrigerator, a stove, and lot of other necessities. This woman was a very caring mother who worked very hard for her child. She would try to get a part time job somewhere, at the GAP, for instance. But the way the system works, her salary would just get deducted from her Welfare. It's a paralyzing system.

Meredith saw the poverty this woman was in, and the commitment she had to her son. So she raised some money. I think Meredith may have contributed some of her own; Kristy did and Tom O'Neill did, too. They ended up buying necessities for this mother right before Christmas. Secretly.

Meredith wouldn't have the mother know that she was behind the gift. So she sent Kristy, Kristy's sister Kerry, and me uptown to the woman's apartment two or three days prior

---

[15]Brendan notes that, thankfully, Tom O'Neill had business on the west coast on the 11th of September.

Christmas. Since we were strangers, we could pose as representatives from a bank, and we told her what was being delivered.

We said, "Congratulations, you won a raffle." We met Meredith's student who was so happy to receive the gifts. Well, the mother stood there in disbelief. All this went on as Meredith waited in the car outside the apartment, anxious to hear about their reaction.

The following year Meredith and Kristy thought, why not start this as a charity? And we've been doing it ever since, keeping with the practice of anonymity. It was, and is, such a beautiful thing.

That's how Secret Smiles was formed.

*   *   *

Kristy has four sisters, three of whom live far away. They all drove to New York as soon as possible – they had to because the airlines were grounded after the 11th. They wanted to support one another and their father, Stu; Kristy's mom had passed away eight years before. So we all gathered in Huntington and the city to support each other.

The days that followed September the 11th were long and filled with rumors. Out of concern for each other - and since we all hoped for survivors - family members from the firm called each other asking questions. "Did Frank get out? Did Bruce get out? Where's Craig? Where's Stacey?"

All these people. Confused. Ridiculous. It was, and still is a true nightmare.

Survivor lists circulated through different hospitals and somebody had put Kristy's name on one of them, as well as two other people from her desk. This created a painful sense of false hope.

I remember someone calling me more than a week after the attacks saying that they're all still alive, in a hospital somewhere in New Jersey. I had to hang up the phone.

Including Kristy, nine people who were at our wedding passed away in the Towers. Everybody at her desk. Gone. Including Stacey McGowan, who was one of Kristy's brides-maids. And it really made me angry, prolonging everything.

There's no blue print for this kind of tragedy. People were and are simply devastated.

*   *   *

It's funny. Kristy went to Meredith's school one time and read children's stories to Meredith's students. Unexpectedly, that mother arrived and noticed Kristy, who was hard to miss because she was so beautiful. Looking at Kristy, the mother said to Meredith, "I know that woman, she looks familiar."

Meredith played dumb. "Oh? Really?"

Meredith and that mother eventually became friends, so the woman attended Meredith's wedding in October of 2001. Even after Kristy's death, she still had no idea that it was Meredith and Kristy's charity who had delivered those items.

I played piano at parts of the wedding, and the woman kept saying to Meredith, "I'm telling you, I know that guy from somewhere."

Good Morning America produced a segment on Kristy and Secret Smiles which aired on Christmas Eve of 2001. It was set up so that the mother could finally meet Kerry and I. So the secret's over.

The mother looked at me and said, "I *knew* you! I *recognized* you!"

I just wished Kristy had been there. She would have loved it.

*   *   *

The Bogmen reunited to play a benefit concert for Secret Smiles in memory of Kristy. We performed two nights at Irving Plaza. Gordon Gano, the singer/songwriter for the Violent Femmes did the shows with us. We're all friends who go to the same bars. He and I wrote a couple songs together with my brother, and I put a CD together with some musician friends in memory of Kristy. I wrote the lyrics to one song *You Make Me Happy* for Kristy.

The band hadn't played together for two and a half years so we were originally going to perform one night. In doing so, we set a high ticket price, but since the first night sold out so fast, we added another. The Bogmen raised $100,000 from those two nights - all proceeds went to Secret Smiles.

We've parlayed Secret Smiles towards what happened downtown. We're getting the word out, and have done some press. We have a website now at www.Secretsmiles.org, and we're still very un-bureaucratic. We're public, but small. We act quickly to get relief right out.

We're not just helping in Harlem, either. We're in Long Island and the tri-State area as well . . . wherever we feel we can help. We're working hand-in-hand with Safe Horizon and some other charities to find out who's really the neediest of the needy and we're focusing on that; the window washers, restaurant workers, and the receptionists in the Towers – their families. The lower income households who may have lost earners.

*   *   *

I think about Kristy all the time. Of course, I do. She was filled with happiness and virtue. Life is hard without her. But the mourning process isn't focused. When a group like hers gets taken out . . . it doesn't make grieving any easier. I think it makes it harder. I know the saying is that 'misery loves company'.

But it doesn't pertain to this situation. It just doesn't.

I talk to family members from Kristy's desk and it's very difficult because the losses are inconceivable. How could so many innocent, young, and talented people be gone?

It's different for everybody. I've talked to some widows - many of whom have kids. They *have* to step it up for their kids, and they're doing it; this takes a tremendous amount of strength.

I don't have any children. I often wish Kristy could have left more of herself behind, an extension of her.

*   *   *

I ran around for the last three and half months, not sure how to approach each day. I didn't sit at home all day crying, I went out a lot and kept moving, doing what I had to do. I planned the shows, worked on the CD, the charity; I started a new job.

But dealing with paper work and certificates is hard because the process is so cold. I've been down to Pier 94 probably eight times now. I've been to surrogate court three times, to Worth Street four or five to visit FEMA, HRA,[16] the Salvation Army, the Red Cross. I get all these letters from Kristy's company saying, "Make sure you register for this, and make sure you call these people. Meanwhile, there's a lot of people out there trying to milk the system who weren't even involved in September 11th. It has a de-humanizing effect, which

---

[16]Human Resources Administration, a city agency.

328

I really don't like.

I kept busy but hated coming home. I dreaded it. I moved to another apartment three weeks ago early December, 2001 and it's helped. I dreaded the other apartment. I slept on the couch for three months with the news on, waiting for the next catastrophe.

* * *

Terrorists piloting a plane to hit American targets is like a midget hitting Mike Tyson in the face and knocking him out. I'm still wondering where our intelligence was, where our defenses were.

For *two* planes to hit the Towers? And another to hit the Pentagon? It's as if our nation's biggest targets sat defenseless. If we sat around a think tank and wondered, "What would someone do if you were an enemy of the United States?" we would probably come up with this scenario.

People believe that what happened that day was inconceivable. I don't. I believe that our government failed Kristy, and all of those people. It's the government's job, first and foremost, to protect its citizens. On the 11th of September, it simply did not do that.

* * *

Things are a little better now, although nights can be rough. It's hard to fall asleep, and my dreams are often difficult. I'm not a pill person, I'm not into medication. Still, the loss of Kristy causes a pain that comes in waves, and it's difficult to control the tempo in which those waves come.

When I wake up, I still smell the fumes from Ground Zero through the bedroom window, and I think, "This isn't really happening." Or, "I'll see Kristy again, she'll come back." Or, "This is just a dirty joke someone's playing on me."

But then I always realize it can't be changed. Like so many others from this catastrophe, my life has changed, and this, unfortunately, is the new world.

I guess I have to do something to make a difference. Kristy did. I can't just stay in bed and do nothing. Some days are really bad, but I get up every morning and try to get *something* done.

Kristy was loved by so many people. She's sorely missed and she always will be. Her friends and family miss her beyond belief. But what I truly find amazing about Kristy is that - even after her death, because of her work with Secret Smiles - people who never even met her feel her presence. And those people miss her too.

*   *   *

The following lyrics are excerpted from the CD produced by The Bogmen, Gordon Gano, and the Knockout Drops for the Irving Plaza benefit, Kristy's Smile.

YOU MAKE ME HAPPY

Walked through the sunbeams from your eyes
Cracked up and laughed all alone
It's not just me on this island
You're with me now to the stone.

You make me happy
You make me happy
You make me happy

It's just a brief separation
Close your eyes, grab onto faith
Rock away all of your demons
Faith is much harder to face
It was too early for sundown
No more predictions of fate

Swam through blue water with dolphins
Kissed a sting ray on the lips
Sailed a boat straight through the ocean
Tried to just get one more kiss

You make me happy
You make me happy
You make me happy . . . 𝄡

MARK LESCOEZEC, 32. A placid guy you'd probably miss in a crowd. But a guy who can keep a company afloat in the middle of a catastrophe by letting his deft fingers work a keyboard.

———

You know, it's funny. People who work in technology? Nobody really knows about us until something goes wrong. Then we're the most important people in the world.

When the Towers went down, the destruction wasn't limited to the physical devastation of the Trade Center buildings. Massive stores of information were annihilated. To me, it's an interesting footnote. That in this age of technology, people and equipment are often replaceable. Information, however, is priceless.

Everybody lost people. Cantor Fitzgerald, you've heard about them? They were huge into bonds. Seven hundred people out of a thousand were lost. I can't fathom that. There were actually concerns over the liquidity of the entire bond market because of one company's sudden destruction, imagine that.

*   *   *

You may have heard that Sandler O'Neill was a company pretty seriously affected by the attack. They were up on the 104th floor of Tower 2. Their offices were . . .well. . .pretty heavily hit.

My boss is Stan Druckamiller, who founded the company I work for, Duchesne Capital. And Stan just asked the folks at Sandler outright, "How can we help you?" See, he knew the guys in upper management at Sandler. I assume they were good friends because our industry is like any other – people get to know one another. One big happy banking family. Sandler wasn't in a position to refuse. And this is the solution we came up with:

We were gonna open up a branch office in San Francisco. I'd already staged and prepped all the necessary equipment at our New York office. It was all set to ship out to San Fran so the guys out there could take the stuff out of the boxes, plug it in, *boom.* Ready to go.

When we heard about the attack, we just . . . well. We basically gave the equipment to Sandler.

*   *   *

My company only has, like, 25 people in New York. So we only have two technology people here. We do the networking, the servers, the T1's, all that. We work with market data. It sounds dry, but imagine a bank without client information. Imagine a broker who loses all his transaction information. The banking industry rides on the back of electronics. State of the art electronics – the faster the better.

Understanding this, our attitude quickly became: "Whatever you need."

For instance, I go over to Sandler after work every day and put in a few hours to get them moving. My time's been donated by my firm. Temporarily, Sandler O'Neill's working out of the Bank of America on 57th Street. Bank of America loaned them space until they get back on their feet and find something long term. It may take two or three months. It might take longer. No one knows. Believe me when I say it's the least of everyone's worries.[17]

So my company gave Sandler everything intended for the San Francisco project and I set up a sequel server for their accounting system. They have a portfolio management system, of course, and I spent a few years in Source Fund Management, so I've worked with those systems in my previous job life. It's all foreign for them. But it's simple for me to come in and do it.

The guys in their accounting office know how to use sequel servers – packages like Solomon database and Nexteva and all that. They just don't know shit about setting them up. Funny, really, what becomes life or death for a company. You follow a question tree of very simple, but very important questions. Were their backup systems good? Were they tested? Did they keep the backups on site or off-site? Fortunately, Sandler was very compliant with all of this.

I'm sure a lot of companies from the Trade Center *didn't* do the procedures that these guys did. And now their business is gone. Wiped out.

*   *   *

That first week after the tragedy, the first week I was helping out, these people, the survivors. They were walking around the office with these . . . eyes. They were lost in a daze. It was an epidemic of white-collar shock. I found one of their portfolio managers working with the computers, actually making things worse - she had no idea what she was doing. It boiled down to advising her and the other people that were there, "Please don't think. Let *us* do the thinking. There's only one goal, now: just get your networks up and running."

I work with these people every day and it's really wild to see. I go outside to have a cigarette

---

[17]This interview was conducted less than three weeks after the attack.

and see the rest of the city scrambling as well, scrambling to get things moving again. Business has to exist. It has to move on. You have to go back to work, keep things running. Accounts are still open, deals are still up in the air for trading firms. And underlying this all is the void of so many lost friends. Faces, once familiar, that no one will ever see again. The disorientation is incalculable.

I go back inside the building and people glance up at me. So thankful. They're so happy we're there to do whatever we can.

*　　*　　*

This past week I went in and you could feel the relief. The network was finally up, the primary server was running smoothly. Given the circumstances, it all happened pretty fast.

Sandler had their tapes - every company backs up their servers, it's something most people don't even think about - and very critical data gets backed up on those tapes.

A lot of companies store them off-site and Sandler was no different. They kept theirs in a vault at HSBC[18] downtown. One little hitch: HSBC was close enough to the disaster so that no one could get into the vaults, the power was cut off.

But somehow they got those tapes. For one second, would you just imagine if they hadn't?

Here's what the scene would look like: you've got all the hardware. You've got rows of talented people sitting in front of dark screens, waiting. But all the data you've been collecting for the past 13 years – spreadsheets, documents, e-mails, portfolios, memos, protocols, payrolls, Christmas card lists. Gone.

We recovered the data from the tapes last Saturday night at two a.m. You can't imagine the huge sigh of relief.

*　　*　　*

Yeah, we still plan on opening San Francisco. But for right now we're just helping out at O'Neill. That's the focus.

I was thinking of volunteering downtown at Ground Zero. But it sounds like they have a lot of people there already. And data is what I do, this is what I *can* do. So I do it. I could dig for bodies, I guess. I could prepare food. But I honestly feel that I'm making a contri-

---

[18]Banking conglomerate.

bution here. Everyone helps in their own way.

Sandler's not out of the woods yet, not by a long shot. I want to get them up to where they can make their own decisions, function independently. They're gonna have to staff up, bring in new people, good people. It's like they're starting all over again.

At least they get the chance.

*   *   *

Let me end with this, because for me? This is how September 11th affected me in both a small and large way at once.

There's a company we use for marketing services. I called them the other day. I often have one of their technician's come in - we're converting to a T-1 line from the system we're using right now, and their guy is very cool. He knows his stuff. He's easy to work with, he solves a lot of problems. The other day I was having difficulties, so I called that service again.

I talked to a woman who answered the phone. I said, "Look, can you send Wade over? I've got a glitch here and I need to finish this conversion."

There was this pause. She said, "Wade was in the World Trade Center."

See, we weren't best friends. I just knew the guy. He was very cool. He knew his stuff. He was easy to work with. But, I mean . . . I mean, you know? ℥

OMAR METWALLY, 28, lives in Brooklyn. He's of Egyptian descent. His dark features and olive complexion might be mistaken for many ethnicities.

His words come easily, but once or twice they catch in his throat and he takes a deep breath before continuing.

———

September 11th, I was working in Mid-town at a temp job. They let us all out when we heard the news, but nobody really knew what to do.

I walked around Central Park. I normally take the F train home to Brooklyn but I couldn't go home, they'd shut the trains down. So I walked around the Park. I looked at people's faces. Lots of blank faces. It was . . . I don't know how to describe it. I was alone. I felt lost. I had nowhere to go. I couldn't get any friends on the phone to set up a place to stay in Manhattan. I didn't know where anyone was. It was awful.

So I went down to the East Side and was walking down First Avenue. I stopped at a pub, just to get off the street for a bit; by that point I'd walked around for a couple hours. There was a crowd of grief-stricken people watching the TV. You couldn't really hear what was being said. You could see the images, though. And also pictures and video of bin Laden. It was the first I'd seen of Osama bin Laden.

I leaned over to this guy next to me. I said: "What's the deal? Did they pin this on the Al Quaeda? Do they know?"

He just watched the TV and nodded. Said: "Yeah, yeah. I think it was them. I think it was bin Laden. We should bomb those fucking Arabs."

He was talking over his shoulder. He wasn't looking at me.

I didn't know what to say. So I turned to him and I said, "You know, I'm Arab."

He didn't say anything for a second. He just sort of stared at me. Frozen. Then he started stammering to apologize. "Sorry. Sorry," he said. "I'm . . . Turkish."

*   *   *

I dealt with that kind of racism growing up all my life. The way the media and films portray people of Arab descent as gun-toting madmen. You know, there was Reagan's war on

Khadaffi. And then the Gulf War in the early 90's. That sentiment's been around and you learn to deal with it. But once I'd left school, I thought I could avoid it. I guess not. It's in there and it's insidious.

How does it make me feel? Hopeless.

I hold the media responsible to a large degree. For years and years there's been a barrage of certain images. If you recall after the Oklahoma City bombing of the Federal building, there was so much speculation. Pictures shown over and over again, pictures that have a very powerful effect. They have a powerful effect on *me*. I'm part of the ethnic group that's being poorly portrayed.

After they found out it that Timothy McVeigh had been responsible – a white American - no apology was ever extended to the Arab community. But the damage had been done already. I think the same thing happened in this situation. The media flooded the nation with images that weren't put into proper context.

You know, already the number of hate crimes on record has skyrocketed. There were only 250 hate crimes reported against Arab Americans last year. Well . . . [laughs] *only* 250. It's up to four or five hundred now. It's doubled and it's growing and it's early.

I'm afraid we're going to war. I'm worried about our basic freedoms. I'm worried about our society. The Bill of Rights. The ideas that we, as a nation, were founded on. They're good ideas. But people have been put into camps in this country.[19] It's a part of our history that lots of people tend to forget. I don't.

I think there are people who are going to take advantage of this situation.

And my fear is that those problems, which are really the root of what happened at the Towers, are going to be ignored so that the government can push the American people into a really frightening right wing agenda.

Fear can be used to such great effect. The problems that need to be addressed in the world

---

[19]Following the attack on Pearl Harbor, Congress passed certain laws and the Executive branch issued certain Exclusion Orders meant to protect the West Coast military areas from sabotage. As a result, over 120,000 Japanese-Americans were required to report to internment camps, regardless of evidence of their loyalty or disloyalty to the U.S. At the time, there was little protest from Americans. The U.S. Supreme Court ruled that the internment camps did not violate the Constitutional rights of Japanese-Americans (in Korematsu vs. United States, 323 U.S. 214, 1942)

are problems that need to be addressed in this country. Problems of social justice, problems of poverty, problems of racial equality, problems of class. But we push it aside, we push it aside, push it aside. And we only reconsider our actions when it's already too late. ⌇

KEN LONGERT is the owner and operator of Ken Longert Lighting, a New York City theatrical lighting business. He's been lighting film; television and commercials; Broadway and Off-Broadway theatre; tradeshows and special events since the 1970s. All of his skills were put to the test when September 11th unexpectedly turned the Chelsea Piers into the Mayor's emergency nerve center.

Ken and his partner, FRED HORNE, review their experiences.

––––––

Ken: Talk about weird luck. The OEM[20] was training cadets at Pier 92 on September 11th. Two or three hundred cadets learning the proper procedures in case some kind of disaster hit New York. Total coincidence. We were booked four or five days before the attack happened – we're the normal subcontractors for the Pier. So we got there about seven o'clock in the morning to set up.

We were doing the job and everything's routine until we look off the south side of Pier 92 and saw smoke coming from the first Tower. Everyone assumed a plane had hit the Trade Center, that it must've been an accident.

Nobody thought much of it until a few minutes later when we witnessed the second plane. It came from the south, we were standing north. So we didn't actually see the impact, but we sure as hell saw the flames gushing out. And within seconds all the people from OEM disappeared. That's when we knew something big was going on. This is 8:45 in the morning.

We took a coffee break about 9:15 and made a decision not to continue setting up because we didn't think the OEM guys would be back. I had 15 or 20 guys floating around the Pier - electricians, carpenters, soundmen. I went up to the roof of Pier 92 to see what was going on and witnessed the buildings come down. Couldn't believe it.

So the job is half-way finished. We're in limbo. Around noon we called it quits and dispersed.

I'm a bike rider, I train every morning in Central Park. I rode my bike from the Pier back up to my home on the Upper West Side. Let me tell you what I saw: there was this peculiar feeling in the air. People were in a daze. Thousands of people walking uptown, like some catharsis had happened and people were in a trance.

*　　*　　*

––––––––––––

[20](OEM) is the New York City Mayor's Office Of Emergency Management

Ken: OEM opened its new Emergency Operations Center in February of '99, this state-of-the-art facility designed to operate as a stand-alone center from which New York City government would operate in a time of crisis. The EOC was in 7 World Trade, within walking distance of City Hall and most city agencies.

That place was an engineering marvel. The EOC facility is powered by three 500 KVA generators that act as emergency power sources totally independent from the building's backup generators. In addition to a 6,000-gallon fuel tank, there's an 11,000-gallon potable water supply for sanitary and domestic water needs, plus a backup system for heating, ventilation and air conditioning. Computers, phone systems, and radios are all individually set with uninterrupted power supplies. The EOC can withstand winds up to, like, 200 mph in the event of a hurricane; the exterior walls are constructed with steel framing, numerous layers of drywall and Kevlar.

Within the EOC is seating for 68 agencies to operate during an emergency, with each agency assigned its own workstation. In the event of a major incident, they can fit out another 40 workstations. These workstations are set up in groups to facilitate interaction with other agencies in the EOC. The groups are broken down into, like: Health & Medical, Utilities, Public Safety, Infrastructure, Human Services, Transportation, Government, and Administration. You have to appreciate the planning this all took.

All of this proved useless. Later on September 11th, 7 World Trade Center collapsed and OEM suddenly found itself homeless.

*　　*　　*

The next day we heard they were going to use Pier 94 as a morgue. This is where our in-house office was. So we scrambled to get the place ready. Put up a lot of curtains. Policemen and firemen started coming in, but we never saw any bodies. Turns out there weren't any to be found right then. Then Mayor Giuiliani showed up.

He came in with Judith Nathan[21] and a whole entourage of people I assume were connected to OEM. A whole parade of suits came through. They were debating what to use the Piers for.

The Piers are owned by the City of New York. Very well located. Basically, the authorities were able to close down the West Side Highway[22] and have one lane open for emergency

---

[21]Mayor Giuliani's girlfriend.

[22]The thruway that runs along the westernmost side of Manhattan alongside the Hudson River.

traffic on its way down to Ground Zero. The Pier's easily accessible from that.

Giuliani had never really seen the Piers set up for a trade show: carpeting laid down, booths set up, the works. I think he was impressed. The upshot is that OEM completely took over Pier 92 for operations. Everything that should have been down at 7 World Trade Center moved in.

I heard later on that they scrambled to find a location as soon as 7 World Trade crumbled on the 11th. I also heard that they moved into two or three places, trying them on, before they settled into the Pier. What's not to like about the Pier? There's parking, windows all around. And it's a ship terminal. If worse came to worse, you could get an aircraft carrier in there.

Keep in mind. At that point? No one knew if we were going to war. Or with whom.

* * *

Ken: So the Family Assistance Center moves in from the 23rd Street Armory to Pier 94. OEM moves into Pier 92. We get the word that they're coming in on the night of the 15th to set up. And we're basically ready to go, our production schedules tend to run like everything is a last-minute emergency anyway. We're used to dealing with this kind of stuff.

Fred: We get calls for big jobs all the time at the last minute. Go into a hotel ballroom; go into a park; into the street; go anywhere. Create an environment, create a production. Work on the fly, that's what we specialize in.

Ken: So we go ahead and start laying in electrical lines and the groups of people start showing up.

Fred: Verizon shows up. They set up hundreds and hundreds of phone and T-1 lines for the OEM.

Ken: Trucks pull in. One of the major telephone companies pulled up and they were letting people make free long distance calls. They needed all sorts of power.

Fred: Fiber optics came in, Time Warner[23] came in laying cable - every OEM office had their own TV set to watch the breaking news. There was no cable at the Pier before this.

---

[23]Time Warner City Cable of NYC, a cable TV and high-speed online service provider.

Ken: We had to take care of the news teams. Television stations, camera crews, ABC, CBS, everybody making requests all at once. The cafeteria needed power lines for refrigeration. Verizon wanted power. People needed lighting. They wanted sound.

On the fly we designed a sound system that would break the place into three zones so whoever was at a podium could switch on Zone 1, Zone 2, or Zone 3. We hung 50 speakers, set up hundreds of track lighting instruments. There was equipment already at the Pier and I have a warehouse in the Bronx where I store the rest of my lighting, staging, sound, audio-visual, and video equipment.

We cracked into everything. Pulled out all the stops. This was serious business. And it was all about saying, "Yes, we can."

*   *   *

Ken: We became the de facto power distribution specialists at the Pier. Really, we had no idea what we were doing. But we put in a very intricate system. I have these multi-cables that drop circuits into quadrants on the Pier, so we just started dropping circuits all over the place, treating the whole place like giant theatrical lighting grid.

Power is universal. How it's distributed is not. There's a million different connectors - two-wire, three-wire, four-wire. Twist locks with the pin in, twist locks with the . . . sheesh. And every connector is rated by voltage and by amperage. Naturally, everybody's got different requirements. But we accommodated everybody.

Fred: We had this huge toy box of everything you could possibly imagine. We outfitted everyone, no matter how weird their request was. They had color Xerox machines, four, five feet wide. Those were 'two-aways', they had weird plugs. But we got that problem solved within three hours; locate the part, send someone to get it, install it, done. If they didn't have it in town, I'd pay for it. I'm still holding the bills.

Ken: Keep in mind that Pier 94 is huge. It's a T-shape, about 600 feet wide with a finger that juts out from the top, about 900 feet. ConEd runs 16,000 Volts into the basement. Then they have substations, which eventually transform the power down to 480 volts. On Pier 94, I installed 480 to 208 volts transformers; the higher the voltage you transport, the smaller the wire you need. And right at specific locations, I broke it down from 208 to the 110 that was needed.

I set it up on a temporary basis to move and accommodate different situations. A certain amount of it is permanent, but there's a whole secondary distribution phase which just moves around as needed per show. We had that same situation on Pier 88, 90 and 92.

Fred: To make sure that the light distribution was right, I marked out a row of Kleig lights in the ceiling. At any one time six were being used. But if any went out, I had it rigged so that six more were ready to go. I had a back-up system, and a *back-up* back-up system. If Number 3 goes down? No problem. *Boom!* You go to Number 4. Absolutely seamless.

*   *   *

Ken: Then they set up the War Room on the mezzanine of Pier 92. That was Giuliani's private conference room. We went in there and set up a sound system, cable mikes, the works. Video monitors outside the room.

They had the top tier of the Mayor's office in the War Room. Department heads sitting up there from every possible area you could imagine - traffic control, sanitation, fire, police, Amtrack, Metro North, Bridge and Tunnel.

Fred: That's what that room was all about. The heads of all the departments would receive an update, figure out who's problem it was, then work together to solve it.

Ken: And that jives with the way we operate. We don't take "no" for an answer. Nothing is impossible for us. Somebody comes to us and they need some obscure, cockamamie electrical connector? It's not like you call your Super and it takes three months to do it. We get it done. Period. It was inspiring to see the city government functioning that way. No politics. No dickering. Just: *Boom!* Get it done.

In fact, I was struck by how amazingly fast the OEM could put a plan in motion. If there was a hole between the walls? They got on the phone and the hole's filled in an hour. In front of Pier 94? If there was a fire hydrant that wasn't working? They got the fire hydrant fixed in *two* hours. This is unheard of for the way the city normally operates. Amazing.

Fred: And then, like a day or two after the whole thing started? Maybe the next weekend, the Comfort[24] arrived. They shipped out from North Carolina or Delaware, I think it was.

Ken: We're saying that overnight, the facility we had worked at for 18 years staging events and trade shows, was turned into a military facility. Overnight. The whole complex, the

---

[24]USNS Comfort (III), hull number T-AH-20, commissioned in 1987. The crew that arrived in New York included some 300 navy medical personnel and 61 civilian mariners. The Comfort actually departed Naval Weapons Station Earle, NJ at three p.m. on September 14th under orders from the Commander in Chief, U.S. Atlantic Fleet. She sailed under Captain Ed Nanartowich.

whole environment changed. For instance, The Comfort's got it's own hospital, operating rooms, emergency rooms, water desalinizing plant. Everything all ready to go.

Fred: You could opt to stay on the ship. They had rooms prepared for you. They had mess halls you could eat in. They had people on duty to do whatever you wanted. You could get your laundry done. It was of great service to the people working at the Pier.

*   *   *

Fred: The thing I'll take away from all this is . . . well, when I was setting up the stage, for instance. You couldn't do anything without somebody asking to help. I'm talking about from different departments. Whether they were walking by with a press folder, in a group, solving some problem . . . a guy from the phone company grabbing a cup of coffee or a janitor passing by with a mop. If you looked like you had a problem putting a ladder up, there were two other guys there helping in the blink of an eye. "Can I hold that ladder for you?" And then off they went. You had time to say "thank you" and that was it. The camaraderie was absolute. The Pier was intense.

The Red Cross showed up every hour with fresh coffee and stuff to eat. "Is there anything special you guys want?"

Ken: Everyone wanted to take part, everyone wanted to do something. From our point of view, we felt that hey, this is what we do best. We're our *own* emergency management for theatrical and trade shows . . . and here we were, a perfect fit. We were able to move into action for the cause. We had our hands full.

Maybe the down side is that we kind of felt isolated. The whole world was down at Ground Zero but we were up at the Pier. And when you work day and night, day and night, day and night . . . eventually, you're working in a fog. It begins to take on its own sense of reality. It really hit home when we lit that Memorial Wall outside the Pier, I think that was a focal point. That became our connection.

Fred: They never had one technical problem. I've done a lot of trade shows in my time, I used to be an equipment rep. I traveled up and down my area - Florida to Maine, hitting every freakin' trade show east of the Mississippi.

In a trade show, you set up your electrical and *sometimes* it works. The thing that really blew me away about what we got done at the Pier . . . there was never a problem with the electrical. The true test? The OEM, FEMA, the Red Cross, run the Piers now 24-7, and they haven't had one problem. The stuff that we built is still working one hundred percent.

Ken: Nothing's done half-assed. Not in my business, in any business. There's no learning curve anymore when you've been on a job 18 years. Not even for something like 9/11. You just put your nose down to the job and get that job done. The rest works itself out.

We were truly proud and happy to make a contribution. ₰

JEAN KNEE has been a social worker for a private school in New Jersey for nine years. She categorizes her school as a "challenging, nurturing, caring atmosphere."

Jean's cousin, MICHAEL CARROLL, was 39 years old, a New York City Fireman for 16 years. He was killed in action on September 11th. Jean tells how her family was affected by the passing of their kinsman.

————

My daughter Elizabeth's wedding was planned for September 15th, 2001. On September 11th, we heard that Michael was one of the first firemen on the scene at the Towers. Soon after that – in the midst of this very confusing day - we understood that he was missing.

My son works in the city. He was on 18th Street and had to evacuate his building. He knew his cousins lived up on 86th Street, so he took off for Michael's mother's apartment. When he got there, the family was trying to find out news about Michael.

Michael came from a family of firemen. This situation was their worst nightmare come true. For the longest time, reports kept repeating, "He's missing." I don't know if you remember, but they kept listing people as 'missing' instead of declaring people dead. So everyone had a tremendous amount of hope that they'd find survivors. But gradually and gradually the hope kept slipping away.

I said, "Michael is safe." I kept telling this to my daughter. "I know Michael's safe. He's somewhere right now and we just don't know where he is."

*   *   *

They closed my school on September 12th, but I met with people from the upper campus to decide what we were going to do. We brought the faculty in early and talked to them about what types of behavior they could expect from children who'd experienced trauma.

"Let the children talk about whatever they want. Don't censor anyone. Let them have their experience." Many of the children had parents who worked either in the city or at the World Trade Center.

When a child is in pain, there's a tendency among adults to say, "It's going to be alright. Don't worry." But the adults sometimes just want children to be quiet. In this case, it was more important to let the children talk about how they felt.

* * *

You know the video clips of the planes hitting the Towers? The ones they played over and over and over again? We found that the young kids - kindergarten and first grade - couldn't distinguish that it was one event played over and over again on the television. They thought it was happening anew each time. So some of them thought that all of Manhattan had been destroyed. This came out in their outside play; they reproduced what they'd seen, smashing into blocks, knocking down towers. Some of the children finished their milk and made planes out of the cartons. (*Plate 16*)

This is all normal. Children express how they're feeling in play. They don't necessarily talk about it. Parents kept asking us, "What are they saying? Are they talking about it?"

No. They weren't. They hadn't formulated it in their heads. And there was nothing they could relate it to, nothing at all.

But my real concern is for the people who survived. They went through horrendous things to get out of those buildings. They walked over dead bodies. They thought they were going to die. It must have been a terrible experience and many of them aren't getting help. They aren't talking because they don't feel they have any right to, because they're still alive.

And if this sort of emotional trauma is allowed to go untreated, there's a very real danger there. Not just to the individual, but to society as a whole.

* * *

On September 14th we heard from Michael's family. They had cancelled their hotel reservations and wouldn't be able to come to Elizabeth's wedding. They were waiting to hear about Michael's condition. Perfectly understandable.

My daughter asked, "Am I really going through with this wedding? Is that right? What should I do?" After a lot of deliberation, we decided to go ahead.

The wedding was on the beach in Provincetown, Cape Cod. Since it was a destination wedding, many people couldn't fly there. The airlines weren't operating yet. Flights were still grounded. A lot of people from the Washington D.C. area drove up instead. It was actually incredible how some people got there.

I almost didn't go myself. I felt that, in my ten years at the school, this was the time I was needed most. The principal finally had to tell me, "Go to the wedding. Nothing's going to fall apart while you're gone for the weekend." So I drove from New Jersey to Massachusetts on Friday night, the 14th.

All the way up to Massachusetts. Every overpass had up flags and signs that said, "God Bless America." I cried the whole way up. It was a six hour ride.

When we got to Provincetown, candles were lit as a memorial in the center of town. People knew people who had died on the planes. This reached everywhere, you know?

*   *   *

On October 20th, the family decided to hold a Memorial Mass for Michael.

The wake was held the day before at Campbell Funeral Home on Madison and 81st. The entire fourth floor was reserved for Michael's wake. The rooms and hallways were filled with firemen, family, and friends.

When the firemen entered the building, they took the stairs - that's what firemen do. They don't take elevators. Stairways are the safest part of the building and I always imagined that Michael was in a stairway at the World Trade Center when he perished. Mayor Giuliani was at the wake Friday night. I think he attended all the services for the uniformed men that died at the World Trade Center, though how he was able to, I don't know.

Elizabeth was at the wake, and her family kept asking about her wedding. She was touched. They had all sent flowers to her wedding with a note saying, "Thinking of you on this day. From your family in New York."

She was so overwhelmed that, in the midst of this difficult time in their lives, *they* had been thinking of *her*.

*   *   *

The day of Michael's memorial, I decided to take the ferry with my children from Hoboken to Ground Zero. As we were going over, I talked to a ferry worker who told me about all the boats that came to help people get away from the area on September 11th.

He said, "It was an incredible scene. People with private boats and anything that could float were pulling up and taking survivors to New Jersey."

We landed and walked over to Broadway.

I had made the decision that morning not to take my camera. The devastation at the site was overwhelming. At that time, thousands of bodies were still missing, but individuals were not yet declared dead. And I thought, "They're here at Ground Zero. Buried in the gray dust."

That dust was everywhere, it was on the leaves of the plants, on the trees, in the planters that line the streets, on the buildings. Window washers were busy trying to clean the façade of a building scheduled to open that week. I stood in silence, wanting to touch the dust, at the same time feeling it was somehow sacred.

*　　*　　*

We went to Ladder 3, on 13th Street, which was Michael's Company. 13 men died from that firehouse. 12 of them worked there and one man had been there waiting for an assignment. I felt compelled to talk to Michael's firemen friends. I know how close these men are; they're like a family unto themselves. I wanted them to know that it was good they were alive.

From there, we took a cab to The Church of Saint Ignatius Loyola.[25] The cab driver asked which side of the street the church was on. I said I didn't know. But as we went over a small rise in the road, we saw hundreds of uniformed firefighters standing in rows on Park Avenue. I said to my children, "This is going to be big."

We got out of the cab, crossed the street and a fireman asked if we were family. He told us to stand to the right side of the church entrance and assured us that seats were being reserved for family. The bagpipers were there. A man with an American bald eagle perched on his arm was standing on the street.

The church was huge. Every seat filled. I didn't know who many of these people were - family, firemen, others. "Carroll" is an Irish name, so we have a large extended family. The women in the family tend to live till their nineties; Michael's grandmother died in her nineties. This is the first death that I could remember in a long time. The first and certainly the most unexpected.

There were several eulogies. Keith Gessner, a long-time friend of Michael's, spoke along with Robert Burmeister, a friend from Ladder Company 3. There were representatives from the Mayor's and Governor's offices. Michael's brother, Billy, spoke; Billy is also a New York City Firefighter. He spoke eloquently about Michael and his love for his wife, Nancy, and their two children: Brendan, six and Olivia, two.

---

[25]Park Avenue at 84th Street.

There wasn't a dry eye throughout the entire ceremony. After a while, I stopped blotting the tears and just let them fall. All around, these big burly firemen had tears running down their faces. The processional hymn was "Be Not Afraid" and we sang "Amazing Grace" and prayed. The recessional hymn was "On Eagle's Wings."

*　*　*

As we left the church, a fire truck pulled up. We, the family, lined up behind it and firemen lined the street, standing at attention, saluting us as we walked behind the fire truck down Park Avenue.

There was so much confusion in my mind between the public events and the personal fact that I was at "little Michael's" funeral. Michael, the little boy in pajamas who used to watch Saturday morning cartoons when I slept over on the couch at this parent's house.

*　*　*

Last week, Michael's body was recovered from the scene. This is a good thing.

Without a body, we all clung to the hope that he would be found safe somehow – many people clung to that hope. Some families are still hoping that their loved ones might be found someplace. That they're unconscious in some hospital somewhere, that they'll wake up and realize they've been missed. That they'll come home.

It's so very sad.

Early on, I told Michael's brother, Billy, "Bill, even now, I keep thinking that they'll find him alive."

He said, "Jean. They're not."

At least now they can bury him. There'll be a grave and a place his family can go, a place his children can visit. That's very important in the grieving process. ❦

JOHN McGRATH, 30, started his law practice at 160 Broadway, less than a full block east of the World Trade Center. He is no stranger to the Trade Center or the particular culture that surrounded it – John worked for the firm of Ohrenstein & Brown on the 85th floor of One World Trade before founding his own company. He talks of the massive damages sustained by the area and the local businesses, as well as the loss of many dear friends.

––––––

O'Hara's. What a place. *Two* bars on the bottom floor, one block from the Trade Center. There was a door on the north side of the room that faced out on the Towers, that's how close you were. They had all Irish bartenders at O'Hara's, except this one Japanese guy, Kato. He always bartended upstairs with my friend Brian McCabe whom we referred to as "The Other Middle Aged Guy with Gout."

You *have* to be a lawyer to go to this bar. Either that or you have to work in the Towers, that's like a rule. So I met up with another lawyer friend of mine that night,. We hung out, watched the game, usual routine. That night: Giants versus the Broncos on Monday Night Football. Great game. Then we got a car to go home.

I remember driving past the Towers and talking about them. I don't remember what we said – a joke as we drove by. That was the last time I ever saw them.

O'Hara's is gone now. The building's still there, the building is sound, I've seen it on the news videos. But the windows are all blown out and the place is filled with shit.

A lot of people from Cantor Fitzgerald hung out there and Cantor lost seven hundred people, I think. Seven hundred. This woman I knew, she was seven months pregnant. She's gone, too.

I still had a lot of friends who worked up there. But I'll get to that in a minute.

*   *   *

You know, I never thought it was a jet liner. When I first heard a plane had hit, I thought it was a Cessna. When you worked in the Trade Center, you *always* saw Cessnas and other little planes flying below you. I figured some idiot had lost control and flown into the building. *(Plate 17)*

In retrospect, I guess that was a little naïve. A Cessna would just bounce off those buildings like a bug.

350

When I watched the attack on TV, the impact of the first plane looked like it might have gone through my old office at Ohrenstein & Brown. It didn't, though. Even when I worked in the Towers, it was always difficult to tell which floor was which when looking at them from the outside. They were just too damned big.

*   *   *

My current office is on the ninth floor of our building at 160 Broadway. Used to be that 70 percent of the view from our window was One Liberty Plaza. The rest was dominated by One World Trade.

Where we once had a relatively nice view out the windows, we now have a view of carnage. And through that: New Jersey. You can see right through where the Towers and 7 World Trade Center were. They're just . . . gone.

Sure, I was concerned that my business was gone. The Wednesday or Thursday after the attack, I was watching the TV coverage and they said that One Liberty Plaza was about to collapse. That's right across the street from my place. But what could you do?

We weren't allowed back in the area until Monday, the 17th. But that was limited access. You had to get past several security checkpoints.

I'd actually tried to go to my office that first Saturday, the 15th. My ID as a local business owner let me in through the first few checkpoints, but we couldn't get to our office because they were still afraid that stuff was falling off One Liberty Plaza. My whole section of Broadway was shut down. No luck.

Turns out my building is structurally sound. But the heating, ventilation and air-conditioning system is probably destroyed. The building owner, before evacuating on the 11th, before the first Tower collapsed - he didn't turn the systems off. The intake fans took in the debris from the collapsed buildings and distributed it.

*   *   *

When we first got into our office on the 17th, everything was covered with dust, but the windows were intact. Which tells you the force of the debris that was flying, that it was strong enough to get through cracks in the ceiling, the window seals. It covered the whole office.

This is a sample of the debris taken out of my office.[26] My girlfriend's father is a Ph.D. in

---

[26]John holds a small vial of gray dust.

chemistry. Retired, but he still has a lot of friends at the University of Connecticut. He volunteered to get this stuff analyzed. The dust has everything in it. Little pieces of paper. Silicates. Concrete and glass fibers.

I don't know why I keep it. I guess I just don't want to throw it away. It's been sitting on the desk in my apartment; I've been working out of there since 9/11. Looking at it, it's kinda hard to believe that the Towers were reduced to that in a heartbeat.

Little things matter a lot now, you know. Like I was going through some old things and found my men's room key from when I worked on the 85th floor of 1 World Trade.

I'm keeping it. I don't think they'll miss it.

*　　*　　*

Things got worse before they got better. I started hearing from people I used to work with and friends from high school. I found out four people from my high school class were killed.

One was a guy I'd gone to high school with. We lost track of each other for a couple of years. Then, the last three years? I started seeing him all the time. Mike Duffy. He became a regular at another place I hang out at. After all this happened, I half-expected to see him. In fact, I found myself looking for him every time I was there. I didn't see him and didn't think much of it until I got a newsletter from my high school.

Another guy I graduated with - John Schroeder, I played lacrosse with him. In my junior year, he was captain of the team. He had gone off to Princeton but we'd see each other occasionally when I was working at the Trade Center. He was on the 87th or 89th floor of 1 World Trade, right where the plane went in.

He'd married a girl in our class and I think they'd been husband and wife for about three months before this happened.

Then there was this friend of mine's father. And the guy who was at my brother's wedding. And my good friend's brother. And this other guy's cousin. Just more and more names. They kept rolling out in the papers ever day. It sucks.

I mean I think the worst part of all this is the number of people we *knew* who are gone. And the people we'll *never* know. Like the guys from Ohrenstein & Brown who used to hang out at O'Hara's – the ones I only knew by their first names. And now we have no idea whether they're with us or not. We may never know.

*   *   *

At first, I was upset with the tourists going downtown. Especially when they first opened Broadway on September 20th or 21st.

There were people climbing on light poles, hefting cameras in the air, taking photographs. Crowding the streets - you couldn't walk on the sidewalk. A three-minute walk to my office ended up taking 20.

I thought it was disrespectful to come as a tourist and gawk. There were people having their photos taken, smiling and posing with what was left of the World Trade Center in the background. At that point, we still thought there were 6,000 people buried. So these people were taking snapshots of a graveyard.

I made comments. One guy was fighting with police to get a picture. I walked up to him and asked, "Where's your family buried?"

He was caught off-guard. I said, "Because, I'd like to dig them up and take their photograph."

He wasn't from New York. But he kinda got the idea.

In fact, one of the restaurants down there printed some signs outside their restaurant. "This is hallowed ground. Show some respect." That was appreciated.

*   *   *

We were out of the office about a month before they cleaned everything up.

When we reopened and started coming to the office again, it was the first time a lot of them had been downtown. Someone involved in litigation is usually not too happy to begin with. But we've had a couple clients come in, look out the window, and start crying. You let them have their moment and then try to get them back on track.

I understand what that's about. It's tough for me to sit here in the office and perform work when I recognize I'm just a couple hundred yards away from a mass grave for thousands of people.

And I know that approximately 20 to 40 percent of the lawyers in New York City either couldn't get into their offices or had them destroyed. The damage to business has been unbelievable. The phones didn't work for six weeks, for instance. Didn't matter, really. We had nothing to do.

That first week we were anticipating about $20,000 in revenue. We got maybe $500. It's only been this last ten days or so that business has picked up again to the levels prior to 9/11. I've already had one case pulled from me; a criminal defense client hired a new lawyer because they couldn't get in touch with us for a week. And I couldn't call them since I had no access to my case files, no phone numbers. ❧

VIEWPOINTS

MUQTEDAR KHAN earned his Ph.D. in international relations, political theory, and Islamic thought from Georgetown University. He is a frequent columnist for the London Daily Telegram, *the* San Francisco Chronicle, *the* Detroit Free Press, *and* Middle East Online. *Currently, he is a professor of Political Science at Adrian College in Michigan where serves on the board of the Center for the Study of Islam and Democracy.*

Following the events of September 11ᵗʰ, Dr. Khan wrote "A Memo to American Muslims" which appeared in national syndication. It accused his fellow Muslims of "practicing hypocrisy on a grand scale" by protesting, among other things, the U.S. support for Israel while maintaining stoic silence on matters of Islamic governmental abuse. "September 11ᵗʰ should never have happened," Khan declared in his Memo, and he charged U.S. Muslims with taking partial responsibility. "We love to live in the U.S.," he said, "but we also love to hate it."

The article inspired a massive controversy. A childhood friend of Dr. Khan's went so far as to accuse him of having "sold out to America." In his interview, however, Khan, refused to back down from his position.

There are reasons why I think that, while the U.S. is not the *only* cause, it is one of the important barriers to democracy in the Middle East:

In 1953, Iran was an elected democracy. The Prime Minister of Iran was interested in nationalizing oil. In order to circumvent that, the United States, in a highly-celebrated CIA coup, basically toppled the government and installed a monarch. You can imagine how much damage this did to Iran. The new monarch was ruthless and his bad government led to the Islamic revolution in 1979.

Iran was a democracy before the revolution. Had it been allowed to progress on its own, it would have shaped itself into a far better democracy by now. The U.S. has tried to do this in Latin America, in Italy and other places during the Cold War. But not aggressively. I wonder: why is America so aggressive in the Middle East? The answer, essentially, is oil; to maintain the kinds of profits that they would like.

Also, because of it's uncritical support for Israel, the U.S. would like to prevent the democratization of the Muslim world. In Islamic countries it's easier to deal with a few insecure puppets than the public opinion. But you will find that the citizens of these two countries are not with the U.S., only their governments are. Imagine if you had an elected President of Saudi Arabia and a *truly* elected President of Egypt. They would say, "Look,

I have no support. My people are not in favor of your bombing of Afghanistan or your support of Israel. We will not cooperate with you."

The U.S. considers Saudi Arabia and Egypt allies. But I consider them puppet governments. In fact, the presence of U.S. troops in Saudi Arabia is seen by many as an arrangement to protect the Saudi monarchy rather than to protect the country from Iraq. The U.S. gives about $2 billion a year to Egyptian President Hasni Mubarak. Much of that money is used to maintain the machinery of the authoritarian Egyptian government.

*　*　*

In 1992, there was an election in Algeria. The military government refused to give power to the elected Islamists. The U.S. simply stood by and watched while France continued to send over $30 billion in military aid over the last seven or eight years to suppress the rebellion. They sabotaged democracy in Algeria - the U.S. put absolutely no pressure on the Algerian government to transfer power to the elected body, as they did in Haiti, for example, when they installed Aristide.

How do other countries fit into the equation? Kuwait is taking steps toward democratization but they are very dependent on U.S. government opinion. The United Arab Emirates are not directly under U.S. influence but some function as American military bases. King Hussein of Jordan and the new king are close U.S. allies. They also receive aid; it's not a lot compared to Egypt, but hundreds of millions of dollars have been given to Jordan since they signed the treaty with Israel in 1993 and gave up their claims to Jerusalem. It's also true that the FBI trained the Jordanian security forces.

Many of the people in these countries feel that if there were a major revolution in the Gulf, especially in the oil countries, the United States would move in quickly. That's why the U.S. has such huge naval and military bases in Oman, Bahrain, Saudi Arabia and Kuwait. Essentially as a precursor to securing the region.

*　*　*

While this goes on the secular elite in the Arab world have imitated a very extreme negative modern model of fascism. Saddam Hussein and Hasni Mubarak are clones of fascist rulers from Europe in the past. Yasir Arafat is as authoritarian as any. If he was to become the President of the Palestinian state, I don't think it would be anything better than Iraq under Hussein. Or Algeria.

But Israel and the U.S. like Arafat. They want to use the authoritarian streak in him to repress Palestinians who oppose the peace process. How can you make peace with a community when 25 percent of the people are opposed? Assuming that Arafat will use force to repress them, the peace process is nothing but Israel subcontracting its repression to Arafat.

Notice that we have catered to every element of Israel's interest during the peace process. We are not doing the same with Palestine. We talk only with those who want to make peace with Israel. Those who do not want peace, we call them terrorists and we throw them in jail.

This brings us to the concept of *jihad*.

*   *   *

The concept of *jihad* is misunderstood by non-Muslims and misused by Muslims.

The word *jihad* itself means 'struggle'. It goes back to the days of the Crusades, after the defeat of the Christian kingdoms. The myth was propagated that Islam led by the sword; that Islam went around conquering people, forcing them to become Muslim and this is the purpose of *jihad*.

But true Islam is the struggle against ignorance. You're supposed to struggle, not through killing, but through argumentation, invitation and dialogue. It's more like missionary work. You're trying to convince people that there is only one God, that we need to be aware of God and our duties toward God.

Jihad is defensive. If you look at a theory of war in Islam, it is identical to the "Just War" theory of Thomas Aquinas. All military action is forbidden in Islam except under three conditions and these three conditions are:

Number one. If you are not allowed to practice your faith, you are allowed to rebel militarily.

Number two. If you are socially oppressed.

Number three. If your lands or properties are taken away from you.

Under these three conditions, you are allowed what is called an 'Inferior *jihad*' or the third category of *jihad*, a military *jihad*. The first two categories of *jihad* are superior categories, essentially a struggle against the self.

*   *   *

For instance, I fast in the month of Ramadan. When I fast, I suppress my appetites for food, sex, and other things, like watching fun TV. I'm concentrating only on God to purify my soul. In spite of the fact that I'm thirsty and hungry, I'm giving you this interview, so this is likened to *jihad* for me. I'm struggling for the image of Islam, I'm struggling for the cause of justice. This is called Supreme *jihad* - the first category.

The second state of *jihad* is Social *jihad*, the struggle to establish social justice within society itself. Like fighting for equal rights, just wages, good conditions in orphanages and so on.

The third category is essentially the defensive military category. But what has happened is that, for various reasons, people in the West have demonized Islam, trying to portray it as an aggressive religion. *Jihad* has served as a useful tool to justify that demonization. But there are also Muslim clerics everywhere - in Kashmir, Palestine, and Egypt - who have used *jihad* as an instrument to demonize 'the other' and have tried to argue that the purpose of Islam is to wage war against non-believers and Muslims alike.

For example, there is a group called Takfiri. They have declared that all Muslims who do not agree with their ideological interpretation of Islam are non-Muslims. That's extreme. They've declared also that any Muslim society which doesn't implement their concept of Islamic law is a non-Islamic society. By doing this, they have declared *jihad* against Muslims.

Mr. bin Laden, and others like him, are not concerned about Muslim casualties. Hundreds of Muslims died in the World Trade Center. In fact, in the embassy affair in North Africa, only 12 Americans died, but hundreds of Muslims died in the bombing. These people have no qualms about killing in the name of Islam.

*   *   *

Extremists favor selective interpretation. If you look at verse 22, chapter 5 of the Qu'ran, it says very clearly: "He who has killed a single innocent human being is as if he has killed all of humanity." There's nothing there to interpret. How much stronger can God get in condemning these actions? Mr. bin Laden chooses to ignore this aspect of the Qu'ran.

The Qu'ran *does* say, "Fight them, those who fight you. And drive them away from the places that they have driven you away from." Which means, if they take your land, you take your land back. Defend yourself. But it has to be done in conjunction with this: that while you're defending yourself, you don't kill innocent people.

Essentially, this is a geo-political problem. Bin Laden is upset with the U.S. military presence in Saudi Arabia and to respond to that, he uses selective Islamic forces to mobilize support. But there are specific passages in the Qu'ran that encourage Muslims to forgive Jews and Christians if they have committed injustice. America is a country of missionary faiths: Christians, Mormons, Jehovah's Witnesses. These people understand that you're not saving any souls by killing people.

I personally believe that to kill a non-believer is a crime and a sin because you have missed out on the opportunity to save someone. I tell my students that, on all issues - not just religious matters - if you find someone who disagrees with you, consider it an opportunity to win over that person through argument. That's a test of your own faith and conviction. This opportunity is a treasure, rather than something that needs to be destroyed.

*   *   *

"While we loudly and consistently condemn Israel for it's ill-treatment of Palestinians, we are silent when Muslim regimes abuse the rights of Muslims and slaughter thousands of them."

- from Mr. Kahn's article, <u>Memo to American Muslims</u>

I come from the position that good values are common to all civilizations. You don't have to be a Muslim to believe that killing innocent people is bad. You don't have to believe in the American Constitution to believe that people have a right to life. For me, being a good Muslim and a good American are one in the same. When people ask me, I say, "I was born American though I was born in India." I came to America at the age of 26. When I came to the U.S., I felt at home. Coming here was like throwing a fish back into a pond.

I've talked to many friends from other parts of the world and they have all felt similarly. They feel at home here. I realized that I did not have to drop any of my Islamic values and beliefs to feel at home in America.

*   *   *

The first time my father came here, we went to Disney World. While we were walking, he turned to me and said, "What is that other line for?"

I looked and said, "That's the shorter line for those who are handicapped."

He said, "They have a different door?"

"Yes," I said, "It's required in every building."

And then we started talking about how handicapped people are taken care of here. I said,

"This country's trying hard to make sure that life is the same for those who are handicapped, too."

My father said, "This is so Islamic! This is more Islamic than even the most Islamic countries I've been to." He was coming from Saudi Arabia.

In fact, in 1900 Muhammad Upto of Egypt went to France, and the first thing he said was, "Aha! This is Islam without Muslims!"

Third World countries, because they are poor, do not have the resources to take care of handicapped people. They tend to discard them from social life. America, however, is concerned. These are good values.

From that point of view, I spoke to American Muslims in my article. "Look, we are critical of Israel, and that's fine. But if you're saying that we are trying to protect the human rights of Palestinians, then the highlight is that we care about human rights. And if we care about human rights, then we should also care about our other brothers who are suffering in Saudi Arabia, Syria, and other places. So if we object to the Israeli violations of human rights, I would like to see similar objections to the violations of human rights by Muslim countries, too. If we are not doing this, we're not truly worried about human rights but economic rights."

*　　*　　*

In that memo, my argument was A) if we care about human rights then we would be objecting to what other Muslim countries are doing. And B) if we care about Palestinians, then why is it that Palestinians get citizenship in Western countries more easily than they do in Arab countries? My argument was: we don't care about Palestinians or human rights. So what is it that we're upset about? It is our enmity toward Israel that drives us rather than our concern for Palestine or human rights. I've taken a lot of heat, but I have not backed away.

*　　*　　*

Saddam Hussein gassed his own people. But I have not seen any Muslim institution created to curb this nemesis. You didn't find any Muslim organizations dedicated to attacking Saddam Hussein while he reigned; we never asked the UN to intervene. Similarly, the Pakistani army committed atrocities in Bangladesh and we didn't cry out about that.

I can run down the list of cover ups. For example, Pakistan sold out the Taliban. They were supporting those people for three or four years, then they suddenly turned around and bumped them. But you don't see much criticism against Pakistan. I have not seen a single American Muslim organization condemn Pakistan for turning their backs on their Muslim brothers.

I think the measure of the ethical quality of any society is consistency. If we are critical of U.S. foreign policy for promoting democracy in Latin America and blocking democracy in the Middle East, fine. We expect the U.S. to be consistent. A true test of ethics is to see how a country behaves when to do so hurts its own interests. To say, "I will speak the truth only when it suits me," means that you are a liar. Hypocritical at the very least.

So, I was saying in my Memo, "Look. We American Muslims also have to be clear. We cannot be critical of the West, the United States or any society without also critiquing ourselves for being clear with our values."

*　*　*

In Ohio, some kid drove a car at extremely high speeds and hit a mosque following September 11ᵗʰ. There were lots of these cases, race-related backlashes.

A large group of Christians came out and held hands around this huge mosque in Parisburg, Ohio, just south of Toledo. This beautiful mosque is on the highway, about ten minutes before you reach Toledo. So it had to be a large number of people who came there to be able to surround it. Thousands of people.

In fact, the *Toledo Blade* had that picture on the front page, the image of a white man holding the hand of a traditionally-dressed Pakistani woman. I found it very moving.

*　*　*

I personally have nothing negative to report. I was flying from Toledo to New York to give an interview to *Time* magazine. I landed in Cincinnati and was going to take a continuation flight. But the flight from Michigan was a half-hour late. When I spoke with the stewardess, she told me, "Don't worry, we'll put you on the next flight." I landed in Ohio, there was somebody waiting there who said, "Dr. Kahn, if you run, we can catch the plane, it's still waiting for you."

So we ran to the next plane. They had held it back for 20 minutes. I climbed into the plane and I saw all these white folks sitting there. And I started laughing, thinking, "These poor guys, they've been waiting for some guy to get on the plane and the *profile* walks in." I have a beard. I look like a Middle Eastern guy.

They were wondering why I was laughing and I explained it to them. They looked pretty sheepish. But that's all.

No, I really haven't experienced any negatives. I've had positive comments from a lot of people because of the Memo, I've received thousands and thousands of e-mails. I got a long letter from a professor at Columbia University. One of the things she said was, "You know, I've seen lots of these interviews on TV where they're asking celebrities, 'Who are your heroes?' I'm no celebrity. But if anyone ever asks me, I will tell them that you are my hero for life."

I also heard that, in one part of the country, some women from a Church decided to wear *hijabs*[1] when they found that Muslim women in their neighborhood were being harassed by young kids in mall parking lots. At Miami University, Ohio some Christian girls started wearing *hijabs* to identify with Muslim women in the first week after September 11th.

I've heard nothing but positives. Which I find encouraging. ֍

---

[1]Traditional garb for Muslim women which covers the entire body save for the eyes, hands, and feet.

Manhattan lawyer STANLEY COHEN, 47, has made his fair share of enemies.[2] As a lawyer, he spent nearly seven years with the Legal Aide Society of New York City's Criminal Defense Division before opening his own practice, where his choice to represent what his colleague Lynne F. Stewart calls "shunned Americans" fostered instant comparisons to the career of William M. Kuntsler.[3]

Since hanging out his shingle in 1989, Cohen has defended Manhattan squatters, alleged cop-killers, IRA members, members of Peru's Shining Path, Native American Indians, and alleged Islamic terrorists. In the mid-1990's, Cohen drew incredible attention and scathing criticism for his choice to defend U.S. resident Mousa Mohammed Abu Marzook from extradition to Israel. Abu Marzook is the political wing leader for Hamas, the militant Palestinian group currently under intense investigation for involvement in the World Trade Center bombings.[4]

Mr. Cohen granted this interview on October 7th, the first day of the Coalition military strike against Afghanistan.

———

I don't defend Islamic terrorists. I represent a lot of Muslims in the United States and overseas. Some are connected to Osama bin Laden or alleged to be terrorists, including the head of the political wing of Hamas, and persons who have struggled for the rights of Palestinian self-determination. Some are resisters who refuse to collaborate with U.S. Government witch-hunts directed at Muslims at home and abroad. None have ever been charged or convicted.

Why do I *do* it? I can give you three answers. The easy answer sounds good but I don't believe it. It's that old story that everyone is entitled to a lawyer and their day in court. If you have an unpopular cause or an unpopular issue, go to the ACLU.

---

[2]If you called the Manhattan headquarters of the Jewish Defense Organization in October of 2001, the taped recording would state bluntly, "Stanley Cohen is a traitor to the Jews, he is a traitor to America and all the victims of the World Trade Center bombing . . . [He is] garbage that needs to be swept into the bag . . . " and " . . . the Jewish Defense Organization intends to do it." Upon discussing this with Cohen, he chuckled and rolled his eyes. "I've actually been called much worse," he says.
[3]William Kuntsler, 1919-1995. Attorney famous for defending the Chicago 7, Leonard Peltier and other high-profile clients. Kuntsler was famous for reveling in his reputation as the most hated lawyer in America. But, in a New York Times article dated September 28, 2001, Stewart notes that Cohen "May go beyond what Bill was . . . Bill would not have wanted to cross over to that level of unpopularity."
[4]On September 26th, 2001, a New York Daily News article quoted Cohen: "If I were approached by him [Osama bin Laden], I believe I would represent him." Another Manhattan attorney noted, "Cohen's a limelight-grabbing hippie freak. He doesn't belong in your book." Mr. Cohen provides a unique response to all that has happened since the September 11t attack, and outlines the method behind his perceived madness.

If folks want the cultural, geopolitical, historical answer . . . I don't join Jews who believe they have a stranglehold on the pains and oppressions of the past. The Holocaust was bad - from a historical perspective, the Jews have certainly felt their share of political pain, repression and genocide. But you've got 100 million Indians who were massacred by discoverers in the Americas. As a Jew it was inculcated in me that we have an obligation to work on behalf of oppressed persons.

So I laugh when people call Palestinians and Arab Muslims anti-Semitic. We're cousins. Palestinians and Jews are family. They're all Semitic. Having been called a 'self-hating Jew', this notion resonates strongly with me.

*   *   *

I predict this new war will end up an extraordinary blunder for the West. I'll get back to that. But let me say this first:

I once sat on the West bank in Gaza at about four in the morning debating with the head of the military wing of Hamas. He said: "You in the West think of history in terms of years. We think of history in terms of millennia. You struggle to focus your eyes for three or four years and move along to the next flimsy cause. We will keep our eye on the millennium and keep fighting until we win."

I think today we have unleashed a wave of resistance, violence and counter-violence that will last a long time. I suspect that in the short run the U.S. will gain what it purports to be its aims. In the long run? We are about to enter an extraordinarily bloody period that will make September 11th pale in comparison. The New War is nothing but a pretext to expand George Bush Sr.'s New World Order into George Bush Jr.'s. We're tinkering with forces that our so-called leaders *can't* understand, and don't *want* to understand.

If Osama bin Laden walked in tomorrow morning with his band of three hundred and said, "I surrender," so what? The U.S. feels it's a perfect opportunity to recreate the East in their own image, whether the East likes it or not. A recent Village Voice piece quoted me about paying back our 'friends in the East'. They thought I was referring specifically to Israel. I wasn't. I was talking more about the Saudis and Egypt. Israel has obviously been the recipient of enormous U.S. support for a long time, but I think that Israel, with or without the United States, would be what Israel is.

I'm not gonna expend a lot of energy trying to redefine Israel. Israel has its own Messianic complex. With or without the United States, they continue to march against the beat of the Universe. The Saudis and the Egyptians, on the other hand, without U.S. support, would collapse in five to ten years.

* * *

Egypt has been the recipient of enormous U.S. support. They have hundreds of thousands of political prisoners; persons, for instance, who dared to stand up against the Saudi government and royalty. People who live in abject poverty. People who are not thrilled that the Saudi government squandered its entire fortune, and that the country is now a debtor nation. Not only do we condone Egypt's keeping of political prisoners, we fund it.

Add Jordan to that. I've called Egypt the fifty-first state and I call Jordan the fifty-second state. I had a client, a U.S. citizen who was picked up and not charged with any crime. He was held incommunicado for five days about a year and a half ago. The U.S. embassy kept insisting they were powerless to do anything, which I found interesting considering that the FBI basically runs the security forces of Jordan and has for about five years now.

So. What we've done is unleash a horrible chain reaction. Osama bin Laden will come in one way or another, although he's not going to be in a prisoner dock in New York City. The U.S. will announce they've killed 157 people secretively when who really knows how many. And we'll wave our flags and say that the people who were tragically slaughtered on September 11th have been vindicated. "The U.S. rid the world of the scourge of terrorism." We'll repeat the same incantations that the West did with the Crusades and we will not have learned our lesson.

* * *

I've traveled extensively in the Middle East and within the Muslim community here in the United States. I've represented folks, *leadership* of different groups. While there are some that describe me as a sophomoric groupie who's titillated by revolutionaries, I'm almost 50 years of age. I'm a lawyer who's been practicing 20 years, a successful litigator. I've fought all the way up to the Supreme Court. My analysis is rooted in understanding and research.

I don't believe the persons behind the September 11th attacks were Islamists *or* Fundamentalists. I assume they were Muslim. But I know of no *true* Muslim who, on his last day on Earth - when he is getting ready to go to Paradise - is gonna go to a club, get drunk on vodka and dance with topless girls.[5] I know of no serious Muslims who, in the weeks prior to their mission, work out at a spa in full view of women. Bin Laden's a secular maniac. But we gotta back up:

---

[5]Investigators claim that Mohammad Atta, the purported ring master of the hijackers, did exactly this on the night of September 10th, 2001.

Palestine. Iraq. Egypt. Saudi Arabia. Kosovo. Bosnia. Chechnya. The list of misdeeds and misconduct by the U.S. government in the Middle East has gone on for *decades*. Afghanistan? We used it as Henry Kissinger used the world, as a huge chessboard. We funded the Mujahadin. They slaughtered everybody, then *they* got slaughtered, millions died and then we said, "We're taking our dog and going home." We left them bankrupt and imperiled at the hands of Afghanistan's Northern Alliance, the first group in history to have mass registration with the sex offender's registry. I'm not concerned about the Taliban. The Northern Alliance are thugs. We've lined them up with the king of Afghanistan who is a Russian Puppet.

Or Algeria! An Islamic state was developing there for years, and in 1990 an election was planned; the Islamists would have won. But the government cancelled the election, locked up hundreds of leaders, slaughtered thousands of people, and the war began. Lord knows there's a checklist of people all over the Middle East who are angry with the United States. There are people, who feel it's appropriate and righteous - in their interpretation of the Qu'ran - that the United States is fair game because the United States has exported terror throughout the world and remains aloof, removed from any retribution or retaliation.

The United States government's known that. Our academics and our intelligence division have known that. But we like to stick our head in the ground like ostriches and say, "Well, we send care and relief packages. We do good things *everywhere*."

Today, October 7th, reminds me of Viet Nam. We had to destroy the village to save it. We're gonna destroy Afghanistan and drop food so the bellies of three million Afghani refugees will be sated for a week. And then they'll be lost. Then we'll have another 20 years of insanity in the Middle East perpetrated by U.S. foreign affairs and policies.

*   *   *

I think 1993, the first attack on the World Trade Center, was the opening salvo.

We never learned our lesson. We've always believed that might is right, and that the biggest gun wins. In Afghanistan that's not true. We have a President who, I dare say, when he first heard the word 'Osama bin Laden' thought it was a religious movement. We have a President who, six or eight weeks ago, in talking about Puerto Rico, said, "They're our friends and our neighbors" - he didn't know they're U.S. citizens. We have a President supported by the same expansionist politicians that guided his father ten years ago, a keen interest that revolves around oil coming out of the Middle East. They have relationships with despotic regimes which control the oil lines.

We believe that the West has some inherent right to lecture, lead, and control the rest of the world. Even though we're a country whose median age is 45 while the rest of the world is 22. We are doomed to repeat mistakes. If you take a look at the Coalition today, it's rooted in the West. The East is sitting silent; they know the unspeakable horror which is going to be released in years to come as a result of this.

*   *   *

I think we have unleashed waves of persons who have absolutely no vested interest in sitting on the sidelines. There's no more conservative, God-fearing and law-abiding community in the U.S. than Muslims. Their view on justice is very orthodox. They have tasted government oppression and harassment in unprecedented numbers. Young Muslims say, "See what happens when you play the game by the rules?" I'm not saying they're gonna go to the next step and pick up a gun or do anything criminal in this country. But overseas?

The Middle East is one of the poorest regions on earth. There's a dichotomy: the people we protect versus the extraordinary power of poverty in the Middle East. Once again they feel victimized by Crusaders from the West. So it's open season. They don't have armies, navies, or air forces, but they have something much more profoundly dangerous: the lack of vested interest.

Whether it's a nine year-old kid in Palestine or an 18 year-old in Afghanistan . . . many of them are so disinvested in the West's policies as to believe that the next world – heaven - will be more comfortable than the current world. They feel obligated to fight and die on behalf of their people. And it's not just the Middle East. Look what's happening in Asia. The world sat back while the Russians committed horrific genocide against the Chechnyans. And Russia's paying us back now by leading us into Afghanistan. The fox returns to the coop. And everyone knows what happened to the Russians in Afghanistan.

*   *   *

I think there's a couple of immediate things that have to be answered.

Number one: the issue of Palestine has got to be resolved. And in order to resolve it, the settlements have to stop. 80 percent of the settlers in the West Bank and Gaza? If the United States offered them a million dollars per house, they'd be gone. The other 20 percent are people from Brooklyn who feel they have a birthright. They have to be removed by force. By Israel, if necessary. Instead of giving Israel a billion dollars a year for guns, we should give Israel a billion dollars to pay the settlers to leave the settlements and bring this all to a close.

The second thing: let each of the Middle Eastern countries know they're on their own. We've got to stop propping up the Saudis. We've got to remove the five thousand troops we have there.

Lastly: we missed a wonderful opportunity to empower the Muslim nations. We should have had the Muslim nations hold court over Osama bin Laden. If a trial had been held by the Muslim states, he would have been convicted, their burden of proof is much lower than ours. He would have been executed. His position as the great Martyr would have been reversed, there would not have been a backlash against the West and it would have set in motion a healthy empowerment in the Middle East.

We've got to call together the best and brightest in the Middle East: academics, intellectuals, religious leaders. Not Western-appointed kings and the chosen. We know who these people are. It's really a matter of choosing to contact them.

But the West remains fueled by economic greed and self-interest. Look at George Bush's inner circle. They come out of oil, industry, and the corporate elite. They continue to direct our policies. They're predators. They talk about fine, egalitarian notions of equality, justice and Christianity - the Judeo-Christian tradition. The reality is that they're concerned about protecting their own self-interests at the expense of everyone else.

The world remains a chess game. As the world becomes browner and younger and more Eastern, we have hopes for survival. As long as it remains basically Western, older and whiter . . . we're destined to fail. ⚎

JENNA LUMBARD is a 13 year-old autistic child. She has never spoken a word, does not make eye contact and lives in her own world. However, she has demonstrated an incredible ability to speed read and retain all she sees. She never sits down to watch television, yet somehow she is up on current events. She's also a gifted writer. Nurtured by friends and family, Jenna has put together a book of her stories and poems.

Jenna's work was submitted to TOWER STORIES by her grandfather in Mill Creek, Washington. He sent a copy of Jenna's latest poem, verses from a "voiceless" young woman to express the weight of a tragedy she uniquely comprehends.

———

Morning shatters with shards of glass
Concrete and dust rains from the heavens
Fire raging from the bowels of Hell
Gone is the sweet September morning
Gone is life as we knew it
Mothers, fathers, sisters and brothers gone forever
No chance to say good-bye

Hatred
Sadistic and senseless
No time to think
No time to pray
Just kill without conscience
Terrorist
Cowardice

People pulling together
Race, creed and color meld
Heroes flourish
One nation under God
Crippled, but still very much alive
Strong in unity
Strong in death
Seeking justice
Not revenge

— Jenna Lumbard, 9/01 🏦

Professor FAWAZ GERGES was born in northern Lebanon in 1959. During the Lebanese civil war, which began in 1975, his town was destroyed by Islamic elements. His family fled to Syria, where they were taken in by Christian monasteries. Prof. Gerges, then a teenager, stayed in Syria for a year before coming to the United States. He studied in California to get his Master's degree and received his Doctorate from Oxford. He left England in 1990 to teach at Harvard and also spent three years at Princeton. Since 1994, he has taught at Sarah Lawrence College in New York where he currently holds the chair in International Affairs and Middle East studies. He also conducts a graduate seminar at Columbia University.

––––––

As you know, the Middle East is a highly volatile and polarized region. They're experiencing now what are called the 'birth pangs of nation building'. And if you look at Middle Eastern history, it's relatively youngish in comparison to other countries in the region.

The Ottoman Empire was defeated in 1918; Britain and France divided the spoils between themselves. They reconstructed the boundaries of the region based on the European notion of 'nation states' between 1918 and 1923. But how alien to that culture! The dominant political categories of the region - tribes, empire, and religion - were forsaken. The economic, strategic, and colonial interests of the British Empire were the tools used to construct national boundaries, not the interests of the indigenous people. It was bloody surgery.

You might say that every single conflict in the region between 1947 and the present is related to the reconstuction of the Middle East.

Osama bin laden has been saying for the last few years, "We wanted you to taste the pain that we have tasted for 80 years." He's referring to that painful chapter in Muslim-Western relations when the colonial powers destroyed the Ottoman Empire, one of the oldest and greatest empires, and imposed their own will upon the region.

*　　*　　*

Americans are angry and they have a right to be. People want justice. They're interested in, "Who are the perpetrators of the 11th?" They're not willing to sit down now and reflect. Where does this antagonism come from? What are the causes of this anger?

Osama bin Laden and other dissidents like him tend to be obscure men. He doesn't have to be a highly-charismatic man. His message is what's important, and it resonates with many Muslims. Unfortunately, since the 11th of September, we've been focusing on the man himself, on the perpetrators. We have lost perspective. What matters, in the eyes of Muslims is bin Laden's *message*.

He's been saying that Muslims have been on the receiving end of abuse for the last hundred years. That their destiny has been determined by Western powers. This anger has been brewing for the last 30 years and is now surfacing against the West. Bin Laden's tapping into what I call an arsenal of accumulated grievances. This explains his ability to recruit thousands of foot soldiers to fight against Westerners. They are willing to join his dream and his bloody organization. But it's essential to understand this arsenal of grievances to tackle the causes of the problem after this particular crisis is over. We need to think in terms of short-term and long-term strategies.

*   *   *

In the long term the critical question is, "How do we show Arabs and Moslems that there's more to America than its foreign policy, military might, and economic power?" That we're not just a bunch of cowboys with guns, that this is a great civil society where genuine people care about human rights?

How do we show this face of America to the Muslim world? I say: investment in education. Investment in civil societies in the Third World in the health and economic conditions of countries we have no military interest in. It requires our diplomats to engage the civilian populations of countries, not just their governments. It requires integration.

It seems to me that right now our two civilizations are not talking to each other, they're really talking *across* each other. *Apart* from each other. This is a tragedy.

The long-term strategy is this question: "How can America reclaim the moral high ground?" America has lost the moral high ground in the eyes of most Muslims. We claim to care about democracy, human rights and the sanctity of human life? So let's practice what we preach, rather than practice economics.

For instance, why not keep our distance from the corrupt leaderships and governments in the Middle East? We go to bed with some of the bloodiest authoritarian regimes, governments who are oppressing their populations. Let's convince the people of the Middle East that we have nothing to do with their oppression.

What happened to the vision of the founding fathers? When we say that democracy is really something for everybody, let's find a way to make that happen. That's the long term.

*   *   *

In the short term? Actions speak louder than words. People have been calling me from the newspapers asking, "How can we fight the propaganda war?" As if somehow we can really deceive and manipulate . . . have a massive media campaign whereby we change people's perceptions of our behavior with superficial advertising. It's the action, not the message that matters. We need to find *initiatives* to tell the people of the Middle East that we are serious about their freedom and, while we're not *responsible* for all their problems, we must start addressing their legitimate grievances.

For example, on the Palestinian-Israeli conflict, I think a Presidential statement defining the contours of affair for the treatment of both sides would not do us a great deal of harm. Tell both sides we are committed to finding a way out of this deadly embrace. Many Israelis will tell you the same thing. Supporting a Palestinian state does not mean we have to give up support for Israel. The question is one of fairness and justice. This is what I call reclaiming the moral high ground.

I'm sure you've heard it: "Why do they hate us so much?" Implying that this hatred is intrinsic or natural. Rubbish! It is neither.

In the late 19th century and the first part of the 20th century, the United States was popular and respected. We were seen as progressive in comparison to European expansion and colonialism. America stood for self-determination. The question in my mind is, "What happened in the last 45 years? How have our policymakers managed to antagonize every social group in the Arab world?" These are questions that need to be deeply considered instead of saying, "They hate us because we're a great democracy."

It doesn't occur to some of our commentators that the people of the Middle East would like to have the human rights we enjoy here. The absence of human rights is the hallmark of political oppression which breeds what I call the 'culture of violence'.

*   *   *

[A note posted anonymously on a bulletin board outside Prof. Gerges' office at the Middle Eastern Institute of Columbia University reads partially:]

To my fellow Americans,

No American actions, however flawed, contributed to the misfortune of the Middle East peoples - nothing in this world ever justifies the slaughter of one, let alone thousands of innocent civilians. This kind of fashionable rationalization for evil is called "blaming the victim" and it must be exposed for what it truly is: mental poison that only adds insult to injury. America shoulders no blame for the evil perpetrated to her on September 11ᵗʰ. The people who freely choose a path of absolute wickedness, of terror, bear complete responsibility.

How do I respond to that? Very bluntly, anyone who tells us that somehow there is moral equivalence between criticism of U.S. foreign policy and what the perpetrators did is engaging in a terrible form of moral relativism.

No criticism of U.S. foreign policy, regardless of what that policy has done, could justify the attack on the 11th of September. I have been highly critical of U.S. foreign policy but my criticism ends when it comes to the sanctity of human life. No foreign policy can stand unless it values human life everywhere. Whether we mean Palestinian children, Iraqi children, Jewish children, or American children.

I'm terrified when I see children in Middle Eastern societies tell you, "Yes. I'd like to kill Americans. My goal in life is to be a suicide bomber." Anti-American sentiment has become deeply entrenched in every single Arab society. I'm terrified that America has no more friends in that part of the world except some of the most corrupt and authoritarian leaderships. And Israel, of course. There was once a wonderful relationship with America and the Middle East that, at some historical junction, turned bloody and tragic. The demonization of Osama bin Laden is actually a distortion of the truth. It's packageable. The truth goes deeper than that.

*   *   *

In 1918 President Wilson seized the moral high ground as one of the greatest advocates of self-determination for the colonized peoples of the Middle East. But Britain and France held the power, exploiting the indigenous people and propagating crimes under the heading of colonialism. Since the mid-1950's, our policies have been perceived by Arabs and Muslims to have inherited a European role in the Third World, perpetuating Western dominance. People have come to see America as the evil source of all problems and failures that have befallen the Middle East in the last 50 years.

And the United States has lost sight of the fact that it's greatest strength is its *soft* power: its accessible pop culture, it's humanism, its open society and individualism. We lost sight that our power does not lie in our economic means and our armies. We've consciously portrayed ourselves in a highly narrow and selfish form, a hegemonic interest perpetuating its own dominance. An economic power looking to exploit the resources of the world.

The people of the Middle East see how the U.S. has taken control of their ancestral lands and armed enemies and allies alike. Not only does the United States have full control of the oil, but, between 1991 and 1998, the Gulf countries bought nearly $100 billion of armament. Billions of dollars, which the countries could spend on their own people. Does the United States invest in the human needs of the country: education and health? No. We give almost $6 billion of our foreign aid budget - about $12 billion a year - and where does it all go? About 70 or 80 percent goes to military tools and toys.

Do you know what you can do with $6 billion? You can give 50,000 fully paid scholarships every year. You can create armies of educated ambassadors for American and global interests throughout the world. Why not build more libraries? Let children read instead of building missiles and tanks. Why not build universities? Fund education? We're already investing the money, but we're investing it in the wrong places. We're investing it in franchising the corrupt military, autocratic leadership. The people of those countries know it. And America is seen as inspiring that unrest.

*   *   *

The Iraqi crisis is one of the most critical issues in how Muslims perceive our country. Since 1991, the United States, using the UN, has imposed draconian measures on Iraqi society. Instead of punishing the bloody dictator of Baghdad, we punished civil society, and children who are themselves oppressed by the dictator. Why?

American policy makers told you it was the fault of Saddam Hussein when he was in power. They told you he had the money to buy food and other resources for his people. *I* know and *you* know that Saddam Hussein is mainly responsible for the plight of the people in Iraq. But the U.S. sanctions did terrible damage, not only to the Iraqi people, but also to the American image as perceived throughout the Arab and Muslim world.

Why did the Bush administration leave Hussein in power after the Gulf War? To counter-balance the power of Iran and maintain relative stability in Iraq. They believed Saddam Hussein, as a military man, could basically maintain order.

55 percent of the Iraqi people are Shiite.[6] Iran is the only Shiite state in the Moslem world. American-Iranian relations are not the best. The U.S. believed that furthering the Iranian influence in Iraq through the Shiite community would make Iran a superpower in the

---

[6]The Shiite branch of Islam accounts for approximately 10 to 15% of the current world Muslim population. Shiite Islam developed as a political movement supporting Ali, the son-in-law of the prophet Muhammad, as the rightful leader of the Islamic state in approximately 650 A.D. The majority of Shiites believe that there have been twelve Imams, and that the 12th Imam never died, but entered a state known as occultation, or disappearance. Clerics of the Shiite faith draw their spiritual power from their role as deputies of this 12th, nonpresent Imam. Shiites believe that the 12th Imam will return at the end of the world to vindicate the righteous, reward his steadfast followers, and see the new kingdom of Islam established for the next age.

Gulf region. When Saddam Hussein invaded Iran in 1980, we believed that Ayatollah Khommani was a bigger *fatwah*.[7] If not for the intelligence and the resources that we provided to Hussein during the 1980's, Iran would have won the war and demolished the Iraqi regime. But the U.S. wanted both countries rendered powerless to threaten the oil resources in Saudi Arabia, Kuwait, and the Gulf.

Not only did we keep Hussein in power, we empowered him to decimate the uprising that happened immediately after the Gulf War. There was a major uprising in Iraq by people of all persuasions who tried to rise up and topple Hussein in 1991. And guess what we did? The Bush administration gave Iraq the green light to use helicopters against the rebels. In two or three weeks Hussein was able to decimate the rebels.

American soldiers on the border between Kuwait and Iraq were ordered to disarm these rebels. We assisted Iraq in the use of air space so the helicopters could destroy rebel outposts. All this against people who were struggling in the same way that our forefathers struggled against the British only 225 years ago. We lacked the political will. We lacked the vision. It was easier for us to keep this dictator in place after we cut him apart and consigned him to the task of caretaker for a society he raped in the first place. We didn't give a moral damn about the people.

* * *

Afghanistan. Another case in point.

The United States invested about $4 billion in the Afghan war against the Soviet occupying forces in the 1980s. We provided money, training, arms and CIA intelligence which soon defeated the Soviet forces. And after the 11th, we pulled a complete turn-around by dropping food under the guise of humanitarian aid. Do you think people really buy this?

Let's not underestimate the intelligence of the Afghan people. If we were concerned about their plight, why did we leave in 1989? I fear, if our nation does *not* take stock of its past behavior, we are doomed to commit the same travesties of justice and sins against humanity that the world will no longer tolerate.

None of the perpetrators of September 11th lived in or even cared about Afghanistan. Their passions lay in the heartland of Islam. To say the problem lies in Afghanistan is misleading.

We had the means and the tools to win the war and decimate the Taliban. But what do you

---

[7]A fatwah (also fatwa) is defined as a ruling on a point of Islamic law which is given by a recognized authority, usually a clergyman.

do after you win the war? Are we willing to glue the country back together? To rebuild Afghan civil society? The reconstruction of Germany and Japan under the Marshall plan after World War II was in our best interest. But how many Americans care about Afghanistan? It's easy to suggest that somehow we will apply our military and material might. But the question is, what comes after we achieve a technical military victory?

We invested in the Mujahadin in Afghanistan against the Soviet forces; look what they did. We invested in Saddam Hussein in the 1980s against Iran; look what he did. In the Gulf War, we *kept* Saddam Hussein in place, imposed the sanctions on Iraq; look what we've done.

*   *   *

I firmly believe that, even if tomorrow the United States decides to say, "Okay, to Hell with the Middle East," Middle Eastern regimes aren't going to collapse overnight. In fact, I would argue that the regimes would become more autocratic, and more authoritarian. Because they don't have to put on the mask of civility at that point. Turkey and Egypt put on a public relations campaign for the rest of the world when they're authoritarian and imprison their opposition elements.

Countries in the Middle East have to take charge of their own political destiny. We are not responsible for the hypocrisies, the absence of human rights, the disempowerment of women for the culture of authoritarianism in many Arab cultures. But when we construct policies, shouldn't the United States, being the greatest power on earth today, remember that justice should lie at heart of every action we put forth? We take in much more of the world's resources than we give out. Much more. What does it take to reinvest a small percentage? Because we know that when people are relatively content - when they have enough to eat and are not persecuted - they behave very differently. Terrorism does not arise from a content culture.

The main victims of terrorism have not been Westerners and Americans. The main victims of terrorism have been Muslims and Arabs. This form of political oppression, this type of terrorism, has resulted in the deaths of hundreds of thousands. This is the second time terrorism has been exported to America? So now it becomes a war of America versus the Middle East? I think not. It is far more complicated than that. ₮

BJ WARD is the author of three volumes of poetry: <u>Gravedigger's Birthday</u>, <u>17 Love Poems with No Despair</u> and <u>Landing in New Jersey with Soft Hands</u>. His work has appeared in Poetry, The New York Times, Puerto Del Sol, and many other publications.

BJ has few things to say about any poem he writes, believing that a poem, ultimately, should speak for itself. However, when asked to comment on the labor of crafting words to explore the tragedy of September 11th, he offered this:

"The Israeli poet Yehuda Amichai once remarked, 'A poet turns bad cholesterol into good cholesterol.' Of course, Amichai's metaphor falls short because the 'bad cholesterol' from September 11th can never be erased; however, if we view the act of writing a poem as an act of creation, and what happened on September 11th as an act of destruction, one might be able to see how the metaphor applies - how one gave rise to another."

――――

For the Children of the World Trade Center Victims

from <u>Gravedigger's Birthday</u> by BJ Ward, published by North Atlantic Books, copyright 2002 by BJ Ward

Nothing could have prepared you—

Note: Every poem I have ever written
     is not as important as this one.

Note: This poem says nothing important.

Clarification of last note:
     This poem cannot save 3,000 lives.

Note: This poem is attempting to pull your father
     out of the rubble, still living and glowing
     and enjoying football on Sunday.

Note: This poem is trying to reach your mother
     in her business skirt, and get her home
     to Ridgewood where she can change
     to her robe and sip Chamomile tea

as she looks through the bay window at the old,
untouched New York City skyline.

Note: This poem is aiming its guns at the sky
to shoot down the terrorists and might
hit God if He let this happen.

Note: This poem is trying to turn
that blooming of orange and black
of the impact into nothing
more than a sudden tiger-lily
whose petals your mother and father
could use as parachutes, float down
to the streets below, a million
dandelion seeds drifting off
to the untrafficked sky above them.

Note: This poem is still doing nothing.

Note: Somewhere in this poem there may be people alive,
and I'm trying like mad to reach them.

Note: I need to get back to writing the poem to reach them
instead of dwelling on these matters, but how
can any of us get back to writing poems?

Note: The sound of this poem: the sound
of a scream in 200 different languages
that outshouts the sounds of sirens and
airliners and glass shattering and
concrete crumbling as steel is bending and
the orchestral tympani of our American hearts
when the second plane hit.

Note: The sound of a scream in 200 languages
is the same sound.
It is the sound of a scream.
Note: In New Jersey over the next four days,
over 30 people asked me

if I knew anyone in the catastrophe.

Yes, I said.
I knew every single one of them.

- BJ Ward ⚓

CODY MAHER, 29. Cody was out of the country when September 11th happened. The overseas perspective of an attack on U.S. soil triggered a unique revelation for him.

———

I took a vacation in Italy for 10 days. We flew into Paris since it was a cheaper alternative. Flying into Rome would have been another 500 bucks per ticket. I had a group of people with me: my sister, my buddy Doug and this woman Sarah I've been dating.

We partied in Paris, and the very next day we got up and took the train to Brussels. From there, we took another train to another airport, flew to Milan, got into a cab and went to the Milan train station where a third train took us all the way to Venice. From Venice, we went to Rome. From Rome, we went to Florence.

We got there in the late evening, September 9th. Went out for a great dinner. Small portions of mozzarella and tomatoes. An excellent red wine. It was my first time in Italy and I was amazed, the food is incredible. We woke up the next morning and hit the town.

Florence is all about awesome architecture. It's a classical Italian city, you know? They've taken a lot of time to put everything together. It's such an aesthetically pleasing place, lots of buildings that I imagine have stood longer than the United States has been in existence. And the people are proud of their city, proud of their heritage. They enjoy life so much more than we do. They take siestas in the middle of the afternoon; spend three or four hours a day just to be with their family. You never see anyone taking a 20 minute lunch and rushing to work until eight in the evening like I usually do.

My sister went shopping and we visited some old cathedrals, saw some ancient paintings. We saw the statue of Michelangelo's David. Have you ever seen it? It's so much bigger than you'd imagine. It's positively huge.

At 5:30 or 5:45 in the evening on September 11th Italy time. We had gotten some Peronis[8] from a bistro on the street downstairs and were relaxing in my sisters room, eating some cheese and thinking about what we were going to do the next day.

*   *   *

When you're checking into a foreign Hotel, you always run into Americans. It's inevitable.

---

[8]An Italian beer.

You're checking in, you're speaking English so immediately any Americans go, "Oh, my God! You speak English? How's it going?" When we checked into the hotel in Florence, we met this couple from New Jersey who were on their honeymoon.

"You're Americans?" the woman said. "Oh, this is soooooo cool."

I mentioned that I'd be moving to New York City in about a month, and we invited them to drop by our room for some wine and cheese when they had a chance. They mentioned they'd been on the road for quite some time. First, they wanted to grab a shower and relax. I didn't think anything of it at the time.

We were staying in a quaint little hotel. More like a pension.[9] They had a little TV set up in the corner over the check-in desk and there was this little Italian guy watching the screen. Everything on TV was in Italian.

*　　*　　*

On the 11th we were in my sister's room, we cracked the beers, we're having a great time, talking about what we could do in Florence the next day. We had left the door to my sister's room ajar and suddenly, the couple we had met in the lobby comes in, both of them, and the woman from New Jersey is fucking freaking out.

Her eyes are tearing up, she's flipping, she's screaming, "Oh my God, they're attacking the United States! They're attacking the United States!"

We're all confused. "What are you talking about?"

She's sobbing. "They're attacking the United States, they just flew a plane into the World Trade Center."

So we went down to the lobby where the TV set was. The little man behind the counter had MSNBC on, dubbed in Italian. As we all walked in, the frame was showing that video shot where the firefighter's working on the street in New York. He looks up like, "What's up? What's that sound?" The camera pans up, and the plane . . . *Boom!* Flies right into the Tower.

We're all standing there, shocked. You could read "MSNBC" on the screen, you could see English running across the zip tape on the bottom of the screen, telling us the time the

---

[9] A tiny European boarding house.

plane crashed, the details. At the same time, the little Italian man knows some English and he's interpreting the newscast that's coming across in Italian, doing the best he can to relay everything he's hearing to us.

Then the picture shows the second plane come around, pivoting, a sharp turn where the top of the plane nearly faced the flank of the buildings. It looked like one of those made-up 3-D digital, computer-generated shots you see in the movies. The angle was so dramatic. But it was real.

The second plane went right in and fire blew out the other side of the building. That's when we all started losing it.

*   *   *

Real quick. A funny story:

In August of 2001, my company flew me to check out New York and see if I wanted to move there. I went on rounds with the New York sales team, met all their regular financial accounts on Wall Street, answered technical questions, got to know the contacts. We had finished all our calls after a really long day's work, and one of the field guys says to me, "Have you ever been to the top of the World Trade Center?"

"Nope. Never."

"Dude, it's an unreal fucking deal."

So we went up. I can't remember what building it was. The South Tower, I think. The one that had the restaurant bar at the top, Windows on the World.

We went up, I looked out those windows, and the first thing I thought was, "Jesus. He's right. This is unreal."

You could see the whole city skyline. From where I was standing, you were looking out towards Queens, northeast, toward LaGuardia airport. You could see the planes coming in and taking off; from as high up as were, the planes were actually below us. Turn your head just a little? You could see Central Park. And it's crazy: geographically those Towers were pretty far away from the Upper West Side and the Upper East Side. But you could see it all laid out before you from up there. Like the whole city was painted on the ground in miniature. (*Plate 18*)

It's funny to think I'll never see a view like that again in my life.

*   *   *

Doug, screaming: "What the Hell is going on?"

My sister: "Oh, my God, oh my God, oh my God."

People shouting, maybe the New Jersey people. "I can't believe this is happening! Why are they doing this? Why are they *doing* this!?"

It was so weird because we were in Italy while everything was going on in a place we were so familiar with, and yet so far away from.

And then it was . . . nothing. Like this thick curtain dropping down over your emotions. You could only sit back and take in what you saw with your eyes, trying to regurgitate everything, trying to think logically.

*   *   *

The next immediate thing was to call my folks who were 2500 miles away from the disaster in California. At the same time, the little Italian guy is relaying to us that there are seven planes unaccounted for in the States. They're airborne and they can't find any of them on radar. We all began to think: what's next? San Fran? San Diego? Or Coronado, specifically, where my Mom was, which is this little island off the San Diego harbor and one of the biggest Naval hubs, a huge military town. Maybe the next Pearl Harbor.

We started trying to get hold of my folks, but it was impossible. The lines were busy, no one could get through. It took us three and a half hours to make the call and in that time I just watched the television screen, over and over again, replaying the same clips. Becoming more and more pissed off, thinking, "I can't believe that you would actually do this, whoever you are."

See, it really got me. I was mad because they were doing this, but at the same time, I'm a pretty logical person. When something happens, I sit back and think, "Okay, *why* did that just happen? Let's *think* about this."

It's what I do for a living, I'm a troubleshooter. I always go through the steps. But I couldn't come up with anything. Not for this.

*   *   *

The very next day, I went to a bookstore in Florence. Most of the texts were in Italian, but I dug around and finally found some in English. I got a book on the Taliban and the Middle East and I started reading it. We were supposed to fly back on the 12th. Our itinerary ran us from Paris to San Francisco International. But now we couldn't do that. When we got to Paris, our 9 p.m. flight had been cancelled.

I kept reading that book on the train ride all the way through Italy to Paris where we stopped overnight in a hotel.

United Airlines told us that England had better relations with the U.S. and urged us to go to London. They could reroute our flight and we'd have a better chance getting back to America sooner if we went to Heathrow airport. United put us up in a hotel; they didn't pay for the whole thing, but they comped some of the fare and it was appreciated. The 11th happened on a Tuesday and we didn't get on a plane until the following Monday, the 17th. We were in that hotel for six days.

I'd finished the book I picked up in Italy and bought three or four more in England. I don't remember the titles, but one was about the Russian invasion of Afghanistan and the fact that the U.S. government had funded the Afghani rebel army, which would eventually become the Taliban. Another was a quick analysis of the Qu'ran. The third was a collection highlighting the significant economic and political sanctions that America had passed over the Middle East since 1960 or so; I skimmed that one.

Why did I read them? I was really pissed off. At that point, I was fuming. But I don't ever make a judgment until I'm informed; I was trying to inform myself. I didn't feel like I knew enough about what was going on.

Here's what I came up with, in a nutshell:

I love the United States of America and everything it stands for. Equality for every individual. I don't care about the color of your skin or your religious beliefs or where you were born or what time - whatever you've got going on, who cares? You have a right to be here. Moreover, you have all the rights that *I* do, so long as you're not an asshole – that is, you don't invade my privacy or screw with me. I like the values this country stands for. We're all composed of the same biological matter and our laws ensure that we therefore all have the same rights.

But if you fly a plane into an economic structure . . . if you fly a plane into a building that houses non-opposing citizens - *my* citizens - who are just going to work to better their own lives? I have a problem with that.

If it were a military site, that might be different. You sign up for the military realizing that you may have to fight for the country you represent, and that – if you fight - you might die. But those bastards flew a plane into a place that contained innocent humans, innocent biological structures. They flew a plane into a house full of monkeys that had no idea what was coming. They were grabbing a bagel, drinking a cup of coffee, getting on with their morning.

* * *

I've heard this argument going around that these rules I'm talking about, these rules of civilization and democracy? This argument says that we, as Americans, can afford to embrace these rules because our country has an economic stature that blinds us to the conditions of the so-called 'real world.' This argument says we're spoiled. This argument says we got what we deserved. This argument says 9/11 was just a leveling of the playing field.

No.

One guy I know says, "Well, take the American Revolution. When *we* were the oppressed party, we fought the British from behind trees. Aren't these people – the terrorists. Aren't they just doing the same thing?"

Not at all. We never killed innocent civilians, we shot at Red Coats[10] from behind trees, it was a revolution confined to the code of military action and nothing more. England wasn't invading the United States, we were trying to claim ourselves as an independent continent. These terrorists sought out an economic location that would get a lot of hype. And they attacked us with our own plane.

Look, this isn't about politics or religion or any of that horseshit. It's about the viability of Democracy as an economic structure and it's about the media and advertising.

* * *

I've got a better analogy for you:

Let's imagine there are two concert stadiums. One of them is colossal; it has capacity for a million people. And the other stadium is more like our current stadiums, it can hold maybe 65,000.

Now, you're a rock and roll band. Your manager comes up to you and says, "Guys, I can

---

[10]Common slang for British soldiers in the era of the American Revolution.

book you in either place. Which stadium would you rather play in?"

Would you rather play in the 65,000 seat stadium? Or would you rather play in the million-seat mega stadium?" Each stadium's great, and the fans are gonna love you in both places. But what are we trying to do by playing music in the first place?

See, it's about sending the *message* of your music. You want to send a message to as many people as you can, as fast as you can, ideally via live television feed. You're looking for the biggest bang for your buck. And in a Capitalist Democracy, the buck always wins. We'll pat each other on the back forever so long as the money keeps getting passed back and forth, that's commerce. Everyone knows Democracy has flaws. But commerce can't be argued with.

That's what I think the terrorists ultimately were after. They were aggressively approaching us with a bid to play in the big game of global economy.

Look at what happened to me. Where was I when the Towers came down? I was in Florence, Italy. And who is Florence, Italy tuning to for their news? MSNBC, Microsoft National Broadcast Company. A United States-owned global cable conglomerate.

You understand? The rest of the world lives and breathes to interpret our culture. American culture. Maybe because, in a way, we are all cultures and none. If anything, we are a Capitalist culture, when you boil it all down.

It's not about right and wrong. It's about, "Let me into the big God-damned stadium, please. Let me in right now! I want to play to an audience of millions. I want to sell lots of tickets and drive fancy cars. I want a Starbucks on every corner."

*　　*　　*

I should have mentioned this:

When we walked into the lobby of that hotel in Florence, I was watching Sam Malone and Diane Chambers arguing with each other. *Cheers*, dubbed in Italian. See, as much as everyone hates to admit it, the United States is the hub of pop culture. And pop culture runs the planet. And pop culture and economy are tied inexplicably to one another.

You want evidence? The *Cheers* cast was making, what – a million bucks an episode? And during commercial breaks on the series the networks hawked McDonalds and Ford and the Super Bowl and MetLife. One half hour of prime time television equals billions of dollars changing hands per day. Who wouldn't want to play in *that* stadium?

The Taliban knew that, if they were to pull something off in the U.S., the biggest bang for their buck would be the Trade Towers. So you can take religion and economics; you can take the sanctions placed on different Middle-Eastern countries; the French and British taking over the Middle Eastern region seventy-five years ago . . . if we take all that out of play and ask ourselves: "What's the real reason they're doing this?" I'd say the answer is that the terrorists are attacking because they know it's going to show up on global television. It's the media. It's advertising. Absolutely. Who grabs the spotlight.

*　*　*

What's funny about the U.S. is that, when you see something on the nightly news or CNN you might think, "Oh, my God, what's all this violence going on in the Middle East or in Ireland or wherever?" You see it, but you're actually very disassociated from it. I know that when I watch things like that on the TV screen, my initial take is always, "Wow. That really sucks. But. At least it's not here."

Next thought: "Thank God I live in a society that's free, a society in which that would never happen."

Next: you begin to take freedom and this great country we live in for granted. This safe harbor that never has to deal with the storm at all.

You get sloppy. You get fat. You get naïve. Then you get stupid.

And then? Something happens.

*　*　*

My life has changed forever. I travel a lot for my job within the continental United States, three or four times a month for three to four days at a time. I've seen the changes at the airport, I've seen the shift in perspective. I never had to unzip my briefcase and pull out my laptop before, never had to take my shoes off, never had to be physically violated by a magnetic wand. But you see, I took those freedoms for granted and now I'll have to pay for it.

I pay for it every time I see a plane in the sky and think, "Hey. That's flying a bit too low." Or I hear a door slam and I jump.

Or I'm doing a product demonstration on the 46th Floor of a Wall Street tower and I think,

"Hmmm. I'm pretty high up. They could fly something right into this."

Or I look at someone who's Islamic American and I think, "What does this guy really think? Really?"

And this is the price of being in a Democracy right now. It's the price of being a human biological unit in America. ₰

CONTRIBUTING PHOTOGRAPHERS

ABBY BULLOCK

FRANK CUTLER

DICK DUANE

ROB EPSTEIN

FRED GEORGE

EDWARD HILLEL

R. ANDREW LEPLEY

BOB LONDON

JESSICA MURROW

DREW NEDERPELT

STEVE OLSEN

MICHAEL RAAB

BOBBIE-JO RANDOLPH

ROBERT RIPPS

SHEPERD SHERBELL

SCOTT SLATER

ROGER SMYTH

ANDREW WALKER

WITH THANKS TO:

Sterling Rome

Revolution Publishing

Martha Kaplan

J. Seward Johnson

The Law Firm of McGrath and Marsh, PC

Mark Woods and Meir Ribalow of New River Dramatists

Darrell Stern, Jersey Visions, Inc.

John Bonomo, Verizon Inc.

Ernesto Mora and Karen Crowe, NYC Union Local 32BJ

Pres. Tom Kean and Deb Meyers, Drew University

Josh Zelman, CNN

NJ Assemblyman William Baroni, Jr.

Cassandra Medley

Patrick Weir

Mike Boyle

Roger Smyth

Jill Corson, President of Advertising Photographers of America

The Modern Gentlemen

Corbis Corporation

Ben Peterson

Robin Siskin

Courtney Cleaver at Muse Media

WITH SPECIAL THANKS:

Compiling TOWER STORIES was not easy. Many of the book's contributors exposed fresh wounds by sharing their stories so recently after the attack on the World Trade Center. The editor would like to thank them for their courage, and offers this page as a place to pause and reflect on the events of September 11th, 2001.

> By the . . . soul, and Him who perfected it
> and inspired it with conscience of what is
> wrong for it and right for it:
> He is indeed successful who causes it to grow, and
> he is indeed a failure who stunts it.
>
> - From Islam, the Qu'ran 91.7-10